DAVID BUSCH CANON® EOS REBEL T1i/500D

GUIDE TO DIGITAL SLR PHOTOGRAPHY

David D. Busch

Course Technology PTR
A part of Cengage Learning

x

COURSE TECHNOLOGY
CENGAGE Learning™

Australia, Brazil, Japan, Korea, Mexico, Singapore, Spain, United Kingdom, United States

COURSE TECHNOLOGY
CENGAGE Learning™

David Busch's Canon® EOS Rebel T1i/500D Guide to Digital SLR Photography
David D. Busch

Publisher and General Manager, Course Technology PTR:
Stacy L. Hiquet

Associate Director of Marketing:
Sarah Panella

Manager of Editorial Services:
Heather Talbot

Marketing Manager:
Jordan Casey

Executive Editor:
Kevin Harreld

Project Editor:
Jenny Davidson

Technical Reviewer:
Michael D. Sullivan

PTR Editorial Services Coordinator:
Jen Blaney

Interior Layout Tech:
Bill Hartman

Cover Designer:
Mike Tanamachi

Indexer:
Katherine Stimson

Proofreader:
Sara Gullion

For product information and technology assistance, contact us at
Cengage Learning Customer & Sales Support, 1-800-354-9706

For permission to use material from this text or product, submit all requests online at **cengage.com/permissions**. Further permissions questions can be e-mailed to **permissionrequest@cengage.com**.

Canon is a registered trademark of Canon Inc. in the United States and other countries.

All other trademarks are the property of their respective owners.

Library of Congress Control Number: 2009929200

ISBN-13: 978-1-4354-5496-5

ISBN-10: 1-4354-5496-0

Course Technology, a part of Cengage Learning
20 Channel Center Street
Boston, MA 02210
USA

Cengage Learning is a leading provider of customized learning solutions with office locations around the globe, including Singapore, the United Kingdom, Australia, Mexico, Brazil, and Japan. Locate your local office at: **international.cengage.com/region**.

Cengage Learning products are represented in Canada by Nelson Education, Ltd.

For your lifelong learning solutions, visit **courseptr.com**.

Visit our corporate Web site at **cengage.com**.

Printed in the United States of America
1 2 3 4 5 6 7 11 10 09

For Cathy

Acknowledgments

Once again thanks to the folks at Course Technology PTR, who have pioneered publishing digital imaging books in full color at a price anyone can afford. Special thanks to executive editor Kevin Harreld, who always gives me the freedom to let my imagination run free with a topic, as well as my veteran production team including project editor Jenny Davidson and technical reviewer Mike Sullivan. Special thanks to long-time Canon shooter Kris Bosworth, who kindly supplied a frozen moment in time worthy of MIT strobe wiz Dr. Harold Edgerton, as well as two other great illustrations. Also thanks to Bill Hartman, layout; Katherine Stimson, indexing; Sara Gullion, proofreading; Mike Tanamachi, cover design; and my agent, Carole Jelen, who has the amazing ability to keep both publishers and authors happy.

About the Author

With more than a million books in print, **David D. Busch** is one of the best-selling authors of books on digital photography and imaging technology, and the originator of popular series like *David Busch's Pro Secrets* and *David Busch's Quick Snap Guides*. He has written eight hugely successful guidebooks for Canon digital SLR models, including the all-time #1 best-sellers for several Canon EOS models, additional user guides for other camera models, as well as many popular books devoted to dSLRs, including *Mastering Digital SLR Photography, Second Edition* and *Digital SLR Pro Secrets*. As a roving photojournalist for more than 20 years, he illustrated his books, magazine articles, and newspaper reports with award-winning images. He's operated his own commercial studio, suffocated in formal dress while shooting weddings-for-hire, and shot sports for a daily newspaper and upstate New York college. His photos have been published in magazines as diverse as *Scientific American* and *Petersen's PhotoGraphic*, and his articles have appeared in *Popular Photography & Imaging, The Rangefinder, The Professional Photographer*, and hundreds of other publications. He's also reviewed dozens of digital cameras for CNet and *Computer Shopper*.

When About.com named its top five books on Beginning Digital Photography, debuting at the #1 and #2 slots were Busch's *Digital Photography All-In-One Desk Reference for Dummies* and *Mastering Digital Photography*. During the past year, he's had as many as five of his books listed in the Top 20 of Amazon.com's Digital Photography Bestseller list—simultaneously! Busch's 100-plus other books published since 1983 include best-sellers like *David Busch's Quick Snap Guide to Digital SLR Lenses*.

Busch is a member of the Cleveland Photographic Society (www.clevelandphoto.org), which has operated continuously since 1887. Visit his website at http://www.dslrguides.com.

Contents

Preface xii
Introduction. xiii

Chapter 1
Getting Started with Your Canon EOS
Rebel T1i/500D   1

Contents of the Box 2
Initial Setup 6
    Battery Included 6
    Final Steps. 10
Selecting a Shooting Mode 17
Choosing a Metering Mode 21
Choosing a Focus Mode 22
Selecting a Focus Point 23
Other Settings. 25
    Adjusting White Balance and ISO 25
    Using the Self-Timer 25
    Using the Built-in Flash. 26
Taking a Picture 28
Reviewing the Images You've Taken 29
    Cruising Through Index Views 30
Transferring Photos to Your Computer. 31

Chapter 2
Canon EOS Rebel T1i/500D Roadmap   35

Front View 36
The Canon EOS Rebel T1i's Business End 41
    Jumping Around 46
Going Topside. 47
Underneath Your Rebel T1i 49
Lens Components 49
LCD Panel Readouts. 51
Looking Inside the Viewfinder 54

Chapter 3
Setting Up Your Canon EOS Rebel T1i/500D   57

Anatomy of the Rebel T1i's Menus. 58
Shooting 1 and 2 Menu Options. 60
    Quality Settings. 60
    Beep 64
    Release Shutter without Card 65
    Review Time 65
    Peripheral Illumination Correction 66
    Red-Eye Reduction 70
    Flash Control 72
    Exposure Compensation/Automatic Exposure Bracketing. 75
    Metering Mode. 77
    Custom White Balance 78
    White Balance Shift and Bracketing 79
    Color Space. 82
    Picture Style 85
    Dust Delete Data. 98
Playback Menu Options 99
    Protect 99
    Rotate. 101
    Erase Images. 102
    Print Order 102
    Transfer Order 102
    Histogram. 102
    Slide Show 104
    Image Jump with Main Dial 106

Setup 1, 2, and 3 Menu Options 107
    Auto Power Off 107
    File Numbering 108
    Auto Rotate 109
    Format 110
    LCD Auto Off 110
    Screen Color 111
    LCD Brightness 111
    Date/Time 111
    Language 113
    Video System 113
    Sensor Cleaning 114
    Live View Function Settings 115
    Custom Functions I/II/III/IV 115
    Clear Settings 128
    Firmware Version 129
My Menu 129
Movie Settings 131

Chapter 4
Fine-Tuning Exposure   133

Understanding Exposure 134
How the Rebel T1i Calculates Exposure 139
Choosing a Metering Method 143
Choosing a Creative Zone Exposure Method 146
    A-DEP 146
    Aperture Priority 148
    Shutter Priority 150
    Program Mode 151
    Making EV Changes 151
    Manual Exposure 152
Basic Zone Modes 153
    Creative Auto 155
Adjusting Exposure with ISO Settings 156
Bracketing 158
    Bracketing and Merge to HDR 160
Dealing with Noise 164
Fixing Exposures with Histograms 165

Chapter 5
Advanced Shooting with Your Canon
EOS Rebel T1i/500D   169

How Focus Works 169
    Phase Detection. 170
    Contrast Detection 172
Getting into Focus 174
    Focus Modes. 175
Focus Pocus 176
    Adding Circles of Confusion. 176
    Making Sense of Sensors. 179
    Your Autofocus Mode Options. 179
    Setting AF Point 181
Introducing Live View. 182
    What You Can/Cannot Do with Live View 184
    Enabling Live View 185
    Activating Live View. 186
Working with Live View 187
    Previewing and Making Settings 188
    Focusing in Live View. 191
Shooting Movies. 195
    Movie Settings 196
    Capturing Video/Sound. 197
Continuous Shooting 198
More Exposure Options 199
A Tiny Slice of Time 199
    Working with Short Exposures 201
Long Exposures 204
    Three Ways to Take Long Exposures 204
    Working with Long Exposures 205
Delayed Exposures 209
    Self-Timer. 210
    Remote Control 210
    Time-Lapse/Interval Photography 211

Chapter 6
Working with Lenses   213

But Don't Forget the Crop Factor 213
Your First Lens 215
    Buy Now, Expand Later 216
What Lenses Can You Use? 220
    EF vs. EF-S 221
Ingredients of Canon's Alphanumeric Soup 223
Your Second (and Third...) Lens 226
    What Lenses Can Do for You 226
    Zoom or Prime? 229
Categories of Lenses 230
Using Wide-Angle and Wide-Zoom Lenses 232
    Avoiding Potential Wide-Angle Problems 235
Using Telephoto and Tele-Zoom Lenses 237
    Avoiding Telephoto Lens Problems 239
    Telephotos and Bokeh 240
Add-ons and Special Features 242
    Lens Hoods 242
    Telephoto Extenders 242
    Macro Focusing 244
    Image Stabilization 245

Chapter 7
Making Light Work for You   247

Continuous Illumination versus Electronic Flash 248
Continuous Lighting Basics 253
    Daylight 254
    Incandescent/Tungsten Light 255
    Fluorescent Light/Other Light Sources 256
    Adjusting White Balance 257
Electronic Flash Basics 257
    How Electronic Flash Works 258

Using the Built-In Flash. 263
    Basic Zone Flash. 264
    Creative Zone Flash 264
    Flash Range 265
    Flash Control Menus 265
    Using FE Lock and Flash Exposure Compensation 269
Using External Electronic Flash 269
    Speedlite 580EX II 269
    Speedlite 430EX II 271
    Speedlite 270EX 271
    Speedlite 220EX 272
More Advanced Lighting Techniques 272
    Diffusing and Softening the Light 272
    Using Multiple Light Sources 274
    Other Lighting Accessories 277

Chapter 8
Downloading and Editing Your Images   281

What's in the Box? 281
    Picture Style Editor 281
    EOS Utility 282
    ZoomBrowser/ImageBrowser 285
    PhotoStitch 285
    Digital Photo Professional. 287
Transferring Your Photos 287
    Direct-Direct Transfer/Indirect-Direct Transfer 288
    Using a Card Reader and Software 292
    Dragging and Dropping 293
Editing Your Photos 293
    Image Editors 294
    RAW Utilities 295
    Adobe Photoshop 298

Chapter 9
Canon EOS Rebel T1i/500D:
Troubleshooting and Prevention   303

Update Your Firmware 304
    Upgrading Your Firmware 305
Protect Your LCD 307
Troubleshooting Memory Cards 309
    All Your Eggs in One Basket? 309
    What Can Go Wrong? 310
    What Can You Do? 311
Clean Your Sensor 313
    Dust the FAQs, Ma'am. 315
    Identifying and Dealing with Dust 316
    Avoiding Dust 317
    Sensor Cleaning 319

Glossary   327

Index   339

Preface

You don't want good pictures from your new Canon EOS Rebel T1i—you demand *outstanding photos*. After all, the Rebel T1i is the most advanced entry-level camera that Canon has ever introduced. It boasts more than 15 megapixels of resolution, blazing-fast automatic focus, and cool new features like the real-time preview system called Live View and honest-to-gosh full HD movie-making capabilities. But your gateway to pixel proficiency is dragged down by the slim little book included in the box as a manual. You know everything you need to know is in there, somewhere, but you don't know where to start. In addition, the camera manual doesn't offer much information on photography or digital photography. Nor are you interested in spending hours or days studying a comprehensive book on digital SLR photography that doesn't necessarily apply directly to your T1i.

What you need is a guide that explains the purpose and function of the T1i's basic controls, how you should use them, and *why*. Ideally, there should be information about file formats, resolution, aperture/priority exposure, and special autofocus modes, but you'd prefer to read about those topics only after you've had the chance to go out and take a few hundred great pictures with your new camera. Why isn't there a book that summarizes the most important information in its first two or three chapters, with lots of illustrations showing what your results will look like when you use this setting or that?

Now there is such a book. If you want a quick introduction to the T1i's focus controls, flash synchronization options, how to choose lenses, or which exposure modes are best, this book is for you. If you can't decide on what basic settings to use with your camera because you can't figure out how changing ISO or white balance or focus defaults will affect your pictures, you need this guide.

Introduction

Canon has done it again! It's packaged up many of the most alluring features of two of its advanced digital SLRs (in this case the Canon EOS 50D and EOS 5D Mark II) and stuffed them into a compact, highly affordable body called the EOS Rebel T1i (in the USA and some other countries; EOS 500D elsewhere except in Japan, where it is the Canon EOS Kiss Digital X3). Your new camera is loaded with capabilities that few would have expected to find in an "entry-level" dSLR. It has 15 megapixels of resolution, like the 50D, and 1920 × 1080-pixel full HD movie-making resolution, like the 5D Mark II.

Yet, the T1i retains the ease of use that smoothes the transition for those new to digital photography. For those just dipping their toes into the digital pond, the experience is warm and inviting. The Rebel T1i isn't a snapshot camera—it's a point-and-shoot (if you want to use it in that mode) for the thinking photographer.

But once you've confirmed that you made a wise purchase decision, the question comes up, *how do I use this thing?* All those cool features can be mind numbing to learn, if all you have as a guide is the manual furnished with the camera. Help is on the way. I sincerely believe that this book is your best bet for learning how to use your new camera, and for learning how to use it well.

If you're a Canon EOS Rebel T1i owner who's looking to learn more about how to use this great camera, you've probably already explored your options. There are DVDs and online tutorials—but who can learn how to use a camera by sitting in front of a television or computer screen? Do you want to watch a movie or click on HTML links, or do you want to go out and take photos with your camera? Videos are fun, but not the best answer.

There's always the manual furnished with the T1i. It's compact and filled with information, but there's really very little about *why* you should use particular settings or features, and its organization may make it difficult to find what you need. Multiple cross-references may send you flipping back and forth between two or three sections of the book to find what you want to know. The basic manual is also hobbled by black-and-white line drawings and tiny monochrome pictures that aren't very good examples of what you can do.

Also available are third-party guides to the T1i, like this one. I haven't been happy with some of these guidebooks, which is why I wrote this one. The existing books range from skimpy and illustrated by black-and-white photos to lushly illustrated in full color but too generic to do much good. Photography instruction is useful, but it needs to be related directly to the Canon EOS Rebel T1i as much as possible.

I've tried to make *David Busch's Canon EOS Rebel T1i/500D Guide to Digital SLR Photography* different from your other T1i learn-up options. The roadmap sections use larger, color pictures to show you where all the buttons and dials are, and the explanations of what they do are longer and more comprehensive. I've tried to avoid overly general advice, including the two-page checklists on how to take a "sports picture" or a "portrait picture" or a "travel picture." Instead, you'll find tips and techniques for using all the features of your Canon EOS Rebel T1i to take *any kind of picture* you want. If you want to know where you should stand to take a picture of a quarterback dropping back to unleash a pass, there are plenty of books that will tell you that. This one concentrates on teaching you how to select the best autofocus mode, shutter speed, f/stop, or flash capability to take, say, a great sports picture under any conditions.

This book is not a lame rewriting of the manual that came with the camera. Some folks spend five minutes with a book like this one, spot some information that also appears in the original manual, and decide "Rehash!" without really understanding the differences. Yes, you'll find information here that is also in the owner's manual, such as the parameters you can enter when changing your T1i's operation in the various menus. Basic descriptions—before I dig in and start providing in-depth tips and information—may also be vaguely similar. There are only so many ways you can say, for example, "Hold the shutter release down halfway to lock in exposure." But not *everything* in the manual is included in this book. If you want a large table showing which settings are available in each of the various Basic Zone and Creative Zone modes, you'd better use the Canon Function Availability Table in the original manual (it's on page 198). But if you need advice on when and how to use the most important functions, you'll find the information here.

David Busch's Canon EOS Rebel T1i/500D Guide to Digital SLR Photography is aimed at both Canon and dSLR veterans as well as newcomers to digital photography and digital SLRs. Both groups can be overwhelmed by the options the T1i offers, while underwhelmed by the explanations they receive in their user's manual. The manuals are great if you already know what you don't know, and you can find an answer somewhere in a booklet arranged by menu listings and written by a camera vendor employee who last threw together instructions on how to operate a camcorder.

Once you've read this book and are ready to learn more, I hope you pick up one of my other guides to digital SLR photography. Four of them are offered by Course Technology PTR, each approaching the topic from a different perspective. They include:

Quick Snap Guide to Digital SLR Photography

Consider this a prequel to the book you're holding in your hands. It might make a good gift for a spouse or friend who may be using your T1i, but who lacks even basic knowledge about digital photography, digital SLR photography, and Canon EOS photography. It serves as an introduction that summarizes the basic features of digital SLR cameras in general (not just the T1i), and what settings to use and when, such as continuous autofocus/single autofocus, aperture/shutter priority, EV settings, and so forth. The guide also includes recipes for shooting the most common kinds of pictures, with step-by-step instructions for capturing effective sports photos, portraits, landscapes, and other types of images.

David Busch's Quick Snap Guide to Using Digital SLR Lenses

A bit overwhelmed by the features and controls of digital SLR lenses, and not quite sure when to use each type? This book explains lenses, their use, and lens technology in easy-to-access two- and four-page spreads, each devoted to a different topic, such as depth-of-field, lens aberrations, or using zoom lenses. If you have a friend or significant other who is less versed in photography, but who wants to borrow and use your Canon EOS Rebel T1i from time to time, this book can save you a ton of explanation.

Mastering Digital SLR Photography, Second Edition

This book is an introduction to digital SLR photography, with nuts-and-bolts explanations of the technology, more in-depth coverage of settings, and whole chapters on the most common types of photography. While not specific to the Rebel T1i, this book can show you how to get more from its capabilities.

Digital SLR Pro Secrets

This is my more advanced guide to dSLR photography with greater depth and detail about the topics you're most interested in. If you've already mastered the basics in *Mastering Digital SLR Photography*, this book will take you to the next level.

Family Resemblance

If you've owned previous models in the Canon EOS digital camera line, and copies of my books for those cameras, you're bound to notice a certain family resemblance. Canon has been very crafty in introducing upgraded cameras that share the best features of the models they replace, while adding new capabilities and options. You benefit in two ways. If you used an EOS Rebel XSi or Rebel XS prior to switching to the latest T1i model, you'll find that parts that haven't changed have a certain familiarity for you, making it easy to make the transition to the newest model. There are lots of features and menu choices of the T1i that are exactly the same as those in the most recent Rebel models, or even "big siblings" like the 40D and 50D. This family resemblance will help level the learning curve for you.

Similarly, when writing books for each new model, I try to retain the easy-to-understand explanations that worked for the earlier cameras, and concentrate on expanded descriptions of things readers have told me they want to know more about, a solid helping of fresh sample photos, and lots of details about the latest and greatest new features. Rest assured, this book was written expressly for you, and tailored especially for the EOS T1i.

Why the Canon EOS Rebel T1i Needs Special Coverage

There are many general digital photography books on the market. Why do I concentrate on books about specific digital SLRs like the Rebel T1i? One reason is that I feel dSLRs are the wave of the future for serious photographers, and those who join the ranks of digital photographers with single lens reflex cameras deserve books tailored to their equipment.

When I started writing digital photography books in 1995, digital SLRs cost $30,000 and few people other than certain professionals could justify them. Most of my readers a dozen years ago were stuck using the point-and-shoot low-resolution digital cameras of the time—even if they were advanced photographers. I took tons of digital pictures with an Epson digital camera with 1024×768 (less than 1 megapixel!) resolution, and which cost $500.

As recently as 2003 (before the original Digital Rebel was introduced), the lowest-cost dSLRs were priced at $3,000 or more. Today, anyone with around $500 can afford one of these basic cameras, and around $800 buys you a sophisticated model like the Canon EOS Rebel T1i (with lens). The digital SLR is no longer the exclusive bailiwick of the professional, the wealthy, or the serious photography addict willing to scrimp and save to acquire a dream camera. Digital SLRs have become the favored camera for anyone who wants to go beyond point-and-shoot capabilities. And Canon cameras have enjoyed a dominating position among digital SLRs because of Canon's innovation in introducing affordable cameras with interesting features and outstanding performance (particularly in the area of high ISO image quality). It doesn't hurt that Canon also provides both full-frame and smaller-format digital cameras and a clear migration path between them (if you stick to the Canon EF lenses that are compatible with both).

You've selected your camera of choice, and you belong in the Canon camp if you fall into one of the following categories:

- Individuals who want to get better pictures, or perhaps transform their growing interest in photography into a full-fledged hobby or artistic outlet with a Rebel T1i and advanced techniques.

- Those who want to produce more professional-looking images for their personal or business website, and feel that the Rebel T1i will give them more control and capabilities.

- Small business owners with more advanced graphics capabilities who want to use the Rebel T1i to document or promote their business.

- Corporate workers who may or may not have photographic skills in their job descriptions, but who work regularly with graphics and need to learn how to use digital images taken with a Canon EOS Rebel T1i for reports, presentations, or other applications.

- Professional webmasters with strong skills in programming (including Java, JavaScript, HTML, Perl, etc.) but little background in photography, but who realize that the T1i can be used for sophisticated photography.

- Graphic artists and others who already may be adept in image editing with Photoshop or another program, and who may already be using a film SLR (Canon or otherwise), but who need to learn more about digital photography and the special capabilities of the T1i dSLR.

Who Am I?

After spending years as the world's most successful unknown author, I've become slightly less obscure in the past few years, thanks to a horde of camera guidebooks and other photographically oriented tomes. You may have seen my photography articles in *Popular Photography & Imaging* magazine. I've also written about 2,000 articles for magazines like *Petersen's PhotoGraphic* (which is now defunct through no fault of my own), plus *The Rangefinder, Professional Photographer*, and dozens of other photographic publications. You might have caught my advice on National Public Radio's *All Tech Considered*. But, first, and foremost, I'm a photojournalist and made my living in the field until I began devoting most of my time to writing books.

Although I love writing, I'm happiest when I'm out taking pictures, which is why I invariably spend several days each week photographing landscapes, people, close-up subjects, and other things. I spend a month or two each year traveling to events, such as Native American "powwows," Civil War re-enactments, county fairs, ballets, and sports (baseball, basketball, football, and soccer are favorites). A few months ago, I took 14 days for a solo visit to Europe, strictly to shoot photographs of the people, landscapes, and monuments that I've grown to love. And just a few weeks before starting on this book, I spent time in Arizona, catching up on baseball spring training and natural wonders like the Sedona Red Rocks and the Grand Canyon. I can offer you my personal advice on how to take photos under a variety of conditions because I've had to meet those challenges myself on an ongoing basis.

Like all my digital photography books, this one was written by someone with an incurable photography bug. My first Canon SLR was a Pellix back in the 1960s, and I've used a variety of newer models since then. I've worked as a sports photographer for an Ohio newspaper and for an upstate New York college. I've operated my own commercial studio and photo lab, cranking out product shots on demand and then printing a few hundred glossy 8 × 10s on a tight deadline for a press kit. I've served as a photo-posing instructor for a modeling agency. People have actually paid me to shoot their weddings and immortalize them with portraits. I even prepared press kits and articles on photography as a PR consultant for a large Rochester, N.Y., company, which shall remain nameless. My trials and travails with imaging and computer technology have made their way into print in book form an alarming number of times, including a few dozen on scanners and photography.

Like you, I love photography for its own merits, and I view technology as just another tool to help me get the images I see in my mind's eye. But, also like you, I had to master this technology before I could apply it to my work. This book is the result of what I've learned, and I hope it will help you master your Rebel T1i digital SLR, too.

As I write this, I'm currently in the throes of upgrading my website and blog, which you can find at www.dslrguides.com/blog, adding tutorials and information about my other books. I'll be adding more tips and recommendations (including a list of equipment and accessories that I can't live without) in the next few months. I hope you'll stop by for a visit.

Getting Started with Your Canon EOS Rebel T1i/500D

Canon has made the migration path through its digital Rebel (formerly Digital Rebel) camera line so seductively easy that it's a safe bet that many of you are jumping to this latest entry-level flagship directly from an earlier EOS model, like the Rebel XT, XTi, or even the relatively new Rebel XSi. The enhanced features of the Canon EOS Rebel T1i/500D are hard to resist, including a whopping 15 megapixels of resolution and honest HDTV movie-making capabilities.

So, if you *do* have experience with a previous Rebel model, it's very likely that by the time you picked up this book, you'd already taken a few hundred or a few thousand photos. And even if you have never picked up a digital SLR (or even a digital camera) before, you still may have conducted some warmly rewarding experiments with your camera before you decided to buckle down with this book and learn all its features.

Well, why not? The T1i is incredibly easy to use. The initial steps, including charging the battery, mounting a lens, attaching a neckstrap, and inserting a Secure Digital memory card aren't exactly rocket science. Every control you need to use to begin snapping pictures is nestled on the top surface, to the right of the viewfinder. There's an On/Off switch, the shutter release button, and a large Mode dial that includes an Auto position labeled with a green icon, plus seven helpful Basic Mode icons picturing a human profile (Portrait mode), a mountain (Landscape mode), blooming flower (Close-up mode), a dashing speedster (Sports mode), a human under night-time illumination (Night scenes), a lightning bolt with the symbol for NO drawn through it (no flash mode), and, finally, an icon that looks suspiciously like an old-fashioned movie camera (Movie mode). The rawest neophyte can turn on the camera, spin the dial to one of those settings, and begin shooting. For an old hand with Canon cameras, getting started with the T1i is even more of a no-brainer.

So, even if you didn't march out of a camera store with a Rebel box under one arm, and my book in hand, you're probably ready to learn more. It's not a bad idea, once you've taken a few orientation pictures with your T1i, to go back and review the basic operations of the camera from the beginning, if only to see if you've missed something. This chapter is my opportunity to review the setup procedures for the camera for those among you who are already veteran users, and to help ease the more timid (and those who have never worked with a digital SLR before) into the basic pre-flight checklist that needs to be completed before you really spread your wings and take off. For the uninitiated, as easy as it is to use initially, the Rebel T1i *does* have lots of dials and buttons and settings that might not make sense at first, but will surely become second nature after you've had a chance to review the instructions in this chapter.

But don't fret about wading through a manual to find out what you must know to take those first few tentative snaps. I'm going to help you hit the ground running with this chapter (or keep on running if you've already jumped right in). If you *haven't* had the opportunity to use your Rebel yet, I'll help you set up your camera and begin shooting in minutes. You won't find a lot of detail in this chapter. Indeed, I'm going to tell you just what you absolutely *must* understand, accompanied by some interesting tidbits that will help you become acclimated. I'll go into more depth and even repeat some of what I explain here in later chapters, so you don't have to memorize everything you see. Just relax, follow a few easy steps, and then go out and begin taking your best shots—ever.

Contents of the Box

You probably spread out on a table or desk the contents of the handsome box that transported the Canon EOS Rebel T1i from its birthplace in Japan. The box is filled with stuff, including connecting cords, booklets, CDs, and lots of paperwork. The first thing you should do (or the *next* thing you should do, if you've already been taking pictures with your camera), is to double-check the contents of the box to make sure nothing was left out, or accidentally removed by the retailer. Someone might have checked out the camera for you as a quality assurance method, or a curious store employee might have rooted through the box to see what this cool new camera actually looks like. In either case, it's entirely possible that something went astray, and it's good to know that *now,* when you can easily bring any missing pieces to the attention of the store that sold you the camera. Otherwise, a month down the road you're going to decide to see what the output of your Rebel T1i looks like on your TV screen, and discover that the video cable you *thought* you had has gone AWOL at some unknown time.

So, check the box at your earliest convenience, and make sure you have (at least) the following:

- **Canon EOS Rebel T1i camera.** This is hard to miss. The camera is the main reason you laid out the big bucks, and it is tucked away inside a nifty bubble-wrap envelope you should save for protection in case the T1i needs to be sent in for repair.

- **Rubber eyecup.** This slide-on soft-rubber eyecup should be attached to the viewfinder when you receive the camera. It helps you squeeze your eye tightly against the window, excluding extraneous light, and also protects your eyeglasses (if you wear them) from scratching.

- **Body cap.** The twist-off body cap keeps dust from entering the camera when no lens is mounted. Even with automatic sensor cleaning built into the T1i, you'll want to keep the amount of dust to a minimum. The body cap belongs in your camera bag if you contemplate the need to travel with the lens removed.

- **Lens (if purchased).** The Rebel T1i may come in a kit with the Canon Zoom Lens EF-S 18-55mm f/3.5-56 IS lens. Or, you may purchase it with another lens. The lens will come with a lens cap on the front, and a rear lens cap aft.

- **Battery pack LP-E5 (with cover).** The power source for your Rebel T1i is packaged separately. You'll need to charge this 7.4V, 1080mAh (milliampere hour) battery before using it. It should be charged as soon as possible (as described next) and inserted in the camera. Save the protective cover. If you transport a battery outside the camera, it's a good idea to re-attach the cover to prevent the electrical contacts from shorting out.

- **Battery charger LC-E5 or LC-E5E.** One of these two battery chargers will be included.

- **Wide strap EW-100DB III.** Canon provides you with a suitable neck strap, emblazoned with Canon advertising. While I am justifiably proud of owning a fine Canon camera, I prefer a low-key, more versatile strap from Optech (www.optech.com) or UPStrap (www.upstrap.com). If you carry your camera over one shoulder, as many do, I particularly recommend the UPStrap shown in Figure 1.1. That patented non-slip pad offers reassuring traction and eliminates the contortions we sometimes go through to keep the camera from slipping off. I know several photographers who refuse to use anything else. If you do purchase an UPStrap, be sure you mention to photographer-inventor Al Stegmeyer that I sent you hence. You won't get a discount, but Al will get yet another confirmation of how much I like his neckstraps.

- **Interface Cable IFC-200U.** You can use this USB cable to transfer photos from the camera to your computer, although I don't recommend that mode, because direct transfer uses a lot of battery power. You can also use the cable to upload and download settings between the camera and your computer (highly recommended), and to operate your camera remotely using the software included on the CD-ROM. This cable is a standard one that works with the majority of digital cameras—Canon and otherwise—so if you already own one, now you have a spare.

■ **AV Cable AVC-DC400.** Use this cable to view your camera's LCD output on a larger television screen, monitor, or other device with a yellow RCA composite input jack.

■ **EOS Digital Solution Disc CD.** The disk contains useful software that will be discussed in more detail in Chapter 9.

■ **Software Instruction manual CD.** While the software itself is easy to use, if you need more help you'll find it in the PDF manuals included on this CD.

■ **Printed instruction manuals.** These include the 228-page Instruction Manual. Even if you have this book, you'll probably want to check the printed user's guide that Canon provides, if only to check the actual nomenclature for some obscure accessory, or to double-check an error code. Google "Canon T1i manual PDF" to find a downloadable, non-printable version that you can store on your laptop, a CD-ROM, or other media in case you want to access this reference when the paper version isn't handy. If you have an old SD card that's too small to be usable on a

Figure 1.1 Third-party neck straps, like this UPStrap model, are often preferable to the Canon-supplied strap.

modern dSLR (I still have some 128MB and 256MB cards), you can store the PDF on that. But an even better choice is to put the manual on a low-capacity USB "thumb" drive, which you can buy for less than $10. You'll then be able to access the reference anywhere you are, because you can always find someone with a computer that has a USB port and Adobe Acrobat Reader available. You might not be lucky enough to locate a computer with an SD card reader.

■ **Pocket guide.** This little booklet tucked away in the camera's paperwork offers a reasonable summary of the Canon T1i's basic commands and settings, and can be stowed in your camera bag more easily than a "field guide" or even this book. There's also a CD-ROM Guide, which details the bundled software.

■ **Warranty and registration card.** Don't lose these! You can register your Canon T1i by mail, although you don't really need to in order to keep your warranty in force, but you may need the information in this paperwork (plus the purchase receipt/invoice from your retailer) should you require Canon service support.

Don't bother rooting around in the box for anything beyond what I've listed previously. There are a few things Canon classifies as optional accessories, even though you (and I) might consider some of them essential. Here's a list of what you *don't* get in the box, but might want to think about as an impending purchase. I'll list them roughly in the order of importance:

■ **Secure Digital (SD) card.** First-time digital camera buyers are sometimes shocked that their new tool doesn't come with a memory card. Why should it? The manufacturer doesn't have the slightest idea of how much storage you require, or whether you want a slow/inexpensive card or one that's faster/more expensive, so why should they pack one in the box and charge you for it? Given the T1i's 15-megapixel resolution, I recommend starting out with a memory card no smaller than 4GB in capacity.

■ **Extra LP-E5 battery.** Even though you might get 500 or more shots from a single battery, it's easy to exceed that figure in a few hours of shooting sports at 3.4 fps. Batteries can unexpectedly fail, too, or simply lose their charge from sitting around unused for a week or two. Buy an extra (I own four, in total), keep it charged, and free your mind from worry.

■ **HDMI Cable HTC-100.** Your camera has an HDMI port for connecting to a high-definition television, but no Type C cable to link the port with your HDTV. Of course, you might not own an HDTV, which is why Canon doesn't include one in the box. But, if you do, you'll want to pick up a cable so you can view your movies and stills in all their glory on the wide screen.

■ **Add-on speedlight.** One of the best uses for your Canon T1i's built-in electronic flash is as a remote trigger for an off-camera speedlight such as the Canon 580EX II, the top of the line model, or the less expensive 270EX and 430EX II, which were designed especially for cameras in this class. Your built-in flash can function as the main illumination for your photo, or be softened and used to fill in shadows. But, you'll have to own one or more external flash units to gain that flexibility. If you do much flash photography at all, consider an add-on speedlight as an important accessory.

- **AC Adapter Kit ACK-E5.** This includes the Compact Power Adapter CA-PS700 and DC Coupler DR-E5, which are used together to power the T1i independently of the batteries. There are several typical situations where this capability can come in handy: when you're cleaning the sensor manually and want to totally eliminate the possibility that a lack of juice will cause the fragile shutter and mirror to spring to life during the process; when indoors shooting tabletop photos, portraits, class pictures, and so forth for hours on end; when using your T1i for remote shooting as well as time-lapse photography; for extensive review of images on your television; or for file transfer to your computer. These all use prodigious amounts of power, which can be provided by this AC adapter. (Beware of power outages and blackouts when cleaning your sensor, however!)

- **Angle Finder C right angle viewer.** This handy accessory fastens in place of the standard rubber eyecup and provides a 90-degree view for framing and composing your image at right angles to the original viewfinder, useful for low-level (or high-level) shooting. (Or, maybe, shooting around corners!)

- **Battery Grip BG-E5.** This add-on vertical grip/battery pack can be outfitted with two LP-E5 batteries or six AA batteries for longer shooting life, and an extra shutter release and control dial for convenient shooting with the camera in a vertical orientation.

Initial Setup

The initial setup of your Canon EOS Rebel T1i is fast and easy. Basically, you just need to charge the battery, attach a lens, and insert a memory card. I'll address each of these steps separately, but if you already feel you can manage these setup tasks without further instructions, feel free to skip this section entirely. You should at least skim its contents, however, because I'm going to list a few options that you might not be aware of.

Battery Included

Your Canon EOS Rebel T1i is a sophisticated hunk of machinery and electronics, but it needs a charged battery to function, so rejuvenating the LP-E5 lithium-ion battery pack furnished with the camera should be your first step. A fully charged power source should be good for approximately 600 shots under normal temperature conditions, based on standard tests defined by the Camera & Imaging Products Association (CIPA) document DC-002. If half your pictures use the built-in flash, you can expect about

500 shots before it's time for a recharge. While those figures sound like a lot of shooting, things like picture review, playing with menus, and using the image stabilization features of your lens can use up more power than you might expect. Shooting in cold weather can reduce the battery's capacity, too. If your pictures are important to you, always take along one spare, fully charged battery.

And remember that all rechargeable batteries undergo some degree of self-discharge just sitting idle in the camera or in the original packaging. Lithium-ion power packs of this type typically lose a few percent of their charge every few days, even when the camera isn't turned on. Li-ion cells lose their power through a chemical reaction that continues when the camera is switched off. So, it's very likely that the battery purchased with your camera, even if charged at the factory, has begun to poop out after the long sea voyage on a banana boat (or, more likely, a trip by jet plane followed by a sojourn in a warehouse), so you'll want to revive it before going out for some serious shooting.

There are many situations in which you'll be glad you have that spare battery:

- **Remote locales.** If you like to backpack and will often be far from a source of electricity, rechargeable cells won't be convenient. They tend to lose some charge over time, even if not used, and will quickly become depleted as you use them. You'll have no way to recharge the cells, lacking a solar-powered charger that might not be a top priority for your backpacking kit.

- **Unexpected needs.** Perhaps you planned to shoot landscapes one weekend, and then are given free front-row tickets to a Major League Soccer game. Instead of a few dozen pictures of trees and lakes, you find yourself shooting hundreds of images of David Beckham and company, which may be beyond the capacity of the single battery you own. If you have a spare battery, you're in good shape.

- **Unexpected failures.** I've charged up batteries and then discovered that they didn't work when called upon, usually because the rechargeable cells had passed their useful life, the charger didn't work, or because of human error. (I *thought* I'd charged them!) That's one reason why I always carry three times as many batteries as I think I will need.

- **Long shooting session.** Perhaps your niece is getting married, and you want to photograph the ceremony, receiving line, and reception. Several extra batteries will see you through the longest shooting session.

Power Options

Several battery chargers and power sources are available for the Canon EOS Rebel T1i. The compact LC-E5, shown in Figure 1.2, plugs directly into a wall socket and is commonly furnished with the camera. Canon also provides the LC-E5E, which is similar, but has a cord. Purchasing one of the optional charging devices offers more than some additional features: You gain a spare that can keep your camera running until you can replace your primary power rejuvenator.

Figure 1.2
The orange status light indicates that the battery is being charged.

Here's a list of your power options:

- **LC-E5.** The standard charger for the T1i, this one is the most convenient, because of its compact size and built-in wall plug prongs that connect directly into your power strip or wall socket and requires no cord. This charger, as well as the LC-E5E, has a switching power module that is fully compatible with 100V to 240V 50/60 Hz AC power, so you can use it outside the US with no problems. When I travel to Europe, for example, I take my charger and an adapter to convert the plug shape for the European sockets. No voltage converter is needed.

- **LC-E5E.** This is similar to the LC-E5, and also charges a single battery, but requires a cord. That can be advantageous in certain situations. For example, if your power outlet is behind a desk or in some other semi-inaccessible location, the cord can be plugged in and routed so the charger itself sits on your desk or another more convenient spot. The cord itself is a standard one that works with many different chargers and devices (including the power supply for my laptop), so I purchased several of them and leave them plugged into the wall in various locations. I can connect my T1i's charger, my laptop computer's charger, and several other electronic components to one of these cords without needing to crawl around behind the furniture. The cord itself draws no power when it's not plugged into a charger.

- **AC Adapter Kit ACK-E5.** This device consists of Compact Power Adapter CA-PS700 and DC Couple DR-E5, and allows you to operate your Rebel T1i directly from AC power, with no battery required. Studio photographers need this capability because they often snap off hundreds of pictures for hours on end and want constant, reliable power. The camera is probably plugged into a flash sync cord (or radio device), and the studio flash are plugged into power packs or AC power, so the extra tether to this adapter is no big deal in that environment. You also might want to use the AC adapter when viewing images on a TV connected to your T1i, or when shooting remote or time-lapse photos.

- **Car Battery Charger CBC-E5.** This is a charger that can juice up your battery when connected to your auto's 12V power source. The vehicle battery option allows you to keep shooting when in remote locations that lack AC power.

- **Battery Grip BG-E5.** This accessory holds two LP-E5 batteries (another reason to own a spare, or two). It can also be equipped with six AA cells with the BGM-E5A battery holder. You can potentially increase your shooting capacity to 1,200 shots, while adding an additional shutter release, Main dial, AE lock/FE lock, and AF point selection controls for vertically oriented shooting.

Charging the Battery

When the battery is inserted into the LC-E5 charger properly (it's impossible to insert it incorrectly), a Charge light begins glowing orange-red. When the battery completes the charge, the lamp turns green, approximately two hours later. When the battery is charged, remove it from the charger, flip the lever on the bottom of the camera and slide the battery in. (See Figure 1.3.) To remove the battery, you must press a white lever, which prevents the pack from slipping out when the door is opened. (See Figure 1.4.)

Figure 1.3 Insert the battery in the camera; it only fits one way.

Figure 1.4 Press the white tab to release the battery when you want to remove it.

Final Steps

Your Canon EOS Rebel T1i is almost ready to fire up and shoot. You'll need to select and mount a lens, adjust the viewfinder for your vision, and insert a memory card. Each of these steps is easy, and if you've used any Canon EOS camera in the past, you already know exactly what to do. I'm going to provide a little extra detail for those of you who are new to the Canon or digital SLR worlds.

Mounting the Lens

As you'll see, my recommended lens mounting procedure emphasizes protecting your equipment from accidental damage, and minimizing the intrusion of dust. If your T1i has no lens attached, select the lens you want to use and loosen (but do not remove) the rear lens cap. I generally place the lens I am planning to mount vertically in a slot in my camera bag, where it's protected from mishaps, but ready to pick up quickly. By loosening the rear lens cap, you'll be able to lift it off the back of the lens at the last instant, so the rear element of the lens is covered until then.

After that, remove the body cap by rotating the cap towards the shutter release button. You should always mount the body cap when there is no lens on the camera, because it helps keep dust out of the interior of the camera, where it can settle on the mirror, focusing screen, the interior mirror box, and potentially find its way past the shutter onto the sensor. (While the T1i's sensor cleaning mechanism works fine, the less dust it has to contend with, the better.) The body cap also protects the vulnerable mirror from damage caused by intruding objects (including your fingers, if you're not cautious).

Once the body cap has been removed, remove the rear lens cap from the lens, set it aside, and then mount the lens on the camera by matching the alignment indicator on the lens barrel (red for EF lenses and white for EF-S lenses) with the red or white dot on the camera's lens mount. (See Figure 1.5.) Rotate the lens away from the shutter release until it seats securely. (You can find out more about the difference between EF and EF-S lenses in Chapter 6.) Set the focus mode switch on the lens to AF (autofocus). If the lens hood is bayoneted on the lens in the reversed position (which makes the lens/hood combination more compact for transport), twist it off and remount with the "petals" facing outward. (See Figure 1.6.) A lens hood protects the front of the lens from accidental bumps, and reduces flare caused by extraneous light arriving at the front element of the lens from outside the picture area.

Adjusting Diopter Correction

Those of us with less than perfect eyesight can often benefit from a little optical correction in the viewfinder. Your contact lenses or glasses may provide all the correction you need, but if you are a glasses wearer and want to use the Rebel T1i without your glasses, or use your glasses with your camera and can benefit from some additional correction, you can take advantage of the camera's built-in diopter adjustment. It can be

Figure 1.5 Match the white dot on EF-S lenses with the white dot on the camera mount to properly align the lens with the bayonet mount. For EF lenses, use the red dots.

Figure 1.6
A lens hood protects the lens from extraneous light and accidental bumps.

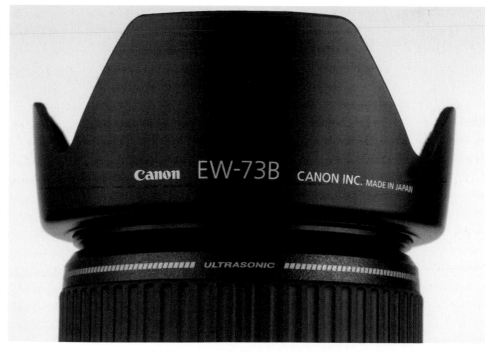

varied from –3 to +1 correction. Press the shutter release halfway to illuminate the indicators in the viewfinder, then rotate the adjacent diopter adjustment wheel (see Figure 1.7) while looking through the window until the indicators appear sharp.

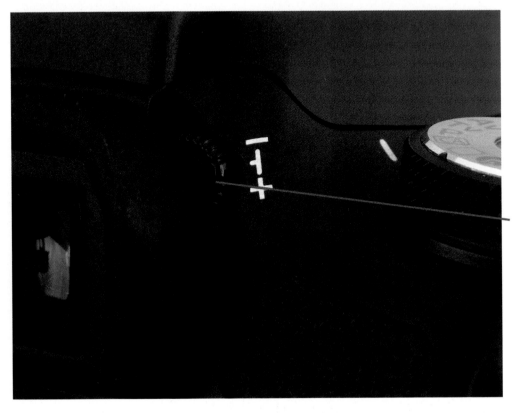

Figure 1.7
Viewfinder diopter correction from –3 to +1 can be dialed in.

diopter correction knob

If the available correction is insufficient, Canon offers 10 different Dioptric Adjustment Lens Series E correction lenses for the viewfinder window. If more than one person uses your T1i, and each requires a different diopter setting, you can save a little time by noting the number of clicks and direction (clockwise to increase the diopter power; counterclockwise to decrease the diopter value) required to change from one user to the other. There are 18 detents in all.

Inserting a Memory Card

You can't take photos without a memory card inserted in your Rebel T1i (although there is a Release Shutter without Card entry in Shooting Menu 1 that enables/disables shutter release functions when a memory card is absent—you'll learn about that in Chapter 3). So, your final step will be to insert a memory card. Slide the door on the right side of the body toward the back of the camera to release the cover, and then open it. (You should only remove the memory card when the camera is switched off, but the T1i will remind you if the door is opened while the camera is still writing photos to the memory card.)

Insert the memory card with the label facing the back of the camera, as shown in Figure 1.8, oriented so the edge with the gold contacts goes into the slot first. Close the door, and your preflight checklist is done! (I'm going to assume you remember to remove the lens cap when you're ready to take a picture!) When you want to remove the memory card later, just press the memory card edge, and it will pop right out.

Figure 1.8
The memory card is inserted with the label facing the back of the camera.

Formatting a Memory Card

There are three ways to create a blank SD card for your T1i, and two of them are at least partially wrong. Here are your options, both correct and incorrect:

- **Transfer (move) files to your computer.** When you transfer (rather than copy) all the image files to your computer from the SD card (either using a direct cable transfer or with a card reader, as described later in this chapter), the old image files are erased from the card, leaving the card blank. Theoretically. This method does *not* remove files that you've labeled as Protected (choosing the Protect Images function in Playback menu) nor does it identify and lock out parts of your memory card that have become corrupted or unusable since the last time you formatted the card.

Therefore, I recommend always formatting the card, rather than simply moving the image files, each time you want to make a blank card. The only exception is when you *want* to leave the protected/unerased images on the card for awhile longer, say, to share with friends, family, and colleagues.

- **(Don't) Format in your computer.** With the SD card inserted in a card reader or card slot in your computer, you can use Windows or Mac OS to reformat the memory card. Don't! The operating system won't necessarily arrange the structure of the card the way the T1i likes to see it (in computer terms, an incorrect *file system* may be installed). The only way to ensure that the card has been properly formatted for your camera is to perform the format in the camera itself. The only exception to this rule is when you have a seriously corrupted memory card that your camera refuses to format. Sometimes it is possible to revive such a corrupted card by allowing the operating system to reformat it first, then trying again in the camera.

- **Setup menu format.** To use the recommended method to format a memory card, press the Menu button, rotate Main dial (located on top of the camera, just behind the shutter release button), choose the Setup Menu 1 (which is represented by a wrench icon with a single dot next to it), use the up/down cross keys to navigate to the Format entry and press the Set button in the center of the cross key pad to access the Format screen. Press the left/right cross keys again to select OK and press the Set button one final time to begin the format process.

LOW LEVEL FORMAT

You can also press the Trash button, located in the lower-right corner of the back of the camera, to mark the Low level format box on the Format screen. This tells the T1i to perform an additional, more thorough, formatting of the card after the initial format is finished. The low level format serves to remove data from all writable portions of your memory card while locking out "bad" sectors, and can be used to restore a memory card that is slowing down as it "trips" over those bad sectors. This extra step takes a bit longer than a standard reformat, and need not be used every time you format your card.

Powering Up/Setting Date and Time

Rotate the On/Off switch on top of the camera to the On position. Automatic sensor cleaning takes place (unless you specifically disable this action) as the T1i powers up. The camera will remain on or in a standby mode until you manually turn it off. After 30 seconds of idling, the T1i goes into the standby mode to save battery power. Just tap the shutter release button to bring it back to life. The automatic sensor cleaning operation does not occur when exiting standby mode.

The first time you use the Rebel T1i, it may ask you to enter the time and date. (This information may have been set by someone checking out your camera on your behalf prior to sale.) Just follow these steps:

1. Press the Menu button, located in the upper-left corner of the back of the T1i.

2. Rotate the Main dial (near the shutter release button on top of the camera) until the Setup 2 menu is highlighted. It's marked by a wrench with two dots next to it, as shown in Figure 1.9.

Figure 1.9
Choose the Date/Time entry from the Setup 2 menu.

3. Use the up/down cross keys to move the highlighting down to the Date/Time entry.

4. Press the Set button in the center of the keypad to access the Date/Time setting screen, shown in Figure 1.10.

5. Use the left/right cross keys to select the value you want to change. When the gold box highlights the month, day, year, hour, minute, or second format you want to adjust, press the Set button to activate that value. A pair of up/down pointing triangles appears above the value.

6. Press the up/down cross keys to adjust the value up or down. Press the Set button to confirm the value you've entered.

Figure 1.10
Adjust the time and date format.

7. Repeat steps 5 and 6 for each of the other values you want to change. The date format can be switched from the default mm/dd/yy to yy/mm/dd or dd/mm/yy.

8. When finished, navigate with the right cross key to select either OK (if you're satisfied with your changes) or Cancel (if you'd like to return to the Setup 2 menu screen without making any changes). Press Set to confirm your choice.

9. When finished setting the date and time, press the Menu button to exit.

Once the Rebel T1i is satisfied that it knows what time it is, the Shooting Settings display, shown in Figure 1.11, should appear on the LCD. It shows the basic settings of the camera, including current shutter speed and lens opening, shooting mode, ISO sensitivity, and other parameters. I'll discuss this display in the next section, after I've had a chance to tell you more about the Basic Zone and Creative Zone modes.

Tip

There is also a Shooting Information display available with several screens of information *about a particular photo* that you have taken. (Just press the DISP button [upper-left corner of the back panel] when the image is presented for your review.) I'll explain the contents of that screen, too, later on.

Figure 1.11

The Shooting Settings display shows the current picture-taking settings of the Rebel T1i.

Selecting a Shooting Mode

You can choose a shooting method from the Mode dial located on the top right of the Canon EOS Rebel T1i. (See Figure 1.12.) There are nine Basic Zone shooting modes, in which the camera makes virtually all the decisions for you (except when to press the shutter), and five Creative Zone modes, which allow you to provide input over the exposure and settings the camera uses. You'll find a complete discussion of both Basic Zone and Creative Zone modes in Chapter 4.

Turn your camera on by flipping the power switch to On. Next, you need to select which shooting mode to use. If you're very new to digital photography, you might want to set the camera to Auto (the green frame on the Mode dial) or P (Program mode) and start snapping away. Either mode will make all the appropriate settings for you for many shooting situations. If you have a specific type of picture you want to shoot, you can try out one of the other Basic Zone modes indicated on the Mode dial with appropriate icons, as shown in Figure 1.13:

- **CA.** This Creative Auto mode is basically the same as the Full Auto option described next, but, unlike the other Basic Zone modes, allows you to change the brightness and other parameters of the image. The T1i still makes most of the decisions for you, but you can make some simple adjustments using the Shooting Setting screen (see Figure 1.14). Press the Set button when this screen is visible, and the Quick Control screen appears. Then use the cross keys to navigate to the adjustable settings.

Figure 1.12
The Mode dial includes both Basic Zone and Creative Zone settings.

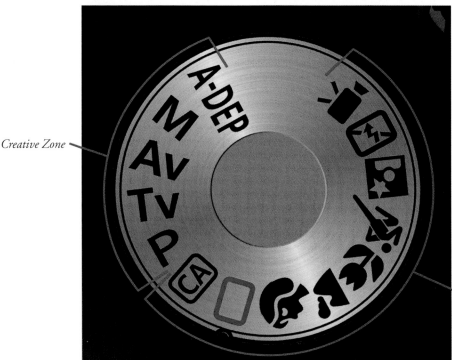

Creative Zone

Basic Zone

Figure 1.13
The Creative Zone modes (left side of dial as shown) let the photographer control how exposures are made, to increase creative options. The Basic Zone settings (right side of the dial) make all the exposure decisions for you.

Figure 1.14
Some settings
can be made
quickly when
the Shooting
Settings display
is visible.

- **Auto.** In this mode, the T1i makes all the exposure decisions for you, and will pop up the flash if necessary under low light conditions.

- **Portrait.** Use this mode when you're taking a portrait of a subject standing relatively close to the camera and want to de-emphasize the background, maximize sharpness, and produce flattering skin tones.

- **Landscape.** Select this mode when you want extra sharpness and rich colors of distant scenes.

- **Close-up.** This mode is helpful when you are shooting close-up pictures of a subject from about one foot away or less.

- **Sports.** Use this mode to freeze fast-moving subjects.

- **Night Portrait.** Choose this mode when you want to illuminate a subject in the foreground with flash, but still allow the background to be exposed properly by the available light. Be prepared to use a tripod or an image-stabilized (IS) lens to reduce the effects of camera shake. (You'll find more about IS and camera shake in Chapter 6.)

- **Flash Off.** This is the mode to use in museums and other locations where flash is forbidden or inappropriate. It otherwise operates exactly like the Auto setting but disables the pop-up internal flash unit.

- **Movie.** Use this mode to shoot videos in Live View.

If you have more photographic experience, you might want to opt for one of the Creative Zone modes. These, too, are described in more detail in Chapter 4. These modes let you apply a little more creativity to your camera's settings. These modes are indicated on the Mode dial by the letters A-DEP, M, Av, Tv, and P:

- **A-DEP (Automatic depth-of-field).** Choose this mode if you want to allow the T1i to select an f/stop that will maximize depth-of-field for the subjects in the frame as it adjusts focus and selects an appropriate shutter speed.

- **M (Manual).** Select when you want full control over the shutter speed and lens opening, either for creative effects or because you are using a studio flash or other flash unit not compatible with the T1i's automatic flash metering.

- **Av (Aperture Priority).** Choose when you want to use a particular lens opening, especially to control sharpness or how much of your image is in focus. The T1i will select the appropriate shutter speed for you. Av stands for *aperture value.*

- **Tv (Shutter Priority).** This mode (Tv stands for *time value*) is useful when you want to use a particular shutter speed to stop action or produce creative blur effects. The T1i will select the appropriate f/stop for you.

- **P (Program).** This mode allows the T1i to select the basic exposure settings, but you can still override the camera's choices to fine-tune your image.

As I mentioned earlier, you can change some settings when the Shooting Settings display is shown on the screen (press the DISP button to the left of the viewfinder window if you want to make the display visible). Press the Set button and then use the cross keys to navigate to the setting you'd like to adjust. The available adjustments depend on what Basic Zone or Creative Zone exposure mode you're using.

- **Basic Zone.** When using Basic Zone modes other than Creative Auto, you can change only the Drive mode (Single Shot, Continuous Shooting and multiple Self-Timer/Remote modes), and Image Quality (Large, Medium, and Small resolutions in Fine or Standard JPEG modes, plus RAW or RAW+JPEG—all explained in detail in Chapter 3). Changeable items will be highlighted.

- **Creative Auto.** You can adjust additional settings, including flash modes, Picture Styles (or image effects), brightness, and depth-of-field (range of sharpness).

- **Creative Zone.** You can adjust any of the settings visible on the Shooting Settings display.

I'll explain these features as well as the Shooting Settings display itself, in later chapters of this book (especially in Chapter 4, which deals with exposure).

Choosing a Metering Mode

You might want to select a particular metering mode for your first shots, although the default Evaluative metering (which is set automatically when you choose a Basic Zone mode) is probably the best choice as you get to know your camera. To change metering modes, you'll need to use the T1i's menu system. (Upgraders beware: the Rebel XSi used the up cross key as a Metering Mode button. That button is now used to set White Balance on the T1i.)

Press the Menu button and navigate to the Shooting 2 menu (a camera icon with two dots next to it). Press Set. A screen pops up on the LCD offering four choices. Keep pressing the Metering Mode button until the choice you want is highlighted. Then press the Set button to confirm your choice. The options are shown in Figure 1.15:

- **Evaluative metering.** The standard metering mode; the T1i attempts to intelligently classify your image and choose the best exposure based on readings from 35 different zones in the frame, with emphasis on the autofocus points.

- **Partial metering.** Exposure is based on a central spot, roughly nine percent of the image area.

Figure 1.15
Metering modes (left to right) Evaluative, Partial, Spot, Center-Weighted.

- **Spot metering.** Exposure is calculated from a smaller central spot, about 3.8 percent of the image area.
- **Center-Weighted Averaging metering.** The T1i meters the entire scene, but gives the most emphasis to the central area of the frame.

You'll find a detailed description of each of these modes in Chapter 4.

Choosing a Focus Mode

You can easily switch between automatic and manual focus by moving the AF/MF switch on the lens mounted on your camera. However, if you're using a Creative Zone shooting mode, you'll still need to choose an appropriate focus mode. (You can read more on selecting focus parameters in Chapter 5.) If you're using a Basic Zone mode, the focus method is set for you automatically.

To set the focus mode, you must first have set the lens to the AF position (instead of the manual focus MF position). Then press the AF button (it's the right cross key) on the back of the camera repeatedly until the focus mode you want is selected (see Figure 1.16). Finally, press Set to confirm your focus mode. The three choices available in Creative Zone modes are

- **One Shot.** This mode, sometimes called *Single Autofocus*, locks in a focus point when the shutter button is pressed down halfway, and the focus confirmation light glows in the viewfinder. The focus will remain locked until you release the button or take the picture. If the camera is unable to achieve sharp focus, the focus confirmation light will blink. This mode is best when your subject is relatively motionless. Portrait, Night Portrait, and Landscape Basic Zone modes use this focus method exclusively.

- **AI Servo.** This mode, sometimes called *Continuous Autofocus*, sets focus when you partially depress the shutter button, but continues to monitor the frame and refocuses if the camera or subject is moved. This is a useful mode for photographing sports and moving subjects. The Sports Basic Zone mode uses this focus method exclusively.

- **AI Focus.** In this mode, the T1i switches between One Shot and AI Servo as appropriate. That is, it locks in a focus point when you partially depress the shutter button (One Shot mode), but switches automatically to AI Servo if the subject begins to move. This mode is handy when photographing a subject, such as a child at quiet play, which might move unexpectedly. The Flash Off Basic Zone mode uses this focus method.

Figure 1.16
Set Autofocus
mode.

Selecting a Focus Point

The Canon EOS Rebel T1i uses nine different focus points to calculate correct focus. In A-DEP, or any of the Basic Zone shooting modes, the focus point is selected automatically by the camera. In the other Creative Zone modes, you can allow the camera to select the focus point automatically, or you can specify which focus point should be used.

There are several methods to set the focus point manually. You can press the AF Point Selection button on the back of the camera (it's in the upper-right corner), and choose a zone from the AF Point Selection screen that pops up when your eye is not pressed against the viewfinder. (See Figure 1.17.) Press the Set button to toggle between automatic focus point selection (the camera does it for you) or manual focus point selection (you need to specify the point yourself). In Manual selection mode, the cross keys are used to highlight the point you want to use. Press the AF Point Selection button again (or just tap the shutter release button) to confirm your choice and exit.

Or, you can look through the viewfinder, press the AF Point Selection button, and rotate the Main dial to move the focus point to the zone you want to use. (See Figure 1.18.) The focus point will cycle among the edge points counterclockwise (if you turn the Main dial to the left) or clockwise (if you spin the Main dial to the right), ending/starting with the center focus point/all nine focus points.

Figure 1.17
Select a focus point and selection mode from the AF point selection screen.

Figure 1.18
Or choose the focus point while looking through the viewfinder.

Other Settings

There are a few other settings you can make if you're feeling ambitious, but don't feel ashamed if you postpone using these features until you've racked up a little more experience with your Rebel T1i.

Adjusting White Balance and ISO

If you like, you can custom-tailor your white balance (color balance) and ISO sensitivity settings. To start out, it's best to set white balance (WB) to Auto, and ISO to ISO 100 or ISO 200 for daylight photos, and ISO 400 for pictures in dimmer light. You'll find complete recommendations for both these settings in Chapter 4. You can adjust either one now by pressing the WB button (the up cross key for white balance) or the ISO button (just aft of the Main dial) and then using the cross keys to navigate until the setting you want appears on the LCD.

If you've been playing with your camera's settings, or your T1i has been used by someone else, you can restore the factory defaults by selecting Clear Settings from the Setup Menu 3. Just press the Menu button (located at the upper-left corner of the back of the camera), press the right cross key until the yellow wrench icon with a vertical row of three dots is highlighted, then press the down cross key to select Clear Settings. A screen will pop up asking whether you'd like to Clear All Camera Settings, or Clear All Custom Func. (C. Fn.). Choose the one you'd like to reset, and press the Set button. I'll explain *why* you might want to reset your camera in more detail (for those who are now wondering why) in Chapter 3.

Using the Self-Timer

If you want to set a short delay before your picture is taken, you can use the self-timer. Press the Drive/left cross key button and then press the right cross key to select from either the 10-second self-timer (which also can be used with the optional RC-1 and RC-5 infrared remote controls), 2-second self-timer, or Self-timer: Continuous, which allows you to press the up/down cross keys to specify a number of shots to be taken (from 2 to 10) once the timer runs its course (see Figure 1.19). Press the Set button to confirm your choice, and a self-timer icon will appear on the Shooting Settings display on the back of the Rebel T1i. Press the shutter release to lock focus and start the timer. The self-timer lamp will blink and the beeper will sound (unless you've silenced it in the menus) until the final two seconds, when the lamp remains on and the beeper beeps more rapidly.

Canon recommends slipping off the eyepiece cup and replacing it with the viewfinder cap, in order to keep extraneous light from reaching the exposure meter through the viewfinder "back door." I usually just shade the viewfinder window with my hand (if I'm using the self-timer to reduce camera shake for a long exposure) or drape something over the back of the camera (if I'm scurrying to get into the picture myself).

Figure 1.19
The Drive modes include (left to right) Single Shot, Continuous, 10-second delay/Remote, 2-second delay, and Self-timer Continuous (which takes multiple shots when the self-timer's delay has elapsed).

Using the Built-in Flash

Working with the EOS T1i's built-in flash (as well as external flash units like the Canon 580EX II) deserves a chapter of its own, and I'm providing one (see Chapter 8). But the built-in flash is easy enough to work with that you can begin using it right away, either to provide the main lighting of a scene, or as supplementary illumination to fill in the shadows. The T1i will automatically balance the amount of light emitted from the flash so that it illuminates the shadows nicely, without overwhelming the highlights and producing a glaring "flash" look. (Think *Baywatch* when they're using too many reflectors on the lifeguards!)

The T1i's flash has a power rating of 13/43 (meters/feet) at ISO 100, using the GN (guide number) system that dates back to the film era and before electronic flash units had any sort of automatic features. I'll explain guide numbers (which can be a little confusing) in more detail in Chapter 8, but in plain terms the flash's rating means that the unit is powerful enough to allow proper illumination of a subject that's 10 feet away at f/4 at the *lowest* ISO (sensitivity) setting of your camera. Boost the ISO (or use a wider f/stop) and you can shoot subjects that are located at a great distance. For example, at

ISO 800, the T1i's flash is good enough for a subject at 20 feet using f/5.6 or, alternatively, you can expose that scene at the original 10 feet distance at f/11. Ordinarily, the T1i takes care of all these calculations for you. If you need a bigger blast of light, you can add one of the Canon external flash units, described in Chapter 8.

The flash will pop up automatically when using any of the Basic Zone modes except for Landscape, Sports, or No Flash modes. In Creative Zone modes, just press the flash button (shown in Figure 1.20). When using these modes, the flash functions in the following way:

- **P (Program mode).** The T1i selects a shutter speed from 1/60th to 1/250th second and appropriate aperture automatically.

- **Tv (Shutter Priority mode).** You choose a shutter speed from 30 seconds to 1/250th second, and the T1i chooses the lens opening for you, while adjusting the flash output to provide the correct exposure.

Figure 1.20
The pop-up electronic flash can be used as the main light source, or for supplemental illumination.

■ **Av (Aperture Priority mode).** You select the aperture you want to use, and the camera will select a shutter speed from 30 seconds to 1/200th second, and adjust the flash output to provide the correct exposure. In low light levels, the T1i may select a very slow shutter speed to allow the flash and background illumination to balance out, so you should use a tripod. (You can disable this behavior using Custom Function I-07 Flash sync. Speed in Av mode, as described in Chapter 3.)

■ **M (Manual mode).** You choose both shutter speed and aperture, and the camera will adjust the flash output to produce a good exposure based on the aperture you've selected.

■ **A-DEP (Automatic Depth-of-Field mode).** When using flash, the A-DEP setting functions exactly the same as the P (Program Mode) setting.

You can read about flash exposure compensation, red-eye reduction options, and other built-in flash features in Chapter 8.

Taking a Picture

Just press the shutter release button halfway to lock in focus at the selected autofocus point for about four seconds. (Remember that you can select a focus point manually when using Creative Zone modes other than A-DEP, while the camera always chooses the focus point in A-DEP and Basic Zone modes.) When the shutter button is in the half-depressed position, the exposure, calculated using the Shooting mode you've selected, is also locked.

Press the button the rest of the way down to take a picture. At that instant, the mirror flips up out of the light path to the optical viewfinder (assuming you're not using Live View mode, discussed in Chapter 6), the shutter opens, the electronic flash (if enabled) fires, and your T1i's sensor absorbs a burst of light to capture an exposure. In moments, the shutter closes, the mirror flips back down restoring your view, and the image you've taken is escorted off the CMOS sensor chip very quickly into an in-camera store of memory called a buffer, and the EOS T1i is ready to take another photo. The buffer continues dumping your image onto the memory card as you keep snapping pictures without pause (at least until the buffer fills and you must wait for it to get ahead of your continuous shooting, or your memory card fills completely).

Reviewing the Images You've Taken

The Canon EOS Rebel T1i has a broad range of playback and image review options, including the ability to jump ahead 10 or 100 images at a time. I'll cover them in more detail in Chapter 3. For now, you'll want to learn just the basics. Here is all you really need to know at this time, as shown in Figure 1.21:

- **Display image.** Press the Playback button (marked with a blue right-pointing triangle just southeast of the color LCD) to display the most recent image on the LCD in full-screen Single Image mode. If you last viewed your images using the thumbnail mode (described later in this list), the Index display appears instead.

- **View additional images.** Use the left and right cross keys to view the next or previous image.

- **Jump ahead or back.** If you want to zip through your shots more quickly to find a specific image, rotate the Main dial to leap ahead or back 10 or 100 images, depending on the increment you've set using the last entry in the Playback 2 menu.

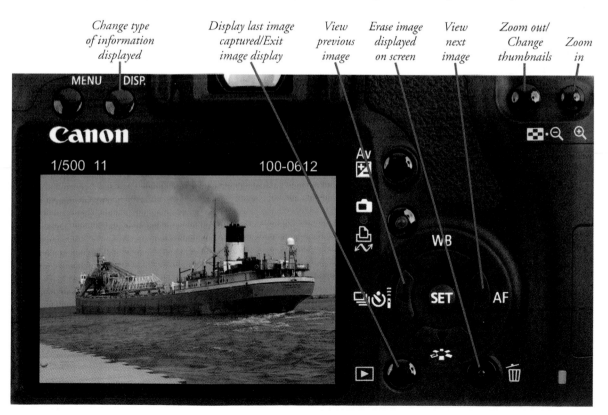

Change type of information displayed   *Display last image captured/Exit image display*   *View previous image*   *Erase image displayed on screen*   *View next image*   *Zoom out/ Change thumbnails*   *Zoom in*

Figure 1.21 Review your images.

(Those migrating from the 40D will note that the earlier camera had a Jump button that was used instead. I find the T1i's use of the Main dial is faster, because you don't have to fumble for the Jump button; just spin the dial.) You can also jump ahead by screens of images, by date, or by folder. I'll show you how to select these options in the discussion of the Playback menu in Chapter 3.

- **View image information.** Press the DISP button repeatedly to cycle among overlays of basic image information, detailed shooting information, or no information at all.

- **Zoom in on an image.** When an image is displayed full-screen on your LCD, press the Magnify/Enlarge button repeatedly to zoom in. The Magnify/Enlarge button is located in the upper-left corner of the back of the camera, marked with a blue magnifying glass with a plus sign in it. The Reduce Image button, located to the right of the Magnify/Enlarge button, zooms back out. Press the Playback button to exit magnified display.

- **Scroll around in a magnified image.** Use the left/right/up/down cross keys to scroll around within a magnified image.

- **View thumbnail images.** You can also rapidly move among a large number of images using the Index mode described in the section that follows this list. The Reduce Image/Zoom Out button in full-frame view switches from single image to display of four or nine reduced-size thumbnails. To change from a larger number of thumbnails to a smaller number (from nine to four to single image, for example), press the Zoom In button until the display you want appears.

Cruising Through Index Views

You can navigate quickly among thumbnails representing a series of images using the T1i's Index mode. Here are your options:

- **Display thumbnails.** Press the Playback button to display an image on the color LCD. If you last viewed your images using Index mode, an Index array of four or nine reduced-size images appears automatically (see Figure 1.22). If an image pops up full-screen in Single Image mode, press the Reduce Image button once to view four thumbnails, or twice to view nine thumbnails. You can switch between four, nine, and single images by pressing the Reduce Image button to see more/smaller versions of your images, and the Magnify/Enlarge button to see fewer/larger versions of your images.

- **Navigate within a screen of index images.** In Index mode, use the up/down/left/right cross keys to move the blue highlight box around within the current Index display screen.

Figure 1.22
Review thumbnails of four or nine images using Index review.

- **View more Index pages.** To view additional Index pages, rotate the Main dial. The display will leap ahead or back by the Jump increment you've set in the Playback 2 menu (as described in Chapter 3), 10 or 100 images, by index page, by date, or by folder.

- **Check image.** When an image you want to examine more closely is highlighted, press the Magnify/Enlarge button until the Single Image version appears full-screen on your LCD.

Transferring Photos to Your Computer

The final step in your picture-taking session will be to transfer the photos you've taken to your computer for printing, further review, or image editing. Your T1i allows you to print directly to PictBridge-compatible printers and to create print orders right in the camera, plus you can select which images to transfer to your computer. I'll outline those options in Chapter 3.

For now, you'll probably want to transfer your images either by using a cable transfer from the camera to the computer or by removing the memory card from the T1i and transferring the images with a card reader. The latter option is usually the best, because it's usually much faster and doesn't deplete the battery of your camera. However, you can use a cable transfer when you have the cable and a computer, but no card reader (perhaps you're using the computer of a friend or colleague, or at an Internet café).

To transfer images from the camera to a Mac or PC computer using the USB cable:

1. Turn off the camera.

2. Pry back the rubber cover that protects the Rebel T1i's USB port, and plug the USB cable furnished with the camera into the USB port. (See Figure 1.23.)

3. Connect the other end of the USB cable to a USB port on your computer.

4. Turn the camera on. Your installed software usually detects the camera and offers to transfer the pictures, or the camera appears on your desktop as a mass storage device, enabling you to drag and drop the files to your computer.

Figure 1.23
Images can be transferred to your computer using a USB cable.

To transfer images from a memory card to the computer using a card reader, as shown in Figure 1.24:

1. Turn off the camera.

2. Slide open the memory card door, and press on the card, which causes it to pop up so it can be removed from the slot.

3. Insert the memory card into your memory card reader. Your installed software detects the files on the card and offers to transfer them. The card can also appear as a mass storage device on your desktop, which you can open, and then drag and drop the files to your computer.

Figure 1.24
A card reader is the fastest way to transfer photos.

2

Canon EOS Rebel T1i/500D Roadmap

One thing that surprises new owners of the Canon EOS Rebel T1i is that the camera has a total of 496 buttons, dials, switches, levers, latches, and knobs bristling from its surface. Okay, I lied. Actually, the real number is closer to two dozen controls and adjustments, but that's still a lot of components to master, especially when you consider that many of these controls serve double-duty to give you access to multiple functions.

Traditionally, there have been two ways of providing a roadmap to guide you through this maze of features. One approach uses two or three tiny 2×3-inch black-and-white line drawings or photos impaled with dozens of callouts labeled with cross-references to the actual pages in the book that tell you what these components do. You'll find this tactic used in the pocket-sized manual Canon provides with the Rebel T1i, and most of the other third-party guidebooks as well. Deciphering one of these miniature camera layouts is a lot like being presented with a world globe when what you really want to know is how to find the capital of Belgium.

I originated a more useful approach in my field guides, providing you, instead of a satellite view, a street-level map that includes close-up full-color photos of the camera from several angles (see Figure 2.1), with a smaller number of labels clearly pointing to each individual feature. And, I don't force you to flip back and forth among dozens of pages to find out what a particular component does. Each photo is accompanied by a brief description that summarizes the control, so you can begin using it right away. Only when a particular feature deserves a lengthy explanation do I direct you to a more detailed write-up later in the book.

So, if you're wondering what the depth-of-field preview does, I'll tell you up front, rather than have you flip to Page 1,282. This book is not a scavenger hunt. But after I explain how to use the ISO button to change the sensitivity of the T1i, I *will* provide a cross-reference to a longer explanation later in the book that clarifies noise reduction, ISO, and its effects on exposure. I think this kind of organization works best for a camera as sophisticated as the Rebel T1i.

By the time you finish this chapter, you'll have a basic understanding of every control and what it does. I'm not going to delve into menu functions here—you'll find a discussion of your setup, shooting, and playback menu options in Chapter 3. Everything here is devoted to the button pusher and dial twirler in you.

Front View

When we picture a given camera, we always imagine the front view. That's the view that your subjects see as you snap away, and the aspect that's shown in product publicity and on the box. The frontal angle is, for all intents and purposes, the "face" of a camera like the Rebel T1i. But, not surprisingly, most of the "business" of operating the camera happens *behind* it, where the photographer resides. The front of the T1i actually has very few controls and features to worry about. Eight of them are readily visible in Figures 2.1 and 2.2:

- **Hand grip.** This provides a comfortable handhold, and also contains the T1i's battery.

- **Memory card door.** Slide this panel towards the back of the camera to gain access to the memory card.

- **DC power port.** You'll find a connector for DC power under this small rubber door in the side of the camera.

- **Shutter release.** Angled on top of the handgrip is the shutter release button. Press this button down halfway to lock exposure and focus (in One Shot mode and AI Focus with nonmoving subjects). The T1i assumes that when you tap or depress the shutter release, you are ready to take a picture, so the release can be tapped to activate the exposure meter or to exit from most menus.

- **Main dial.** This dial is used to change shooting settings. When settings are available in pairs (such as shutter speed/aperture), this dial will be used to make one type of setting, such as shutter speed. The other setting, say, the aperture, is made using an alternate control, such as spinning the Main dial while holding down an additional button like the Exposure Compensation button (which resides conveniently under the thumb on the back of the camera).

Figure 2.1

hand grip

memory card
access door

DC power port

Figure 2.2

Main dial

shutter release

Red-eye
reduction/
Self-timer lamp

remote control
sensor

microphone

- **Red-eye reduction/self-timer lamp.** This LED provides a blip of light shortly before a flash exposure to cause the subjects' pupils to close down, reducing the effect of red-eye reflections off their retinas. When using the self-timer, this lamp also flashes to mark the countdown until the photo is taken.

- **Remote control sensor.** The sensor behind this window receives signals from the optional Canon RC-1 and RC-5 infrared remote controls. The RC-1 trips the shutter immediately or after a two-second delay, while the RC-5 always initiates a two-second delay before taking the picture. Note that the sensor is on the hand grip and thus would be blocked if you happened to be holding the T1i when trying to take a picture. In practice, of course, the camera will be mounted on a tripod or supported in some other way when using the remote control. The remote control generally must be used from in front of the camera for the sensor to detect its signal.

- **Microphone.** This is a monaural (non-stereo) microphone for recording the audio track of your HDTV movies.

You'll find more controls on the other side of the T1i, shown in Figure 2.3.

- **Flash button.** This button releases the built-in flash so it can flip up (see Figure 2.4) and start the charging process. If you decide you do not want to use the flash, you can turn it off by pressing the flash head back down.

- **Lens Release button.** Press and hold this button to unlock the lens so you can rotate the lens to remove it from the camera.

- **Depth-of-Field Preview button.** This button, adjacent to the lens mount, stops down the lens to the aperture that will be used to take the picture, so you can see in the viewfinder how much of the image is in focus. The view grows dimmer as the aperture is reduced.

- **Lens switches.** Canon autofocus lenses have a switch to allow changing between automatic focus and manual focus, and, in the case of IS lenses, another switch to turn image stabilization on and off.

The main feature on this side of the Rebel T1i is a rubber cover (see Figure 2.5) that protects the three connector ports underneath from dust and moisture, plus one of two neck strap mounts (the other is on the other side of the camera). The three connectors, shown in Figure 2.6, are as follows:

- **Remote control terminal.** You can plug various Canon remote release switches, timers, and wireless controllers into this connector.

- **USB /Video out port.** Plug in the USB cable furnished with your Rebel T1i and connect the other end to a USB port in your computer to transfer photos. Or, connect the AV cable and connect your camera to a television to view your photos on

Figure 2.3

lens switches

Lens Release
button

Depth-of-Field
Preview button

Figure 2.4

Pressing the
Flash button
(which has an
arrow/lightning
bolt symbol)
pops up the
built-in flash
unit and starts
the charging
process.

Pop-up electronic flash

Flash button

Figure 2.5

neck strap
mount

terminal cover

Figure 2.6

remote control

USB port/Video out

HDMI out

a large screen. Note that previous Rebel models used two separate ports with different connectors for this pair of functions. They were combined in the T1i to make room for the HDMI port.

■ **HDMI port.** Use a Type C HDMI cable (not included in the box with your camera) to direct the video and audio output of the T1i to a high-definition television (HDTV) or HD monitor.

The Canon EOS Rebel T1i's Business End

The back panel of the Rebel T1i (see Figure 2.7) bristles with more than a dozen different controls, buttons, and knobs. That might seem like a lot of controls to learn, but you'll find, as I noted earlier, that it's a lot easier to press a dedicated button and spin a dial than to jump to a menu every time you want to change a setting.

Figure 2.7

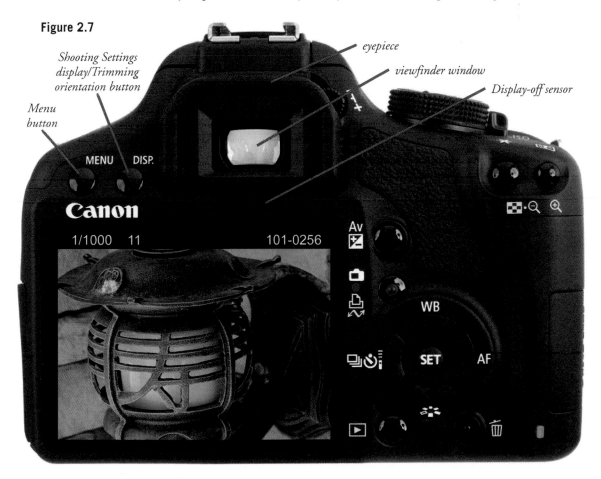

Shooting Settings display/Trimming orientation button

Menu button

eyepiece

viewfinder window

Display-off sensor

You can see the controls clustered on the left side of the T1i in Figure 2.7. The key buttons and components and their functions are as follows:

■ **Viewfinder eyepiece.** You can frame your composition by peering into the viewfinder. It's surrounded by a soft rubber frame that seals out extraneous light when pressing your eye tightly up to the viewfinder, and it also protects your eyeglass lenses (if worn) from scratching. It can be removed and replaced by the cap attached to your neck strap when you use the camera on a tripod, to ensure that light coming from the back of the camera doesn't venture inside and possibly affect the exposure reading.

■ **Menu button.** Summons/exits the menu displayed on the rear LCD of the T1i. When you're working with submenus, this button also serves to exit a submenu and return to the main menu.

■ **DISP button.** When pressed repeatedly, changes the amount of picture information displayed. In Playback mode, pressing the DISP button cycles among basic display of the image; a detailed display with a thumbnail of the image, shooting parameters, and a brightness histogram; and a display with less detail but with separate histograms for brightness, red, green, and blue channels. (I'll show you what these look like later in the chapter.) When setting Picture Styles, the DISP button is used to select a highlighted Picture Style for modification. In Live View mode, the DISP button adjusts the amount of information overlaid on the live image that appears on the LCD screen. When the camera is connected to a printer, you can trim an image; in that mode, the DISP button selects the orientation. If you press the DISP button after you press the Menu button, you are shown a media Freespace, My Menu settings, and date and time display. All these options are explained in Chapter 3.

■ **Display-off sensor.** This sensor detects when your face or some other object approaches the viewfinder, and turns off the Shooting Settings display on the LCD, and activates the viewfinder display.

■ **LCD.** This is the three-inch display that shows your Live View preview, image review after the picture is taken, Shooting Setting display before the photo is snapped, and all the menus used by the Rebel T1i.

The most-used controls reside on the right side of the Rebel T1i (see Figure 2.8). There are 11 buttons in all, many of which do double-duty to perform several functions. I've divided them into two groups; here's the first:

■ **Cross keys.** This array of four-directional keys provides left/right/up/down movement to navigate menus, and is used to cycle among various options (usually with the left/right buttons) and to choose amounts (with the up/down buttons). The four cross keys also have secondary functions to adjust White Balance, Autofocus mode, Picture Styles, and drive mode (I'll describe these separately).

Figure 2.8

- **Set button.** Used to confirm a selection or activate a feature.

- **Aperture value (AV)/Exposure compensation button.** When using Manual exposure mode, hold down this button and rotate the Main dial to specify a lens aperture; rotate the Main dial alone to choose the shutter speed. In other Creative Zone exposure modes—Aperture Priority (Av), Shutter Priority (Tv), or Program (P)—hold down this button and rotate the Main dial to the right to add Exposure Compensation (EV) to an image (making it brighter), or rotate to the left to subtract EV and make the image darker.

- **Live View/Print/Share/Movie button.** Press this button to activate Live View when using a Creative Zone mode (Live View cannot be used with Basic Zone modes). The button can also be used when the T1i is connected to a printer or personal computer to initiate transfer, as described in Chapter 8. To shoot movies, turn the Mode dial to the Movie position, and then press this button to start/stop video/audio recording.

- **Playback button.** Displays the last picture taken. Thereafter, you can move back and forth among the available images by pressing the left/right cross keys to advance or reverse one image at a time, or the Main dial, to jump forward or back using the jump method you've selected. (See the section below for more on jumping.) To quit playback, press this button again. The T1i also exits Playback mode automatically when you press the shutter button (so you'll never be prevented from taking a picture on the spur of the moment because you happened to be viewing an image).

- **Erase button.** Press to erase the image shown on the LCD. A menu will pop up displaying Cancel and Erase choices. Use the left/right cross buttons to select one of these actions, then press the Set button to activate your choice.

The next group of buttons allow you to change settings:

- **AE/FE (Auto exposure/Flash exposure) Lock/Thumbnail Index/Zoom Out button.** This button, which has a * label above it, has several functions, which differ depending on the AF point and metering mode. You can find more about these variations in Chapter 4.

  In Shooting mode, it locks the exposure or flash exposure that the camera sets when you partially depress the shutter button. In Evaluative exposure mode, exposure is locked at the AF point that achieved focus. In Partial, Spot, or Center-Weighted modes, exposure is locked at the AF center point. The exposure lock indication (*) appears in the viewfinder and on the Shooting Settings display. If you want to recalculate exposure with the shutter button still partially depressed, press the * button again. The exposure will be unlocked when you release the shutter button or take the picture. To retain the exposure lock for subsequent photos, keep the * button pressed while shooting.

  When using flash, pressing the * button fires an extra preflash that allows the unit to calculate and lock exposure prior to taking the picture. The characters FEL will appear momentarily in the viewfinder, and the exposure lock indication and a flash indicator appear. (See the description of the viewfinder display later in this chapter.)

  In Playback mode, press this button to switch from single-image display to nine-image thumbnail index. (See Figure 2.9.) Move highlighting among the thumbnails with the cross keys or Main dial. To view a highlighted image, press the Zoom In button.

  In Playback mode, when an image is zoomed in, press this button to zoom out.

Figure 2.9
The Thumbnail Index/Zoom Out button changes the playback display from single image to four or nine thumbnails.

■ **AF Point Selection/Zoom In button.** In Shooting mode, this button activates autofocus point selection. (See Chapter 4 for information on setting autofocus/exposure point selection.) In Playback mode, if you're viewing a single image, this button zooms in on the image that's displayed. If thumbnail indexes are shown, pressing this button switches from nine thumbnails to four thumbnails, or from four thumbnails to a full screen view of a highlighted image.

■ **White Balance/Jump method button.** The White Balance function has been moved to the up cross key for the T1i. With the most recent Rebels, the up cross key was used as the Metering Mode button, and White Balance was set using the (now) overworked Print/Share button. Press the WB button when using one of the Creative Zone modes (A-DEP, M, Av, Tv, or P) to produce the White balance screen. Use the left/right cross keys to select a white balance, and press Set to confirm. (I'll explain more about white balance in Chapter 3.) You can also choose a Jump method by pressing the up cross key while an image is being played back on the LCD. Keep pressing the up key until the Jump method you prefer is selected. (I describe jumps in more detail in the next section.)

■ **AF Mode.** Press the right cross key to produce a screen that allows choosing Autofocus mode from among One Shot, AI Focus, and AI Servo. Press repeatedly until the focus mode you want is selected. Then press Set to confirm your focus mode. (See Figure 1.12 in the previous chapter.)

- **Drive mode.** Press the left cross key to produce a screen that allows choosing a drive mode. Then press the right cross key to select the 10-second self-timer (which also can be used with the optional IR remote controls), 2-second self-timer, or Self-timer: Continuous, which allows you to specify a number of shots to be taken (from 2 to 10) with the up/down keys. Press Set to confirm your choice.

- **Picture Styles Selection button.** Press the down cross key to pop up the Picture Styles menu on the LCD, so you can select a given style, or gain access to user-defined styles. To modify a Picture Style, you'll need to use Shooting 2 menu, as described in Chapter 3.

- **Set button.** Selects a highlighted setting or menu option.

- **Memory card access lamp.** When lit or blinking, this lamp indicates that the memory card is being accessed.

Jumping Around

When a photo you've taken is displayed on the color LCD, you can change the method used to jump with the Main dial. To select a Jump method, when viewing a single full-screen image during playback, press the up cross key. An overlay appears that allows you to choose the method. (See Figure 2.10.) Keep pressing the up key until the method you want to use is shown, then press Set to confirm your choice.

Figure 2.10
Choose a Jump method by pressing the up cross key while viewing an image.

You can also choose a Jump method using the Playback 2 menu (using the procedure described with all the other menus in Chapter 3). The advantage of using the menu is that you can set both the number of images to jump and the type of jump. The Jump feature allows you to leap forward and backward among the images on your memory card using the increment/method you have chosen by rotating the Main dial. The Jump method is shown briefly on the screen as you leap ahead to the next image displayed. Your options are as follows:

- **1 image.** Rotating the Main dial one click jumps forward or back one image.

- **10 images.** Rotating the Main dial one click jumps forward or back ten images.

- **100 images.** Rotating the Main dial one click jumps forward or back one hundred images.

- **Date.** Rotating the Main dial one click jumps forward or back to the first image taken on the next or previous calendar date.

- **Movies.** Tells the T1i to jump only among movie images when using a card that contains both video clips and still images. This option is useful when you prefer to view only one kind of file.

- **Stills.** Specifies jumping only between still images when using a card that has both video clips and still images.

Going Topside

The top surface of the Canon EOS Rebel T1i has a few frequently accessed controls of its own. The key controls, shown in Figure 2.11, are as follows:

- **Mode dial.** Rotate this dial to switch among Basic Zone and Creative Zone modes. You'll find these modes and options described in more detail in Chapter 4.

- **Sensor focal plane.** Precision macro and scientific photography sometimes requires knowing exactly where the focal plane of the sensor is. The symbol on the side of the pentaprism marks that plane.

- **Flash hot shoe.** Slide an electronic flash into this mount when you need a more powerful speedlight. A dedicated flash unit, like those from Canon, can use the multiple contact points shown to communicate exposure, zoom setting, white balance information, and other data between the flash and the camera. There's more on using electronic flash in Chapter 7.

- **ISO.** Press this button (just aft of the Main dial) and use the cross keys to navigate until the setting you want appears on the LCD. Press the Set button to confirm your choice. You'll find more about ISO options in Chapter 3, and flash EV settings in Chapter 7.

Figure 2.11

shutter release

Main dial

sensor plane

hot shoe

Mode dial

On/Off switch

ISO button

- **Main dial.** This dial is used to make many shooting settings. When settings come in pairs (such as shutter speed/aperture in Manual shooting mode), the Main dial is used for one (for example, shutter speed), while some other control, such as the AV button (when shooting in Manual exposure mode), is used for the other (aperture).

- **Shutter release button.** Partially depress this button to lock in exposure and focus. Press all the way to take the picture. Tapping the shutter release when the camera has turned off the auto exposure and autofocus mechanisms reactivates both. When a review image is displayed on the back-panel color LCD, tapping this button removes the image from the display and reactivates the autoexposure and autofocus mechanisms.

- **On/Off switch.** Flip forward to turn the Rebel T1i on, and back to turn it off again.

Underneath Your Rebel T1i

There's not a lot going on with the bottom panel of your Rebel T1i. You'll find a tripod socket, which secures the camera to a tripod, and is also used to lock on the optional BG-E5 battery grip, which provides more juice to run your camera to take more exposures with a single charge. It also adds a vertically oriented shutter release, Main dial, AE Lock/FE Lock, and AF point selection controls for easier vertical shooting. To mount the grip, slide the battery door latch to open the door, then push gently towards the outside edge of the camera to free the hinge pins from their sockets. That will let you remove the battery door. Then slide the grip into the battery cavity, aligning the pin on the grip with the small hole on the other side of the tripod socket. Tighten the grip's tripod socket screw to lock the grip onto the bottom of your T1i. Figure 2.12 shows the underside view of the camera.

Figure 2.12

tripod socket

aligning pin hole

battery cover door   *latch*

Lens Components

The typical lens, like the ones shown in Figures 2.13 and 2.14, has seven or eight common features. Not every component appears on every lens. The 18-55mm lens on the right, for example, lacks the distance scale and distance indicator that the 17-85mm lens on the left has. Lenses that lack image stabilization will not have a stabilization switch.

- **Filter thread.** Lenses have a thread on the front for attaching filters and other add-ons. Some also use this thread for attaching a lens hood (you screw on the filter first, and then attach the hood to the screw thread on the front of the filter).

Figure 2.13

Filter threads

lens hood bayonet

focus ring

zoom ring

zoom scale

focus ring

zoom position

Autofocus/
Manual
focus switch

focus distance

focus scale

lens mounting
index mark

image stabilizer switch

Figure 2.14

electrical contacts

lens mount bayonet

- **Lens hood bayonet.** This is used to mount the lens hood for lenses that don't use screw-mount hoods (the majority).

- **Zoom ring.** Turn this ring to change the zoom setting.

- **Zoom scale.** These markings on the lens show the current focal length selected.

- **Focus ring.** This is the ring you turn when you manually focus the lens.

- **Distance scale.** This is a readout that rotates in unison with the lens's focus mechanism to show the distance at which the lens has been focused. It's a useful indicator for double-checking autofocus, roughly evaluating depth-of-field, and for setting manual focus guesstimates.

- **Autofocus/Manual switch.** Allows you to change from automatic focus to manual focus.

- **Image stabilization switch.** Lenses with IS include a separate switch for adjusting the stabilization feature.

- **Electrical contacts.** On the back of the lens (see Figure 2.14) are electrical contacts that the camera uses to communicate focus, aperture setting, and other information.

- **Lens bayonet.** This mount is used to attach the lens to a matching bayonet on the camera body.

LCD Panel Readouts

The Rebel T1i does not have a monochrome status LCD, like the one found on the top panel of the mid- and upper-level EOS cameras, like the 50D and 5D Mark II. Nor does it have such a monochrome panel underneath the color LCD on the back, as the original Digital Rebel and Rebel XT did. Lacking this auxiliary information display, the T1i uses the generously expansive three-inch color LCD to show you everything you need to see, from images to a collection of informational data displays. Here's an overview of these displays, and how to access them:

- **Image playback displays.** When the T1i shows you a picture for review, you can select from among four different information overlays. To switch among them, press the DISP button while the image is on the screen. The LCD will cycle among the Single Image Display (Figure 2.15); Single Image Display with Recording Quality (Figure 2.16); Histogram Display, which shows basic shooting information as well as a brightness histogram at bottom right, with individual histograms for the red, green, and blue channels above (Figure 2.17); and a complete Shooting Information Display (Figure 2.18), which includes most of the relevant shooting settings, plus a brightness histogram. I'll explain how to work with histograms in Chapter 4.

- **Shooting Settings display.** While you are taking pictures, this screen will be shown, with information like that in Figure 2.19. Not all of the data pictured will be seen at one time; only the settings that are appropriate for the current shooting mode will be displayed. I'll explain how to make and use each of these settings later in this book. You can turn this display off by pressing the DISP button, and restore it again by pressing the DISP button a second time. When the Shooting Settings display is active, you can return to it when there is a menu screen or image review on the LCD by tapping the shutter release button. If you want to make adjustments, press the Set button to activate the Quick Control screen, and use the cross keys to navigate to the setting you want to change. As I mentioned in Chapter 1, when using Basic Zone modes other than Creative Auto, you can change only the drive mode and Image Quality. When using Creative Auto, you can adjust additional settings, such as flash modes, Picture Styles (or image effects), brightness, and depth-of-field (range of sharpness). With Creative Zone modes, you can change any of the settings visible in the Quick Control screen.

- **Camera function settings.** When any menu is displayed, you can switch to the Camera Functions settings screen by pressing the DISP button. A screen like the one shown in Figure 2.20 will appear, with key camera function settings arrayed.

Figure 2.15, 2.16, 2.17, 2.18 Image playback displays include Single image, Single image with recording quality, Histogram, and Shooting information.

Figure 2.19
Shooting
Settings
display.

shutter
speed

lens
aperture

white
balance

flash exposure
compensation

ISO
setting

Metering
mode

Exposure
level/exposure
compensation
amount/auto-
matic exposure
bracketing range

Exposure mode

Picture Control

image quality

Access Quick
Control screen

white
balance
correction

white
balance
bracketing

Autofocus
mode

battery
level

shots remaining/shots remaining
during WB bracketing/Self-timer
countdown/bulb exposure time

Drive
mode

Figure 2.20
Camera func-
tions display.

Sensor cleaning

auto power off

beeper

current
date/time

remaining
memory card
capacity

color space

white balance
correction

Live View
shooting

Red-eye
reduction

auto rotate
display

LCD monitor
auto off

Looking Inside the Viewfinder

Much of the important shooting status information is shown inside the viewfinder of the Rebel T1i. As with the displays shown on the color LCD, not all of this information will be shown at any one time. Figure 2.21 shows what you can expect to see. I'll explain all of these readouts later in this book, with those pertaining to exposure in Chapter 4, and those relating to flash in Chapter 7. These readouts include:

- **Spot metering reference circle.** Shows the circle that delineates the metered area when Spot metering is activated. (The reference circle is visible at all times, even when you're not using Spot metering.)

- **Autofocus zones.** Shows the nine areas used by the T1i to focus. The camera can select the appropriate focus zone for you, or you can manually select one or all of the zones, as described in Chapters 1 and 4.

AE Lock/ automatic exposure bracketing in progress *FE Lock/flash exposure bracketing in progress* *AF point display indicator* *Spot metering circle* *AF points*

Figure 2.21

shutter speed/card full warning

ISO speed

White balance correction

maximum burst

focus confirmation

flash-ready/ improper FE lock warning *high-speed sync* *flash exposure compensation* *aperture* *exposure level indicator/exposure compensation amount/autoexposure bracketing range/red-eye reduction lamp on indicator* *Black-and-white shooting*

- **Auto exposure lock.** Shows that exposure has been locked. This icon also appears when an automatic exposure bracketing sequence is in process.

- **Flash-ready indicator.** This icon appears when the flash is fully charged. It also shows when the flash exposure lock has been applied for an inappropriate exposure value.

- **Flash status indicator.** Appears along with the flash-ready indicator: The H is shown when high speed (focal plane) flash sync is being used. The * appears when flash exposure lock or a flash exposure bracketing sequence is underway.

- **Flash exposure compensation.** Appears when flash EV changes have been made.

- **Shutter speed/aperture readouts.** Most of the time, these readouts show the current shutter speed and aperture. This pair can also warn you of memory card conditions (full, error, or missing), ISO speed, flash exposure lock, and a buSY indicator when the camera is busy doing other things (including flash recycling).

- **Exposure level indicator.** This scale shows the current exposure level, with the bottom indicator centered when the exposure is correct as metered. The indicator may also move to the left or right to indicate under- or overexposure (respectively). The scale is also used to show the amount of EV and flash EV adjustments, the number of stops covered by the current automatic exposure bracketing range, and is used as a red-eye reduction lamp indicator.

- **ISO Sensitivity.** This useful indicator shows the current ISO setting value. Those who have accidentally taken dozens of shots under bright sunlight at ISO 1600 because they forgot to change the setting back after some indoor shooting will treasure this addition.

- **B/W indicator.** Illuminates when the Monochrome Picture Style is being used. There's no way to restore color when you're shooting JPEGs without RAW, so this indicator is another valuable warning.

- **White balance correction.** Shows that white balance has been tweaked.

- **Maximum burst available.** Changes to a number to indicate the number of frames that can be taken in Continuous mode using the current settings.

- **Focus confirmation.** This green dot appears when the subject covered by the active autofocus zone is in sharp focus.

3

Setting Up Your Canon EOS Rebel T1i/500D

For an entry-level camera, the Rebel T1i has a remarkable number of options and settings you can use to customize the way your camera operates. Not only can you change shooting settings used at the time the picture is taken, but you can adjust the way your camera behaves. Indeed, if your T1i doesn't operate in exactly the way you'd like, chances are you can make a small change in the pair of Shooting menus, the Playback menu, or three (count 'em) Setup menus to tailor the camera to your needs. If you don't like the organization of the menus themselves, you can collect your favorite functions into one group called My Menu.

This chapter will help you sort out the settings for all the T1i's menus. These include the aforementioned Shooting and Playback menus, which determine how the T1i uses many of its shooting features to take a photo and how it displays images on review. Later in the chapter, I'll show you how to use the Setup menu to adjust power-saving timers, specify Live View options, control your built-in flash, and work with the Rebel T1i's 13 useful Custom Functions.

As I've mentioned before, this book isn't intended to replace the manual you received with your T1i, nor have I any interest in rehashing its contents. You'll still find the original manual useful as a standby reference that lists every possible option in exhaustive (if mind-numbing) detail—without really telling you how to use those options to take better pictures. There is, however, some unavoidable duplication between the Canon manual and this chapter, because I'm going to explain all the key menu choices and the options you may have in using them. You should find, though, that I will give you the information you need in a much more helpful format, with plenty of detail on why you should make some settings that are particularly difficult to understand.

I'm not going to waste a lot of space on some of the more obvious menu choices in these chapters. For example, you can probably figure out, even without my help, that the Beep option deals with the solid-state beeper in your camera that sounds off during various activities (such as the self-timer countdown). You can certainly decipher the import of the two options available for the Beep entry (On and Off). In this chapter, I'll devote no more than a sentence or two to the blatantly obvious settings and concentrate on the more confusing aspects of T1i setup, such as autofocus. I'll start with an overview of using the T1i's menus themselves.

Anatomy of the Rebel T1i's Menus

The T1i has one of the best-designed menu systems of any digital SLR in its price class, with a remarkable amount of consistency (finally!) with other cameras in the Canon product line. In fact, if you used any other newer Canon dSLR before you purchased your Rebel T1i, you're probably already familiar with the basic menu lineup. The Rebel T1i has a series of seven separate tabbed menus, plus My Menu, each with a single screen of entries, arranged in rows (so you won't need to scroll within a menu to see all the entries). The new menus are much cleaner, too.

With the revamped system, just press the Menu button, located in the upper-left corner of the back of the camera, and use either the left/right cross keys or spin the Main dial to highlight the menu tab you want to access. Then, scroll up and down within a menu with the up/down cross keys. What could be easier?

Pressing the Menu button brings up a typical menu like the one shown in Figure 3.1. (If the camera goes to "sleep" while you're reviewing a menu, you may need to wake it up again by tapping the shutter release button.) There are eight menu tabs: Shooting 1, Shooting 2, Playback 1, Playback 2, Setup 1, Setup 2, Setup 3, and My Menu. (When using Basic exposure modes, Shooting 2, Setup 3, and My Menu tabs do not appear, and options in those menus are not available to you.) The tabs are color-coded: red for Shooting menus, blue for the Playback menu, yellow for Setup menus, and green for the My Menu tab. The currently selected menu's icon is white within a white border, on a background corresponding to its color code. All the inactive menus are grayed out and the icon and their borders are color-coded. The top line of the menu screen also has a DISP indicator to remind you that you can press the DISP button at any time to switch to a screen that shows many of the current settings. (Review Figure 2.20 in the previous chapter; I'm not going to repeat that figure here.)

Here are the things to watch for as you navigate the menus:

- **Menu tabs.** In the top row of the menu screen, the menu that is currently active will be highlighted as described earlier. One, two, or three dots in the tab lets you know if you are in, say Setup 1, Setup 2, or Setup 3. Just remember that the two red camera icons stand for shooting options; the blue right-pointing triangle represents playback options; the three yellow wrench/hammer icons stand for setup options; and the green star stands for personalized menus defined for the star of the show—you.

■ **Selected menu item.** The currently selected menu item will have a black background and will be surrounded by a box the same hue as its color code.

■ **Other menu choices.** The other menu items visible on the screen will have a medium or dark gray background (alternating).

■ **Current setting.** The current settings for visible menu items are shown in the right-hand column, until one menu item is selected (by pressing the Set key). At that point, all the settings vanish from the screen except for those dealing with the active menu choice.

Selected menu   *Inactive menus*   *Current setting*

Figure 3.1
The Rebel T1i's menus are arranged in a series of eight tabs.

Selected menu item

Other menu choices

When you've moved the menu highlighting with the up/down cross keys to the menu item you want to work with, press the Set button to select it. A submenu with a list of options for the selected menu item will appear. Within the submenu options, you can scroll up or down with the up/down cross keys to choose a setting, and then press Set to confirm the choice you've made. Press the Menu button again to exit.

Shooting 1 and 2 Menu Options

The various direct setting buttons on the top and back panels of the camera, for Autofocus mode, white balance, Drive mode, ISO sensitivity, metering mode, and flash, along with exposure compensation (EV) adjustments are likely to be the most common settings changes you make, with changes during a particular session fairly common. You'll find that the Shooting menu options are those that you access second-most frequently when you're using your Rebel T1i. You might make such adjustments as you begin a shooting session, or when you move from one type of subject to another. Canon makes accessing these changes very easy.

This section explains the options of the two Shooting menus and how to use them. As with most of the T1i's menu listings, the order has changed since the introduction of models like the XSi. If you used an earlier Rebel, the entries may not be where you expected to find them, and several new choices have been added. The options you'll find in these red-coded menus include:

- Quality
- Beep
- Release shutter without card
- Review time
- Peripheral illumin. Correct.
- Red-Eye On/Off
- Flash control
- Expo. Comp./AEB (Automatic Exposure Bracketing)
- Metering mode
- Custom WB
- WB Shift/BKT
- Color Space
- Picture Style
- Dust Delete Data

Quality Settings

You can choose the image quality settings used by the T1i to store its files. You have three choices to make:

- **Resolution.** The number of pixels captured determines the absolute resolution of the photos you shoot with your Rebel T1i. Your choices range from 15 megapixels (Large or L), measuring 4,752 × 3,168 pixels; 8 megapixels (Medium or M), measuring 3,456 × 2,304 pixels; to 3.7 megapixels (Small or S), 2,352 × 1,568 pixels.

- **JPEG compression.** To reduce the size of your image files and allow more photos to be stored on a given memory card, the T1i uses JPEG compression to squeeze the images down to a smaller size. This compacting reduces the image quality a little, so you're offered your choice of Fine compression and Normal compression. The symbols help you remember that Fine compression (represented by a quarter-circle) provides the smoothest results, while Normal compression (signified by a stair-step icon) provides "jaggier" images.

■ **JPEG, RAW, or both.** You can elect to store only JPEG versions of the images you shoot (5MB each at the Large Fine resolution setting) or you can save your photos as uncompressed, loss-free RAW files, which consume about four times as much space on your memory card (up to 20MB per file). Or, you can store both at once as you shoot. Many photographers elect to save *both* a JPEG and a RAW file, so they'll have a JPEG version that might be usable as-is, as well as the original "digital negative" RAW file in case they want to do some processing of the image later. You'll end up with two different versions of the same file: one with a .jpg extension, and one with the .cr2 extension that signifies a Canon RAW file.

To choose the combination you want, access the menus, scroll to Quality, and press the Set button. A screen similar to the one shown in Figure 3.2 will appear. Use the cross keys to cycle among the eight choices. In practice, you'll probably use only the Large (Fine), RAW+L (Large Fine), or RAW selections if you want the best quality images.

There are some limited advantages to using the Medium and Small resolution settings, and Normal JPEG compression setting. They all allow stretching the capacity of your memory card so you can shoehorn quite a few more pictures onto a single memory card. That can come in useful when on vacation and you're running out of storage, or when you're shooting non-critical work that doesn't require full resolution (such as photos taken for real estate listings, web page display, photo ID cards, or similar applications).

Figure 3.2
Choose your resolution, JPEG compression, and file format from this screen.

Some photographers like to record RAW+JPEG Fine so they'll have a JPEG file for review, while retaining access to the original RAW file for serious editing.

For most work, using lower resolution and extra compression is false economy. You never know when you might actually need that extra bit of picture detail. Your best bet is to have enough memory cards to handle all the shooting you want to do until you have the chance to transfer your photos to your computer or a personal storage device.

However, reduced image quality can sometimes be beneficial if you're shooting sequences of photos rapidly, as the T1i is able to hold more of them in its internal memory buffer before transferring to the memory card. Using the RAW+L or RAW settings, the largest burst you can expect will be 4 to 9 shots. Eschew RAW and go for JPEG Fine at maximum resolution, and you might get more than 170 photos in a single burst. Canon says that with a JPEG Medium setting, bursts of up to 740 shots are feasible. (I've never checked this out, because I don't have the patience or inclination to fire off 740 pictures at one time.) For most sports and other applications, you'd probably rather have better, sharper pictures than longer periods of continuous shooting, so the JPEG Fine setting will work best.

JPEG vs. RAW

You'll sometimes be told that RAW files are the "unprocessed" image information your camera produces, before it's been modified. That's nonsense. RAW files are no more unprocessed than your camera film is after it's been through the chemicals to produce a negative or transparency. A lot can happen in the developer that can affect the quality of a film image—positively and negatively—and, similarly, your digital image undergoes a significant amount of processing before it is saved as a RAW file. Canon even applies a name (Digic 4) to the digital image processing (DIP) chip used to perform this magic in the Rebel T1i.

A RAW file is more similar to a film camera's processed negative. It contains all the information, captured in 14-bit channels per color (and stored in a 16-bit space), with no compression, no sharpening, no application of any special filters or other settings you might have specified when you took the picture. Those settings are *stored* with the RAW file so they can be applied when the image is converted to a form compatible with your favorite image editor. However, using RAW conversion software such as Adobe Camera Raw or Canon's Digital Photo Professional, you can override those settings and apply settings of your own. You can select essentially the same changes there that you might have specified in your camera's picture-taking options.

RAW exists because sometimes we want to have access to all the information captured by the camera, before the camera's internal logic has processed it and converted the image to a standard file format. RAW doesn't save as much space as JPEG. What it does do is preserve all the information captured by your camera after it's been converted from analog to digital form.

So, why don't we always use RAW? Although some photographers do save only in RAW format, it's more common to use either RAW plus the JPEG option or just shoot JPEG and eschew RAW altogether. While RAW is overwhelmingly helpful when an image needs to be fine-tuned, in other situations working with a RAW file can slow you down significantly. RAW images take longer to store on the memory card, and require more post-processing effort, whether you elect to go with the default settings in force when the picture was taken, or make minor adjustments.

As a result, those who depend on speedy access to images or who shoot large numbers of photos at once may prefer JPEG over RAW. Wedding photographers, for example, might expose several thousand photos during a bridal affair and offer hundreds to clients as electronic proofs for inclusion in an album. Wedding shooters take the time to make sure that their in-camera settings are correct, minimizing the need to post process photos after the event. Given that their JPEGs are so good, there is little need to get bogged down shooting RAW. Sports photographers also eschew RAW files for similar reasons.

JPEG was invented as a more compact file format that can store most of the information in a digital image, but in a much smaller size. JPEG predates most digital SLRs and was initially used to squeeze down files for transmission over slow dialup connections. Even if you were using an early dSLR with 1.3 megapixel files for news photography, you didn't want to send them back to the office over a modem at 1,200 bps.

But, as I noted, JPEG provides smaller files by compressing the information in a way that loses some image data. JPEG remains a viable alternative because it offers several different quality levels. At the highest quality Fine level, you might not be able to tell the difference between the original RAW file and the JPEG version, even though the RAW file occupies, by Canon's estimate, 20.2MB on your memory card, while the highest quality JPEG takes up only 5.2MB of space. You've squeezed the image by two-thirds without losing much visual information at all. If you don't mind losing some quality, you can use more aggressive Standard compression with JPEG to cut the size in half again, to 2.5MB.

In my case, I shoot virtually everything at RAW+L. Most of the time, I'm not concerned about filling up my memory cards, as I usually have a minimum of three 8GB memory cards with me. If I know I may fill up all those cards, I have a tiny battery-operated personal storage device that can copy an 8GB card in about 15 minutes. As I mentioned earlier, when shooting sports I'll shift to JPEG FINE (with no RAW file) to squeeze a little extra speed out of my T1i's Continuous Shooting mode, and to reduce the need to wade through eight photo bursts taken in RAW format. On my last trip to Europe, I took only RAW photos (rather than shooting both RAW and JPEG), to fit more images onto my 60GB personal storage device, shown in Figure 3.3, as I planned on doing at least some post-processing on many of the images for a travel book I was working on.

Figure 3.3
If RAW storage space is a concern, consider a portable storage device like this one.

MANAGING LOTS OF FILES

The only long-term drawback to shooting everything in RAW+JPEG is that it's easy to fill up your computer's hard drive if you are a prolific photographer. Here's what I do. My most recent photos are stored on my working hard drive in a numbered folder, say T1i-01, with subfolders named after the shooting session, such as 090601Trees, for pictures of trees taken on June 1, 2009. An automatic utility copies new and modified photos to a different hard drive for temporary backup four times daily.

When the top-level folder accumulates about 30GB of images, I back it up to DVDs and then move the folder to a 1.5TB (1500GB) drive dedicated solely for storage of folders that have already been backed up onto DVD. Then I start a new folder, such as T1i-02, on the working hard drive and repeat the process. I always have at least one backup of every image taken, either on another hard drive or on a DVD.

Beep

The Rebel T1i's internal beeper provides a helpful chirp to signify various functions, such as the countdown of your camera's self-timer. You can switch it off if you want to avoid the beep because it's annoying, impolite, or distracting (at a concert or museum), or undesired for any other reason. (I've actually had new dSLR owners ask me how to turn off the "shutter sound" the camera makes; such an option was available in the point-and-shoot camera they'd used previously.) Select Beep from the menu, press Set, and use the cross keys to choose On or Off, as you prefer, as shown in Figure 3.4. Press Set again to activate your choice.

Figure 3.4
Silence your camera's beep when it might prove distracting.

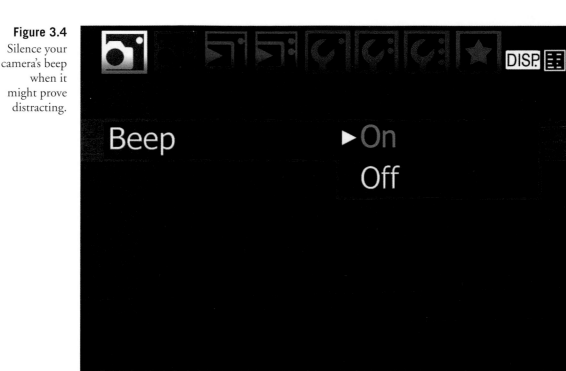

Release Shutter without Card

This entry in the Shooting 1 menu (see Figure 3.5) gives you the ability to snap off "pictures" without a memory card installed—or to lock the camera shutter release if that is the case. It is sometimes called Play mode, because you can experiment with your camera's features or even hand your T1i to a friend to let him fool around, without any danger of pictures actually being taken. Back in our film days, we'd sometimes finish a roll, rewind the film back into its cassette surreptitiously, and then hand the camera to a child to take a few pictures—without actually wasting any film. It's hard to waste digital film, but Shoot without Card mode is still appreciated by some, especially camera vendors who want to be able to demo a camera at a store or trade show, but don't want to have to equip each and every demonstrator model with a memory card. Choose this menu item, press Set, select On or Off, and press Set again to enable or disable this capability.

Review Time

You can adjust the amount of time an image is displayed for review on the LCD after each shot is taken. You can elect to disable this review entirely (Off), or choose display times of 2, 4, or 8 seconds. You can also select Hold, an indefinite display, which will keep your image on the screen until you use one of the other controls, such as the shutter button or Main dial. Turning the review display off or choosing a brief duration can help preserve battery power. However, the T1i will always override the review display

Figure 3.5
You can enable triggering the shutter even when no memory card is present.

when the shutter button is partially or fully depressed, so you'll never miss a shot because a previous image was on the screen. Choose Review Time from the Shooting 1 menu, and select Off, 2 sec., 4 sec., 8 sec., or Hold, as shown in Figure 3.6, and press Set. If you want to retain an image on the screen for a longer period, but don't want to use Hold as your default, press the Erase button located just southeast of the cross keys. The image will display until you choose Cancel or Erase from the menu that pops up at the bottom of the screen. While those choices remain on the screen, they generally don't obscure much of the picture area.

Peripheral Illumination Correction

With certain lenses, under certain conditions, your images might suffer from a phenomenon called *vignetting*, which is a darkening of the four corners of the frame because of a slight amount of fall-off in illumination at those nether regions. This menu option allows you to activate a clever feature built into the EOS T1i that partially (or fully) compensates for this effect. Depending on the f/stop you use, the lens mounted on the camera, and the focal length setting, vignetting can be non-existent, slight, or may be so strong that it appears you've used a too-small hood on your camera. (Indeed, the wrong lens hood can produce a vignette effect of its own.) Vignetting can be affected by the use of a telephoto converter.

Figure 3.6
Adjust the time
an image is dis-
played on the
LCD for review
after a picture
is taken.

Peripheral illumination drop-off, even if pronounced, may not be much of a problem. I actually *add* vignetting, sometimes, when shooting portraits and some other subjects. Slightly dark corners tend to focus attention on a subject in the middle of the frame. On the other hand, vignetting with subjects that are supposed to be evenly illuminated, such as landscapes, is seldom a benefit.

To minimize the effects of corner light fall-off, you can process RAW files using Digital Photo Professional (described in Chapter 8), or, if you want your JPEG files fixed as you shoot them, by using this menu option. Figure 3.7 shows an image without peripheral illumination correction at top, and a corrected image at the bottom. I've exaggerated the vignetting a little to make it more evident on the printed page. Keep in mind that the amount of correction available with Digital Photo Pro can be a little more intense than that applied in the camera. In addition, the higher the ISO speed, the less correction is applied. If you see severe vignetting with a particular lens, focal length, or ISO setting, you might want to turn this feature off, shoot RAW, and apply correction using DPP instead.

When you select this menu option from the Shooting 1 menu, the screen shown in Figure 3.8 appears. The lens currently attached to the camera is shown, along with a notation whether correction data needed to brighten the corners is already registered in the camera. (Information about 20 of the most popular lenses is included in the T1i's firmware.) If so, you can select Enable to activate the feature, or Disable to turn it off.

Figure 3.7
Vignetting (top) is undesirable in a landscape photo. You can correct this defect in the camera or by using Digital Photo Pro software.

Figure 3.8
Peripheral illumination correction can fix dark corners.

Press the Set button to confirm your choice. Note that in-camera correction must be applied *before* you take the photo.

If your lens is not registered in the camera, you can remedy that deficit using the EOS Utility (also described in Chapter 8). Just follow these steps:

1. Connect your T1i to your computer using the USB cable supplied with the camera.

2. Load the EOS Utility and click on Camera Settings/Remote Shooting from the splash screen that appears.

3. Choose the Shooting menu from the menu bar located about midway in the control panel that appears on your computer display. The panel is shown at left in Figure 3.9. The Shooting menu icon is the white camera on a red background.

4. Click on the Peripheral Illumin. Correct. choice to produce the screen shown at right in Figure 3.9.

5. Select the category containing the lens you want to register from the panels at the top of the new screen, then place a check mark next to all the lenses you'd like to register in the camera.

6. Click OK to send the data from your computer to the T1i and register your lenses.

7. When a newly registered lens is mounted on the camera, you will be able to activate the anti-vignetting feature for that lens from the Shooting 1 menu.

Figure 3.9
Select the lenses to be corrected.

Red-Eye Reduction

Your Rebel T1i has a fairly effective Red-Eye Reduction flash mode. Unfortunately, your camera is unable, on its own, to *eliminate* the red-eye effects that occur when an electronic flash (or, rarely, illumination from other sources) bounces off the retinas of the eye and into the camera lens. Animals seem to suffer from yellow or green glowing pupils, instead; the effect is equally undesirable. The effect is worst under low-light conditions (exactly when you might be using a flash) as the pupils expand to allow more light to reach the retinas. The best you can hope for is to *reduce* or minimize the red-eye effect.

The best way to truly eliminate red-eye is to raise the flash up off the camera so its illumination approaches the eye from an angle that won't reflect directly back to the retina and into the lens. The extra height of the built-in flash may not be sufficient, however. Gaining a bit of extra height alone may be a good reason for using an external flash. If you're working with your T1i's built-in flash, your only recourse may be to switch the Red-Eye Reduction feature on with the menu choice shown in Figure 3.10. It causes a lamp on the front of the camera to illuminate with a half-press of the shutter release button, which may cause your subjects' pupils to contract, decreasing the amount of the red-eye effect. You may have to ask your subject to look at the lamp to gain maximum effect. Avoid blocking the lamp as your fingers wrap around the grip. Figure 3.11 shows the effects of wider pupils (left) and those that have been contracted using the T1i's Red-Eye Reduction feature.

Figure 3.10
Turn on your camera's Red-Eye Reduction feature to help eliminate demon-red pupils.

Figure 3.11 Red-eye is tamed (right), thanks to the Rebel T1i's Red-Eye reduction lamp.

Flash Control

This multi-level menu entry, creatively moved to this location from its slot in the Setup 2 menu in earlier Rebel models, includes five settings for controlling the Canon EOS Rebel T1i's built-in, pop-up electronic flash unit, as well as accessory flash units you can attach to the camera (see Figure 3.12). Here are your main options:

Flash Firing

Use this option to enable or disable the built-in or attached accessory electronic flash when working with Creative Zone modes. You might want to totally disable the T1i's flash (both built-in and accessory flash) when shooting in sensitive environments, such as concerts, in museums, or during religious ceremonies. When disabled, the flash cannot fire even if you accidentally elevate it, or have an accessory flash attached and turned on when using Creative Zone modes.

Built-in Flash Function Setting

There are three choices for this menu choice. The Flash mode entry is grayed out and cannot be selected when using the built-in flash, which has a fixed E-TTL-II mode. This entry is available only when an external flash is attached.

- **Shutter sync.** You can choose 1st Curtain sync, which fires the flash as soon as the shutter is completely open (this is the default mode). Alternatively, you can select 2nd Curtain sync, which fires a pre-flash used to measure exposure as soon as the

Flash control

Flash firing   Enable

Built-in flash func. setting

External flash func. setting

External flash C. Fn. setting

Clear ext. flash C. Fn. set.

MENU

Figure 3.12
The Flash Control menu entry has five setting sub-menus.

shutter release is pressed down all the way, but before the shutter opens, and then triggers a second flash at the end of the exposure, just before the shutter starts to close. This action allows photographing a blurred trail of light of moving objects with sharp flash exposures at the beginning and the end of the exposure. This type of flash exposure is slightly different from what some other cameras produce using 2nd Curtain sync. I'll explain how it works in Chapter 6.

■ **Flash exp. comp.** This entry is an alternate method of setting flash exposure compensation. Select this option with the Set button, then dial in the amount of flash EV compensation you want using the left/right cross keys. The EV that was in force prior to your adjustment is shown with a blue indicator. Press Set again to confirm your change, and then press the Menu button to exit.

■ **E-TTL II.** You can choose Evaluative or Average metering modes for the electronic flash exposure meter. Evaluative looks at selected areas in the scene to calculate exposure, while Average calculates flash exposure by reading the entire scene.

Tip

If you've activated the Rebel T1i's Auto Lighting Optimizer (described later in this chapter), any Flash EV changes you make may not provide the brightening effect you're looking for. Disable Auto Lighting Optimizer (C.Fn II-7 in the Setup 3 menu).

External Flash Function Setting

You can access this menu only when you have a compatible electronic flash attached and switched on. The settings available are shown in Figure 3.13. If you press the DISP button while adjusting flash settings, both the changes made to the settings of an attached external flash and to the built-in flash will be cleared.

■ **Flash mode.** This entry allows you to set the flash mode for the external flash, from E-TTL II, A-TTL, or TTL when using a flash that includes these modes. All three provide through-the-lens flash metering, but with different degrees of sophistication. E-TTL (Evaluative Through-the-Lens) uses a preflash just prior to taking the picture to allow the camera's metering sensor to read the flash exposure and compare it with ambient light to provide the best exposure. A-TTL (Advanced Through-the-Lens) metering is an earlier system used with some Canon speedlights to read illumination through the lens, but concentrate sensitivity on the active focus point, also using a preflash. The TTL (Through-the-Lens) system is a less sophisticated flash exposure control system used by some flash units. It doesn't use a preflash. You should always choose E-TTL if your flash supports it, or select one of the other systems compatible with the Speedlite you are using.

(As I'll explain in Chapter 7, you should be careful when using non-dedicated and non-Canon flash units, because their triggering voltage may be too high for your camera's electronics.)

- **Shutter sync.** As with the T1i's internal flash, you can choose 1st Curtain sync, which fires the flash as soon as the shutter is completely open (this is the default mode). Alternatively, you can select 2nd Curtain sync, which fires the flash as soon as the shutter opens, and then triggers a second flash at the end of the exposure, just before the shutter starts to close.

- **FEB.** Flash Exposure Bracketing (FEB), available with compatible flash units, operates similarly to ordinary exposure bracketing, providing a series of different exposures to improve your chances of getting the exact right exposure, or to provide alternative renditions for creative purposes.

- **Flash exposure compensation.** You can adjust flash exposure using a menu here. Select this option with the Set button, then dial in the amount of flash EV compensation you want using the cross keys. The EV that was in place before you started to make your adjustment is shown as a blue indicator, so you can return to that value quickly. Press Set again to confirm your change, then press the Menu button twice to exit.

External flash func. setting

Flash mode	E-TTL II
Shutter sync.	1st. curtain
FEB	‾3..2..1..0..1..2.‡3
Flash exp. comp	‾2..1..0..1.‡2
E-TTL II	Evaluative
Zoom	Auto

DISP. Clear Speedlite settings

Figure 3.13
External flash units can be controlled from the Canon EOS Rebel T1i using this menu.

■ **E-TTL II.** You can choose Evaluative (Matrix) or Average metering modes for the electronic flash exposure meter. Evaluative looks at selected areas in the scene to calculate exposure, while Average calculates flash exposure by reading the entire scene.

■ **Zoom.** Some flash units can vary their coverage to better match the field of view of your lens at a particular focal length. You can allow the external flash to zoom automatically, based on information provided, or manually, using a zoom button on the flash itself.

External Flash Custom Function Setting

Many external Speedlites from Canon include their own list of Custom Functions, which can be used to specify things like flash metering mode and flash bracketing sequences, as well as more sophisticated features, such as modeling light/flash (if available), use of external power sources (if attached), and functions of any slave unit attached to the external flash. This menu entry allows you to set an external flash unit's Custom Functions from your T1i's menu.

Clear External Flash Custom Function Setting

This entry allows you to zero-out any changes you've made to your external flash's Custom Functions, and return them to their factory default settings.

Exposure Compensation/Automatic Exposure Bracketing

The first entry on the Shooting 2 menu (see Figure 3.14) is Exposure Compensation/ AEB (Automatic Exposure Bracketing). As you'll learn in Chapter 4, exposure compensation is a way to add or subtract a fixed amount of exposure to all shots taken while exposure compensation is active. Bracketing using the T1i's AEB feature is a way to shoot several consecutive exposures using *different* exposure settings, to improve the odds that one will be exactly right.

I'll explain both options in detail in Chapter 4. But if you want a crash course, here's how to use this menu option. Just select Exposure Comp./AEB, press Set, and then:

■ **Add or subtract exposure compensation.** When the screen shown in Figure 3.15 is visible, press the left/right cross keys to subtract or add exposure. You can bypass the menu entirely when the Shooting Settings screen is visible by pressing the Av button (to the right of the LCD) and rotating the Main dial.

■ **Activate exposure bracketing.** When the screen is visible, rotate the Main dial to spread the three blocks representing the bracketed exposures by the size of the bracket increment you want. Then, optionally, use the left/right cross keys to shift the bracket so the center exposure is less or more than the base exposure calculated by the camera. (See Figure 3.16, and jump ahead to the full explanation in Chapter 4 if you're hopelessly confused.)

Figure 3.14
The Shooting 2 menu.

Figure 3.15
Add or subtract exposure compensation.

Figure 3.16
Set the range of
the three brack-
eted exposures.

Select this menu choice, then use the Main dial to spread or contract the three dots beneath the –2/+2 scale until you've defined the range you want the bracket to cover, shown as two-thirds-stop jumps in Figure 3.16. Use the cross keys to move the bracket to Darker or Brighter.

As you take pictures, the amount of bracketing will be shown as three indicators in the analog exposure display that flash when the shutter release button is pressed halfway. When AEB is activated, the three bracketed shots will be exposed in this sequence: metered exposure, decreased exposure, increased exposure. To cancel bracketing, select this menu option again, and use the left cross key to converge all the bracket indicators once more. You'll find more information about exposure bracketing in Chapter 4.

Metering Mode

Use this menu option to switch among Evaluative, Partial, Spot, and Center-Weighted average metering. Earlier Rebels had a button that could be pressed to allow setting metering mode without entering the menu system. Canon felt that this setting isn't changed often enough by the average user to merit that convenience, and moved Metering mode here.

Custom White Balance

If Automatic white balance or one of the six preset settings available by pressing the WB button (Auto, Daylight, Shade, Cloudy/Twilight/Sunset, Tungsten, White Fluorescent, or Flash) aren't suitable, you can set a custom white balance using this menu option. The custom setting you establish will then be applied whenever you select Custom using the WB button.

To set the white balance to an appropriate color temperature under the current ambient lighting conditions, follow these steps:

1. Focus manually (with the lens set on MF) on a plain white or gray object, such as a card or wall, making sure the object fills the spot metering circle in the center of the viewfinder.

2. Take a photo.

3. Press the Menu button and select Custom WB from the Shooting 2 menu.

4. The reference image you just took appears. If you want to use a different picture, use the left/right cross keys to navigate to the photo you'd like to use.

5. Press the Set button to store the white balance of the image as your custom setting.

6. Henceforth, you can access this customized setting by pressing the WB button and choosing the Custom icon. It's the one at the extreme left of the screen that pops up.

Figure 3.17 Adjusting color temperature can provide different results of the same subject at 3400K (left), 5000K (middle), and 2800K (right).

A WHITE BALANCE LIBRARY

Shoot a selection of blank-card images under a variety of lighting conditions on a spare memory card. If you want to "recycle" one of the color temperatures you've stored, insert the card and set the Custom white balance to one of the images in your white balance library, as described above.

White Balance Shift and Bracketing

White balance shift allows you to dial in a white balance color bias along the Blue/Amber (yellow) dimensions, and/or Magenta/Green scale. In other words, you can set your color balance so that it is a little bluer or yellower (only), a little more magenta or green (only), or a combination of the two bias dimensions. You can also bracket exposures, taking several consecutive pictures each with a slightly different color balance biased in the directions you specify.

The process is a little easier to visualize if you look at Figure 3.18. The center intersection of lines BA and GM (remember high school geometry!) is the point of zero bias. Move the point at that intersection using the left/right and up/down cross keys to locate it at any point on the graph using the Blue/Amber (yellow) and Green/Magenta coordinates. The amount of shift will be displayed in the SHIFT box to the right of the graph.

Figure 3.18
Use the Main dial to specify color balance bracketing using Green-Magenta bias or to specify Blue/Amber (yellow) bias.

White balance bracketing is like white balance shifting, only the bracketed changes occur along the bias axis you specify. The three squares in Figure 3.18 show that the white balance bracketing will occur in two stop steps along the Blue/Amber (yellow) axis. The amount of the bracketing is shown in the lower box to the right of the graph.

This form of bracketing is similar to exposure bracketing, but with the added dimension of hue instead of brightness/darkness. Bias bracketing can be performed in any JPEG-only mode. You can't use RAW or RAW+JPEG, because the RAW files already contain the information needed to fine-tune the white balance and white balance bias.

White Balance Bracketing

Follow these steps to bracket white balance.

1. **Activate white balance shift/bracketing.** Select WB SHIFT/BKT from the Shooting 2 menu.

2. **Choose the amount of the WB bracketing.** Rotate the Main dial to select the amount of shift (how much each photo will vary). Spin to the right to separate the three indicator dots by 1 to 3 increments in the horizontal Blue/Amber axis. Spin to the left to separate the three dots in the vertical Green/Magenta direction. The bracket amount (BA) will be shown in the BKT box at the right side of the screen.

3. **Select the WB bias.** Unless you adjust the white balance bias, the bracketing will take place along one axis only; that is, blue-to-amber changes or green-to-magenta changes, either progressing from the center neutral point that's the intersection of axes BA and GM. You can use the left/right and up/down cross keys to add some *bias* to the white balance bracketing (described next).

4. **Confirm your white balance bracketing.** Press DISP to cancel the WB shift/bracketing changes you've made, or press Set to confirm the setting and return to the Shooting 2 menu.

5. **Take your bracket sets.** Subsequent pictures you take will have their white balance bracketed in sets of three, using the parameters you've just entered. The order will be Standard WB (representing the middle dot of the three); More Blue/More Magenta (either the left or top dot, depending on whether you used the Blue/Amber or Magenta/Green axes); More Amber/More Green.

> ### Tip
>
> If you use the Rebel T1i's continuous shooting feature, you can snap off all three shots in a bracket set quickly and automatically. Note that if High ISO speed noise reduction is set to On in the Custom Functions menu (described later in this chapter), WB bracketing is disabled.

BIASING YOUR WHITE BALANCE

White balance bracketing is confusing enough, until you start adding some bias to the equation. Fortunately, the concept is easy to understand with a little explanation. As I noted above, white balance bracketing usually proceeds along a single axis, either the Blue/Amber (horizontal) or Green/Magenta (vertical axis). If you stick to those directions, the bracketing dot indicators will confine themselves to the thicker center lines that bisect the grid shown in Figure 3.18. You can move the bracket dots along either center line with the left/right (for horizontal movement) or up/down (for vertical movement) cross keys to give your bracketing an unambiguous bias towards the blue, amber, green, or magenta tones.

The potentially confusing part comes into play when you use the up/down keys to adjust the bracket range for Blue/Amber (horizontal) bracketing, or the left/right keys to adjust the bracket range for the Green/Magenta (vertical bracketing). When you do that, the bracket indicators drift into one of the four quadrants of the grid, so you end up with Blue/Amber bracketing that has a bit of a green or magenta bias as well, or a Green/Magenta bracketing with some blue or amber bias, as shown in Figure 3.19. This is the kind of ultra-fine tuning that the Rebel T1i makes available to you, and of which you might want to afford yourself as you gain experience. In most cases, it's fairly easy to determine if you want your image to be more green, more magenta, more blue, or more yellow, although judging your current shots on the LCD screen can be tricky unless you view the screen in a darkened location so it will be bright and easy to see. You'll find more about bracketing in Chapter 4.

Figure 3.19
The up/down and left/right cross keys can be used to maneuver the bracketing into any quadrant.

Color Space

When you are using one of the Creative Zone modes, you can select one of two different color spaces (also called *color gamuts*) using this menu entry. One color space is named *Adobe RGB* (because it was developed by Adobe Systems in 1998), while the other is called *sRGB* (supposedly because it is the *standard* RGB color space). These two color gamuts define a specific set of colors that can be applied to the images your T1i captures.

The color space menu choice applies directly to JPEG images shot using Creative Zone exposure modes (P, Tv, Av, M, and A-DEP). When you're using Basic Zone modes, the T1i uses the sRGB color space for all the JPEG images you take. RAW images are a special case. They have the information for *both* sRGB and Adobe RGB, but when you load such photos into your image editor, it will default to sRGB (with Basic Zone shots) or the color space specified here (for Creative Zone pictures) unless you change that setting while importing the photos. (See the Best of Both Worlds sidebar which follows for more information.)

You may be surprised to learn that the T1i doesn't automatically capture *all* the colors we see. Unfortunately, that's impossible because of the limitations of the sensor and the filters used to capture the fundamental red, green, and blue colors, as well as that of the phosphors used to display those colors on your camera and computer monitors. Nor is it possible to *print* every color our eyes detect, because the inks or pigments used don't absorb and reflect colors perfectly. In short, your sensor doesn't capture all the colors that we can see, your monitor can't display all the colors that the sensor captures, and your printer outputs yet another version.

On the other hand, the T1i does capture quite a few more colors than we need. The original 14-bit RAW image contains a possible 4.4 *trillion* different hues, which are condensed down to a mere 16.8 million possible colors when converted to a 24-bit (eight bits per channel) image. While 16.8 million colors may seem like a lot, it's a small subset of 4.4 trillion captured, and an even smaller subset of all the possible colors we can see. The set of colors, or gamut that can be reproduced or captured by a given device (scanner, digital camera, monitor, printer, or some other piece of equipment) is represented as a color space that exists within the larger full range of colors.

That full range is represented by the odd-shaped splotch of color shown in Figure 3.20, as defined by scientists at the International Commission on Illumination (usually known as the CIE for its French name *Commission internationale de l'éclairage*) back in 1931. The colors possible with Adobe RGB are represented by the larger, black triangle in the figure, while the sRGB gamut is represented by the smaller white triangle.

Regardless of which triangle—or color space—is used by the T1i, you end up with some combination of 16.8 million different colors that can be used in your photograph. (No

Figure 3.20
The outer figure shows all the colors we can see; the two inner outlines show the boundaries of Adobe RGB (black triangle) and sRGB (white triangle).

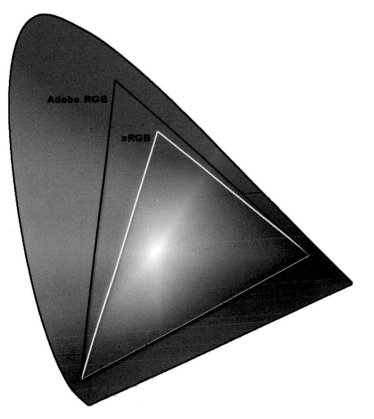

one image will contain all 16.8 million! If each and every pixel in a 15-megapixel photo were a different color—which is extremely unlikely—you'd need only 15 million different colors.) But, as you can see from the figure, the colors available will be *different*.

Adobe RGB is what is often called an *expanded* color space, because it can reproduce a range of colors that is spread over a wider range of the visual spectrum. Adobe RGB is useful for commercial and professional printing. You don't need this range of colors if your images will be displayed primarily on your computer screen or output by your personal printer.

The other color space, sRGB, is recommended for images that will be output locally on the user's own printer, as this color space matches that of the typical inkjet printer fairly closely. While both Adobe RGB and sRGB can reproduce the exact same 16.8 million absolute colors, Adobe RGB spreads those colors over a larger portion of the visible spectrum, as you can see in the figure. Think of a box of crayons (the jumbo 16.8 million crayon variety). Some of the basic crayons from the original sRGB set have been removed and replaced with new hues not contained in the original box. Your "new" box contains colors that can't be reproduced by your computer monitor, but which work just fine with a commercial printing press.

BEST OF BOTH WORLDS

As I mentioned, if you're using a Basic Zone mode, the T1i selects the sRGB color space automatically. In addition, you may choose to set the sRGB color space with this menu entry to apply that gamut to all your Creative Zone photos as well. But, in either case, you can still easily obtain Adobe RGB versions of your photos if you need them. Just shoot using RAW+JPEG. You'll end up with sRGB JPEGs suitable for output on your own printer, but you can still extract an Adobe RGB version from the RAW file at any time. It's like capturing two different color spaces at once—sRGB and Adobe RGB—and getting the best of both worlds.

Of course, choosing the right color space doesn't solve the problems that result from having each device in the image chain manipulating or producing a slightly different set of colors. To that end, you'll need to investigate the wonderful world of *color management*, which uses hardware and software tools to match or *calibrate* all your devices, as closely as possible, so that what you see more closely resembles what you capture, what you see on your computer display, and what ends up on a printed hardcopy. Entire books have been devoted to color management, and most of what you need to know doesn't directly involve your Canon EOS T1i, so I won't detail the nuts and bolts here.

To manage your color, you'll need, at the bare minimum, some sort of calibration system for your computer display, so that your monitor can be adjusted to show a standardized set of colors that is repeatable over time. (What you see on the screen can vary as the monitor ages, or even when the room light changes). I use Pantone's Huey monitor color correction system for my computer's main 26-inch wide-screen LCD display, as well as for the smaller 20-inch wide-screen secondary display that flanks it. The Huey checks room light levels every five minutes, and reminds me to recalibrate every week or two, using the small sensor device shown in Figure 3.21, which attaches temporarily to the front of the screen with tiny suction cups, and interprets test patches that the Huey software displays during calibration. The rest of the time, the Huey sensor sits in the stand shown, measuring the room illumination, and adjusting my monitors for higher or lower ambient light levels.

Figure 3.21 Pantone's Huey monitor color correction system is an inexpensive device for calibrating your display.

The Huey (www.pantone.com) is an inexpensive (under $100) system that does a good job of calibrating a single monitor. You can upgrade it, as I did, for use with multiple monitors using a $40 software download. If you're serious about accurate color and make prints, you'll want a more advanced system (up to $500) like the various Spyder products from Datacolor (www.datacolor.com), or Colormunki from X-Rite (www.colormunki.com).

Picture Style

The Picture Styles feature, introduced to the EOS camera line with the Canon EOS 30D back in February, 2006, is one of the most important tools for customizing the way your T1i renders its photos. Picture Styles are extremely flexible. If you don't like one of the predefined styles, you can adjust it to suit your needs. You can also use those three User Definition files to create styles that are all your own. If you want rich, bright colors to emulate Velvia film or the work of legendary photographer Pete Turner, you can build your own color-soaked style. If you want soft, muted colors and less sharpness to create a romantic look, you can do that, too. Perhaps you'd like a setting with extra contrast for shooting outdoors on hazy or cloudy days.

Once your styles are set up, Picture Styles are easy to access, and there's no need to visit this menu just to swap one style for another. Just press the Picture Styles button (the down cross key) next to the color LCD, and use the left/right cross keys to move through the list of available styles. As each style is highlighted, its current settings for Sharpness, Contrast, Saturation, and Color Tone are shown at the top of the screen. Press Set to activate the style of your choice.

You can also select a Picture Style from the Shooting 2 menu entry (although it takes a few seconds longer). You'll primarily use this menu item to define or redefine your Picture Styles. (See Figure 3.22.) You can also set up Picture Styles using the T1i's Picture Styles Editor.

Tip

As with the Color Space menu entry, Picture Styles can be applied directly *only* to JPEG images shot using Creative Zone exposure modes (P, Tv, Av, M, and A-DEP). When using a Basic Zone mode, the Canon EOS T1i selects the Standard Picture Style automatically, except when shooting Portrait or Landscape Basic Zone modes (in which case the Portrait and Landscape Picture Styles will be used, respectively). RAW images can be adjusted to any Picture Style you want when the photo is imported into your image editor.

Figure 3.22
Nine different
Picture Styles
are available
from this
scrolling menu;
these six plus
three User Def
styles not
shown.

The parameters applied when using Picture Styles follow. Figure 3.23 shows exaggerated examples of the first four (color photo) attributes, as applied by Picture Styles (your real-world tweaks may not be quite this drastic, but lesser modifications are more difficult to represent on the printed page):

■ **Sharpness.** This parameter determines the apparent contrast between the outlines or edges in an image, which we perceive as image sharpness. You can adjust the sharpness of the image between values of 0 (no sharpening added) to 7 (dramatic additional sharpness). When adjusting sharpness, remember that more is not always a good thing. A little softness is necessary (and is introduced by a blurring "anti-alias" filter in front of the sensor) to reduce or eliminate the moiré effects that can result when details in your image form a pattern that is too close to the pattern, or frequency, of the sensor itself. The default (0) level sharpening was chosen by Canon to allow most moiré interference to be safely blurred to invisibility, at the cost of a little sharpness. As you boost sharpness (either using a Picture Style or in your image editor), moiré can become a problem, plus, you may end up with those noxious "halos" that appear around the edges of images that have been oversharpened. Use this adjustment with care.

Figure 3.23 These sets of photos represent the main color image Picture Styles parameters: sharpness (upper-left pair); contrast (upper-right pair); saturation (lower-left pair); and color tone (lower-right pair).

■ **Contrast.** Use this control, with values from −4 (low contrast) to +4 (higher contrast) to change the number of middle tones between the deepest blacks and brightest whites. Low contrast settings produce a flatter-looking photo, while high contrast adjustments may improve the tonal rendition while possibly losing detail in the shadows or highlights.

■ **Saturation.** This parameter, adjustable from −4 (low saturation) to +4 (high saturation) controls the richness of the color, making, say, a red tone appear to be deeper and fuller when you increase saturation, and tend more towards lighter, pinkish hues when you decrease saturation of the reds. Boosting the saturation too much can mean that detail may be lost in one or more of the color channels, producing what is called "clipping." You can detect this phenomenon when using the RGB histograms, as described in Chapter 4.

■ **Color Tone.** This adjustment has the most effect on skin tones, making them either redder (0 to –4) or yellower (0 to +4).

■ **Filter effect (Monochrome only).** Filter effects do not add any color to a black-and-white image. Instead, rather, they change the rendition of gray tones as if the picture were taken through a color filter. I'll explain this distinction more completely in the sidebar "Filters vs. Toning" later in this section.

■ **Toning effect (Monochrome only).** Using toning effects preserves the monochrome tonal values in your image, but adds a color overlay that gives the photo a sepia, blue, purple, or green cast.

The predefined Picture Styles are these:

■ **Standard.** This Picture Style, the default, applies a set of parameters useful for most picture taking, and which are applied automatically when using Basic Zone modes other than Portrait or Landscape.

■ **Portrait.** This style boosts saturation for richer colors when shooting portraits, particularly of women and children, while reducing sharpness slightly to provide more flattering skin texture. The Basic Mode Portrait setting uses this Picture Style. You might prefer the Faithful style for portraits of men when you want a more rugged or masculine look, or when you want to emphasize character lines in the faces of older subjects of either gender.

■ **Landscape.** This style increases the saturation of blues and greens, and increases both color saturation and sharpness for more vivid landscape images. The Basic Zone Landscape mode uses this setting.

■ **Neutral.** This Picture Style is a less saturated and lower contrast version of the Standard style. Use it when you want a more muted look to your images, or when the photos you are taking seem too bright and contrasty (say, at the beach on a sunny day).

■ **Faithful.** The goal of this style is to render the colors of your image as accurately as possible, roughly in the same relationships as seen by the eye.

■ **Monochrome.** Use this Picture Style to create black-and-white photos in the camera. If you're shooting JPEG only, the colors are gone forever. But if you're shooting JPEG+RAW you can convert the RAW files to color as you import them into your image editor, even if you've shot using the Monochrome Picture Style. Your T1i displays the images in black-and-white on the screen during playback, but the colors are there in the RAW file for later retrieval.

> **Tip**
>
> You can use the Monochrome Picture Style even if you are using one of the RAW formats alone, without a JPEG version. The EOS T1i displays your images on the screen in black-and-white, and marks the RAW image as monochrome so it will default to that style when you import it into your image editor. However, the color information is still present in the RAW file and can be retrieved, at your option, when importing the image.

Selecting Picture Styles

Canon makes selecting a Picture Style very easy, and, to prevent you from accidentally changing an existing style when you don't mean to, divides *selection* and *modification* functions into two separate tasks. There are actually two different ways to choose from among your existing Picture Styles.

One way is to choose Picture Styles from the Shooting 2 menu and press Set to produce the main Picture Style menu screen. Use the up/down cross keys to choose from the nine choices (Neutral, Faithful, Monochrome and User Def. 1, User Def. 2, and User Def. 3 are shown in Figure 3.24; the rest appear as you scroll.) The current settings for each Picture style are shown on the right half of the screen. Press Set to activate your

Figure 3.24
You can select a style from the Picture Style menu in Setup 2 menu.

choice. Then press the Menu button to exit the menu system. You can see that even with this method, switching among Picture Styles is fast and easy enough to allow you to shift gears as often as you like during a shooting session.

But your T1i offers an even simpler way to activate a Picture Style. Press the Picture Styles button (the down cross key) and scroll through the list of available styles on the screen that appears, shown in Figure 3.25. When you use this method, the current settings for a particular style are shown *only* when you've highlighted that style. Press Set to activate the style of your choice.

Figure 3.25
Press the Picture Style button under the LCD to choose a style from this fast-access screen.

Defining Picture Styles

Canon makes interpreting current Picture Style settings and applying changes very easy. As you saw in Figures 3.24 and 3.25, the current settings of the visible Picture Style options are shown as numeric values on the menu screen. Some camera vendors use word descriptions, like Sharp, Extra Sharp, or Vivid, More Vivid that are difficult to relate to. The T1i's settings, on the other hand, are values on uniform scales, with seven steps (from 1 to 7) for sharpness, and plus/minus four steps clustered around a zero (no change) value for contrast and saturation (so you can change from low contrast/low saturation, –4, to high contrast/high saturation, +4), as well as color tone (–4/reddish to +4/yellowish). The individual icons at the top of Figures 3.22, 3.24, and 3.25 represent (left to right) Sharpness, Contrast, Saturation, and Color Tone.

You can change one of the existing Picture Styles or define your own whenever the Shooting 2 menu version of the Picture Styles menu or the pop-up selection screen shown are visible. Just press the DISP button when either screen is on the LCD. Follow these steps:

1. Use the cross keys to scroll to the style you'd like to adjust.

2. Press the DISP button to choose Detail set. If you're coming from the Shooting 2 menu, the screen that appears next will look like the one shown in Figure 3.26 for the five color styles or three User Def styles. If you've accessed the adjustment screen by pressing the Picture Styles button first, the screen looks much the same, but has blue highlighting instead of red.

3. Use the cross keys to scroll among the four parameters. Default set. at the bottom of the screen restores the values to the preset numbers.

4. Press Set to change the values of one of the four parameters. If you're redefining one of the default presets, the menu screen will look like the figure, which represents the Landscape Picture Style.

5. Use the left/right cross keys to move the triangle to the value you want to use. Note that the previous value remains on the scale, represented by a gray triangle. This makes it easy to return to the original setting if you want.

6. Press the Set button to lock in that value, then press the Menu button three times to back out of the menu system.

Figure 3.26
Each parameter can be changed separately.

Any Picture Style that has been changed from its defaults will be shown in the Picture Style menu with blue highlighting the altered parameter. You don't have to worry about changing a Picture Style and then forgetting that you've modified it. A quick glance at the Picture Style menu will show you which styles and parameters have been changed.

Making changes in the Monochrome Picture Style is slightly different, as the Saturation and Color Tone parameters are replaced with Filter Effect and Toning Effect options. (Keep in mind that once you've taken a photo using a Monochrome Picture Style, you can't convert the image back to full color.) You can choose from Yellow, Orange, Red, Green filters, or None, and specify Sepia, Blue, Purple, or Green toning, or None. You can still set the Sharpness and Contrast parameters that are available with the other Picture Styles. Figure 3.27 shows filter effects being applied to the Monochrome Picture Style.

Figure 3.27
Apply changes to the Monochrome Picture Style.

FILTERS VS. TONING

Although some of the color choices overlap, you'll get very different looks when choosing between Filter Effects and Toning Effects. Filter Effects add no color to the monochrome image. Instead, they reproduce the look of black-and-white film that has been shot through a color filter. That is, Yellow will make the sky darker and the clouds will stand out more, while Orange makes the sky even darker and sunsets more full of detail. The

Red filter produces the darkest sky of all and darkens green objects, such as leaves. Human skin may appear lighter than normal. The Green filter has the opposite effect on leaves, making them appear lighter in tone. Figure 3.28 shows the same scene shot with no filter, then Yellow, Green, and Red filters.

The Sepia, Blue, Purple, and Green toning effects, on the other hand, all add a color cast to your monochrome image. Use these when you want an old-time look or a special effect, without bothering to recolor your shots in an image editor. Figure 3.29 shows the various toning effects available.

Figure 3.28
No filter (upper left); yellow filter (upper right); green filter (lower left); and red filter (lower right).

Figure 3.29
Select from among four color filters in the Monochrome Picture Style, including sepia (top left); blue (top right); purple (lower left); and green (lower right).

Adjusting Styles with the Picture Style Editor

The Picture Style Editor, shown in Figure 3.30, allows you to create your own custom Picture Styles, or edit existing styles, including the Standard, Landscape, Faithful, and other predefined settings already present in your EOS T1i. You can change sharpness, contrast, color saturation, and color tone—and a lot more—and then save the modifications as a .PF2 file that can be uploaded to the camera, or used by Digital Photo Professional (described in Chapter 9) to modify a RAW image as it is imported.

To create and load your own Picture Style, just follow these steps:

1. **Load the editor.** Launch the Picture Style Editor (PSE, not to be confused with the *other* PSE, Photoshop Elements).

2. **Access a RAW file.** Load a RAW .CR2 image you'd like to use as a reference into PSE. You can drag a file from a folder into the editor's main window, or use the Open command in the File menu.

3. **Choose an existing style to base your new style on.** Select any of the base styles except for Standard. Your new style will begin with all the attributes of the base style you choose, so start with one that already is fairly close to the look you want to achieve ("tweaking" is easier than building a style from the ground up).

Figure 3.30 The Picture Style Editor lets you create your own Picture Styles for use by the T1i or Digital Photo Professional when importing image files.

4. **Split the screen.** You can compare the appearance of your new style with the base style you are working from. Near the lower-left edge of the display pane are three buttons you can click to split the old/new styles vertically, horizontally, or return to a single image.

5. **Dial in basic changes.** Click the Advanced button in the Tool palette, shown at right in Figure 3.30 to pop up the Advanced Picture Style Settings dialog box that appears at left in the figure. These are the same parameters you can change in the camera. Click OK when you're finished.

6. **Make advanced changes.** The Tool palette has additional functions for adjusting hue, tonal range, and curves. Use of these tools is beyond the scope of a single chapter, let alone a notation in a bulleted list, but if you're familiar with the advanced tools in Photoshop, Photoshop Elements, Digital Photo Pro, or another image editor, you can experiment to your heart's content. Note that these modifications go way beyond what you can do with Picture Styles in the camera itself, so learning how to work with them is worth the effort.

7. **Save your Picture Style.** When you're finished, choose Save Picture Style File from the File menu to store your new style as a .PF2 file on your hard disk. Add a caption and copyright information to your style in the boxes provided. If you click Disable Subsequent Editing, your style will be "locked" and protected from further changes, and the modifications you did make will be hidden from view (just in case you dream up your own personal, "secret" style). But you'll be unable to edit that style later on. If you think you might want to change your custom Picture Style, save a second copy without marking the Disable Subsequent Editing box.

Now it's time to upload your new style to your Canon EOS T1i using one of your three User Def slots in the Picture Style array. Just follow these steps:

1. **Link your camera for upload.** Connect your camera to your computer using the USB cable, turn the T1i on, launch the EOS Utility, and click the Camera Settings/Remote Shooting choice in the splash screen.

2. **Choose the shooting menu.** It's marked with an icon of a white camera on a red background, from the menu bar located about midway in the control panel that appears on your computer display.

3. **Access the Picture Style.** Click on the Picture Style choice to produce the screen shown at left in Figure 3.31. Highlight one of the three User Def choices and click Detail set. (Note that you could also click one of the predefined Picture Styles, such as Standard or Landscape, and change their parameters, too.) The Picture Style settings dialog box, at right in Figure 3.31, appears.

4. **Specify your new style.** In the Picture Style settings dialog box, click the Open button, and navigate to the new Picture Style that you named and saved in Step 7 above.

Figure 3.31
Upload your
new style to
your EOS T1i
using the EOS
Utility.

5. **Upload to your camera.** Click the Apply button and your Picture Style will be uploaded to the T1i into the User Def slot indicated at the top of the dialog box.

6. **Exit EOS Utility.** Click Close to quit the Picture Style settings dialog, and exit the EOS Utility. Disconnect your camera from your computer, and your new style is ready to use.

Get More Picture Styles

I've found that careful Googling can unearth other Picture Styles that helpful fellow EOS owners have made available, and even a few from the helpful Canon company itself. My own search turned up this link: http://web.canon.jp/imaging/picturestyle/file /index.html, where Canon offers a half dozen or more useful PF2 files you can download and install on your own. Remember that Picture Style files are compatible between various Canon EOS camera models (that is, you can use a style created for the Canon 50D with your T1i), but you should be working with the latest software versions to work with the latest cameras and Picture Styles. If you installed your software from the CDs that came with your EOS T1i, you're safe. If you owned an earlier EOS and haven't re-installed the software since your camera upgrade, you might need to re-install the software.

Try the additional styles Canon offers for yourself. They include:

- **Studio Portrait.** Compared to the Portrait style built into the camera, this one, Canon says, expresses translucent skin in smooth tones, but with less contrast. (Similar to films in the pre-digital age that were intended for studio portraiture.)

- **Snapshot Portrait.** This is another "translucent skin" style, with enhanced contrast indoors or out.

- **Nostalgia.** This style adds an amber tone to your images, while reducing the saturation of blue and green tones.

- **Clear.** This style adds contrast for what Canon says is additional "depth and clarity."

- **Twilight.** Adds a purple tone to the sky just before and after sunset or sunrise.

- **Emerald.** Emphasizes blues and greens.

- **Autumn Hues.** Increases the richness of browns and red tones seen in Fall colors.

Dust Delete Data

This menu choice lets you "take a picture" of any dust or other particles that may be adhering to your sensor. The T1i will then append information about the location of this dust to your photos, so that the Digital Photo Professional software can use this reference information to identify dust in your images and remove it automatically. You should capture a Dust Delete Data photo from time to time as your final line of defense against sensor dust.

To use this feature, select Dust Delete Data to produce the screen shown in Figure 3.32. Select OK and press the Set button. The camera will first perform a self-cleaning operation by applying ultrasonic vibration to the low-pass filter that resides on top of the sensor. Then, a screen will appear asking you to press the shutter button. Point the T1i at a solid white card with the lens set on Manual focus and rotate the focus ring to infinity. When you press the shutter release, the camera takes a photo of the card using aperture priority and f/22 (which provides enough depth-of-field [actually, in this case *depth-of-focus*] to image the dust sharply). The "picture" is not saved to your memory card but, rather, is stored in a special memory area in the camera. Finally, a "Data obtained" screen appears. If the Rebel T1i was unable to capture the data, you'll be asked to repeat the process. Make sure the camera is pointed at a plain white surface that's evenly illuminated.

The Dust Delete Data information is retained in the camera until you update it by taking a new "picture." The T1i adds the information to each image file automatically.

Figure 3.32
Capture
updated dust
data for your
sensor to allow
Digital Photo
Professional to
remove it
automatically.

Playback Menu Options

The single blue-coded Playback menu is where you select options related to the display, review, transfer, and printing of the photos you've taken (see Figure 3.33). The choices you'll find include:

- Protect images
- Rotate
- Erase images
- Print order

- Transfer order
- Histogram
- Slide show
- Image jump with main dial

Protect

If you want to keep an image from being accidentally erased (either with the Erase button or by using the Erase images menu), you can mark that image for protection. To protect one or more images, press the Menu button and choose Protect. Then use the left/right cross keys to view the image to be protected. Press the Set button to apply the protection. A key icon will appear at the upper edge of the information display while still in the protection screen, and when reviewing that image later (see Figure 3.34). To remove protection, repeat the process. You can scroll among the other images on your memory card and protect/unprotect them in the same way. Image protection will not save your images from removal when the card is reformatted.

Figure 3.33
The Playback menu includes options for viewing, printing, and transferring images.

Figure 3.34
Protected images can be locked against accidental erasure (but not preserved from formatting).

Rotate

While you can set the Rebel T1i to automatically rotate images taken in a vertical orientation using the Auto Rotate option in the Setup menu, you can manually rotate an image during playback using this menu selection. Select Rotate from the Playback menu, use the left/right cross keys to page through the available images on your memory card until the one you want to rotate appears, then press Set. The image will appear on the screen rotated 90 degrees, as shown in Figure 3.35. Press Set again, and the image will be rotated 270 degrees.

Figure 3.35
A vertically oriented image that isn't rotated appears larger on the LCD, but rotation allows viewing the photo without turning the camera.

Erase Images

Choose this menu entry and you'll be given two choices: Select and Erase Images and All Images on Card. The former option displays the most recent image. Press the up/down cross keys to mark or unmark an image for deletion (a check mark will appear in a box in the upper-left corner). Then, use the left/right cross keys to view other images and mark/unmark them for deletion. If you try to mark a protected image for deletion, a warning Protected appears on the screen.

When finished marking pictures, press the Trash button, and you'll see a screen that says Erase Selected Images with two options, Cancel and OK. Choose OK, then press the Set button to erase the images, or select Cancel and press the Set button to return to the selection screen. Press the Menu button to unmark your selections and return to the menu.

The All Images on Card choice removes all the pictures on the card, except for those you've marked with the Protect command, and does not reformat the memory card.

Print Order

The Rebel T1i supports the DPOF (Digital Print Order Format) that is now almost universally used by digital cameras to specify which images on your memory card should be printed, and the number of prints desired of each image. This information is recorded on the memory card, and can be interpreted by a compatible printer when the camera is linked to the printer using the USB cable, or when the memory card is inserted into a card reader slot on the printer itself. Photo labs are also equipped to read this data and make prints when you supply your memory card to them.

Transfer Order

You can specify which images are to be transferred to your personal computer when the Rebel T1i is linked to the computer with the USB cable. Individual images are "marked" using a review and selection system similar to the one used to specify print orders. You'll find more about creating a transfer order in Chapter 8.

Histogram

This entry is the first on the Playback 2 menu. (See Figure 3.36.) The T1i can show either a Brightness histogram or a set of three separate Red, Green, and Blue histograms in the full information display during picture review, or, it can show you both types of histogram in the partial information display.

Brightness histograms give you information about the overall tonal values present in the image. The RGB histograms can show more advanced users valuable data about specific channels that might be "clipped" (details are lost in the shadows or highlights).

Figure 3.36
The Playback 2
menu has three
entries.

This menu choice determines only how they are displayed during picture review. The amount of information displayed cycles through the following list as you repeatedly press the DISP button:

- **Single Image Display.** Only the image itself is shown, with basic shooting information displayed in a band across the top of the image, as you can see at upper left in Figure 3.37.

- **Single Image Display+Image-Recording Quality.** Identical to Single Image Display, except that the image size, RAW format (if selected), and JPEG compression (if selected) are overlaid on the image in the lower-left corner of the frame.

- **Histogram Display.** Both RGB and brightness histograms are shown, along with partial shooting information. This menu choice has no effect on the histograms shown in this display, which you can see at upper right in Figure 3.37.

- **Shooting Information Display.** Full shooting data is shown, along with either a brightness histogram (bottom left in Figure 3.37) or RGB histogram (bottom right in Figure 3.37). The type of histogram on view in this screen is determined by the setting you make in this menu choice. Select Histogram from the Playback 2 menu and choose Brightness or RGB. You can read more about *using* histograms in Chapter 5.

Figure 3.37 Press the DISP button to cycle between Single Image Display (upper left); Single Image Display+Image-Recording Quality (not shown); Histogram Display (upper right); or Shooting Information Displays with brightness histogram (bottom left) or RGB histogram (bottom right).

Slide Show

Slide Show is a convenient way to review images one after another, without the need to manually switch between them. To activate, just choose Slide Show from the Playback 2 menu. During playback, you can press the Set button to pause the "slide show" (in case you want to examine an image more closely), or the DISP button to change the amount of information displayed on the screen with each image. For example, you might want to review a set of images and their histograms to judge the exposure of the group of pictures. To set up your slide show, follow these steps:

1. **Begin set up.** Choose Slide Show from the Playback 2 menu, pressing Set to display the screen shown in Figure 3.38.

Figure 3.38
Set up your
slide show
using this
screen.

2. **Choose image selection method.** Rotate the cross keys to All Images, and press Set. Then use the cross keys to choose from All Images, Folder, or Date. Press Set to activate that selection mode. If you selected All Images, skip to Step 4.

3. **Choose images.** If you've selected Folder or Date, press the DISP button to produce a screen that allows you to select from the available folders, or the available image creation dates on your memory card. When you've chosen a folder or date, press Set to confirm your choice.

4. **Choose Play time and Repeat options.** Navigate to highlight Setup and press Set to produce a screen with playing time (1, 2, 3, or 5 seconds per image), and repeating options (On or Off). When you've specified either value, press the Menu button to confirm your choice, and then Menu once more to go back to the main Slide Show screen.

5. **Start the show.** Highlight Start and press Set to begin your show. (If you'd rather cancel the show you've just set up, press Menu instead.)

6. **Use show options during display.** Press Set to pause/restart; Info to cycle among the four information displays described in the section before this one; Menu to stop the show.

Image Jump with Main Dial

As first described in Chapter 1, you can leap ahead or back during picture review by rotating the Main dial, using a variety of increments, which you can select using this menu entry. The jump method is shown briefly on the screen as you leap ahead to the next image displayed, as shown in Figure 3.39.

Your options are as follows:

- **1 image.** Rotating the Main dial one click jumps forward or back one image.

- **10 images.** Rotating the Main dial one click jumps forward or back ten images.

- **100 images.** Rotating the Main dial one click jumps forward or back one hundred images.

- **Date.** Rotating the Main dial one click jumps forward or back to the first image taken on the next or previous calendar date.

- **Movies.** Rotating the Main dial one click jumps forward or back to display only motion picture clips.

- **Stills.** Rotating the Main dial one click jumps forward or back one to display only still images.

Figure 3.39
The Jump method is shown on the LCD briefly when you leap forward or back using the Main dial.

Setup 1, 2, and 3 Menu Options

There are three yellow/gold-coded Setup menus where you make adjustments on how your camera *behaves* during your shooting session, as differentiated from the Shooting menu, which adjusts how the pictures are actually taken. Your choices include:

- Auto power off
- File numbering
- Auto rotate
- Format
- LCD auto off
- Screen color
- LCD brightness
- Date/Time

- Language
- Video system
- Sensor cleaning
- Live View function settings
- Custom Functions (C.Fn)
- Clear settings
- Firmware Ver.

Auto Power Off

This menu entry is the first in the Setup 1 menu (see Figure 3.40). It allows you to determine how long the Rebel T1i remains active before shutting itself off. You can select 30 seconds, 1, 2, 4, 8, or 15 minutes, or Off, which leaves the camera turned on

Figure 3.40
Select an automatic shut-off period to save battery power.

indefinitely—or until 30 minutes have passed. However, even if the camera has shut itself off, if the power switch remains in the On position, you can bring the camera back to life by pressing the shutter button halfway, or the DISP, Playback, or Set buttons.

SAVING POWER WITH THE Rebel T1i

There are three settings and several techniques you can use to help you stretch the longevity of your T1i's battery. The first setting is the Review Time option described earlier under the Shooting 1 menu. That big 3-inch LCD uses a lot of juice, so reducing the amount of time it is used (either for automatic review or for manually playing back your images) can boost the effectiveness of your battery. Auto Power Off turns off most functions (metering and autofocus shut off by themselves about six seconds after you release the shutter button or take a picture) based on the delay you specify. The third setting is the LCD Brightness adjustment described below. If you're willing to shade the LCD with your hand, you can often get away with lower brightness settings outdoors, which will further increase the useful life of your battery. The techniques? Use the internal flash as little as possible; no flash at all or fill flash use less power than a full blast. Turn off image stabilization if your lens has that feature and you feel you don't need it. When transferring pictures from your T1i to your computer, use a card reader instead of the USB cable. Linking your camera to your computer and transferring images using the cable takes longer and uses a lot more power.

File Numbering

The Rebel T1i will automatically apply a file number to each picture you take, using consecutive numbering for all your photos over a long period of time, spanning many different memory cards, starting over from scratch when you insert a new card, or when you manually reset the numbers. Numbers are applied from 0001 to 9999, at which time the camera creates a new folder on the card (100, 101, 102, and so forth), so you can have 0001 to 9999 in folder 100, then numbering will start over in folder 101.

The camera keeps track of the last number used in its internal memory. That can lead to a few quirks you should be aware of. For example, if you insert a memory card that had been used with a different camera, the T1i may start numbering with the next number after the highest number used by the previous camera. (I once had a brand new T1i start numbering files in the 8,000 range.) I'll explain how this can happen next.

On the surface, the numbering system seems simple enough: In the menu, you can choose Continuous, Automatic Reset, or Manual Reset. Here is how each works:

- **Continuous.** If you're using a blank/reformatted memory card, the T1i will apply a number that is one greater than the number stored in the camera's internal memory. If the card is not blank and contains images, then the next number will be one greater than the highest number on the card *or* in internal memory. (In other words, if you want to use continuous file numbering consistently, you must always use a card that is blank or freshly formatted.) Here are some examples.

■ You've taken 4,235 shots with the camera, and you insert a blank/reformatted memory card. The next number assigned will be 4,236, based on the value stored in internal memory.

■ You've taken 4,235 shots with the camera, and you insert a memory card with a picture numbered 2,728. The next picture will be numbered 4,236.

■ You've taken 4,235 shots with the camera, and you insert a memory card with a picture numbered 8,281. The next picture will be numbered 8,282, and that value will be stored in the camera's menu as the "high" shot number (and will be applied when you next insert a blank card).

■ **Automatic Reset.** If you're using a blank/reformatted memory card, the next photo taken will be numbered 0001. If you use a card that is not blank, the next number will be one greater than the highest number found on the memory card. Each time you insert a memory card, the next number will either be 0001 or one higher than the highest already on the card.

■ **Manual Reset.** The T1i creates a new folder numbered one higher than the last folder created, and restarts the file numbers at 0001. Then, the camera uses the numbering scheme that was previously set, either Continuous or Automatic Reset, each time you subsequently insert a blank or non-blank memory card.

Auto Rotate

You can turn this feature On or Off. When activated, the Rebel T1i rotates pictures taken in vertical orientation on the LCD screen so you don't have to turn the camera to view them comfortably. However, this orientation also means that the longest dimension of the image is shown using the shortest dimension of the LCD, so the picture is reduced in size. You have three options, shown in Figure 3.41. The image can be autorotated when viewing in the camera *and* on your computer screen using your image editing/viewing software. The image can be marked to autorotate *only* when reviewing your image in your image editor or viewing software. This option allows you to have rotation applied when using your computer, while retaining the ability to maximize the image on your LCD in the camera. The third choice is Off. The image will not be rotated when displayed in the camera or with your computer. Note that if you switch Auto Rotate off, any pictures shot while the feature is disabled will not be automatically rotated when you turn Auto Rotate back on; information embedded in the image file when the photo *is taken* is used to determine whether autorotation is applied.

Figure 3.41
Choose autorotation both in the camera and on your computer display (top); only on your computer display (middle); or no automatic rotation (bottom).

Format

Use this item to erase everything on your memory card and set up a fresh file system ready for use. When you select Format, you'll see a display like Figure 3.42, showing the capacity of the card, how much of that space is currently in use, and two choices at the bottom of the screen to Cancel or OK (proceed with the format). A blue-green bar appears on the screen to show the progress of the formatting step. (The optional Low Level format invoked with the Trash button is a slower, but more thorough reformatting that can help restore a memory card that has picked up some bad sectors that aren't locked out by the normal format step.)

LCD Auto Off

The Display Off sensor under the viewfinder eyepiece senses when you have brought the camera to your eye (or when another object approaches the viewfinder) and turns off the Shooting Settings display on the LCD. If you'd like to cancel this behavior and have the LCD display visible at all times (unless you turn it off manually by pressing the DISP button), use this menu option. Selecting Enable activates the auto-off feature. Disable turns it off.

Figure 3.42
You must confirm the format step before the camera will erase a memory card.

Format

Format card
All data will be lost!

10.7MB used   7.74 GB
🗑 ✔ Low level format

Cancel   OK

Screen Color

If you find the default color scheme for the Shooting Settings display (black text on white) distracting or hard to read, you can change to one of three alternates: white text on black, white text on dark blue, and black text on tan.

LCD Brightness

This menu option is the first on the second Setup menu tab (see Figure 3.43). Select it to view a thumbnail image accompanied by a grayscale strip, as shown in Figure 3.44. Use the left/right cross keys to adjust the brightness to a comfortable viewing level. Brighter settings use more battery power, but can allow you to view an image on the LCD outdoors in bright sunlight. When you have the brightness you want, press the Set button to lock it in and return to the menu.

Date/Time

Use this option to set the date and time, which will be embedded in the image file along with exposure information and other data. I showed you how to do this in Chapter 1. See Figure 1.10 if you need a refresher.

Figure 3.43
The Setup 2 menu.

Figure 3.44
Adjust LCD brightness for easier viewing under varying ambient lighting conditions.

Language

Choose from 25 languages for menu display, rotating the cross keys until the language you want to select is highlighted. Press the Set button to activate. Your choices include English, German, French, Dutch, Danish, Portuguese, Finnish, Italian, Ukrainian, Norwegian, Swedish, Spanish, Greek, Russian, Polish, Czech, Magyar, Romanian, Turkish, Arabic, Thai, Simplified Chinese, Traditional Chinese, Korean, and Japanese.

If you accidentally set a language you don't read and find yourself with incomprehensible menus, don't panic. Just choose the third option from the top of the Setup 2 menu, and select the idioma, sprache, langue, or kieli of your choice.

Video System

This setting controls the output of the T1i through the AV cable when you're displaying images on an external monitor. You can select either NTSC, used in the United States, Canada, Mexico, many Central, South American, and Caribbean countries, much of Asia, and other countries; or PAL, which is used in the UK, much of Europe, Africa, India, China, and parts of the Middle East.

VIEWING ON A TELEVISION

Canon makes it quite easy to view your images on a standard television screen, and not much more difficult on a high definition television (HDTV). (You have to buy a separate cable for HDTV.) For regular TV, just open the right port cover on the left side of the camera, plug in the cable supplied with the camera into the socket labeled Video, and connect the other end to the yellow VIDEO RCA composite jack on your television or monitor.

For HDTV display, purchase the optional HDMI Cable HTC-100 and connect it to the HDMI OUT terminal just below the standard video terminal on the left side of the camera. Connect the other end to an HDMI input port on your television or monitor (my 42-inch HDTV has three of them; my 26-inch monitor has just two). Then turn on the camera and press the Playback button. The image will appear on the external TV/HDTV/monitor and will not be displayed on the camera's LCD. HDTV systems automatically show your images at the appropriate resolution for that set.

Sensor Cleaning

One of the Canon EOS Rebel T1i's best features is the automatic sensor cleaning system that reduces or eliminates the need to clean your camera's sensor manually using brushes, swabs, or bulb blowers (you'll find instructions on how to do that in Chapter 9). Canon has applied anti-static coatings to the sensor and other portions of the camera body interior to counter charge build-ups that attract dust. A separate filter over the sensor vibrates ultrasonically each time the T1i is powered on or off, shaking loose any dust, which is captured by a sticky strip beneath the sensor.

Use this menu entry to enable or disable automatic sensor cleaning on power up (select Auto Cleaning to choose power-up cleaning) or to activate automatic cleaning during a shooting session (select Clean Now). You can also choose the Clean Manually option to flip up the mirror and clean the sensor yourself with a blower, brush, or swab, as described in Chapter 9. If the battery level is too low to safely carry out the cleaning operation, the T1i will let you know and refuse to proceed, unless you use the optional AC adapter kit. (See Figure 3.45.)

Figure 3.45

Use this menu choice to activate automatic sensor cleaning or enable/disable it on power up.

Live View Function Settings

Here is where you adjust the Rebel T1i's Live View functions, which enable you to work with a real-time LCD display as you preview and compose your image. I'm going to provide detailed instructions for using Live View in Chapter 5, as some functions are controlled here, and some are set in the Custom Functions menus (described later in this chapter). You'll want to review the Live View section of Chapter 5 for detailed information on how to use the four settings you can make from this menu entry.

■ **Live View shoot.** Enables Live View. Choose Disable to turn the feature off; select Enable and Live View will be activated when you press the Set (Live View) button.

■ **Grid Display.** Overlays a "rule of thirds" grid on the LCD to help with alignment and composition.

■ **Metering Timer.** This option turns off the exposure meter after a specified period of time (4, 16, or 30 seconds, plus 1, 10, and 30 minutes) to save power, as Live View can be quite a juice hog when you're displaying an image on the LCD for more than a few seconds at a time.

■ **AF mode.** Indicates the autofocus mode used for Live View shooting: Live Mode, Live Mode with face detection activated, and Quick Mode.

Custom Functions I/II/III/IV

Custom Functions, the first choice in the Setup 3 menu (see Figure 3.46), let you customize the behavior of your camera in a variety of different ways, ranging from whether or not the flash fires automatically to the function carried out when the Set button is pressed. If you don't like the default way the camera carries out a particular task, you just may be able to do something about it. You can find the Custom Functions in their own screen with 13 choices, divided into four groups of settings: Exposure (I, C.Fn 01, 02, and 03); Image (II, C.Fn 04-07); Autofocus/Drive (III C.Fn 08-09); and Operation/Others (IV, C.Fn. 10-13). The Roman numeral divisions within a single screen with a single line of choices seem odd until you realize that other Canon EOS models, from the EOS 40D up, separate each of these groups into separate screens (with larger numbers of options).

Each of the Custom Functions is set in exactly the same way, so I'm not going to bog you down with a bunch of illustrations showing how to make this setting or that. One quick run-through using Figure 3.47 should be enough. Here are the key parts of the Custom Function screen:

■ **Custom Function category.** At the top of the Settings screen is a label that tells you which category that screen represents.

■ **Current Function name.** Use the left/right cross keys to select the function you want to adjust. The name of the function currently selected appears at the top of

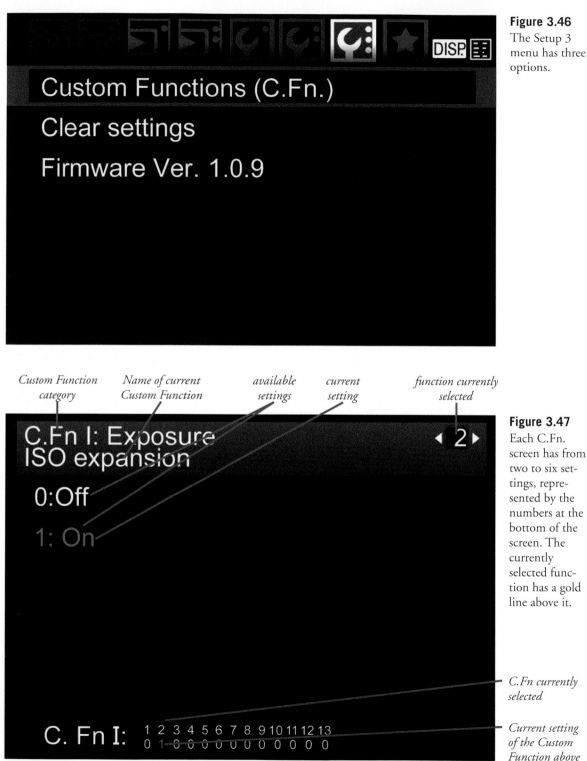

Figure 3.46
The Setup 3 menu has three options.

Custom Function category

Name of current Custom Function

available settings

current setting

function currently selected

Figure 3.47
Each C.Fn. screen has from two to six settings, represented by the numbers at the bottom of the screen. The currently selected function has a gold line above it.

C.Fn currently selected

Current setting of the Custom Function above

the screen, and its number is marked with an over score in the row of numbers at the bottom of the screen. You don't need to memorize the function numbers.

- **Function currently selected.** The function number appears in two places. In the upper-right corner you'll find a box with the current function clearly designated. In the lower half of the screen are two lines of numbers. The top row has numbers from 1 to 13, representing the Custom Function. The second row shows the number of the current setting. If the setting is other than the default value (a zero), it will be colored blue, so you can quickly see which Custom Functions have been modified. The currently selected function will have a gold line above it.

- **Available settings.** Within the alternating medium gray/dark gray blocks appear numbered setting options. The current setting is highlighted in blue. You can use the up/down cross keys to scroll to the option you want and then press the Set button to select it; then press the Menu button twice to back out of the Custom Functions menus.

- **Current setting.** Underneath each Custom Function is a number from 0 to 5 that represents the current setting for that function.

- **Option selection.** When a function is selected, the currently selected option appears in a highlighted box. As you scroll up and down the option list, the setting in the box changes to indicate an alternate value.

In the listings that follow, I'm going to depart from the sometimes-cryptic labels Canon assigns to each Custom Function in the menu, and instead categorize them by what they actually do. I'm also going to provide you with a great deal more information on each option and what it means to your photography.

C.Fn I-01: Size of Exposure Adjustments

Exposure level increments. This setting tells the Rebel T1i the size of the "jumps" it should use when making exposure adjustments—either one-third or one-half stop. The increment you specify here applies to f/stops, shutter speeds, EV changes, and autoexposure bracketing.

- **0: 1/3 stop.** Choose this setting when you want the finest increments between shutter speeds and/or f/stops. For example, the T1i will use shutter speeds such as 1/60th, 1/80th, 1/100th, and 1/125th second, and f/stops such as f/5.6, f/6.3, f/7.1, and f/8, giving you (and the autoexposure system) maximum control.

- **1: 1/2 stop.** Use this setting when you want larger and more noticeable changes between increments. The T1i will apply shutter speeds such as 1/60th, 1/125th, 1/250th, and 1/500th second, and f/stops including f/5.6, f/6.7, f/8, f/9.5, and f/11. These coarser adjustments are useful when you want more dramatic changes between different exposures.

C.Fn I-02: Whether ISO 3200 Is Available or Disabled

ISO expansion. Ordinarily, only ISO settings from 100 to 3200 are available (ISO 200-3200 if Highlight tone priority [C.Fn. II-3] is enabled). The ISO Expansion function is disabled by default to prevent you from unintentionally using ISO settings higher than ISO 1600. If you want to use the H1 (ISO 6400) or H2 (ISO 12800) settings, they must be activated using this Custom Function. I've found the noise produced at the ISO 6400 setting on my EOS 50D to be quite acceptable under certain situations, and ISO 12800 can be useable. That's particularly so with images of subjects that have a texture of their own that tends to hide or mask the noise. Figure 3.48 is an example

Figure 3.48 This enlargement shows that noise levels can be acceptable even at ISO 3200.

of this type of shot. It was taken indoors at a jellyfish exhibit, with the back illumination so dim and ethereal that I needed a high ISO 6400 setting to provide shutter speed fast enough to freeze the pulsating motion of the creature. Although there is a fair amount of noise in the image, the multicolored speckles are not objectionable.

CAUTION

Be aware that if you've activated Highlight Tone Priority (described later), the H1 and H2 settings (and ISO values less than ISO 200) will not be available even if you have enabled ISO expansion.

- **0:Off.** The H1 and H2 (ISO 6400 and 12800) settings are locked out and not available when using the ISO button or menu options.

- **1: On.** The H1 and H2 settings (equivalent to ISO 6400 and ISO 12800) can be selected.

C.Fn I-03: Flash Synchronization Speed When Using Aperture Priority

Flash sync. Speed in Av mode. You'll find this setting useful when using flash. When you're set to Aperture Priority mode (Av), you select a fixed f/stop and the Rebel T1i chooses an appropriate shutter speed. That works fine when you're shooting by available light. However, when you're using flash, the flash itself provides virtually all of the illumination that makes the main exposure, and the shutter speed determines how much, if any, of the ambient light contributes to a second, non-flash exposure. Indeed, if the camera or subject is moving, you can end up with two distinct exposures in the same frame: the sharply defined flash exposure, and a second, blurry "ghost" picture created by the ambient light.

If you *don't* want that second exposure, you should use the highest shutter speed that will synchronize with your flash (that's 1/200th second with the Rebel T1i). If you do want the ambient light to contribute to the exposure (say, to allow the background to register in night shots, or to use the ghost image as a special effect), use a slower shutter speed. For brighter backgrounds, you'll need to put the camera on a tripod or other support to avoid the blurry ghosts.

- **0:Auto.** The T1i will vary the shutter speed in Av mode, allowing ambient light to partially illuminate the scene in combination with the flash exposure, as at right in Figure 3.49. Use a tripod, because shutter speeds slower than 1/60th second may be selected.

Figure 3.49
At left, a 1/200th second shutter speed eliminated ambient light so only the flash illuminated the scene; at right, a 1/60th second shutter speed let the ambient light supplement the electronic flash.

- **1: 1/200-1/60 sec. (auto).** The camera will use a shutter speed from 1/200th second (to virtually eliminate ambient light) to 1/60th second (to allow ambient light to illuminate the picture). This compromise allows a slow enough shutter speed to permit ambient light to contribute to the exposure, but blocks the use of shutter speeds slower than 1/60, to minimize the blurriness of the secondary, ambient light exposure.

- **2: 1/200th sec. (fixed).** The camera always uses 1/200th second as its shutter speed in Av mode, reducing the effect of ambient light and, probably, rendering the background dark.

C.Fn II-04: Reducing Noise Effects at Shutter Speeds of One Second or Longer

Long exposure noise reduction. Visual noise is that graininess that shows up as multicolored specks in images, and this setting helps you manage it. In some ways, noise is like the excessive grain found in some high-speed photographic films. However, while photographic grain is sometimes used as a special effect, it's rarely desirable in a digital photograph.

The visual noise-producing process is something like listening to a CD in your car, and then rolling down all the windows. You're adding sonic noise to the audio signal, and while increasing the CD player's volume may help a bit, you're still contending with an unfavorable signal to noise ratio that probably mutes tones (especially higher treble notes) that you really want to hear.

The same thing happens when the analog signal is amplified: You're increasing the image information in the signal, but boosting the background fuzziness at the same time. Tune in a very faint or distant AM radio station on your car stereo. Then turn up the volume. After a certain point, turning up the volume further no longer helps you hear better. There's a similar point of diminishing returns for digital sensor ISO increases and signal amplification as well.

These processes create several different kinds of noise. Noise can be produced from high ISO settings. As the captured information is amplified to produce higher ISO sensitivities, some random noise in the signal is amplified along with the photon information. Increasing the ISO setting of your camera raises the threshold of sensitivity so that fewer and fewer photons are needed to register as an exposed pixel. Yet, that also increases the chances of one of those phantom photons being counted among the real-life light particles, too.

Fortunately, the Rebel T1i's sensor and its digital processing chip are optimized to produce the low noise levels, so ratings as high as ISO 800 can be used routinely (although there will be some noise, of course), and even ISO 1600 can generate good results.

A second way noise is created is through longer exposures. Extended exposure times allow more photons to reach the sensor, but increase the likelihood that some photosites will react randomly even though not struck by a particle of light. Moreover, as the sensor remains switched on for the longer exposure, it heats, and this heat can be mistakenly recorded as if it were a barrage of photons. This Custom Function can be used to tailor the amount of noise-canceling performed by the digital signal processor.

- **0: Off.** Disables long exposure noise reduction. Use this setting when you want the maximum amount of detail present in your photograph, even though higher noise levels will result. This setting also eliminates the extra time needed to take a picture caused by the noise reduction process. If you plan to use only lower ISO settings (thereby reducing the noise caused by ISO amplification), the noise levels produced by longer exposures may be acceptable. For example, you might be shooting a river spilling over rocks at ISO 100 with the camera mounted on a tripod, using a neutral density filter and long exposure to cause the pounding water to blur slightly, as shown in Figure 3.50. To maximize detail in the non-moving portions of your photos, you can switch off long exposure noise reduction.

Figure 3.50
When lower ISO settings are used, as in this 30-second exposure of the Virgin River in Zion National Park (made through a neutral density filter), long exposure noise reduction might not be needed.

- **1: Auto.** The Rebel T1i examines your photo taken with an exposure of one second or longer, and if long exposure noise is detected, a second, blank exposure is made and compared to the first image. Noise found in the "dark frame" image is subtracted from your original picture, and only the noise-corrected image is saved to your memory card. Because the noise-reduction process effectively doubles the time required to take a picture, this is a good setting to use when you want to avoid this delay when possible, but still have noise reduction applied when appropriate.

- **2: On.** When this setting is activated, the T1i applies dark frame subtraction to all exposures longer than one second. You might want to use this option when you're working with high ISO settings (which will already have noise boosted a bit) and want to make sure that any additional noise from long exposures is eliminated, too. Noise reduction will be applied to some exposures that would not have caused it to kick in using the Auto setting.

Tip

While the "dark frame" is being exposed, the LCD screen will be blank during Live View mode, and the number of shots you can take in Continuous shooting mode will be reduced. White balance bracketing is disabled during this process.

C.Fn II-05: Eliminating Noise Caused by Higher ISO Sensitivities

High ISO speed noise reduct'n. This setting applies noise reduction that is especially useful for pictures taken at high ISO sensitivity settings. The default is 0 (Standard noise reduction), but you can specify 1 (low) or 2 (strong) noise reduction, or disable noise reduction entirely. At lower ISO values, noise reduction improves the appearance of shadow areas without affecting highlights; at higher ISO settings, noise reduction is applied to the entire photo. Note that when the 2: Strong option is selected, the maximum number of continuous shots that can be taken will decrease significantly, because of the additional processing time for the images.

- **0: Standard.** At lower ISO values, noise reduction is applied primarily to shadow areas; at higher ISO settings, noise reduction affects the entire image.

- **1: Low.** A smaller amount of noise reduction is used. This will increase the grainy appearance, but preserve more fine image detail.

- **2: Strong.** More aggressive noise reduction is used, at the cost of some image detail, adding a "mushy" appearance that may be noticeable and objectionable.

- **3. Disable.** No additional noise reduction will be applied.

C.Fn II-06: Improving Detail in Highlights

Highlight Tone priority. This setting concentrates the available tones in an image from the middle grays up to the brightest highlights, in effect expanding the dynamic range of the image at the expense of shadow detail. You'd want to activate this option when shooting subjects in which there is lots of important detail in the highlights, and less detail in shadow areas. Highlight tones will be preserved, while shadows will be allowed to go dark more readily (and may exhibit an increase in noise levels). Bright beach or snow scenes, especially those with few shadows (think high noon, when the shadows are smaller) can benefit from using Highlight Tone priority.

- **0: Disable.** The Rebel T1i's normal dynamic range is applied.

- **1: Enable.** Highlight areas are given expanded tonal values, while the tones available for shadow areas are reduced. The ISO 100 sensitivity setting is disabled and only ISO 200-ISO 1600 are available. You can tell that this restriction is in effect by checking the final zero in the ISO speed displayed in the viewfinder and in the Shooting Information display for a particular image—the zero will be rendered in a smaller size.

C.Fn II-07: Fixing Dark, Low Contrast Images.

Auto lighting optimizer. This setting automatically provides a partial fix for images that are too dark or flat (low in contrast) by boosting the brightness and contrast as required. The feature is used automatically in Basic Zone modes, but can be activated here for Creative Zone modes, Program, Aperture Priority, and Shutter Priority modes (but not Manual mode).

- **0: Standard.** Adjusts brightness and contrast of dark, flat images.

- **1: Low.** Adjusts brightness and contrast of dark, flat images.

- **2: Strong.** Adjusts brightness and contrast of dark, flat images.

- **3: Disable.** No adjustments are applied.

C.Fn III-08: Activation of the Autofocus Assist Lamp

Activation of Autofocus Assist Beam. This setting determines when the AF assist lamp in the camera or an external flash is activated to emit a pulse of light prior to the main exposure that helps provide enough contrast for the Rebel T1i to focus on a subject.

- **0: Emits.** The AF assist light is emitted by the camera's built-in flash whenever light levels are too low for accurate focusing using the ambient light.

- **1: Does not emit.** The AF assist illumination is disabled. You might want to use this setting when shooting at concerts, weddings, or darkened locations where the light might prove distracting or discourteous.

- **2: Only external flash emits.** The built-in AF assist light is disabled, but if a Canon EX dedicated flash unit is attached to the camera, its AF assist feature (a flash pulse) will be used when needed. Because the flash unit's AF assist is more powerful, you'll find this option useful when you're using flash and are photographing objects in dim light that are more than a few feet away from the camera (and thus not likely to be illuminated usefully by the Rebel T1i's built-in light source). Note that if AF-assist beam firing is disabled within the flash unit's own Custom Functions, this setting will not override that.

C.Fn III-09: Whether It Is Possible to Lock Up the Viewing Mirror Prior to an Exposure

Mirror lockup. The Mirror lockup function determines whether the reflex viewing mirror will be flipped up out of the way in advance of taking a picture, thereby eliminating any residual blurring effects caused by the minuscule amount of camera shake that can be produced if (as is the case normally) the mirror is automatically flipped up an instant before the actual exposure. When shooting telephoto pictures with a very long lens, or close-up photography at extreme magnifications, even this tiny amount of vibration can have an impact.

You'll want to make this adjustment immediately prior to needing the mirror lockup function, because once it's been enabled, the mirror *always* flips up, and picture taking becomes a two-press operation. That is, you press the shutter release once to lock exposure and focus, and to swing the mirror out of the way. Your viewfinder goes blank (of course, the mirror's blocking it). Press the shutter release a second time to actually take the picture. Because the goal of mirror lockup is to produce the sharpest picture possible, and because of the viewfinder blackout, you can see that the camera should be mounted on a tripod prior to taking the picture, and, to avoid accidentally shaking the camera yourself, using an off-camera shutter release mechanism is a good idea.

- **0: Disable.** Mirror lockup is not possible.

- **1: Enable.** Mirror lockup is activated and will be used for every shot until disabled.

Canon lists some important warnings and techniques related to using mirror lockup in the Rebel T1i manual, and I want to emphasize them here and add a few of my own, even if it means a bit of duplication. Better safe than sorry!

- **Don't use ML for sensor cleaning.** Though locked up, the mirror will flip down again automatically after 30 seconds, which you don't want to happen while you're poking around the sensor with a brush, swab, or air jet. There's a separate menu item—sensor cleaning—for sensor housekeeping. You can find more about this topic in Chapter 9.

- **Avoid long exposure to extra-bright scenes.** The shutter curtain, normally shielded from incoming light by the mirror, is fully exposed to the light being focused on the focal plane by the lens mounted on the T1i. When the mirror is locked up, you certainly don't want to point the camera at the sun, and even beach or snow scenes may be unsafe if the shutter curtain is exposed to their illumination for long periods. (This advice also applies to Live View, of course, because the sensor is similarly exposed while you're previewing the image on the LCD.)

- **ML can't be used in continuous shooting modes.** The Rebel T1i will use Single Shot mode for mirror lockup exposures, regardless of the sequence mode you've selected.

- **Use self-timer to eliminate second button press.** If you've activated the self-timer, the mirror will flip up when you press the shutter button down all the way, and then the picture will be taken two seconds later. This technique can help reduce camera shake further if you don't have a remote release available and have to use a finger to press the shutter button. You can also use the Remote Controller RC-1 or RC-5. Set the RC-1 to a two-second delay. With the RC-5, press the transmit button to lock up the mirror; the shot will be taken automatically two seconds later.

C.Fn IV-1O: What Happens When You Partially Depress the Shutter Release/Press the AE Lock Button

Shutter button/AE Lock button (*). This setting controls the behavior of the shutter release and the AE Lock button (*) when you are using Creative Zone exposure modes. With Basic Zone modes, the Rebel T1i always behaves as if it has been set to Option 0, described below. Options 1, 2, and 3 are designed to work with AI Servo mode, which locks focus as it is activated, but refocuses if the subject begins to move. The options allow you to control exactly when focus and exposure are locked when using AI Servo mode.

In the option list, the first action in the pair represents what happens when you press the shutter release; the second action says what happens when the AE Lock button is pressed.

- **0: AF/AE lock.** With this option, pressing the shutter release halfway locks in focus; pressing the * button locks exposure. Use this when you want to control each of these actions separately.

- **1: AE lock/AF.** Pressing the shutter release halfway locks exposure; pressing the * button locks autofocus. This setting swaps the action of the two buttons compared to the default 0 option.

- **2: AF/AF lock, no AE lock.** Pressing the AE lock button interrupts the autofocus and locks focus in AI Servo mode. Exposure is not locked at all until the actual moment of exposure when you press the shutter release all the way. This mode is handy when moving objects may pass in front of the camera (say, a tight end crosses your field of view as you focus on the quarterback) and you want to be able to avoid change of focus. Note that you can't lock in exposure using this option.

- **3: AE/AF, no AE lock.** Pressing the shutter release halfway locks in autofocus, except in AI Servo mode, in which you can use the * button to start or stop auto-focus. Exposure is always determined at the moment the picture is taken, and cannot be locked.

C.Fn IV-11: Using the Set Button as a Function Key

Assign SET button. You already know that the Set button is used to select a choice or option when navigating the menus. However, when you're taking photos, it has no function at all. You can easily remedy that with this setting. This setting allows you to assign one of five different actions to the Set key. Because the button is within easy reach of your right thumb, that makes it quite convenient for accessing a frequently used function. When this Custom Function is set to 5, the Set button has no additional function during shooting mode (except to activate Live View when it is turned on), and options 0 through 4 assign an action to the button during shooting.

CAUTION

One thing to keep in mind when redefining the behavior of controls (including other controls that can be modified within the Custom Functions menus) is that any non-standard customization you do will definitely be confusing to others who use your camera, and may even confuse you if you've forgotten that you've changed a control from its default function.

- **0: Quick Control Screen.** This is the default during shooting. Activates the Quick Control screen. Press the cross keys to choose the function to adjust, then rotate the Main dial to change the setting.

- **1: Image quality.** Pressing the Set button produces the Shooting 1 menu's Quality menu screen on the color LCD. You can cycle among the various quality options with the up/down and left/right cross keys. Press Set again to lock in your choice.

- **2: Flash exposure comp.** The Set button summons the Flash Exposure Compensation screen. Use the left/right cross keys to adjust flash exposure plus or minus two stops. If you're using an external flash unit, its internal flash exposure compensation settings override those set from the camera. Press Set to confirm your choice.

- **3: LCD monitor On/Off.** Assigns to the Set button the same functions as the DISP button. Because the Set button can be accessed with the thumb, you may find it easier to use when turning the LCD monitor on or off.

- **4: Menu display.** Pressing Set produces the T1i's Menu screen on the LCD, with the last menu entry you used highlighted. Press Set again to work with that menu normally, or press the Menu button to cancel and back out of the menus. This setting duplicates the Menu button's function, but some find it easier to locate the Set button with their thumb.

- **5: Disable.** When chosen, nothing happens when you press the Set button while shooting.

C.Fn IV-12: LCD Display When Power On

LCD display when power on. Controls the behavior of the LCD when the Rebel T1i is switched on. There are two options:

- **0: Display.** When the T1i is powered on, the Shooting Settings screen will be shown. You can turn this screen on and off by pressing the DISP button. Use this option if you always want the settings screen to be displayed when the camera is turned on.

- **1: Retain power OFF status.** When the Rebel T1i is turned on, the LCD monitor will display the Shooting Settings screen if it was turned on when the camera was last powered down. If the screen had been turned off (by pressing the DISP button), it will not be displayed when the T1i is next powered up. Use this option if you frequently turn off the settings screen, and want the camera to "remember" whether the screen was on display when the T1i was last powered down.

C.Fn IV-13: Activating Data Verification Feature

Add original decision data. The Rebel T1i has a special feature that allows determining whether a specific image has been modified using a special Canon Original Data Security Kit OSK-E3. The Data Verification Kit DVK-E2 is a nifty $650 add-on which consists of a data security card and a dedicated USB card reader-writer and verification software that must be used with a computer to verify an image. The Add Original Decision Data function determines whether the information needed to verify an image is included in the image file. Data verification is especially useful for law enforcement, legal, and scientific purposes, but not required for everyday shooting (which is why the feature is turned off by default).

- **0: Off.** Data verification information is not added to the image file.
- **1: On.** Data verification information is included in the image file.

Clear Settings

This menu choice resets all the settings to their default values. You can choose Clear All Camera Settings, Clear All Custom Func. (C.Fn.), or Delete Copyright Information. When you choose Clear All Camera Settings, regardless of how you've set up your Rebel T1i, it will be adjusted for One Shot AF mode, automatic AF point selection, Evaluative metering, JPEG Fine Large image quality, automatic ISO, sRGB color mode, automatic white balance, and Standard Picture Style. Any changes you've made to exposure compensation, flash exposure compensation, and white balance will be canceled, and any bracketing for exposure or white balance nullified. Custom white balances and Dust Delete Data will be erased.

The Clear All Custom Func. (C.Fn.) choice can be used to clear all camera Custom Functions. Press the Set button, then rotate the left/right cross keys to either Cancel or OK. Press the Set button to confirm. All Custom Functions will be reset to their default 0 values.

Copyright information can be embedded in your camera using the Canon EOS Utility (see Figure 3.51). If you've added that information to your T1i, it will be included in the Exif information stored with each image that you take. If you decide you no longer want to include this information in your image files, you can use the Delete Copyright Information choice to remove it from your camera. If you haven't uploaded a copyright string to your camera with the EOS Utility, this menu choice will be grayed out and unavailable.

Figure 3.51
Copyright
information
can be
uploaded to
your camera
with the EOS
Utility.

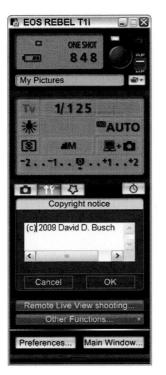

Firmware Version

You can see the current firmware release in use in the menu listing. If you want to update to a new firmware version, insert a memory card containing the binary file, and press the Set button to begin the process. You can read more about firmware updates in Chapter 9.

My Menu

The Canon EOS Rebel T1i has a great new feature that allows you to define your own menu, with just the items listed that you want. Remember that the T1i always returns to the last menu and menu entry accessed when you press the Menu button. So you can set up My Menu to include just the items you want, and jump to those items instantly by pressing the Menu button. To create your own My Menu, you have to *register* the menu items you want to include. Just follow these steps:

1. Press the Menu button and use the left/right cross keys to select the My Menu tab. When you first begin, the personalized menu will be empty except for the My Menu Settings entry. Press the Set button to select it. You'll then see a screen like the one shown in Figure 3.52.

2. Use the up/down cross keys to select Register, then press the Set button.

Figure 3.52
In the My Menu Settings screen you can add menu items, delete them, and specify whether My Menu always pops up when the Menu button is pressed.

Figure 3.53
You can add one to six menu entries to My Menu. Four added entries are shown.

3. Use the up/down cross keys to scroll down through the continuous list of all menu entries that can be registered to find one you would like to add. Press Set.

4. Confirm your choice by selecting OK in the next screen and pressing Set again.

5. Continue to select up to six menu entries for My Menu.

6. When you're finished, press the Menu button twice to return to the My Menu screen to see your customized menu, which might look like Figure 3.53.

In addition to registering menu items, you can perform other functions at the My Menu Settings screen:

■ **Changing the Order.** Choose Sort to reorder the items in My Menu. Select the menu item to be moved and press the Set button. Press the up/down cross keys to move the item up and down within the menu list. When you've placed it where you'd like it, press the Menu button to lock in your selection and return to the previous screen.

■ **Delete/Delete All Items.** Use these to remove an individual menu item or all menu items you've registered in My Menu.

■ **Display from My Menu.** As I mentioned earlier, the T1i (almost) always shows the last menu item accessed. That's convenient if you used My Menu last, but if you happen to use another menu, then pressing the Menu button will return to that item instead. If you enable the Display from My Menu option, pressing the Menu button will *always* display My Menu first. You are free to switch to another menu tab if you like, but the next time you press the Menu button, My Menu will come up again. Use this option if you work with My Menu a great deal and make settings with other menu items less frequently.

Movie Settings

The Rebel T1i has one additional "hidden" menu called Movie Settings, which appears only when the Mode dial is set to the Movie position (rotate the Mode dial as far as it will go in the clockwise direction). You won't be using this menu when shooting still pictures, so I'm going to leave the discussion of its functions for Chapter 5, which discusses the camera's movie-making and Live View capabilities in more detail.

4

Fine-Tuning Exposure

The Canon EOS Rebel T1i offers the best of two worlds when it comes to capturing exactly the right exposure—a picture with the optimum balance of tones and colors that are neither too light nor too dark to reveal all the detail in the original subject. You can select one of the Basic Zone modes suitable for your subject matter—Portrait, Landscape, Close-up, Sports, or Night-time subjects, and the camera will do an excellent job of calculating the right settings to give you an outstanding picture with little input on your part beyond the initial Mode dial selection. If you can't decide which Basic Zone mode is best, you can select the green Auto icon or Creative Auto instead, and the T1i will still do a fine job.

So, why do I include an entire chapter titled "Fine-Tuning Exposure" in all my Canon books? As you learn to use your T1i creatively, you're going to find that the right settings—as determined by the camera's exposure meter and intelligence—need to be *adjusted* to account for your creative decisions or special situations.

For example, when you shoot with the main light source behind the subject, you end up with *backlighting*, which results in an overexposed background and/or an underexposed subject. The Rebel T1i recognizes backlit situations nicely, and can properly base exposure on the main subject, producing a decent photo. Features like Highlight Priority and the Auto Lighting Optimizer (discussed in Chapter 3) can fine-tune exposure to preserve detail in the highlights and shadows.

But what if you *want* to underexpose the subject, to produce a silhouette effect? Or, perhaps, you might want to flip up the T1i's built-in flash unit to fill in the shadows on your subject. The more you know about how to use your T1i, the more you'll run into situations where you want to creatively tweak the exposure to provide a different look than you'd get with a straight shot.

This chapter shows you the fundamentals of exposure, so you'll be better equipped to override the EOS T1i's default settings when you want to, or need to. After all, correct exposure is one of the foundations of good photography, along with accurate focus and sharpness, appropriate color balance, freedom from unwanted noise and excessive contrast, as well as pleasing composition.

Understanding Exposure

Exposure determines the look, feel, and tone of an image, in more ways than one. Incorrect exposure can impair even the best-composed image by cloaking important tones in darkness, or by washing them out so they become featureless to the eye. On the other hand, correct exposure brings out the detail in the areas you want to picture, and provides the range of tones and colors you need to create the desired image. However, getting the perfect exposure can be tricky, because digital sensors can't capture all the tones we are able to see. If the range of tones in an image is extensive, embracing both inky black shadows and bright highlights, the sensor may not be able to capture them all. Sometimes, we must settle for an exposure that renders most of those tones—but not all—in a way that best suits the photo we want to produce. You'll often need to make choices about which details are important, and which are not, so that you can grab the tones that truly matter in your image. That's part of the creativity you bring to bear in realizing your photographic vision.

For example, look at the two typical tourist snapshots presented side by side in Figure 4.1. The camera was mounted on a tripod for both, so the only way you can really see that they are two different images is by examining the differences in the way the water flows over the rocks. However, the pair of pictures does vary in exposure. The version on the left was underexposed, which helps bring out detail in the ridges and sky in the background, but makes the water and foreground look murky and dark. The overexposed version on the right offers better exposure for the foreground area, but now the ridges and sky are too light.

With digital camera sensors, it's tricky to capture detail in both highlights and shadows in a single image, because the number of tones, the *dynamic range* of the sensor is limited. The solution in this particular case was to combine the two photos using Photoshop. For the image on the left, the camera calculated exposure based—mostly—on the cliffs in the background. The harsh shadows are underexposed. The second exposure correctly exposed for the shadows, giving them the right amount of exposure, but the cliffs in the background and the sky are now badly overexposed. The camera's sensor simply can't capture detail in both dark areas and bright areas in a single shot.

The solution, in this particular case, was to resort to a technique called High Dynamic Range (HDR) photography, in which the two exposures from Figure 4.1 were combined in an image editor such as Photoshop, or a specialized HDR tool like Photomatix (about $100 from www.hdrsoft.com). The resulting shot is shown in Figure 4.2. I'll explain more about HDR photography later in this chapter. For now, though, I'm going to concentrate on showing you how to get the best exposures possible without resorting to such tools, using only the features of your Canon EOS T1i.

To understand exposure, you need to understand the six aspects of light that combine to produce an image. Start with a light source—the sun, an interior lamp, or the glow from a campfire—and trace its path to your camera, through the lens, and finally to the sensor that captures the illumination. Here's a brief review of the things within our control that affect exposure.

■ **Light at its source.** Our eyes and our cameras—film or digital—are most sensitive to that portion of the electromagnetic spectrum we call *visible light*. That light has several important aspects that are relevant to photography, such as color, and harshness (which is determined primarily by the apparent size of the light source as it illuminates a subject). But, in terms of exposure, the important attribute of a light source is its *intensity*. We may have direct control over intensity, which might be the case with an interior light that can be brightened or dimmed. Or, we might have

Figure 4.1
At left, the image is exposed for the background highlights, losing shadow detail. At right, the exposure captures detail in the shadows, but the background highlights are washed out.

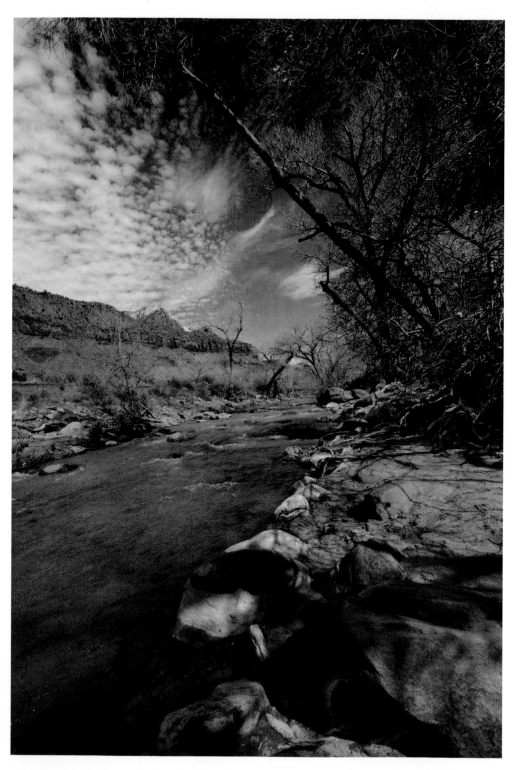

Figure 4.2
Combining the two exposures produces the best compromise image.

only indirect control over intensity, as with sunlight, which can be made to appear dimmer by introducing translucent light-absorbing or reflective materials in its path.

- **Light's duration.** We tend to think of most light sources as continuous. But, as you'll learn in Chapter 7, the duration of light can change quickly enough to modify the exposure, as when the main illumination in a photograph comes from an intermittent source, such as an electronic flash.

- **Light reflected, transmitted, or emitted light.** Once light is produced by its source, either continuously or in a brief burst, we are able to see and photograph objects by the light that is reflected from our subjects towards the camera lens; transmitted (say, from translucent objects that are lit from behind); or emitted (by a candle or television screen). When more or less light reaches the lens from the subject, we need to adjust the exposure. This part of the equation is under our control to the extent we can increase the amount of light falling on or passing through the subject (by adding extra light sources or using reflectors), or by pumping up the light that's emitted (by increasing the brightness of the glowing object).

- **Light passed by the lens.** Not all the illumination that reaches the front of the lens makes it all the way through. Filters can remove some of the light before it enters the lens. Inside the lens barrel is a variable-sized diaphragm called an *aperture* that dilates and contracts to control the amount of light that enters the lens. You, or the T1i's autoexposure system, can control exposure by varying the size of the aperture. The relative size of the aperture is called the *f/stop*.

- **Light passing through the shutter.** Once light passes through the lens, the amount of time the sensor receives it is determined by the T1i's shutter, which can remain open for as long as 30 seconds (or even longer if you use the Bulb setting) or as briefly as 1/4,000th second.

- **Light captured by the sensor.** Not all the light falling onto the sensor is captured. If the number of photons reaching a particular photosite doesn't pass a set threshold, no information is recorded. Similarly, if too much light illuminates a pixel in the sensor, then the excess isn't recorded or, worse, spills over to contaminate adjacent pixels. We can modify the minimum and maximum number of pixels that contribute to image detail by adjusting the ISO setting. At higher ISOs, the incoming light is amplified to boost the effective sensitivity of the sensor.

These factors—the quantity of light produced by the light source; the amount reflected or transmitted towards the camera; the light passed by the lens; the amount of time the shutter is open; and the sensitivity of the sensor—all work proportionately and reciprocally to produce an exposure. That is, if you double the amount of light that's available, increase the aperture by one stop, make the shutter speed twice as long, or boost the ISO setting 2X, you'll get twice as much exposure. Similarly, you can increase any of these factors while decreasing one of the others by a similar amount to keep the same exposure.

F/STOPS AND SHUTTER SPEEDS

If you're *really* new to more advanced cameras, you might need to know that the lens aperture, or f/stop, is a ratio, much like a fraction, which is why f/2 is larger than f/4, just as 1/2 is larger than 1/4. However, f/2 is actually *four times* as large as f/4. (If you remember your high school geometry, you'll know that to double the area of a circle, you multiply its diameter by the square root of two: 1.4.)

Lenses are usually marked with intermediate f/stops that represent a size that's twice as much/half as much as the previous aperture. So, a lens might be marked:

f/2, f/2.8, f/4, f/5.6, f/8, f/11, f/16, f/22

with each larger number representing an aperture that admits half as much light as the one before, as shown in Figure 4.3.

Shutter speeds are actual fractions (of a second), but the numerator is omitted, so that 60, 125, 250, 500, 1,000, and so forth represent 1/60th, 1/125th, 1/250th, 1/500th, and 1/1,000th second. To avoid confusion, Canon uses quotation marks to signify longer exposures: 2", 2"5, 4", and so forth represent 2.0, 2.5, and 4.0 second exposures, respectively.

Figure 4.3 Top row (left to right): f/2, f/2.8, f/4; bottom row, f/5.6, f/8, f11.

Most commonly, exposure settings are made using the aperture and shutter speed, followed by adjusting the ISO sensitivity if it's not possible to get the preferred exposure (that is, the one that uses the "best" f/stop or shutter speed for the depth-of-field or action-stopping we want). Table 4.1 shows equivalent exposure settings using various shutter speeds and f/stops.

Table 4.1 Equivalent Exposures

Shutter speed	f/stop	Shutter speed	f/stop
1/30th second	f/22	1/500th second	f/5.6
1/60th second	f/16	1/1,000th second	f/4
1/125th second	f/11	1/2,000th second	f/2.8
1/250th second	f/8	1/4,000th second	f/2

When the T1i is set for P mode, the metering system selects the correct exposure for you automatically, but you can change quickly to an equivalent exposure when the exposure meters are active by spinning the Main dial until the desired equivalent exposure combination is displayed. If the meters have gone to sleep, tap the shutter release first to wake them up. This program shift mode does not work when you're using flash.

In Aperture Priority (Av) and Shutter Priority (Tv) modes, you can change to an equivalent exposure, but only by adjusting either the aperture (in AV mode the camera chooses the shutter speed) or the shutter speed (in Tv mode the camera selects the aperture). I'll cover all these exposure modes later in the chapter.

How the Rebel T1i Calculates Exposure

Your Canon Rebel T1i calculates exposure by measuring the light that passes through the lens and is bounced up by the mirror to sensors located near the focusing surface, using a pattern you can select (more on that later) and based on the assumption that each area being measured reflects about the same amount of light as a neutral gray card with 18-percent reflectance. That assumption is necessary, because different subjects reflect different amounts of light. In a photo containing a white cat and a dark gray cat, the white cat might reflect five times as much light as the gray cat. An exposure based on the white cat will cause the gray cat to appear to be black, while an exposure based only on the gray cat will make the white cat washed out. Light-measuring devices handle this by assuming that the areas being measured average a standard value of 18-percent gray, a figure that's been used as a rough standard (most vendors don't calibrate their metering for exactly 18-percent gray; the actual figure may be closer to 13 or 14 percent) for many years.

You could, in many cases, arrive at a reasonable exposure by pointing your T1i at an evenly lit object, such as an actual 18-percent gray card (available at any camera store) or the palm of your hand (the backside of the hand is too variable). It's more practical though, to use your T1i's system to meter the actual scene, using the options available to you when using one of the Creative Zone modes (P, Tv, Av, M, and A-DEP). (In Basic Zone modes, the metering decisions are handled by the camera's programming.) (See Figure 4.4.)

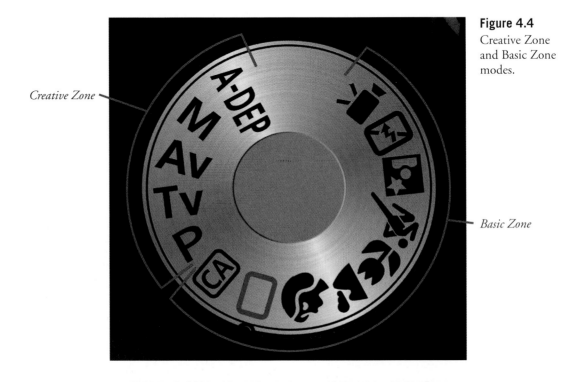

Creative Zone

Basic Zone

Figure 4.4
Creative Zone and Basic Zone modes.

Tip

Of course, if you work with a gray card, strictly speaking, you need to use about one-half stop *more* exposure than metered, because the T1i is calibrated for a lighter tone, rather than the 18-percent gray you just measured. If you're using a human palm instead, add one full stop more exposure. (This is true of palms of any race or ethnic group.)

To meter properly in the Creative Zone, you'll want to choose both the *metering method* (how light is evaluated) and *exposure method* (how the appropriate shutter speeds and apertures are chosen). I'll describe both in the following sections. But first, let's clear up that black cat/gray cat/white cat conundrum you may have heard of before, without using any actual cats. Black, white, and gray cats have been a standard metaphor for many years, as well, so I'm going to explain this concept using a different, and more cooperative, life form: fruit.

Figure 4.5 shows three ordinary pieces of fruit. The yellow banana at left represents a white cat, or any object that is very light but which contains detail that we want to see in the light areas. The orange in the middle is a stand-in for a gray cat, because it has most of its details in the middle tones. The deep purple plum serves as our black cat, because it is a dark object with detail in its shadows.

Figure 4.5
The yellow banana, orange, and deep-purple plum represent light, middle, and dark tones.

The colors confuse the issue, so I'm going to convert our color fruit to black-and-white. For the version shown in Figure 4.6, the exposure (measured by spot metering) was optimized for the white (yellow) banana, changing its tonal value to a medium, 18-percent gray. The dark (purple) and medium-toned (orange) fruit are now *too* dark. For Figure 4.7, the exposure was optimized for the dark (purple) plum, making most of its surface, now, fall into the middle-tone, 18-percent gray range. The light yellow banana and mid-tone orange are now too light.

The solution, of course, is to measure exposure from the object with the middle tones that most closely correspond to the 18-percent gray "standard." Do that, and you wind up with a picture that more closely resembles the original tonality of the yellow, orange, and purple fruit, which looks, in black-and-white, like Figure 4.8.

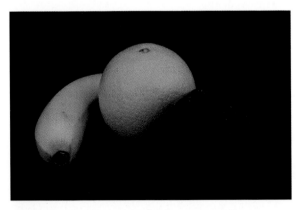

Figure 4.6 Exposing for the light-colored banana at left renders the other two fruit excessively dark.

Figure 4.7 Exposing for the dark plum (right) causes the two fruit at left to become too light.

Figure 4.8
Exposing for the middle-toned orange produces an image in which the tones of all three subjects appear accurately.

To meter properly in the Creative Zone, you'll want to choose both the *metering method* (how light is evaluated) and *exposure method* (how the appropriate shutter speeds and apertures are chosen). I'll describe both in the following sections.

Choosing a Metering Method

The T1i has four different schemes for evaluating the light received by its exposure sensors. You can choose among them by pressing the Metering Mode button (up cross key) and rotating the Main dial until the mode you want is selected.

- **Evaluative.** The T1i slices up the frame into 35 different zones, shown in Figure 4.9 (the LCD icon is shown in the upper-left corner for reference; it does not appear in the viewfinder). The camera evaluates the measurements, paying special attention to the metering zones that indicate sharp focus, to make an educated guess about what kind of picture you're taking, based on examination of thousands of different real-world photos. For example, if the top sections of a picture are much lighter than the bottom portions, the algorithm can assume that the scene is a landscape photo with lots of sky. This mode is the best all-purpose metering method for most pictures.

Figure 4.9
Evaluative metering uses 35 zones, linked to the autofocus points shown as red brackets.

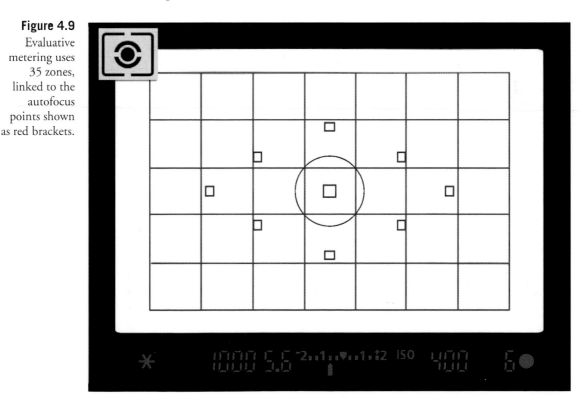

CHOOSE EXPOSURE "ZONE"

If you're using P, Av, Tv, or M shooting modes and Evaluative metering, you can select the autofocus zone manually. (See "Setting AF Point" in Chapter 5.) The camera will link its exposure calculations when using Evaluative metering to the focus zone you've selected.

■ **Partial.** This is a *faux* Spot mode, using roughly nine percent of the image area to calculate exposure, which, as you can see in Figure 4.10, is a rather large spot. The status LCD icon is shown in the upper-left corner. One of the improvements brought by the introduction of the T1i was a true Spot mode, described later. Use this mode if the background is much brighter or darker than the subject.

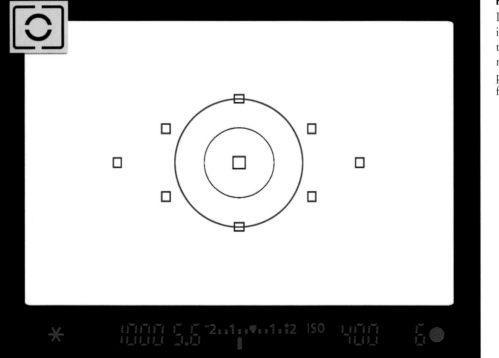

Figure 4.10
Partial metering uses a center spot that's roughly nine percent of the frame area.

■ **Spot.** This mode confines the reading to a limited area in the center of the viewfinder, as shown in Figure 4.11, making up only 3.8 percent of the image. This mode is useful when you want to base exposure on a small area in the frame. If that area is in the center of the frame, so much the better. If not, you'll have to make your meter reading and then lock exposure by pressing the shutter release halfway, or by pressing the AE-Lock button.

Figure 4.11
Spot metering calculates exposure based on a center spot that's only 3.5 percent of the image area.

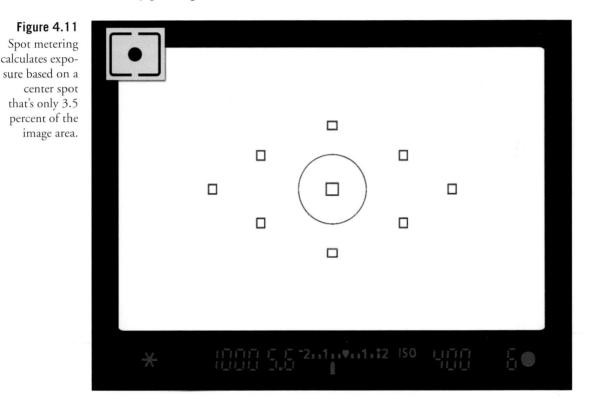

■ **Center-Weighted.** In this mode, the exposure meter emphasizes a zone in the center of the frame to calculate exposure, as shown in Figure 4.12, on the theory that, for most pictures, the main subject will be located in the center. Center-weighting works best for portraits, architectural photos, and other pictures in which the most important subject is located in the middle of the frame. As the name suggests, the light reading is *weighted* towards the central portion, but information is also used from the rest of the frame. If your main subject is surrounded by very bright or very dark areas, the exposure might not be exactly right. However, this scheme works well in many situations if you don't want to use one of the other modes.

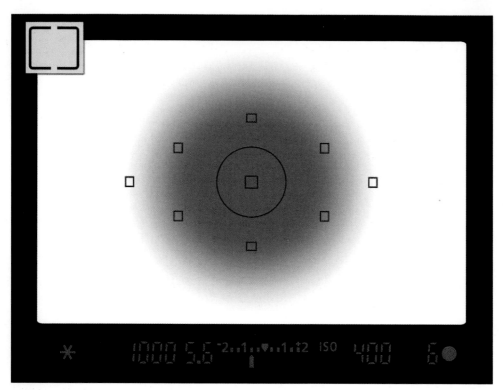

Figure 4.12
Center-Weighted metering calculates exposure based on the full frame, but emphasizes the center area.

Choosing a Creative Zone Exposure Method

You'll find five methods for choosing the appropriate shutter speed and aperture within the Creative Zone settings. Just spin the Mode dial to choose the method you want to use. Your choice of which is best for a given shooting situation will depend on things like your need for lots of (or less) depth-of-field, a desire to freeze action or allow motion blur, or how much noise you find acceptable in an image. Each of the EOS T1i's exposure methods emphasizes one aspect of image capture or another. This section introduces you to all five.

A-DEP

The Automatic Depth-of-Field exposure mode is a handy method to use when you want to maximize the range of sharpness in your image. The camera actually selects an f/stop that will allow as much of the subject matter you've framed as possible to be in sharp focus, and then applies the shutter speed necessary to provide a good exposure at that aperture. The disadvantage of this mode is that you relinquish control over shutter speed, f/stop, and focus distance (which makes A-DEP a bit more like a Basic Zone scene mode than a true Creative Zone mode). You might end up with the required depth-of-field, but a blurry photo because the T1i has selected a shutter speed that's too slow for hand-holding!

A-DEP performs its magic by examining the nine autofocus points in the viewfinder to discover the nearest and farthest objects in the frame. Then, it chooses an aperture and focus point that supplies the required DOF (if possible) and sets the appropriate shutter speed. The focus zones that can be rendered in sharp focus will flash red; other zones that can't be included in the focus range remain black, as shown in Figure 4.13. Press the DOF button on the front of the camera to check the range of focus, if you want. This mode won't work under all conditions, for example, with flash (in which case the T1i acts as if you've selected P mode) or if you're using manual focus. The viewfinder provides you with status information:

- **Flashing red AF points.** Shows the subjects covered by the DOF range set.

- **Blinking aperture indicator in viewfinder.** The desired DOF range cannot be set because the subjects are separated too widely for sufficient depth-of-field at the smallest available aperture.

- **Blinking 30 shutter speed in viewfinder.** Illumination is too dim to provide requested DOF at the current ISO setting.

- **Blinking 4000 shutter speed in viewfinder.** Illumination is too bright to provide requested DOF at the current ISO setting.

Figure 4.13
A-DEP mode can provide automatic depth-of-field for many types of subjects.

Because of the limitations of A-DEP mode, I don't favor it. However, it's fun to play with and may come in handy in certain situations, especially when you're shooting quickly and don't have time to manipulate depth-of-field manually.

A-DEP AND HYPERFOCAL DISTANCE

A-DEP is a simplified version of a related mode found in some higher-end Canon digital and film models called DEP. DEP allows you to manually select the nearest and farthest points you want in focus, and the camera will then adjust the focus point to a setting known as the *hyperfocal distance*. At the hyperfocal distance, everything from half that distance to infinity will be in acceptable focus.

Although many photographers elect to set hyperfocal distance themselves, the exact distance varies by the lens focal length and aperture selected, so, unless you carry a hyperfocal distance chart around with you, it's usually easy to let A-DEP do its simplified calculations (you don't get to choose the near/far focus points) for you. Both DEP and A-DEP were developed around the time depth-of-field scales were starting to be omitted from lenses. While DOF scales can show you the approximate near and far acceptable focus points, as zoom lenses replaced fixed focal length (or *prime* lenses, as discussed in Chapter 7), such scales became too complicated for easy use. Thus, we have A-DEP as a "replacement."

Aperture Priority

In Av mode, you specify the lens opening used, and the T1i selects the shutter speed. Aperture Priority is especially good when you want to use a particular lens opening to achieve a desired effect. Perhaps you'd like to use the smallest f/stop possible to maximize depth-of-field in a close-up picture. Or, you might want to use a large f/stop to throw everything except your main subject out of focus, as in Figure 4.14, a chilling portrait of a menacing lizard, taken by talented Cleveland photographer Kris Bosworth. Maybe you'd just like to "lock in" a particular f/stop because it's the sharpest available aperture with that lens. Or, you might prefer to use, say, f/2.8 on a lens with a maximum aperture of f/1.4, because you want the best compromise between speed and sharpness.

Aperture Priority can even be used to specify a *range* of shutter speeds you want to use under varying lighting conditions, which seems almost contradictory. But think about it. You're shooting a soccer game outdoors with a telephoto lens and want a relatively high shutter speed, but you don't care if the speed changes a little should the sun duck behind a cloud. Set your T1i to Av, and adjust the aperture until a shutter speed of, say, 1/1,000th second is selected at your current ISO setting. (In bright sunlight at ISO 400,

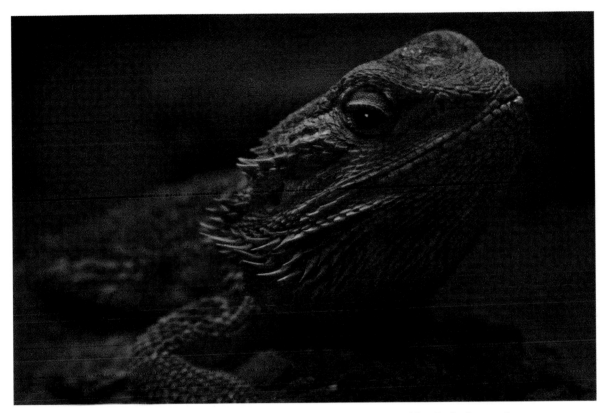

Figure 4.14 Use Aperture Priority to "lock in" a large f/stop when you want to blur the background.

that aperture is likely to be around f/11.) Then, go ahead and shoot, knowing that your T1i will maintain that f/11 aperture (for sufficient DOF as the soccer players move about the field), but will drop down to 1/750th or 1/500th second if necessary should the lighting change a little.

A blinking 30 or 4000 shutter speed in the viewfinder indicates that the T1i is unable to select an appropriate shutter speed at the selected aperture and that over- and under-exposure will occur at the current ISO setting. That's the major pitfall of using Av: you might select an f/stop that is too small or too large to allow an optimal exposure with the available shutter speeds. For example, if you choose f/2.8 as your aperture and the illumination is quite bright (say, at the beach or in snow), even your camera's fastest shutter speed might not be able to cut down the amount of light reaching the sensor to provide the right exposure. Or, if you select f/8 in a dimly lit room, you might find yourself shooting with a very slow shutter speed that can cause blurring from subject movement or camera shake. Aperture Priority is best used by those with a bit of experience in choosing settings. Many seasoned photographers leave their T1i set on Av all the time.

Shutter Priority

Shutter Priority (Tv) is the inverse of Aperture Priority: you choose the shutter speed you'd like to use, and the camera's metering system selects the appropriate f/stop. Perhaps you're shooting action photos and you want to use the absolute fastest shutter speed available with your camera; in other cases you might want to use a slow shutter speed to add some blur to a sports photo that would be mundane if the action were completely frozen. Or, you might want to give a feeling of motion, as with another Kris Bosworth image of an antique auto cruising down the parkway at dozens of miles per hour (see Figure 4.15). Shutter Priority mode gives you some control over how much action-freezing capability your digital camera brings to bear in a particular situation.

You'll also encounter the same problem as with Aperture Priority when you select a shutter speed that's too long or too short for correct exposure under some conditions. I've shot outdoor soccer games on sunny Fall evenings and used Shutter Priority mode to lock in a 1/1,000th second shutter speed, only to find my T1i refused to shoot when the sun dipped behind some trees and there was no longer enough light to shoot at that speed, even with the lens wide open.

Figure 4.15 Lock the shutter at a slow speed to introduce blur, as with this panned image of an antique automobile.

Like Av mode, it's possible to choose an inappropriate shutter speed. If that's the case, the maximum aperture of your lens (to indicate underexposure) or the minimum aperture (to indicate overexposure) will blink.

Program Mode

Program mode (P) uses the T1i's built-in smarts to select the correct f/stop and shutter speed using a database of picture information that tells it which combination of shutter speed and aperture will work best for a particular photo. If the correct exposure cannot be achieved at the current ISO setting, the shutter speed indicator in the viewfinder will blink 30 or 4000, indicating under- or overexposure (respectively). You can then boost or reduce the ISO to increase or decrease sensitivity.

The T1i's recommended exposure can be overridden if you want. Use the EV setting feature (described later, because it also applies to Tv and Av modes) to add or subtract exposure from the metered value. And, as I mentioned earlier in this chapter, you can change from the recommended setting to an equivalent setting (as shown in Table 4.1) that produces the same exposure, but using a different combination of f/stop and shutter speed. To accomplish this:

1. Press the shutter release halfway to lock in the current base exposure, or press the AE-Lock button (*) on the back of the camera (in which case the * indicator will illuminate in the viewfinder to show that the exposure has been locked).

2. Spin the Main dial to change the shutter speed (the T1i will adjust the f/stop to match).

Your adjustment remains in force for a single exposure; if you want to change from the recommended settings for the next exposure, you'll need to repeat those steps.

Making EV Changes

Sometimes you'll want more or less exposure than indicated by the T1i's metering system. Perhaps you want to underexpose to create a silhouette effect, or overexpose to produce a high key look. It's easy to use the T1i's Exposure Compensation system to override the exposure recommendations, available in any Creative Zone mode except Manual. There are two ways to make exposure value (EV) changes with the Rebel T1i. One method is fast and a bit clumsy to use, especially if your fingers aren't well coordinated. The other method takes a few seconds longer, but can be done smoothly by the most fumble-fingered among us.

Fast EV Changes

Activate the exposure meters by tapping the shutter release button. Then, just hold down the AV button (located on the back next to the upper-right corner of the LCD) and rotate the Main dial to the right to make the image brighter (add exposure), and to the left to make the image darker (subtract exposure). The exposure scale in the viewfinder and on the LCD indicates the EV change you've made. The EV change you've made remains for the exposures that follow, until you manually zero out the EV setting with the AV button+Main dial. EV changes are ignored when using M or any of the Basic Zone modes.

Slower EV Changes

If you find yourself not turning the Main dial quickly enough after you tap the shutter release button, try the second method for making EV changes with the T1i. It can be a little slower, but gives you more time to dial in your EV adjustment. You also have the option of setting exposure bracketing at the same time:

1. Press the Menu button and navigate to the Expo. Comp./AEB entry on the Shooting 2 menu.

2. When the screen appears, press the left/right cross keys to add or subtract EV adjustment. The screen has helpful labels (Darker on the left and Brighter on the right) to make sure you're adding/subtracting when you really want to. Note that you can also set exposure bracketing, as discussed in Chapter 3, by rotating the Main dial while viewing this screen.

3. Press Set to confirm your choice.

Manual Exposure

Part of being an experienced photographer comes from knowing when to rely on your Rebel T1i's automation (including P mode and Basic Zone settings), when to go semi-automatic (with Tv or Av), and when to set exposure manually (using M). Some photographers actually prefer to set their exposure manually, as the T1i will be happy to provide an indication of when its metering system judges your manual settings provide the proper exposure, using the analog exposure scale at the bottom of the viewfinder and on the status LCD.

Manual exposure can come in handy in some situations. You might be taking a silhouette photo and find that none of the exposure modes or EV correction features give you exactly the effect you want. For example, when I shot the ballet dancer in Figure 4.16 in front of a mostly dark background highlighted by an illuminated curtain off to the right, there was no way any of my Rebel T1i's exposure modes would be able to interpret the scene the way I wanted to shoot it, even with Spot metering, which didn't have a narrow enough field of view from my position. So, I took a couple test exposures, and set the exposure manually to using the exact shutter speed and f/stop I needed. You might be working in a studio environment using multiple flash units. The additional flash are triggered by slave devices (gadgets that set off the flash when they sense the light from another flash, or, perhaps from a radio or infrared remote

Figure 4.16
Manual mode allowed setting the exact exposure for this starkly-lit shot.

control). Your camera's exposure meter doesn't compensate for the extra illumination, and can't interpret the flash exposure at all, so you need to set the aperture manually.

Because, depending on your proclivities, you might not need to set exposure manually very often, you should still make sure you understand how it works. Fortunately, the Rebel T1i makes setting exposure manually very easy. Just set the Mode dial to M, turn the Main dial to set the shutter speed, and hold down the Av button while rotating the Main dial to adjust the aperture. Press the shutter release halfway or press the AE-Lock button, and the exposure scale in the viewfinder shows you how far your chosen setting diverges from the metered exposure.

Basic Zone Modes

The final tools in your exposure repertoire are the seven Basic Zone shooting modes, which can automatically make all the basic settings needed for certain types of shooting situations, such as portraits, landscapes, close-ups, sports, night portraits, and "no-flash zone" pictures. These "autopilot" modes are especially useful when you suddenly encounter a picture-taking opportunity and don't have time to decide exactly which

Creative Zone mode you want to use. Instead, you can spin the Mode dial to the appropriate Basic Zone mode and fire away, knowing that, at least, you have a fighting chance of getting a good or usable photo.

Basic Zone modes are also helpful when you're just learning to use your T1i. Once you've learned how to operate your camera, you'll probably prefer one of the Creative Zone modes that provide more control over shooting options. The Basic Zone scene modes may give you few options or none at all. The AF mode, Drive mode, and metering mode are all set for you. Here are the modes available (I'll cover Creative Auto separately):

- **Full Auto.** This is the mode to use when you hand your camera to a total stranger and ask him or her to take your picture posing in front of the Eiffel Tower. All the photographer has to do is press the shutter release button. Every other decision is made by the camera's electronics.

- **Portrait.** This mode tends to use wider f/stops and faster shutter speeds, providing blurred backgrounds and images with no camera shake. If you hold the shutter release down, the T1i will take a continuous sequence of photos, which can be useful in capturing fleeting expressions in portrait situations.

- **Landscape.** The T1i tries to use smaller f/stops for more depth-of-field, and boosts saturation slightly for richer colors.

- **Close-up.** This mode is similar to the Portrait setting, with wider f/stops to isolate your close-up subjects, and high shutter speeds to eliminate the camera shake that's accentuated at close focusing distances. However, if you have your camera mounted on a tripod or are using an image-stabilized (IS) lens, you might want to use the Creative Zone Aperture Priority (Av) mode instead, so you can specify a smaller f/stop with additional depth-of-field.

- **Sports.** In this mode, the T1i tries to use high shutter speeds to freeze action, switches to High-Speed Continuous drive to allow taking a quick sequence of pictures with one press of the shutter release, and uses AI Servo AF to continually refocus as your subject moves around in the frame. You can find more information on autofocus options in Chapter 5.

- **Night Portrait.** Combines flash with ambient light to produce an image that is mainly illuminated by the flash, but the background is exposed by the available light. This mode uses longer exposures, so a tripod, monopod, or image-stabilized lens is a must.

- **Flash Off.** Absolutely prevents the flash from flipping up and firing, which you might want in some situations, such as religious ceremonies, museums, classical music concerts, and your double-naught spy activities. This mode is identical to Full Auto, but with the flash disabled.

Creative Auto

This mode is a hybrid between the Basic Zone Auto mode, and the Creative Zone Program mode. When you've selected this mode, the T1i makes most of the exposure decisions for you (just as in true Auto mode), but allows you to make some adjustments to other parameters, as described next.

When you set the Mode dial to the CA position, a screen resembling the one shown in Figure 4.17 appears (the currently set shutter speed and aperture appear only when the exposure meters are activated; turn them on by tapping the shutter release). The basic settings are the same as those produced by the Full Auto Basic Zone mode. Just follow these steps:

1. Press the Set button to switch into Settings mode.

2. Use the cross keys to navigate to the setting you want to change. A description of that setting appears at the bottom of the screen when that option is highlighted.

3. Press the Set button again to activate the setting.

Figure 4.17 In Creative Auto mode, this screen appears to allow making quick adjustments to some parameters.

4. Use Main dial to choose the option you want.

5. Press the Set button to confirm your choice.

6. Press the DISP button or tap the shutter release to exit the settings mode.

The settings you may adjust include:

- **Flash.** Auto Flash, Flash On, or Flash Off.

- **Blur/sharpen background.** Rotate the Main dial to the left to blur the background (which causes the T1i to select a larger f/stop for the same exposure), or towards the right to sharpen the background (ending up with a smaller f/stop for the same exposure).

- **Adjust image brightness.** Rotate the Main dial to the left to reduce the overall exposure, making the image darker, or towards the right to increase exposure and make the image brighter.

- **Picture Style.** You can select Standard, Portrait, Landscape, or Monochrome Picture Styles, which, in the Creative Auto mode are equated to "standard images," "smooth skin tones," "vivid blues and greens," and "monochrome image." (The actual name of the Picture Style is not shown, and the other pre-set styles, plus User Def. styles are not available from this screen in Creative Auto mode.)

- **Drive mode.** You can switch from single, continuous, or self-timer drive modes.

- **Image quality.** When you highlight this section, you can use the Main dial to cycle among the various combinations of image size/JPEG quality/RAW options.

Adjusting Exposure with ISO Settings

Another way of adjusting exposures is by changing the ISO sensitivity setting. Sometimes photographers forget about this option, because the common practice is to set the ISO once for a particular shooting session (say, at ISO 100 or 200 for bright sunlight outdoors, or ISO 800 when shooting indoors) and then forget about ISO. The reason for that is that ISOs higher than ISO 100 or 200 are seen as "bad" or "necessary evils." However, changing the ISO is a valid way of adjusting exposure settings, particularly with the Canon EOS Rebel T1i, which produces good results at ISO settings that create grainy, unusable pictures with some other camera models.

Indeed, I find myself using ISO adjustment as a convenient alternate way of adding or subtracting EV when shooting in Manual mode, and as a quick way of choosing equivalent exposures when in Automatic or Semiautomatic modes. For example, I've selected a Manual exposure with both f/stop and shutter speed suitable for my image using, say, ISO 200. I can change the exposure in full-stop increments by pressing the ISO button on top of the camera, and spinning the Main dial one click at a time. The difference in image quality/noise at the base setting of ISO 200 is negligible if I dial in ISO 100 to reduce exposure a little, or change to ISO 400 to increase exposure. I keep my preferred f/stop and shutter speed, but still adjust the exposure.

Or, perhaps, I am using Tv mode and the metered exposure at ISO 200 is 1/500th second at f/11. If I decide on the spur of the moment I'd rather use 1/500th second at f/8, I can press the ISO button and spin the Main dial to switch to ISO 100. Of course, it's a good idea to monitor your ISO changes, so you don't end up at ISO 1,600 accidentally. ISO settings can, of course, also be used to boost or reduce sensitivity in particular shooting situations. The Rebel T1i can use ISO settings from ISO 100 up to 12,800 when you're choosing a sensitivity manually and you've selected the Expanded ISO range, as described in Chapter 3. The camera will choose ISO 100 to 1,600 automatically in Basic Zone modes or from ISO 100 to 3,200 in Creative Zone Auto mode— and up to 12,800 with the Expanded ISO range available.

The camera can adjust the ISO automatically as appropriate for various lighting conditions. In Basic Zone modes, ISO is normally set between ISO 100-800. When you choose the Auto ISO setting, the T1i adjusts the sensitivity dynamically to suit the subject matter. In Basic Zone Auto, Landscape, Close-Up, Sports, Night Portrait, and Flash Off modes, the T1i adjusts ISO between ISO 100-1600 as required. In Portrait mode, ISO is fixed at ISO 100, because the T1i attempts to use larger f/stops to blur the background, and the lower ISO setting lends itself to those larger stops.

When Auto ISO is chosen when using Creative Zone modes, sensitivity will be generally set to ISO 100-1600 in Program, Av, and A-DEP modes. In Manual exposure mode, Auto ISO is fixed at ISO 400.

When using flash, Auto ISO produces a setting of ISO 400 automatically, except when overexposure would occur (as when shooting subjects very close to the camera), in which case a lower setting (down to ISO 100) will be used. If you have an external dedicated flash attached, the T1i can set ISO in the range 400-1600 automatically. That capability can be useful when shooting outdoor field sports at night and other "long distance" flash pictures, particularly with a telephoto lens, because you want to extend the "reach" of your external flash as far as possible (to dozens of feet or more), and boosting the ISO does that. Remember that if the Auto ISO ranges aren't suitable for you, individual ISO values can also be selected in any of the Creative Zone modes.

Tip

Find yourself locked out of ISO settings lower than 200? Check Custom Function C.Fn II 06 Highlight tone priority. When set to 1:Enable, only ISO 200-1600 can be selected.

Bracketing

Bracketing is a method for shooting several consecutive exposures using different settings, as a way of improving the odds that one will be exactly right. Before digital cameras took over the universe, it was common to bracket exposures, shooting, say, a series of three photos at 1/125th second, but varying the f/stop from f/8 to f/11 to f/16. In practice, smaller than whole-stop increments were used for greater precision. Plus, it was just as common to keep the same aperture and vary the shutter speed, although in the days before electronic shutters, film cameras often had only whole increment shutter speeds available.

Today, cameras like the T1i can bracket exposures much more precisely, and bracket white balance as well. While WB bracketing is sometimes used when getting color absolutely correct in the camera is important, auto exposure bracketing (AEB) is used much more often. When this feature is activated, the T1i takes three consecutive photos: one at the metered "correct" exposure, one with less exposure, and one with more exposure, using an increment of your choice up to plus 2/minus 2 stops. (Choose between increments by setting Custom Function I-01 to 0 [1/3 stop] or 1 [1/2 stop].) In Av mode, the shutter speed will change, while in Tv mode, the aperture speed will change.

Using AEB is trickier than it needs to be, but has been made more flexible with the upgrade from the Rebel XSi's bracketing system (with the T1i you can now choose to bracket only overexposures or underexposures—a very useful improvement!). Just follow these steps:

1. **Activate the EV/AEB screen.** Press the Menu button and navigate to the Shooting 2 menu, where you'll find the Expo.comp/AEB option. Press Set to select this choice.

2. **Set the bracket range.** Rotate the Main dial to spread out or contract the three dots to include the desired range you want to cover. For example, with the dots clustered tightly together, the three bracketed exposures will be spread out over a single stop. Separating the cluster produces a wider range and larger exposure change between the three shots in the bracket set, as shown in Figure 4.18.

3. **Adjust zero point.** By default, the bracketing is zeroed around the center of the scale, which represents the correct exposure. But you might want to have your three bracketed shots all biased towards overexposure or underexposure. Perhaps you feel that the metered exposure will be too dark or too light, and you want the bracketed shots to lean in the other direction. Use the left/right cross keys to move the bracket spread towards one end of the scale or the other, as shown in Figure 4.19.

Figure 4.18
Rotate the Main dial to set the increment between bracketed shots.

Figure 4.19
Use the left/right cross keys to bias the bracketing towards more or less exposure.

NON-BRACKETING IS EXPOSURE COMPENSATION

When the three bracket indicators aren't separated, using the left/right cross keys simply, in effect, adds or subtracts exposure compensation. You'll be shooting a "bracketed" set of one picture, with the zero point placed at the portion of the scale you indicated. Until you rotate the Main dial to separate the three bracket indicators by at least one indicator, this screen just supplies EV adjustment. Also keep in mind that the increments shown will be either 1/3 stop or 1/2 stop, depending on how you've set C.Fn. I-01.

4. **Confirm your choice.** Press the Set button to enter the settings.

5. **Take your three photos.** You can use Single shooting mode to take the trio of pictures yourself, use the self-timer (which will expose all three pictures after the delay), or switch to Continuous Shooting mode to take the three pictures in a burst.

6. **Monitor your shots.** As the images are captured, three indicators will appear on the exposure scale in the viewfinder, with one of them flashing for each bracketed photo, showing when the base exposure, underexposure, and overexposure are taken.

7. **Turn bracketing off when done.** Bracketing remains in effect when the set is taken so you can continue shooting bracketed exposures until you use the electronic flash, turn off the camera, or return to the menu to cancel bracketing.

Bracketing and Merge to HDR

HDR (High Density Range) photography is, at the moment, an incredibly popular fad. There are even entire books that do nothing but tell you how to shoot HDR images. If you aren't familiar with the technique, HDR involves shooting two or three or more images at different bracketed exposures, giving you an "underexposed" version with lots of detail in highlights that would otherwise be washed out; an "overexposed" rendition that preserves detail in the shadows; and several intermediate shots. These are combined to produce a single image that has an amazing amount of detail throughout the scene's entire tonal range.

I call this technique a fad because the reason it exists in the first place is due to a (temporary, I hope) defect in current digital camera sensors. It's presently impossible to capture the full range of brightness that we perceive; digital cameras, including the EOS T1i, can't even grab the full range of brightness that *film* can see, as I showed you in Figures 4.1 and 4.2 at the beginning of this chapter.

But as the megapixel race slows down, sensor designers have already begun designing capture electronics that have larger density (dynamic) ranges, and I fully expect to see cameras within a few years that can produce images similar to what we're getting now with HDR manipulation in image editors.

HDR works like this: Suppose you wanted to photograph a dimly-lit room that had a bright window showing an outdoors scene. Proper exposure for the room might be on the order of 1/60th second at f/2.8 at ISO 200, while the outdoors scene probably would require f/11 at 1/400th second. That's almost a 7 EV step difference (approximately 7 f/stops) and well beyond the dynamic range of any digital camera, including the EOS T1i.

When you're using Merge to HDR, a feature found in Adobe Photoshop (similar functions are available in other programs, including the Mac/PC utility Photomatix [www.hdrsoft.com; free to try, $99 to buy]), you'd take several pictures. As I mentioned earlier, one would be exposed for the shadows, one for the highlights, and perhaps one for the midtones. Then, you'd use the Merge to HDR command (or the equivalent in other software) to combine all of the images into one HDR image that integrates the well-exposed sections of each version. You can use the EOS T1i's bracketing feature to produce those images.

The images should be as identical as possible, except for exposure. So, it's a good idea to mount the T1i on a tripod, use a remote release, and take all the exposures in one burst. Just follow these steps:

1. Mount the T1i on a tripod and connect either the remote release cable or use the optional infrared remote.

2. Set the camera to shoot RAW images, as described in Chapter 3.

3. Set bracketing to a 2-stop increment, as described above and in Chapter 3.

4. Manually focus or autofocus the T1i.

5. Trigger the camera to expose your set of three images.

6. Copy your images to your computer and continue in Photoshop with the Merge to HDR steps listed next.

The next steps show you how to combine the separate exposures into one merged high dynamic range image. The sample images shown in Figures 4.20, 4.21, and 4.23 show the results you can get from a two-shot bracketed sequence. I merged only two pictures for simplicity, because the differences between three or more bracketed exposures, even when taken at exposures that are 2 stops apart, can be too subtle to show up well on the printed page.

1. If you use an application to transfer the files to your computer, make sure it does not make any adjustments to brightness, contrast, or exposure. You want the real raw information for Merge to HDR to work with. If you do everything correctly, you'll end up with at least two photos like the ones shown in Figures 4.20 and 4.21.

2. Load the images into Photoshop using your preferred RAW converter.

3. Save as .PSD files.

Figure 4.20 Make one exposure for the shadow areas.

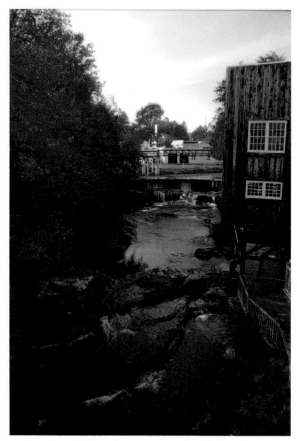

Figure 4.21 Make a second exposure for the highlights, such as the sky.

4. Activate Merge to HDR by choosing File > Automate > Merge to HDR.

5. Select the photos to be merged, as shown in Figure 4.22, where I have specified the two .PSD files. You'll note a checkbox that can be used to automatically align the images if they were not taken with the T1i mounted on a rock-steady support.

6. Once HDR merge has done its thing, you must save in .PSD, to retain the file's full color information, in case you want to work with the HDR image later. Otherwise, you can convert to a normal 24-bit file and save in any compatible format.

Figure 4.22 Use the Merge to HDR command to combine the two images.

If you do everything correctly, you'll end up with a photo like the one shown in Figure 4.23, which has the properly exposed foreground of the first shot, and the well-exposed sky of the second image. Note that, ideally, nothing should move between shots. In the example pictures, the river is moving, but the exposures were made so close together that, after the merger, you can't really tell.

Figure 4.23
You'll end up with an extended dynamic range photo like this one.

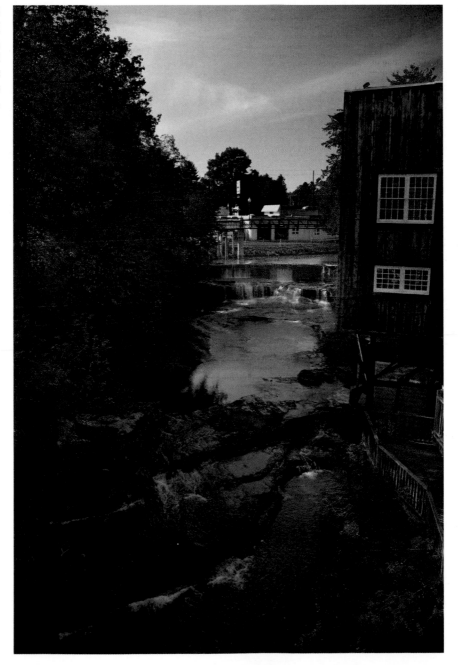

What if you don't have the opportunity, inclination, or skills to create several images at different exposures, as described? If you shoot in RAW format, you can still use Merge to HDR, working with a *single* original image file. What you do is import the image into Photoshop several times, using Adobe Camera Raw to create multiple copies of the file at different exposure levels.

For example, you'd create one copy that's too dark, so the shadows lose detail, but the highlights are preserved. Create another copy with the shadows intact and allow the highlights to wash out. Then, you can use Merge to HDR to combine the two and end up with a finished image that has the extended dynamic range you're looking for.

Dealing with Noise

Image noise is that random grainy effect that some like to use as a visual effect, but which, most of the time, is objectionable because it robs your image of detail even as it adds that "interesting" texture. Noise is caused by two different phenomena: high ISO settings and long exposures.

High ISO noise commonly appears when you raise your camera's sensitivity setting above ISO 400. With Canon cameras, which are renown for their good ISO noise characteristics, noise may become visible at ISO 800, and is usually fairly noticeable at ISO 1,600. This kind of noise appears as a result of the amplification needed to increase the sensitivity of the sensor. While higher ISOs do pull details out of dark areas, they also amplify non-signal information randomly, creating noise.

A similar noisy phenomenon occurs during long time exposures, which allow more photons to reach the sensor, increasing your ability to capture a picture under low-light conditions. However, the longer exposures also increase the likelihood that some pixels will register random phantom photons, often because the longer an imager is "hot" the warmer it gets, and that heat can be mistaken for photons. There's also a special kind of noise that CMOS sensors like the one used in the T1i are potentially susceptible to. With a CCD, the entire signal is conveyed off the chip and funneled through a single amplifier and analog-to-digital conversion circuit. Any noise introduced there is, at least, consistent. CMOS imagers, on the other hand, contain millions of individual amplifiers and A/D converters, all working in unison. Because all these circuits don't necessarily all process in precisely the same way all the time, they can introduce something called fixed-pattern noise into the image data.

Fortunately, Canon's electronics geniuses have done an exceptional job minimizing noise from all causes in the T1i. Even so, you might still want to apply the optional long exposure noise reduction that can be activated using Custom Function II-04. This type of noise reduction involves the T1i taking a second, blank exposure, and comparing the random pixels in that image with the photograph you just took. Pixels that coincide in the two represent noise and can safely be suppressed. This noise reduction system, called *dark frame subtraction,* effectively doubles the amount of time required to take a picture, and is used only for exposures longer than one second. Noise reduction can reduce the amount of detail in your picture, as some image information may be removed along with the noise. So, you might want to use this feature with moderation.

To activate your T1i's noise reduction features, go to the Custom Function menu, choose C.Fn. II: Image, and select either C.Fn. II-04 (Long exposure noise reduction) or C.Fn. II-05 (High ISO noise reduction) as explained in Chapter 3.

You can also apply noise reduction to a lesser extent using Photoshop, and when converting RAW files to some other format, using your favorite RAW converter, or an industrial-strength product like Noise Ninja (www.picturecode.com) to wipe out noise after you've already taken the picture.

Fixing Exposures with Histograms

While you can often recover poorly exposed photos in your image editor, your best bet is to arrive at the correct exposure in the camera, minimizing the tweaks that you have to make in post-processing. However, you can't always judge exposure just by viewing the image on your T1i's LCD after the shot is made. Nor can you get a 100 percent accurately exposed picture by using the T1i's Live View feature. Ambient light may make the LCD difficult to see, and the brightness level you've set can affect the appearance of the playback image.

Instead, you can use a histogram, which is a chart displayed on the Rebel T1i's LCD that shows the number of tones being captured at each brightness level. You can use the information to provide correction for the next shot you take. The T1i offers two histogram variations that can be shown while viewing images: one that shows overall brightness levels for an image and an alternate version that separates the red, green, and blue channels of your image into separate histograms.

DISPLAYING HISTOGRAMS

To view histograms on your screen, press the DISP button while an image is shown on the LCD. Keep pressing the button until the histogram(s) are shown. The display will cycle between several levels of information, including flashing highlights and two histograms. One histogram shows overall brightness levels (Figure 4.24), while the second type of histogram screen shows both brightness levels and levels for each of the red, green, and blue channels (Figure 4.25). During histogram display, you'll also see a thumbnail at the left side of the screen with your image displayed. Overexposed areas will blink, which is your prompt to use negative exposure compensation if you want to salvage those areas. (See "Making EV Changes" above.) To change your default histogram type from Brightness to RGB, use the Histogram setting in the Playback 2 menu.

Figure 4.24
A brightness histogram shows the relationship of tones in an image.

Figure 4.25
Individual red, green, and blue histograms show the exposure for each color channel.

Both types are charts that include a representation of up to 256 vertical lines on a horizontal axis that show the number of pixels in the image at each brightness level, from 0 (black) on the left side to 255 (white) on the right. (The 3-inch LCD doesn't have enough pixels to show each and every one of the 256 lines, but, instead provides a representation of the shape of the curve formed.) The more pixels at a given level, the taller the bar at that position. If no bar appears at a particular position on the scale from left to right, there are no pixels at that particular brightness level.

A typical histogram produces a mountain-like shape, with most of the pixels bunched in the middle tones, with fewer pixels at the dark and light ends of the scale. Ideally, though, there will be at least some pixels at either extreme, so that your image has both a true black and a true white representing some details. Learn to spot histograms that represent over- and underexposure, and add or subtract exposure using an EV modification to compensate.

For example, Figure 4.26 shows the histogram for an image that is badly underexposed. You can guess from the shape of the histogram that many of the dark tones to the left of the graph have been clipped off. There's plenty of room on the right side for additional pixels to reside without having them become overexposed. Or, a histogram might look like Figure 4.27, which is overexposed. In either case, you can increase or decrease the exposure (either by changing the f/stop or shutter speed in Manual mode or by adding or subtracting an EV value in Autoexposure mode) to produce the corrected histogram shown in Figure 4.28, in which the tones "approach" the right side of the histogram to produce as many highlight details as possible. See "Making EV Changes" above for information on dialing in exposure compensation.

Figure 4.26 This histogram shows an underexposed image.

Figure 4.27 This histogram reveals that the image is overexposed.

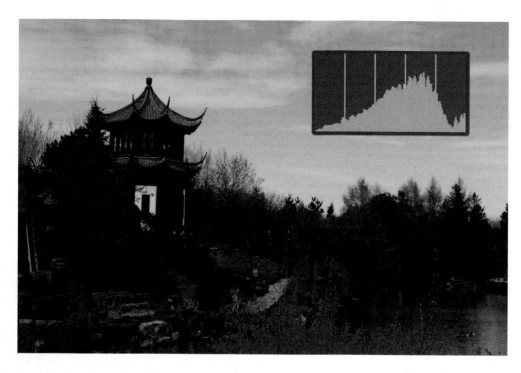

Figure 4.28
A histogram for
a properly
exposed image
should look
like this.

The histogram can also be used to aid in fixing the contrast of an image, although gauging incorrect contrast is more difficult. For example, if the histogram shows all the tones bunched up in one place in the image, the photo will be low in contrast. If the tones are spread out more or less evenly, the image is probably high in contrast. In either case, your best bet may be to switch to RAW (if you're not already using that format) so you can adjust contrast in post processing. However, you can also change to a user-defined Picture Style (User Def. 1, User Def. 2, or User Def. 3 in the Picture Style menu) with contrast set lower (–1 to –4) or higher (+1 to +4) as required.

Advanced Shooting with Your Canon EOS Rebel T1i/500D

Getting the right exposure is one of the foundations of a great photograph, but a lot more goes into a compelling shot than good tonal values. A sharp image, proper white balance, good color, and other factors all can help elevate your image from good to exceptional. So, now that you've got a good understanding of exposure tucked away, you'll want to learn how to work with some additional exposure options, use the automatic and manual focusing controls available with the Canon EOS Rebel T1i, and master some of the many ways you can fine-tune your images.

How Focus Works

Although Canon added autofocus capabilities in the 1980s, back in the day of film cameras, prior to that focusing was always done manually. Honest. Even though viewfinders were bigger and brighter than they are today, special focusing screens, magnifiers, and other gadgets were often used to help the photographer achieve correct focus. Imagine what it must have been like to focus manually under demanding, fast-moving conditions such as sports photography.

Focusing was problematic because our eyes and brains have poor memory for correct focus, which is why your eye doctor must shift back and forth between sets of lenses and ask "Does that look sharper—or was it sharper before?" in determining your correct prescription. Similarly, manual focusing involves jogging the focus ring back and forth, as you go from almost in focus, to sharp focus, to almost focused again. The little clockwise and counterclockwise arcs decrease in size until you've zeroed in on the point of correct focus. What you're looking for is the image with the most contrast between the edges of elements in the image.

The camera also looks for these contrast differences among pixels to determine relative sharpness. There are two ways that sharp focus is determined.

Phase Detection

In this mode, the autofocus sampling area is divided into two halves by a lens in the sensor. The two halves are compared, much like (actually, exactly like) a two-window rangefinder used in surveying, weaponry—and non-SLR cameras like the venerable Leica M film models. The contrast between the two images changes as focus is moved in or out, until sharp focus is achieved when the images are "in phase," or lined up.

The T1i's nine autofocus sensors are located in the "floor" of the mirror box, just under the flip-up mirror, which is partially silvered so that most of the light reaching it from the lens is bounced upwards to the viewfinder, while some light is directed downward towards the focus sensors. If you lock up the mirror of your camera (using the Sensor Cleaning option in the Setup 2 menu), you can see where these sensors are located.

Figure 5.1 When an image is out of focus, the split lines don't align precisely.

Figure 5.2 Using phase detection, the T1i is able to align the features of the image and achieve sharp focus quickly.

You can visualize how phase detection autofocus works if you look at Figures 5.1 and 5.2. (However, your camera's actual autofocus sensors don't look like this; I'm providing a greatly simplified view just for illustration.) In Figure 5.1, a typical horizontally oriented focus sensor is looking at a series of parallel vertical lines in a weathered piece of wood. The lines are broken into two halves by the sensor's rangefinder prism, and you can see that they don't line up exactly; the image is slightly out of focus.

Fortunately, the rangefinder approach of phase detection tells the T1i exactly how out of focus the image is, and in which direction (focus is too near, or too far) thanks to the amount and direction of the displacement of the split image. The camera can quickly and precisely snap the image into sharp focus and line up the vertical lines, as shown in Figure 5.2. Of course, this scenario—vertical lines being interpreted by a horizontally oriented sensor—is ideal. When the same sensor is asked to measure focus for, say, horizontal lines that don't split up quite so conveniently, or, in the worst case, subjects such as the sky (which may have neither vertical or horizontal lines), focus can slow down drastically, or even become impossible.

Phase detection is the normal mode used by the T1i (and is also applied when using Live View in Quick mode, discussed later in this chapter). As with any rangefinder-like function, accuracy is better when the "base length" between the two images is larger. (Think back to your high school trigonometry; you could calculate a distance more accurately when the separation between the two points where the angles were measured was greater.) For that reason, phase detection autofocus is more accurate with larger (wider) lens openings—especially those with maximum f/stops of f/2.8 or better—than with smaller lens openings, and may not work at all when the f/stop is smaller than f/5.6. As I noted, the T1i is able to perform these comparisons very quickly.

Improved Cross-Type Focus Point

One improvement that new Canon EOS Rebel T1i owners sometimes overlook is the upgrade to a cross-type focus point at the center position. Why is this important? It helps to take a closer look at the phase detection system when presented with a non-ideal subject.

Figure 5.3 shows the same weathered wood pictured earlier, except in this case we've chosen to rotate the camera 90 degrees (say, because we want a vertically oriented composition). In the illustration, the image within the focus sensor's area is split in two and displaced slightly side-to-side, but the amount and direction of the misalignment is far from obvious. A horizontally oriented focus sensor will be forced to look for less obvious vertical lines to match up. Our best-case subject has been transformed into a *worst-case* subject for a horizontal focus sensor.

The value of the cross-type focus sensor, which can interpret contrast in both horizontal and vertical directions, can be seen in Figure 5.4. The horizontal lines are still giving the horizontal portion of the cross sensor fits, but the vertical bar can easily split and align the subject to achieve optimum focus. Cross-type sensors can handle horizontal and vertical lines with equal aplomb and, if you think about it, lines at any diagonal angle as well. In lower light levels, with subjects that were moving, or with subjects that have no pattern and less contrast to begin with, the cross-type sensor not only works faster but can focus subjects that a horizontal- or vertical-only sensor can't handle at all.

Figure 5.3 A horizontal focus censor doesn't handle horizontal lines very well.

Figure 5.4 Cross-type sensors can evaluate contrast in both horizontal and vertical directions, as well as diagonally.

So, you can see that having a center cross-type focus sensor that is extra-sensitive with faster lenses is a definite advantage.

Contrast Detection

This is a slower mode, suitable for static subjects, and used by the Canon T1i with Live View and Live Face Detection modes. It's a bit easier to understand, and is illustrated by Figure 5.5. At top in the figure, the transitions between the edges found in the image are soft and blurred because of the low contrast between them. Although the illustration uses the same vertical lines used with the phase detection example, the orientation of the features doesn't matter. The focus system looks only for contrast between edges, and those edges can run in any direction.

Figure 5.5

Focus in
Contrast
Detection
mode evaluates
the increase in
contrast in the
edges of sub-
jects, starting
with a blurry
image (top)
and producing
a sharp, con-
trasty image
(bottom).

At the bottom of Figure 5.5, the image has been brought into sharp focus, and the edges have much more contrast; the transitions are sharp and clear. Although this example is a bit exaggerated so you can see the results on the printed page, it's easy to understand that when maximum contrast in a subject is achieved, it can be deemed to be in sharp focus. Although achieving focus with contrast detection is generally quite a bit slower, there are several advantages to this method:

- **Works with more image types.** Contrast detection doesn't require subject matter rotated 90 degrees from the sensor's orientation to operate optimally. Any subject that has edges will work.

- **Focus on any point.** While phase detection focus can be achieved *only* at the points that fall under one of the nine autofocus sensors, with contrast detection, any portion of the image can be used. Focus is achieved with the actual sensor image, so focus point selection is simply a matter of choosing which part of the sensor image to use.

- **Potentially more accurate.** Phase detection can fall prey to the vagaries of uncooperative subject matter: if suitable lines aren't available, the system may have to hunt for focus or achieve less than optimal focus. Contrast detection is more clearcut. The camera can clearly see when the highest contrast has been achieved.

The T1i's autofocus mechanism, like all such systems found in SLR cameras, evaluates the degree of focus, but, unlike the human eye, it is able to remember the progression perfectly, so that autofocus can lock in much more quickly and, with an image that has sufficient contrast, more precisely. Unfortunately, while the T1i's focus system finds it easy to measure degrees of apparent focus at each of the focus points in the viewfinder, it doesn't really know with any certainty *which* object should be in sharpest focus. Is it the closest object? The subject in the center? Something lurking *behind* the closest subject? A person standing over at the side of the picture? Many of the techniques for using autofocus effectively involve telling the Rebel T1i exactly what it should be focusing on, by choosing a focus zone or by allowing the camera to choose a focus zone for you. I'll address that topic shortly.

Getting into Focus

Learning to use the Canon EOS Rebel T1i's autofocus system is easy, but you do need to fully understand how the system works to get the most benefit from it. Once you're comfortable with autofocus, you'll know when it's appropriate to use the manual focus option, too. The important thing to remember is that focus isn't absolute. For example, some things that look in sharp focus at a given viewing size and distance might not be in focus at a larger size and/or closer distance. In addition, the goal of optimum focus isn't always to make things look sharp. Not all of an image will be or should be sharp. Controlling exactly what is sharp and what is not is part of your creative palette. Use of depth-of-field characteristics to throw part of an image out of focus while other parts are sharply focused is one of the most valuable tools available to a photographer. But, selective focus works only when the desired areas of an image are in focus properly. For the digital SLR photographer, correct focus can be one of the trickiest parts of the technical and creative process.

To make your job easier, the Rebel T1i has a precision nine-point autofocus system that uses a separate CMOS sensor in the viewing system (described earlier) to focus the image using phase detection. When the contrast is highest at the active autofocus point(s), that part of the image is in sharp focus. The active focus points are represented by the nine sets of brackets visible in the viewfinder (see Figure 5.6), and can be selected automatically by the camera, or manually by you, the photographer. The center autofocus point is of the advanced "cross" type (that is, it measures in both horizontal and vertical directions) I just described that works with all Canon lenses having a maximum aperture of f/5.6 or larger, but has enhanced sensitivity when used with a lens having a maximum aperture of f/2.8 or larger.

Your camera's autofocus sensors require a minimum amount of light to operate, which is why autofocus capabilities are possible only with lenses having an f/5.6 or larger maximum aperture. If necessary, the AF assist beam built into the T1i and Canon's dedicated flash units provide additional light that helps assure enough illumination for autofocus.

Figure 5.6
Any of the nine
autofocus
points can be
selected by the
photographer
manually or by
the camera
automatically.

Focus Modes

The T1i has three AF modes: One Shot AF (also known as Single Autofocus), AI Servo
(Continuous Autofocus), and AI Focus AF (which switches between the two as appropriate). I'll explain all of these in more detail later in this section.

MANUAL FOCUS

With Manual focus activated by sliding the switch on the lens, your T1i lets you set the
focus yourself. There are some advantages and disadvantages to this approach. While your
batteries will last slightly longer in Manual focus mode, it will take you longer to focus
the camera for each photo, a process that can be tricky. Modern digital cameras, even
dSLRs, depend so much on autofocus that the viewfinders of models that have less than
full-frame-sized sensors are no longer designed for optimum Manual focus. The T1i provides .87 magnification, compared with .80 magnification with some earlier Rebels. That
means that with a 50mm focal length, the image appears to be 87 percent of life size. You
see 95 percent of the actual image area through the T1i's viewfinder.

Focus Pocus

The T1i's autofocus mechanism, like all such systems found in SLR cameras, also evaluates these increases and decreases in sharpness, but it is able to remember the progression perfectly, so that autofocus can lock in much more quickly and, with an image that has sufficient contrast, more precisely. Unfortunately, while the T1i's focus system finds it easy to measure degrees of apparent focus at each of the focus points in the viewfinder, it doesn't really know with any certainty *which* object should be in sharpest focus. Is it the closest object? The subject in the center? Something lurking *behind* the closest subject? A person standing over at the side of the picture? Many of the techniques for using autofocus effectively involve telling the Rebel T1i exactly what it should be focusing on.

Adding Circles of Confusion

But there are other factors in play, as well. You know that increased depth-of-field brings more of your subject into focus. But more depth-of-field also makes autofocusing (or manual focusing) more difficult because the contrast is lower between objects at different distances. So, autofocus with a 200mm lens (or zoom setting) may be easier than at a 28mm focal length (or zoom setting) because the longer lens has less apparent depth-of-field. By the same token, a lens with a maximum aperture of f/1.8 will be easier to autofocus (or manually focus) than one of the same focal length with an f/4 maximum aperture, because the f/4 lens has more depth-of-field *and* a dimmer view. That's why lenses with a maximum aperture smaller than f/5.6 can give your T1i's autofocus system fits.

To make things even more complicated, many subjects aren't polite enough to remain still. They move around in the frame, so that even if the T1i is sharply focused on your main subject, it may change position and require refocusing. An intervening subject may pop into the frame and pass between you and the subject you meant to photograph. You (or the T1i) have to decide whether to lock focus on this new subject, or remain focused on the original subject. Finally, there are some kinds of subjects that are difficult to bring into sharp focus because they lack enough contrast to allow the T1i's AF system (or our eyes) to lock in. Blank walls, a clear blue sky, or other subject matter may make focusing difficult.

If you find all these focus factors confusing, you're on the right track. Focus is, in fact, measured using something called a *circle of confusion*. An ideal image consists of zillions of tiny little points, which, like all points, theoretically have no height or width. There is perfect contrast between the point and its surroundings. You can think of each point as a pinpoint of light in a darkened room. When a given point is out of focus, its edges decrease in contrast and it changes from a perfect point to a tiny disc with blurry edges (remember, blur is the lack of contrast between boundaries in an image). (See Figure 5.7.)

Figure 5.7
When a pin-point of light (left) goes out of focus, its blurry edges form a circle of confusion (center and right).

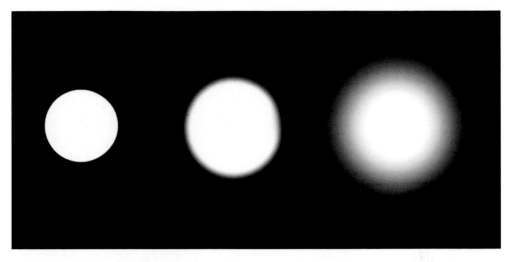

If this blurry disc—the circle of confusion—is small enough, our eye still perceives it as a point. It's only when the disc grows large enough that we can see it as a blur rather than a sharp point that a given point is viewed as out of focus. You can see, then, that enlarging an image, either by displaying it larger on your computer monitor or by making a large print, also enlarges the size of each circle of confusion. Moving closer to the image does the same thing. So, parts of an image that may look perfectly sharp in a 5 × 7-inch print viewed at arm's length, might appear blurry when blown up to 11 × 14 and examined at the same distance. Take a few steps back, however, and it may look sharp again.

To a lesser extent, the viewer also affects the apparent size of these circles of confusion. Some people see details better at a given distance and may perceive smaller circles of confusion than someone standing next to them. For the most part, however, such differences are small. Truly blurry images will look blurry to just about everyone under the same conditions.

Technically, there is just one plane within your picture area, parallel to the back of the camera (or sensor, in the case of a digital camera), that is in sharp focus. That's the plane in which the points of the image are rendered as precise points. At every other plane in front of or behind the focus plane, the points show up as discs that range from slightly blurry to extremely blurry, as you can see in Figure 5.8. In practice, the discs in many of these planes will still be so small that we see them as points, and that's where we get depth-of-field. Depth-of-field is just the range of planes that include discs that we perceive as points rather than blurred splotches. The size of this range increases as the aperture is reduced in size and is allocated roughly one-third in front of the plane of sharpest focus, and two-thirds behind it. The range of sharp focus is always greater behind your subject than in front of it.

Figure 5.8
The model is in focus, but the area behind her appears blurry because the depth-of-field is limited.

Making Sense of Sensors

The number and type of autofocus sensors can affect how well the system operates. As I mentioned, the Canon EOS Rebel T1i has nine AF points. The original Digital Rebel and Digital Rebel XT had seven autofocus points, and Canon's high-end cameras, like the 21MP Canon EOS-1Ds Mark III has a whopping 45 autofocus points. These focus sensors can consist of vertical or horizontal lines of pixels, cross-shapes, and often a mixture of these types within a single camera, although, as I mentioned, the Rebel T1i includes a cross-type sensor at the center position. The more AF points available, the more easily the camera can differentiate among areas of the frame, and the more precisely you can specify the area you want to be in focus if you're manually choosing a focus spot.

As the camera collects contrast information from the sensors, it then evaluates it to determine whether the desired sharp focus has been achieved. The calculations may include whether the subject is moving, and whether the camera needs to "predict" where the subject will be when the shutter release button is fully depressed and the picture is taken. The speed with which the camera is able to evaluate focus and then move the lens elements into the proper position to achieve the sharpest focus determines how fast the autofocus mechanism is. Although your T1i will almost always focus more quickly than a human, there are types of shooting situations where that's not fast enough. For example, if you're having problems shooting sports because the T1i's autofocus system manically follows each moving subject, a better choice might be to switch autofocus modes or shift into Manual and prefocus on a spot where you anticipate the action will be, such as a goal line or soccer net. At night football games, for example, when I am shooting with a telephoto lens almost wide open, I often focus manually on one of the referees who happens to be standing where I expect the action to be taking place (say, a halfback run, or a pass reception). When I am less sure about what is going to happen, I may switch to AI Servo autofocus and let the camera decide.

Your Autofocus Mode Options

Choosing the right autofocus mode and the way in which focus points are selected is your key to success. Using the wrong mode for a particular type of photography can lead to a series of pictures that are all sharply focused—on the wrong subject. When I first started shooting sports with an autofocus SLR (back in the film camera days), I covered one game alternating between shots of base runners and outfielders with pictures of a promising young pitcher, all from a position next to the third-base dugout. The base runner and outfielder photos were great, because their backgrounds didn't distract the autofocus mechanism. But all my photos of the pitcher had the focus tightly zeroed in on the fans in the stands behind him. Because I was shooting film instead of a digital camera, I didn't know about my gaffe until the film was developed. A simple change, such as locking in focus or focus zone manually, or even manually focusing, would have done the trick.

To save battery power, your T1i doesn't start to focus the lens until you partially depress the shutter release. But, autofocus isn't some mindless beast out there snapping your pictures in and out of focus with no feedback from you after you press that button. There are several settings you can modify that return at least a modicum of control to you. Your first decision should be whether you set the T1i to One Shot, AI Servo AF, or AI Focus AF. With the camera set for one of the Creative Zone modes, press the AF button (the right cross key) and use the Main dial or left/right cross keys to select the focus mode you want (see Figure 5.9). Press Set to confirm your choice. (The AF/M switch on the lens must be set to AF before you can change autofocus mode.)

Figure 5.9
Press the left/right cross keys or rotate the Main dial until the AF choice you want is selected.

One Shot AF

In this mode, also called *Single Autofocus*, focus is set once and remains at that setting until the button is fully depressed, taking the picture, or until you release the shutter button without taking a shot. For non-action photography, this setting is usually your best choice, as it minimizes out-of-focus pictures (at the expense of spontaneity). The drawback here is that you might not be able to take a picture at all while the camera is seeking focus; you're locked out until the autofocus mechanism is happy with the current setting. One Shot AF/Single Autofocus is sometimes referred to as *focus priority* for that reason. Because of the small delay while the camera zeroes in on correct focus, you might experience slightly more shutter lag. This mode uses less battery power.

When sharp focus is achieved, the selected focus point will flash red in the viewfinder, and the focus confirmation light at the lower right will flash green. If you're using Evaluative metering, the exposure will be locked at the same time. By keeping the shutter button depressed halfway, you'll find you can reframe the image while retaining the focus (and exposure) that's been set. With other metering methods, you can use the AE lock/FE lock button to retain your exposure while reframing.

AI Servo AF

This mode, also known as *Continuous Autofocus*, is the mode to use for sports and other fast-moving subjects. In this mode, once the shutter release is partially depressed, the camera sets the focus but continues to monitor the subject, so that if it moves or you move, the lens will be refocused to suit. Focus and exposure aren't really locked until you press the shutter release down all the way to take the picture. You'll often see Continuous Autofocus referred to as *release priority.* If you press the shutter release down all the way while the system is refining focus, the camera will go ahead and take a picture, even if the image is slightly out of focus. You'll find that AI Servo AF produces the least amount of shutter lag of any autofocus mode: press the button and the camera fires. It also uses the most battery power, because the autofocus system operates as long as the shutter release button is partially depressed.

AI Servo AF uses a technology called *predictive AF*, which allows the T1i to calculate the correct focus if the subject is moving toward or away from the camera at a constant rate. It uses either the automatically selected AF point or the point you select manually to set focus.

AI Focus AF

This setting is actually a combination of the first two. When selected, the camera focuses using One Shot AF and locks in the focus setting. But, if the subject begins moving, it will switch automatically to AI Servo AF and change the focus to keep the subject sharp. AI Focus AF is a good choice when you're shooting a mixture of action pictures and less dynamic shots and want to use One Shot AF when possible. The camera will default to that mode, yet switch automatically to AI Servo AF when it would be useful for subjects that might begin moving unexpectedly.

Setting AF Point

You can change which of the nine focus points the Canon EOS Rebel T1i uses to calculate correct focus, or allow the camera to select the point for you. As I mentioned in Chapter 1, in A-DEP, or any of the Basic Zone shooting modes, the focus point is always selected automatically by the camera. In the other Creative Zone modes, you can allow the camera to select the focus point automatically, or you can specify which focus point should be used.

To review, there are several methods to set the focus point manually. You can press the AF point selection button on the back of the camera, look through the viewfinder, and use the cross keys to move the focus point to the zone you want to use. It is not necessary to *hold* the AF point selection button down. Just press it once, and the cross keys become active for about four seconds, or until you stop moving the focus point around. For example, press the cross keys straight up or down, and the top or bottom focus points are selected. To the left or right, and the side points are selected. Press the Set button, and the center focus point becomes active. Press the Set button twice, and automatic focus is selected with all focus points active.

You can also choose a focus point by pressing the AF point selection button and then rotating the Main dial. The focus point will cycle among the edge points counterclockwise (if you turn the Main dial to the left) or clockwise (if you spin the Main dial to the right). At each end of the cycle the center focus point and then all nine focus points will be active. When all nine are "live" auto point selection will be switched back on.

Figure 5.10
When selecting focus points manually, rotate the Main dial to select specific points. Continue rotating until all nine points are visible, and the T1i switches back to automatic AF point selection mode.

Introducing Live View

Live View is one of those features that experienced SLR users (especially those dating from the film era) sometimes think they don't need—until they try it. It's also one of those features (like truly "silent" shooting, without any shutter click) that point-and-shoot refugees are surprised that digital SLRs (until recently) have lacked. As I noted earlier, SLRs have actual, mechanical shutters that can't be completely silenced, as can be done with point-and-shoot cameras. I've fielded almost as many queries from those who want to know how to preview their images on the LCD—just as they did with their point-and-shoot cameras. Indeed, many point-and-shoot models don't even *have* optical viewfinders, engendering a whole generation of amateur photographers who think the only way to frame and compose an image is to hold the camera out at arm's length so the back panel LCD can be viewed more easily.

While dSLR veterans didn't really miss what we've come to know as Live View, it was at least, in part, because they didn't have it and couldn't miss what they never had. After all, why would you eschew a big, bright, magnified through-the-lens optical view that showed depth-of-field fairly well, and which was easily visible under virtually all ambient light conditions? LCD displays, after all, were small, tended to wash out in bright light, and didn't really provide you with an accurate view of what your picture was going to look like.

There were technical problems, as well. Real-time previews theoretically disabled a dSLR's autofocus system, as focus was achieved by measuring contrast through the optical viewfinder, which is blocked when the mirror is flipped up for a live view. Extensive previewing had the same effect on the sensor as long exposures: the sensor heated up, producing excess noise. Pointing the camera at a bright light source when using a real-time view could damage the sensor. The list of potential problems goes on and on.

Most of those problems have been at least partially overcome.

The Canon EOS Rebel T1i has a gorgeous 3-inch LCD that can be viewed under a variety of lighting conditions and from wide-ranging angles, so you don't have to be exactly behind the display to see it clearly. (See Figure 5.11.) It offers a 100-percent view of the sensor's capture area (the optical viewfinder shows just 95 percent of the sensor's field of view). It's large enough to allow manual focusing—but if you want to use automatic focus, there's an option that allows briefly flipping the mirror back down for autofocusing, interrupting Live View, and then restoring the sensor preview image after focus is achieved. You still have to avoid pointing your T1i at bright light sources (especially the Sun) when using Live View, but the real-time preview can be used for fairly long periods without frying the sensor. (Image quality can degrade, but the camera issues a warning when the sensor starts to overheat.)

Unlike some of the previous attempts at a Live View-type mode by other sensors (and including Canon with its EOS 20Da, designed for astrophotography), the T1i's Live View works. No beam-splitting prisms that divert some light to the sensor, no grainy black-and-white real-time preview, no need for a spare sensor to provide a simulated Live View. Canon's system works just like you'd want it to: the mirror flips up, the shutter opens, and what the sensor sees is displayed in full color on the LCD on the back of the camera. You can expect every new camera introduced by Canon and every other

Figure 5.11
Live View
really shines on
the Canon
EOS Rebel
T1i's large
3-inch LCD.

vendor to include Live View features from now on. And, expect Live View to get better. Canon has made some significant improvements in its Live View implementation in the interim between its original introduction on the EOS 40D, and the unveiling of the upgraded version offered with the Rebel T1i.

What You Can/Cannot Do with Live View

You may not have considered just what you can do with Live View, because the capability is so novel. But once you've played with it, you'll discover dozens of applications for this capability, as well as a few things that you can't do. Here's a list of Live View Do's/Don'ts/Cans/Cant's.

- **Shoot stills and movies.** You can take still pictures or movies using Live View.

- **Preview your images on a TV.** Connect your Rebel T1i to a television using the video cable or HDMI cable, and you can preview your image on a large television or HDTV screen.

- **Preview remotely.** Extend the cable between the camera and TV screen, and you can preview your images some distance away from the camera.

- **Shoot from your computer.** Canon gives you the software you need to control your camera from your computer, so you can preview images and take pictures without physically touching the Rebel T1i.

- **Continuous shooting.** You can shoot bursts of images using Live View, but all shots will use the focus and exposure setting established for the first picture in the series.

- **Shoot from tripod or handheld.** Of course, holding the camera out at arm's length to preview an image is poor technique, and will introduce a lot of camera shake. If you want to use Live View for handheld images, use an image-stabilized lens and/or a high shutter speed. A tripod is a better choice if you can use one.

- **Watch your power.** Live View uses a lot of juice and will deplete your battery rapidly. Canon estimates that you can get 130-170 shots per battery when using Live View, depending on the temperature. The optional AC adapter is a useful accessory.

Enabling Live View

You need to take some steps before using Live View. This workflow prevents you from accidentally using Live View when you don't mean to, thus potentially losing a shot, and it also helps ensure that you've made all the settings necessary to successfully use the feature efficiently. Here are the steps to follow:

1. **Choose a shooting mode.** Select a Creative Zone shooting mode. Live View doesn't work with any of the Basic Zone modes. You can choose A-DEP, but the T1i will behave as if you selected P, instead, and A-DEP's automatic focus point selection (like all autofocus features) will be disabled.

2. **Enable Live View.** You'll need to activate Live View by choosing Live View function settings from the Setup 2 menu. Use the up/down cross keys to select Enable and press the Set button to exit.

3. **Choose other Live View functions.** Select from the other Live View functions (described next), then press the menu button to exit from the Live View function settings menu.

Several other optional functions can be set from the Live View function settings menu. (See Figure 5.12). They include:

- **Grid display (Off, Grid 1, Grid 2).** Overlays Grid 1, a "rule of thirds" grid on the screen to help you compose your image and align vertical and horizontal lines; or Grid 2, which consists of four rows of six boxes, which allow finer control over placement of images in your frame.

- **Metering timer (4 sec. to 30 min).** This option allows you to specify how long the Rebel T1i's metering system will remain active before switching off.

- **Autofocus mode (Quick mode, Live mode, Live "Face Detection" mode).** This option, explained next, lets you choose between phase detection, contrast detection, and contrast detection with "face" recognition.

Figure 5.12
You can choose grids, metering timeout, and autofocus mode when using Live View.

Activating Live View

Once you've enabled Live View, you can continue taking pictures normally through the T1i's viewfinder. When you're ready to activate Live View, press the Print/Share/Live View button on the back of the camera, to the immediate right of the viewfinder window. The mirror will flip up, and the sensor image will appear on the LCD. Here are some things you should keep in mind when Live View is active:

- **Shooting functions don't interrupt.** You can change settings or review images normally when in Live View mode. Press the WB, AF/Drive, or ISO-Flash Compensation buttons on the top of the camera, and an overlay appears superimposed on the Live View screen. You can use the cross keys to change those settings.

- **Live View continues.** When you press the shutter release, the T1i will take a photo, then display the image you just shot for review, as normal. When picture review is finished, the camera returns to Live View mode. You can take as many consecutive shots using Live View as you like, barring sensor overheating. To exit Live View entirely, press the Live View button.

- **Metering mode cannot be changed.** Evaluative metering linked to the focus frame is used. You cannot change to Partial, Spot, or Center-Weighted metering when Live View is active.

- **Press DOF button to check focus and exposure.** If you press the depth-of-field button while using Live View, the lens will stop down to the taking aperture and you'll see the effective focus range, as well as approximate image brightness. It may not show the relative brightness of the image accurately under very low or very bright lighting conditions.

- **Some functions disabled.** Live View disables some Custom Function settings: C.Fn III-2, -3, -6 (Lens AF stop button function; AF point selection method; Mirror lockup); and C.Fn IV-1, -3 (Shutter button/AF-ON button; Assign Set button). In addition, if C.Fn II-4 (Auto Lighting Optimizer) is enabled, the image will look bright even if a negative EV value has been set.

- **Flash OK.** You can use flash when working with Live View, but the FE (flash exposure) Lock, modeling flash, and test firing of the flash are not possible. In addition, to change the Speedlite's own custom functions, you'll need to use the camera's menus in the Flash Control section of the Setup 2 menu. The flash's own Custom Function setting capability is disabled.

- **Watch for overheating.** Leaving Live View on for extended periods increases the temperature of the sensor, potentially causing noise or odd colors in your image. If you want to take a long exposure, turn off Live View for several minutes before shooting, to allow your sensor to cool. Live View will shut off automatically after 30 minutes.

- **Information display.** During Live View, useful information is shown on the screen, such as battery status, Picture Style, and most of the shooting information (shutter speed, f/stop, ISO setting, number of exposures remaining) you'd see through the viewfinder. Press the DISP button to change the amount of information shown.

Working with Live View

I'm going to go over each of the aspects of using Live View one at a time, because working with Live View is quite different from the routines you have become accustomed to with the T1i's conventional shooting modes. I'm going to cover viewing, shooting, and focusing separately.

Previewing and Making Settings

Once you've set up your camera to enable Live View, as described in the previous section, you're ready to begin using this feature. Set the T1i to one of the Creative Zone modes. Remember that Live View will not work with any of the Basic Zone modes, not even Creative Auto. Mount your camera on a tripod, if desired, and then press the Print/Share/Live View button, located just northwest of the up cross key. A reminder to press the AE Lock (*) button to activate autofocus appears briefly. Then, you're presented with a screen image like the one shown in Figure 5.13.

Not all the information shown in the figure will appear on the screen at the same time. You can adjust the amount of info by pressing the DISP button, exactly as you can with the Shooting Information screen, as explained in Chapter 2. As you press the DISP

Autofocus mode　Picture Style　White balance　Drive mode　Image quality　AF Points (Quick mode)　AF Point (Live mode)　Histogram

flash ready

Autoexposure bracketing

Flash exposure bracketing

Exposure simulation

Battery level

Shutter speed　f/stop　Autoexposure Lock indicator　Exposure level indicator Autoexposure bracketing range　Flash exposure compensation　Exposures remaining　ISO setting　Highlight tone priority

Figure 5.13
Some or all of this information can be displayed when you're using Live View.

button repeatedly, the Live View display cycles among no additional information (basically a blank screen with the Magnifying Frame and grid—if you've enabled it); a single line of data (shown at the bottom of the screen in the figure); a display with quick settings icons at the left; and an "all of the above" screen that adds an honest-to-gosh real-time histogram.

I recommend going for the minimalist display most of the time, or, if you can't live without basic data, the version with the line of data at the bottom of the screen. The icon overlays make it difficult to see your subject, and, in any case, you can summon the quick settings icons any time you want to make an adjustment by pressing the Set button. Here's a summary of what you can do with all this screen information. I'll start with the info that's overlaid on the image area of the screen. Seven of them are informational indicators showing the status of some feature:

- **Histogram.** Use this display to view the arrangement of tones in your image-to-be, and make exposure adjustments to compensate, as explained under the detailed histogram section at the end of Chapter 4.

- **AF point for contrast detect focusing.** A white vertically oriented rectangle appears when you're using AF Live autofocus. The area within the box is used to detect contrast when achieving sharp focus using contrast detection.

- **AF Points for phase detect focusing.** When you're using AF Quick, the AF point box changes to a horizontally oriented "magnifying frame" rectangle, and the nine focus points appear, enabling you to choose a focus point manually, as I will describe shortly.

- **AEB/FEB indicators.** These appear when you've activated the full screen of information and you are using automatic exposure bracketing and flash exposure bracketing, respectively.

- **Exposure simulation.** This indicator appears in three different forms: white, blinking, and gray. When shown in white, the Live View image brightness approximates what you'll get in the final image. Under very bright or very dim conditions, this indicator will blink, indicating that the Live View on the LCD may not closely represent the brightness of the picture you'll take. This indicator is shown in gray if you're using flash or the bulb (manually timed long exposure) setting as a reminder that the view on the LCD may not represent the exposure of the actual picture.

- **AE Lock indicator.** This icon appears on the full informational screen when you've locked exposure using the AE Lock button in the upper-right corner of the back of the camera.

- **Flash ready.** This icon appears when your camera's built-in flash is charged and ready to go.

Five of the icons represent settings you can change. They are:

- **AF mode.** Choose between AF Live; AF Face Detection Live; and AF Quick mode. I'll describe these in an upcoming section of this chapter.

- **Picture Style.** Choose from among Standard, Portrait, Landscape, Neutral, Faithful, Monochrome, User Def. 1, User Def. 2, or User Def. 3, as described in Chapter 3.

- **White Balance.** You can select from Auto, Daylight, Shade, Cloudy, Tungsten, White Fluorescent, Flash, or Custom white balances.

- **Drive mode.** Choose from Single Shooting, Continuous Shooting, Self-Timer/Remote control, and Self-Timer/2 seconds.

- **Image recording quality.** You select Large, Medium, and Small Resolution JPEG images, with either Fine or Standard compression, plus RAW or RAW+JPEG.

To change any of the five settings just described, and shown at the left side of the LCD, just follow these steps:

1. **Press the Set button.** The settings that can be modified will appear, with the last setting you adjusted highlighted in blue.

2. **Select setting.** Use the up/down cross keys to highlight the setting you want to change.

3. **Make an adjustment.** To modify a highlighted setting, rotate the Main dial until the option you want appears. A line of text appears at the bottom of the screen describing the currently selected option.

4. **Exit.** Press the Set button again to back out of the Quick Settings screen.

The strip along the bottom of the frame is purely an informational display. Left to right, it shows the currently set shutter speed; f/stop; an exposure scale that can also indicate the automatic exposure bracketing range; an indicator that shows when flash exposure compensation has been activated; the number of shots remaining; current ISO sensitivity setting; whether highlight tone priority has been activated; and a battery status check.

Many of these indicators duplicate what you see in the viewfinder when not using Live View. The most noticeable omission is the focus confirmation indictor that tells you when the image is in sharp focus.

Making Other Settings

Even while using Live View, you can still make other settings using the conventional menu system (press the Menu button), or even review images you've already taken using the Playback button. Exit either of these modes when finished, and you'll be returned to Live View. However, if you select Dust Delete Data from the Shooting 2 menu, Sensor Cleaning from the Setup 2 menu, or either Clear Settings or Firmware Ver. From the Setup 3 menu, Live View will be aborted, and the T1i will return to normal operation.

Focusing in Live View

Press the AE Lock button to activate autofocus using the currently set Live View autofocus mode. Those modes are Quick mode, Live mode, and Live "Face Detection" mode. You can also use Manual focus. I'll describe each of these separately.

Quick Mode

This mode uses phase detection, as described earlier in the chapter. It temporarily interrupts Live View mode to allow the Rebel T1i to focus the same AF sensor used when you focus through the viewfinder. Because the step takes a second or so, you may get better results using this autofocus mode when the camera is mounted on a tripod. If you handhold the T1i, you may displace the point of focus achieved by the autofocus system. It also simplifies the operation if you use One Shot focus and center the focus point. You can use AI-Servo and Automatic or Manual focus point selection, but if the focus point doesn't coincide with the subject you want to focus on, you'll end up with an out-of-focus image. Just follow these steps.

1. **Set lens to Autofocus.** Make sure the focus switch on the lens is set to AF.

2. **Activate Live View.** Press the Live View button.

3. **Choose AF Quick mode.** Press the Set button, then use the cross keys to highlight the AF icon at the top of the left-hand column on the screen. Press Set again, then rotate the Main dial until AF Quick is displayed in blue as the current autofocus mode. (If the camera has already been set for AF Quick mode, you won't need to change the focus mode setting.)

OR CHOOSE FOCUS MODE IN MENU

You can also select the Live View focus mode using the Live View function settings option in the Setup 2 menu.

4. **Choose AF point.** With the nine focus points illuminated, rotate the Main dial to choose which of the nine AF points to use. They turn blue on the screen when active.

5. **Select subject.** Compose the image on the LCD so the selected focus point is on the subject.

6. **Press and hold the AE Lock button.** The LCD will blank as the mirror flips down, reflecting the view of the subject to the phase detection AF sensor.

7. **Wait for focus.** When the T1i is able to lock in focus using phase detection, a beep will sound. If you are handholding the T1i, you may hear several beeps as the AF system focuses and refocuses with each camera movement. Then, the mirror will flip back up, and the Live View image reappears. The AF focus point will be highlighted in red on the LCD.

8. **Take picture.** Press the shutter release to take the picture. (You can't take a photo while Quick mode AF is in process, until the mirror flips back up.)

Live Mode

This mode uses contrast detection, using the relative sharpness of the image as it appears on the sensor to determine focus. This method is less precise, and usually takes longer than Quick mode. To Autofocus using Live mode, follow these steps:

1. **Set lens to Autofocus.** Make sure the focus switch on the lens is set to AF.

2. **Activate Live View.** Press the Set button and choose Live mode with the Main dial as outlined above.

3. **Choose AF point.** Use the cross keys to move the AF point box (shown as a vertically oriented rectangle) anywhere you like on the screen, except for the edges. Press the Trash button to return the AF point to the center of the screen.

4. **Select subject.** Compose the image on the LCD so the selected focus point is on the subject.

5. **Press and hold the AE Lock button.** When focus is achieved, the AF point turns green, and you'll hear a beep. If the T1i is unable to focus, the AF point turns red instead.

6. **Take picture.** Press the shutter release to take the picture.

Live (Face Detection) Mode

This mode also uses contrast detection, using the relative sharpness of the image as it appears on the sensor to determine focus. The T1i will search the frame for a human face and attempt to focus on the face. Like Live Mode, this method is less precise, and usually takes longer than Quick mode. To Autofocus using Live (Face Detection) mode, follow these steps:

1. **Set lens to Autofocus.** Make sure the focus switch on the lens is set to AF.

2. **Activate Live View.** Press the Set button and choose Live (Face Detection) mode with the Main dial.

3. **Face detection.** A frame will appear around a face found in the image. (See Figure 5.14.) If more than one face is found, a frame with "ears" (actually left/right pointing triangles) appears. In that case, use the cross keys to move the frame to the face you want to use for focus. If no face is detected, the AF point will be locked into the center.

Figure 5.14
In Face Detection mode, the T1i can locate human faces and focus on them.

4. **Troubleshoot (if necessary).** If you experience problems in Face Detection mode, press down on the Set button and switch to standard Live mode. Face Detection is far from perfect. The AF system may fail to find a face if the person's visage is too large/small or light/dark in the frame, tilted, or located near an edge of the picture. You can press the Trash button to switch from Live (Face Detection) mode to standard Live AF mode. If you like, you can press the Trash button once more to switch back to Live (Face Detection) mode and try again.

5. **Press and hold the AE Lock button.** When focus is achieved, the AF point turns green, and you'll hear a beep. If the T1i is unable to focus, the AF point turns red instead.

6. **Take picture.** Press the shutter release to take the picture.

Manual Mode

Focusing manually on an LCD screen isn't as difficult as you might think, but Canon has made the process even easier by providing a magnified view. Just follow these steps to focus manually.

1. **Set lens to Manual focus.** Make sure the focus switch on the lens is set to MF.

2. **Move magnifying frame.** Use the cross keys to move the focus frame that's superimposed on the screen to the location where you want to focus. You can press the Trash button to center the focus frame in the middle of the screen.

3. **Press the Zoom button.** The area of the image inside the focus frame will be magnified 5X. (See Figure 5.15.) Press the Zoom button (at the top-right corner of the back of the camera) again to increase the magnification to 10X. A third press will return you to the full-frame view. The enlarged area is artificially sharpened to make it easier for you to see the contrast changes, and simplify focusing. When zoomed in, the current shutter speed and aperture are shown in orange-red.

4. **Focus manually.** Use the focus ring on the lens to focus the image. When you're satisfied, you can zoom back out by pressing the Zoom button.

Figure 5.15
You can manually focus the center area, which can be zoomed in 5X or 10X.

Shooting Movies

The Canon EOS Rebel T1i can shoot full HDTV movies with monaural sound at 1920 × 1080 resolution. In some ways, the camera's movie mode is closely related to the T1i's Live View still mode. In fact, the T1i uses Live View type imaging to show you the video clip on the LCD as it is captured. Many of the functions and setting options are the same, so the information in the previous sections will serve you well as you branch out into shooting movies with your camera.

You'll want to keep the following things in mind before you start:

- **Choose your resolution.** The T1i can capture movies in Full High Definition (1920 × 1080 pixel) resolution, but at a slower frame rate of 20 fps. If you want to capture at the video standard of 30 fps, you must use High Definition (1280 × 720) or Standard Definition (640 × 480) resolution. I'll show you how to specify resolution in the next section.

- **You can still shoot stills.** Press the shutter release all the way down at any time while filming movies in order to capture a still photo. The T1i will use the Image Quality settings you specify in the Shooting 1 menu, operate only in Single-Shot drive mode (continuous shooting or self-timer delays are not possible), and flash is disabled. You can also extract a 2MP, 1MP, or .3MP image from your movie clips using ZoomBrowser. Still photos are stored as separate files.

- **Use the right card.** You'll want to use an SD Class 6 memory card or better to store your clips; slower cards may not work properly. Chose a memory card with at least 4GB capacity (8GB or 16GB are even better). If the card you are working with is too slow, a five-level thermometer-like "buffer" indicator may appear at the right side of the LCD, showing the status of your camera's internal memory. If the indicator reaches the top level because the buffer is full, movie shooting will stop automatically.

- **Use a fully charged battery.** Canon says that a fresh battery will allow about one hour of filming at normal (non-Winter) temperatures.

MOVIE TIME

I've standardized on 16GB SDHC cards when I'm shooting movies; these cards will give you 49 minutes of recording at 1920 × 1080 Full HD resolution. (Figure 330MB per minute of capture.) A 4GB card, in contrast, offers just 12 minutes of shooting at the Full HD setting.

Movie Settings

The Movie Settings menu, shown in Figure 5.16, can be summoned by the Menu button only when the T1i has been set to Movie mode (turn the Mode dial as far as it will go in the clockwise direction). There are six settings available:

- **Grid display (Off, Grid 1, Grid 2).** Overlays Grid 1, a "rule of thirds" grid on the screen to help you compose your image and align vertical and horizontal lines; or Grid 2, which consists of four rows of six boxes, which allow finer control over placement of images in your frame.

- **Metering timer (4 sec. to 30 min).** This option allows you to specify how long the Rebel T1i's metering system will remain active when the ISO button is pressed before switching off.

- **Movie recording size.** Choose 1920 × 1080 (Full HD), 1280 × 720 (HD), or 640 × 480 pixel (Standard) resolutions.

- **Autofocus mode (Quick mode, Live mode, Live "Face Detection" mode).** This option, explained earlier in the Live View section, lets you choose between phase detection, contrast detection, and contrast detection with "face" recognition.

Figure 5.16
The Movie Settings menu has six entries.

Grid display	Off
Metering timer	4 sec.
Movie rec. size	1920 x 1080
AF mode	Live mode
Sound recording	On
Remote control	Disable

- **Sound recording.** Set to On to record audio with your video clips; choose Off when you want to record silent movies (especially if you plan to add your own narration or music track(s) later on).

- **Remote control.** Use this setting to enable/disable use of an optional RC-1 or RC-5 remote control device (which plugs into the Remote Control Terminal under the rubber cover on the left edge of the camera) while using Movie mode. The remote can be used to stop and start recording, or to take a still photo during movie shooting.

Capturing Video/Sound

To shoot movies with your camera, just follow these steps:

1. **Change to Movie mode.** Set the Mode dial to the Movie setting (turn the dial as far as it will go in a clockwise direction).

2. **Focus.** Use the autofocus or manual focus techniques described in the preceding sections to achieve focus on your subject. As before, you can activate the current AF mode by pressing the AE Lock button.

3. **Begin filming.** Press the Print/Share/Live View button to begin shooting. A red dot appears in the upper-right corner of the screen to show that video/sound are being captured. The access lamp also flashes during shooting.

4. **Lock exposure.** You can lock in exposure by pressing the ISO button on top of the T1i, located just aft of the Main dial. Unlock exposure again by pressing the ISO button once more.

5. **Stop filming.** Press the Print/Share/Live View button again to stop filming.

6. **View your clip.** Press the Playback button (located to the bottom right of the LCD). You will see a still frame with the clip timing and a symbol telling you to press the Set button to see the clip. A series of video controls appear at the bottom of the frame. Press Set again and the clip begins. A blue thermometer bar progresses in the upper-left corner as the timing counts down. Press Set to stop at any time.

GETTING INFO

The information display shown on the LCD screen when shooting movies is almost identical to the one displayed during Live View shooting. (See Figure 5.13 for reference.) The settings icons in the left column show the same options, which can be changed in Movie mode, too, except that the Drive mode choice is replaced by an indicator that shows the current movie resolution and time remaining on your memory card.

Continuous Shooting

The Canon EOS Rebel T1i's pair of Continuous Shooting modes remind me how far digital photography has brought us. The first accessory I purchased when I worked as a sports photographer some years ago was a motor drive for my film SLR. It enabled me to snap off a series of shots in rapid succession, which came in very handy when a full-back broke through the line and headed for the end zone. Even a seasoned action photographer can miss the decisive instant when a crucial block is made, or a baseball superstar's bat shatters and pieces of cork fly out. Continuous shooting simplifies taking a series of pictures, either to ensure that one has more or less the exact moment you want to capture or to capture a sequence that is interesting as a collection of successive images.

The T1i's "motor drive" capabilities are, in many ways, much superior to what you get with a film camera. For one thing, a motor-driven film camera can eat up film at an incredible pace, which is why many of them are used with cassettes that hold hundreds of feet of film stock. At three frames per second (typical of film cameras), a short burst of a few seconds can burn up as much as half of an ordinary 36-exposure roll of film. Digital cameras, in contrast, have reusable "film," so if you waste a few dozen shots on non-decisive moments, you can erase them and shoot more. Save only the best shots, like the series shown in Figure 5.17.

To use the T1i's Continuous Shooting modes, press the Drive button (the left cross key). Spin the Main dial until the Continuous Shooting (3.4 frames per second) icon is highlighted. Then, press Set. When you partially depress the shutter button, the viewfinder will display a number representing the maximum number of shots you can take at the current quality settings. (If your battery is low, this figure will be lower.) The larger buffer in the T1i will generally allow you to take as many as 170 JPEG shots in a single burst, 9 RAW photos, or 4 RAW+JPEG images.

To increase this number, reduce the image-quality setting by switching to JPEG only (from JPEG+RAW), to a lower JPEG quality setting, or by reducing the T1i's resolution from L to M or S. The reason the size of your bursts is limited is that continuous images are first shuttled into the T1i's internal memory buffer, then doled out to the Secure Digital card as quickly as they can be written to the card. Technically, the T1i takes the RAW data received from the digital image processor and converts it to the output format you've selected—either .JPG or .CR2 (RAW)—and deposits it in the buffer ready to store on the card.

This internal "smart" buffer can suck up photos much more quickly than the SD card and, indeed, some memory cards are significantly faster or slower than others. When the buffer fills, you can't take any more continuous shots (a buSY indicator appears in the viewfinder and LCD status panel) until the T1i has written some of them to the card, making more room in the buffer. (You should keep in mind that faster memory cards write images more quickly, freeing up buffer space faster.)

Figure 5.17 Continuous shooting allows you to capture an entire sequence of exciting moments as they unfold.

More Exposure Options

In Chapter 4, you learned techniques for getting the *right* exposure, but I haven't explained all your exposure options just yet. You'll want to know about the *kind* of exposure settings that are available to you with the Canon EOS Rebel T1i. There are options that let you control when the exposure is made, or even how to make an exposure that's out of the ordinary in terms of length (time or bulb exposures). The sections that follow explain your camera's special exposure features, and even discuss a few it does not have (and why it doesn't).

A Tiny Slice of Time

Exposures that seem impossibly brief can reveal a world we didn't know existed. In the 1930s, Dr. Harold Edgerton, a professor of electrical engineering at MIT, pioneered high-speed photography using a repeating electronic flash unit he patented called the *stroboscope.* As the inventor of the electronic flash, he popularized its use to freeze objects in motion, and you've probably seen his photographs of bullets piercing balloons and drops of milk forming a coronet-shaped splash.

Electronic flash freezes action by virtue of its extremely short duration—as brief as 1/50,000th second or less. Although the Rebel T1i's built-in flash unit can give you these ultra-quick glimpses of moving subjects, an external flash, such as one of the Canon Speedlites, offers even more versatility. You can read more about using electronic flash to stop action in Chapter 7.

Of course, the T1i is fully capable of immobilizing all but the fastest movement using only its shutter speeds, which range all the way up to a speedy 1/4,000th second. Indeed, you'll rarely have need for such a brief shutter speed in ordinary shooting. If you wanted to use an aperture of f/1.8 at ISO 100 outdoors in bright sunlight, for some reason, a shutter speed of 1/4,000th second would more than do the job. You'd need a faster shutter speed only if you moved the ISO setting to a higher sensitivity (but why would you do that?). Under less than full sunlight, 1/4,000th second is more than fast enough for any conditions you're likely to encounter.

Most sports action can be frozen at 1/2,000th second or slower, and for many sports a slower shutter speed is actually preferable—for example, to allow the wheels of a racing automobile or motorcycle, or the propeller on a classic aircraft to blur realistically. But if you want to do some exotic action-freezing photography without resorting to electronic flash, the T1i's top shutter speed is at your disposal. Here are some things to think about when exploring this type of high-speed photography:

- **You'll need a lot of light.** High shutter speeds cut very fine slices of time and sharply reduce the amount of illumination that reaches your sensor. To use 1/4,000th second at an aperture of f/6.3, you'd need an ISO setting of 1,600—even in full daylight. To use an f/stop smaller than f/6.3 or an ISO setting lower than 1,600, you'd need *more* light than full daylight provides. (That's why electronic flash units work so well for high-speed photography when used as the sole illumination; they provide both the effect of a brief shutter speed and the high levels of illumination needed.)

- **Forget about reciprocity failure.** If you're an old-time film shooter, you might recall that very brief shutter speeds (as well as very high light levels and very *long* exposures) produced an effect called *reciprocity failure,* in which given exposures ended up providing less than the calculated value because of the way film responded to very short, very intense, or very long exposures of light. Solid-state sensors don't suffer from this defect, so you don't need to make an adjustment when using high shutter speeds (or brief flash bursts).

- **No elongation effect.** This is another old bugaboo that has largely been solved through modern technology, but I wanted to bring it to your attention anyway.

In olden times, cameras used shutters that traveled horizontally. To achieve faster shutter speeds, focal plane shutters (located just in front of the plane of the sensor) opened only a smaller-than-frame-sized slit so that, even though the shutter is already traveling at its highest rate of speed, the film/sensor is exposed for a briefer period of time as the slit moves across the surface. At very short shutter speeds, and with subjects moving horizontally at very fast velocities, it was possible for the subject to partially "keep up" with the shutter if it were traveling in the same direction as the slit, producing an elongated effect. Conversely, subjects moving in the opposite direction of shutter motion could be compressed. Today, shutters like those in the T1i move vertically and at a higher maximum rate of speed. So, unless you're photographing a rocket blasting into space, and holding the camera horizontally to boot (or shooting a racing car in vertical orientation), it's almost impossible to produce unwanted elongation/compression.

- **Don't combine high shutter speeds with electronic flash.** You might be tempted to use an electronic flash with a high shutter speed. Perhaps you want to stop some action in daylight with a brief shutter speed and use electronic flash only as supplemental illumination to fill in the shadows. Unfortunately, under most conditions you can't use flash in subdued illumination with your T1i at any shutter speed faster than 1/200th second. That's the fastest speed at which the camera's focal plane shutter is fully open: at shorter speeds, the "slit" described above comes into play, so that the flash will expose only the small portion of the sensor exposed by the slit during its duration. (Check out "High Speed Sync" in Chapter 7 if you want to see how you *can* use shutter speeds shorter than 1/250th second with certain Canon Speedlites, albeit at much-reduced effective power levels.)

Working with Short Exposures

You can have a lot of fun exploring the kinds of pictures you can take using very brief exposure times, whether you decide to take advantage of the action-stopping capabilities of your built-in or external electronic flash or work with the Canon EOS Rebel T1i's faster shutter speeds. Here are a few ideas to get you started:

- **Take revealing images.** Fast shutter speeds can help you reveal the real subject behind the façade, by freezing constant motion to capture an enlightening moment in time. Legendary fashion/portrait photographer Philippe Halsman used leaping photos of famous people, such as the Duke and Duchess of Windsor, Richard Nixon, and Salvador Dali to illuminate their real selves. Halsman said, "*When you ask a person to jump, his attention is mostly directed toward the act of jumping and the mask falls so that the real person appears.*" Try some high-speed portraits of people you know in motion to see how they appear when concentrating on something other than the portrait.

■ **Create unreal images.** High-speed photography can also produce photographs that show your subjects in ways that are quite unreal. A helicopter in mid-air with its rotors frozen or a motocross cyclist leaping over a ramp, but with all motion stopped so that the rider and machine look as if they were frozen in mid-air, make for an unusual picture. The college football players never stopped to pose for the tableaux you see in Figure 5.18, but a fast shutter speed froze them in place.

Figure 5.18
A football moment frozen in time captures a confrontation that actually lasted only a few seconds.

■ **Capture unseen perspectives.** Some things are *never* seen in real life, except when viewed in a stop-action photograph. MIT professor Dr. Harold Edgerton's often-seen balloon bursts were only a starting point. Freeze a hummingbird in flight for a view of wings that never seem to stop. Or, capture the splashes as liquid falls into a bowl, as shown in Figure 5.19. No electronic flash was required for this image (and wouldn't have illuminated the water in the bowl as evenly). Instead, a clutch of high intensity lamps and an ISO setting of 1,600 allowed the Rebel T1i to capture this image at 1/2,000th second.

Figure 5.19
A large amount of artificial illumination and an ISO 1,600 sensitivity setting allowed capturing this shot at 1/2,000th second without use of an electronic flash.

■ **Vanquish camera shake and gain new angles.** Here's an idea that's so obvious it isn't always explored to its fullest extent. A high enough shutter speed can free you from the tyranny of a tripod, making it easier to capture new angles, or to shoot quickly while moving around, especially with longer lenses. I tend to use a monopod or tripod for almost everything when I'm not using an image-stabilized lens, and I end up missing some shots because of a reluctance to adjust my camera support to get a higher, lower, or different angle. If you have enough light and can use an f/stop wide enough to permit a high shutter speed, you'll find a new freedom to choose your shots. I have a favored 170mm-500mm lens that I use for sports and wildlife photography, almost invariably with a tripod, as I don't find the "reciprocal of the focal length" rule particularly helpful in most cases. (I would *not* handhold this hefty lens at its 500mm setting with a 1/500th second shutter speed under most circumstances.) However, at 1/2,000th second or faster, it's entirely possible for a steady hand to use this lens without a tripod or monopod's extra support, and I've found that my whole approach to shooting animals and other elusive subjects changes in high-speed mode. Selective focus allows dramatically isolating my prey wide open at f/6.3, too.

Long Exposures

Longer exposures are a doorway into another world, showing us how even familiar scenes can look much different when photographed over periods measured in seconds. At night, long exposures produce streaks of light from moving, illuminated subjects like automobiles or amusement park rides. Extra-long exposures of seemingly pitch-dark subjects can reveal interesting views using light levels barely bright enough to see by. At any time of day, including daytime (in which case you'll often need the help of neutral density filters to make the long exposure practical), long exposures can cause moving objects to vanish entirely, because they don't remain stationary long enough to register in a photograph.

Three Ways to Take Long Exposures

There are actually three common types of lengthy exposures: *timed exposures, bulb exposures,* and *time exposures.* The Rebel T1i offers only the first two, but once you understand all three, you'll see why Canon made the choices it did. Because of the length of the exposure, all of the following techniques should be used with a tripod to hold the camera steady.

- **Timed exposures.** These are long exposures from 1 second to 30 seconds, measured by the camera itself. To take a picture in this range, simply use Manual or Tv modes and use the Main dial to set the shutter speed to the length of time you want, choosing from preset speeds of 1.0, 1.5, 2.0, 3.0, 4.0, 6.0, 8.0, 10.0, 15.0, 20.0, or 30.0 seconds (if you've specified 1/2 stop increments for exposure adjustments), or 1.0, 1.3, 1.6, 2.0, 2.5, 3.2, 4.0, 5.0, 6.0, 8.0, 10.0, 13.0, 15.0, 20.0, 25.0, and 30.0 seconds (if you're using 1/3 stop increments). The advantage of timed exposures is that the camera does all the calculating for you. There's no need for a stopwatch. If you review your image on the LCD and decide to try again with the exposure doubled or halved, you can dial in the correct exposure with precision. The disadvantage of timed exposures is that you can't take a photo for longer than 30 seconds.

- **Bulb exposures.** This type of exposure is so-called because in the olden days the photographer squeezed and held an air bulb attached to a tube that provided the force necessary to keep the shutter open. Traditionally, a bulb exposure is one that lasts as long as the shutter release button is pressed; when you release the button, the exposure ends. To make a bulb exposure with the T1i, set the camera on Manual mode and use the Main dial to select the shutter speed immediately after 30 seconds—buLB. Then, press the shutter to start the exposure, and press it again to close the shutter. If you'd like to simulate a time exposure (described below), you can use the Canon remote controls that attach to the terminal on the left side of the camera under the rubber cover. If you are able to link your camera to a computer, the EOS Utility allows taking long exposures up to 99 minutes and 59 seconds.

■ **Time exposures.** This is a setting found on some cameras to produce longer exposures. With cameras that implement this option, the shutter opens when you press the shutter release button, and remains open until you press the button again. Usually, you'll be able to close the shutter using a mechanical cable release or, more commonly, an electronic release cable. The advantage of this approach is that you can take an exposure of virtually any duration without the need for special equipment (the tethered release is optional). You can press the shutter release button, go off for a few minutes, and come back to close the shutter (assuming your camera is still there). The disadvantages of this mode are exposures must be timed manually, and with shorter exposures it's possible for the vibration of manually opening and closing the shutter to register in the photo. For longer exposures, the period of vibration is relatively brief and not usually a problem—and there is always the release cable option to eliminate photographer-caused camera shake entirely. While the T1i does not have a built-in time exposure capability, you can simulate it with the bulb exposure technique, described previously.

WATCH OUT FOR AMP NOISE

When exposures extend past 30 seconds into the realm of several minutes—or more—all digital cameras are theoretically susceptible to a phenomenon called *amp noise*, which manifests itself as a purplish glow, often around the edges of an image, creating an aurora borealis-style ghost effect. Amp noise happens when the sensor heats up during a long exposure, and some cameras fall victim more readily than others. The Rebel T1i resists this phenomenon better than most dSLRs, but you should be aware it exists, even if you'd need to use an outlandish exposure (on the order of 30 minutes or so) to create the effect with your camera.

Working with Long Exposures

Because the Rebel T1i produces such good images at longer exposures, and there are so many creative things you can do with long-exposure techniques, you'll want to do some experimenting. Get yourself a tripod or another firm support and take some test shots with long exposure noise reduction both enabled and disabled (to see whether you prefer low noise or high detail) and get started. Here are some things to try:

■ **Make people invisible.** One very cool thing about long exposures is that objects that move rapidly enough won't register at all in a photograph, while the subjects that remain stationary are portrayed in the normal way. That makes it easy to produce people-free landscape photos and architectural photos at night or, even, in full daylight if you use a neutral density filter (or two or three) to allow an exposure of at least a few seconds. At ISO 100, f/22, and a pair of 8X (three-stop) neutral density filters you can use exposures of nearly two seconds; overcast days and/or even more neutral density filtration would work even better if daylight people-vanishing is your goal. They'll have to be walking *very* briskly and across the field of view (rather than directly toward the camera) for this to work. At night, it's much easier to achieve this effect with the 20- to 30-second exposures that are possible, as you can see in Figures 5.20 and 5.21.

Figure 5.20 This alleyway is thronged with people, as you can see in this two-second exposure using only the available illumination.

Figure 5.21 With the camera still on a tripod, a 30-second exposure rendered the passersby almost invisible.

- **Create streaks.** If you aren't shooting for total invisibility, long exposures with the camera on a tripod can produce some interesting streaky effects, as shown in Figure 5.22. You don't need to limit yourself to indoor photography, however. Even a single 8X ND filter will let you shoot at f/22 and 1/6th second in full daylight.

- **Produce light trails.** At night, car headlights and taillights and other moving sources of illumination can generate interesting light trails. Your camera doesn't even need to be mounted on a tripod; handholding the T1i for longer exposures adds movement and patterns to your trails. If you're shooting fireworks, a longer exposure may allow you to combine several bursts into one picture, as shown in Figure 5.23.

- **Blur waterfalls, etc.** You'll find that waterfalls and other sources of moving liquid produce a special type of long-exposure blur, because the water merges into a fantasy-like veil that looks different at different exposure times, and with different waterfalls. Cascades with turbulent flow produce a rougher look at a given longer exposure than falls that flow smoothly. Although blurred waterfalls have become almost a cliché, there are still plenty of variations for a creative photographer to explore, as you can see in Figure 5.24.

Figure 5.22
This Korean dancer produced a swirl of color as she spun during the 1/4 second exposure.

Figure 5.23
A long exposure allows capturing several bursts of fireworks in one image.

Figure 5.24 A 1/4-second exposure blurred the falling water, as the cooperative bird remained still.

■ **Show total darkness in new ways.** Even on the darkest, moonless nights, there is enough starlight or glow from distant illumination sources to see by, and, if you use a long exposure, there is enough light to take a picture, too. I was visiting a lakeside park after dark and saw that the dim light from the lamps in the parking lot provided sufficient light to see a distant stand of trees. A 30-second exposure with the lens almost wide open revealed the scene shown in Figure 5.25, even though in real life, there was barely enough light to make out the closest tree. Although the photo appears as if it were taken at twilight or sunset, in fact the shot was made at 11 p.m. It was a new moon that night, so the main illumination was starlight, spill light from the parking lot, and a distant city (which added a sunset-like effect to the sky at the horizon that shows at the far side of the lake).

Figure 5.25 A 30-second exposure on a dark night revealed this lakeside setting, illuminated only by starlight, spill light from a parking lot adjacent to the shore, and distant city lights.

Delayed Exposures

Sometimes it's desirable to have a delay of some sort before a picture is actually taken. Perhaps you'd like to get in the picture yourself, and would appreciate it if the camera waited 10 seconds after you press the shutter release to actually take the picture. Maybe you want to give a tripod-mounted camera time to settle down and damp any residual vibration after the release is pressed to improve sharpness for an exposure with a relatively slow shutter speed. It's possible you want to explore the world of time-lapse photography. The next sections present your delayed exposure options.

Self-Timer

The Rebel T1i has a built-in self-timer with 10-second and 2-second delays. (Remember that the 10-second timer can also be used with a remote control and is marked with a "remote" icon in the Drive mode screen.) Your camera also has a self-timer/multiple setting that allows taking 2 to 10 shots after the delay. All these options were described in Chapter 2.

Activate the timer by pressing the Drive button (left cross key) and pressing the left/right cross keys to choose one of the three self-timer icons. Press the Set button to confirm your choice. Then, press the shutter release button halfway to lock in focus on your subjects (if you're taking a self-portrait, focus on an object at a similar distance and use focus lock). When you're ready to take the photo, continue pressing the shutter release the rest of the way. The lamp on the front of the camera will blink slowly for eight seconds (when using the 10-second timer) and the beeper will chirp (if you haven't disabled it in the Shooting 1 menu, as described in Chapter 3). During the final two seconds, the beeper sounds more rapidly and the lamp remains on until the picture is taken. The LCD displays a countdown in the lower-right corner of the screen while all this is going on.

Another way to use the self-timer is with the mirror lockup feature (C.Fn III-09). This is something you might want to do if you're shooting close-ups, landscapes, or other types of pictures using the self-timer only to trip the shutter in the most vibration-free way possible. Forget to bring along your tripod, but still want to take a close-up picture with a precise focus setting? Set your digital camera to the self-timer function, then put the camera on any reasonably steady support, such as a fence post or a rock. When you're ready to take the picture, press the shutter release. The camera might totter back and forth for a second or two, but it will settle back to its original position before the self-timer activates the shutter. The self-timer remains active until you turn it off—even if you power down the T1i.

Remote Control

As outlined in the "Bulb Exposure" description earlier, your Canon EOS Rebel T1i can be triggered using a plug-in remote control with an electronic or infrared connection. For example, the Remote Switch RS-80N3 allows triggering a camera attached to the end of its cable. More versatile is the Canon TC-80N3, a remote switch with a 2.6-foot cord (you can add a 33-foot extension cable) and includes a more flexible self-timer that can be set to trip the camera after a delay of anywhere from 1 second to 99 hours, 59 minutes, and 59 seconds (in other words, one second less than 100 hours). It has an LCD display that makes it easy to make and view settings.

Time-Lapse/Interval Photography

Who hasn't marveled at a time-lapse photograph of a flower opening, a series of shots of the moon marching across the sky, or one of those extreme time-lapse picture sets showing something that takes a very, very long time, such as a building under construction.

You probably won't be shooting such construction shots, unless you have a spare T1i you don't need for a few months (or are willing to go through the rigmarole of figuring out how to set up your camera in precisely the same position using the same lens settings to shoot a series of pictures at intervals). However, other kinds of time-lapse photography are entirely within reach.

Although the Rebel T1i can't take time-lapse/interval photographs all by itself, if you're willing to tether the camera to a computer (a laptop will do) using the USB cable, you can take time-lapse photos using the EOS Utility software furnished with your camera. (See Figure 5.26.) For example, you can set the self-timer for a specific period of time, then take a specified number of exposures at one-second intervals. Or, you can set a delay period that must elapse before the T1i begins a long exposure. Finally, you can choose to shoot a set number of pictures at intervals from 1 second to 99 hours, 59 minutes, and 59 seconds.

Figure 5.26
The EOS Utility can control time-lapse photography with a tethered camera.

Timer shooting settings

Keep the following for prolonged shooting using interval timer shooting.
Use household AC outlets for the camera and PC. Release the PC's power-saving function.

Delay setting
  Delay time (00:00 - 99:59)   00 : 10

☑ Interval timer shooting
  Shooting interval (00:05 - 99:59)   02 : 10

  Shots (minimum 2)   10

Bulb Shooting
  Exposure time (00:05 - 99:59)   00 : 05

Start   Cancel

If you want freedom to shoot anywhere, Opteka (www.opteka.com) offers a reasonably affordable add-on (around $100) with much more than the self-timer and remote control features mentioned previously. In fact, it has several different modes with an interesting array of delay/interval combinations for time-lapse photography and interval shooting. For example, you can set a delay period that must elapse before the T1i begins an exposure. Or, you can choose to shoot a set number of pictures at intervals from 1 second to 99 hours, 59 minutes, and 59 seconds. Canon offers a similar controller for other cameras in its line (the TC-80N3), so until an equivalent model becomes available for the T1i, the Opteka device is your best option.

Here are some tips for effective time-lapse photography:

- **Use AC power.** If you're shooting a long sequence, consider connecting your camera to an AC adapter, as leaving the T1i on for long periods of time will rapidly deplete the battery. Use the Canon AC Adapter kit ACK-E5, which consists of the Compact Power Adapter CA-PS700 and the DC Coupler DR-E5.

- **Make sure you have enough storage space.** Unless your memory card has enough capacity to hold all the images you'll be taking, you might want to change to a higher compression rate or reduced resolution to maximize the image count.

- **Make a movie.** While time-lapse stills are interesting, you can increase your fun factor by compiling all your shots into a motion picture using your favorite desktop movie-making software.

- **Protect your camera.** If your camera will be set up for an extended period of time (longer than an hour or two), make sure it's protected from weather, earthquakes, animals, young children, innocent bystanders, and theft.

- **Vary intervals.** Experiment with different time intervals. You don't want to take pictures too often or less often than necessary to capture the changes you hope to image.

Working with Lenses

In April 2008, Canon announced that it had produced its 40 millionth EF-series lens, a mere 21 years after the company's current autofocus mount was introduced (back in the film era). Considering that it took 11 years for Canon to sell its first 10 million copies of its EF lens line, but only two years and three months to peddle its most recent 10 million lenses, it's easy to see that the digital photography revolution can take credit for the most recent explosion.

With more than five dozen lenses in its current lineup, Canon is catering to the wide-ranging needs of a broad user base, from novice photo enthusiasts to advanced amateur and professional photographers. It's this mind-bending assortment of high quality lenses available to enhance the capabilities of cameras like the Canon EOS Rebel T1i. Thousands of current and older lenses introduced by Canon and third-party vendors since 1987 can be used to give you a wider view, bring distant subjects closer, let you focus closer, shoot under lower light conditions, or provide a more detailed, sharper image for critical work. Other than the sensor itself, the lens you choose for your dSLR is the most important component in determining image quality and perspective of your images.

This chapter explains how to select the best lenses for the kinds of photography you want to do.

But Don't Forget the Crop Factor

From time to time you've heard the term *crop factor*, and you've probably also heard the term *lens multiplier factor*. Both are misleading and inaccurate terms used to describe the same phenomenon: the fact that cameras like the Rebel T1i (and most other affordable digital SLRs) provide a field of view that's smaller and narrower than that produced by certain other (usually much more expensive) cameras, when fitted with exactly the same lens.

Figure 6.1 quite clearly shows the phenomenon at work. The outer rectangle, marked 1X, shows the field of view you might expect with a 28mm lens mounted on a Canon 5D Mark II camera, a so-called "full-frame" model. The rectangle marked 1.3X shows the effective field of view from the same vantage point with the exact same lens mounted on a Canon 1D Mark III camera, while the area marked 1.6X shows the field of view you'd get with that 28mm lens installed on a Rebel T1i. It's easy to see from the illustration that the 1X rendition provides a wider, more expansive view, while the other two are, in comparison, *cropped*.

The cropping effect is produced because the sensors of the latter two cameras are smaller than the sensors of the 1Ds Mark III. The "full-frame" camera has a sensor that's the size of the standard 35mm film frame, 24mm × 36mm. Your Rebel T1i's sensor does *not* measure 24mm × 36mm; instead, it specs out at 22.2mm × 14.8mm, or about 62.5 percent of the area of a full-frame sensor, as shown by the yellow boxes in the figure. You can calculate the relative field of view by dividing the focal length of the lens by .625. Thus, a 100mm lens mounted on a Rebel T1i has the same field of view as a

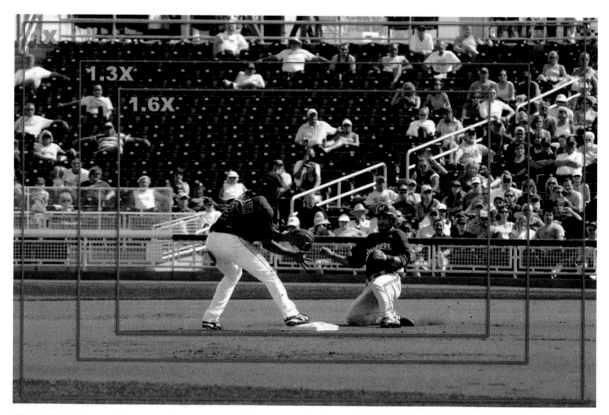

Figure 6.1 Canon offers digital SLRs with full-frame (1X) crops, as well as 1.3X and 1.6X crops.

160mm lens on the 1Ds Mark III. We humans tend to perform multiplication operations in our heads more easily than division, so such field of view comparisons are usually calculated using the reciprocal of .625—1.6—so we can multiply instead. (100 / .625=160; 100 × 1.6=160.)

This translation is generally useful only if you're accustomed to using full-frame cameras (usually of the film variety) and want to know how a familiar lens will perform on a digital camera. I strongly prefer *crop factor* over *lens multiplier*, because nothing is being multiplied; a 100mm lens doesn't "become" a 160mm lens—the depth-of-field and lens aperture remain the same. (I'll explain more about these later in this chapter.) Only the field of view is cropped. But *crop factor* isn't much better, as it implies that the 24 × 36mm frame is "full" and anything else is "less." I get e-mails all the time from photographers who point out that they own full-frame cameras with 36mm × 48mm sensors (like the Mamiya 645ZD or Hasselblad H3D-39 medium format digitals). By their reckoning, the "half-size" sensors found in cameras like the 1Ds Mark III are "cropped."

If you're accustomed to using full-frame film cameras, you might find it helpful to use the crop factor "multiplier" to translate a lens's real focal length into the full-frame equivalent, even though, as I said, nothing is actually being multiplied. Throughout most of this book, I've been using actual focal lengths and not equivalents, except when referring to specific wide-angle or telephoto focal length ranges and their fields of view.

Your First Lens

The Canon EOS Rebel T1i is frequently purchased with a lens, often the Canon EF-S 18-55mm f/3.5-5.6 IS autofocus lens, which adds only about $100 to the price tag of the body alone, and is thus an irresistible bargain. You can sometimes buy the T1i body alone if you already have some lenses and find a dealer that doesn't stock only kits. Other Canon models, including the EOS 1D Mark III, EOS 1Ds Mark III, and EOS 5D Mark II, are generally purchased without a lens by veteran Canon photographers who already have a complement of optics to use with their cameras.

I bought my EOS 50D as a body-only, because I already had a collection of lenses, but when it came time to pick up my T1i, I went with the kit that included the 18-55 image-stabilized lens. Who can turn down an IS lens for only $100? However, you'll also find many purchasers who fall into one of the following categories: Those who are upgrading from other Canon models; from a Canon film camera; or who are buying the T1i as a second camera body to complement their other Canon camera. These owners, too, generally already have lenses they can use with their new T1i.

So, depending on which category you fall into, you'll need to make a decision about what kit lens to buy, or decide what other kind of lenses you need to fill out your complement of Canon optics. This section will cover "first lens" concerns, while later in the chapter we'll look at "add-on lens" considerations.

When deciding on a first lens, there are several factors you'll want to consider:

- **Cost.** You might have stretched your budget a bit to purchase your Rebel T1i, so you might want to keep the cost of your first lens fairly low. Fortunately, there are excellent lenses available that will add from $100 to $300 to the price of your camera if purchased at the same time.

- **Zoom range.** If you have only one lens, you'll want a fairly long zoom range to provide as much flexibility as possible. Fortunately, the two most popular basic lenses for the T1i have 3X to 5X zoom ranges, extending from moderate wide-angle/normal out to medium telephoto. Either is fine for everyday shooting, portraits, and some types of sports.

- **Adequate maximum aperture.** You'll want an f/stop of at least f/3.5 to f/4 for shooting under fairly low light conditions. The thing to watch for is the maximum aperture when the lens is zoomed to its telephoto end. You may end up with no better than an f/5.6 maximum aperture. That's not great, but you can often live with it.

- **Image quality.** Your starter lens should have good image quality, because that's one of the primary factors that will be used to judge your photos. Even at a low price, the several different lenses sold with the T1i as a kit include extra-low dispersion glass and aspherical elements that minimize distortion and chromatic aberration; they are sharp enough for most applications. If you read the user evaluations in the online photography forums, you know that owners of the kit lenses have been very pleased with their image quality.

- **Size matters.** A good walking-around lens is compact in size and light in weight.

- **Fast/close focusing.** Your first lens should have a speedy autofocus system (which is where the ultrasonic motor/USM found in all but the bargain basement lenses is an advantage). Close focusing (to 12 inches or closer) will let you use your basic lens for some types of macro photography.

You can find comparisons of the lenses discussed in the next section, while evaluations of both Canon optics and third-party lenses from Sigma, Tokina, Tamron, and other vendors, are available in online groups and websites. I'll provide my recommendations for Canon lenses, but more information is always helpful.

Buy Now, Expand Later

The T1i is commonly available with several good, basic lenses that can serve you well as a "walk-around" lens (one you keep on the camera most of the time, especially when you're out and about without your camera bag). The number of options available to you is actually quite amazing, even if your budget is limited to about $100-$350 for your first lens. One other vendor, for example, offers only 18mm-70mm and 18mm-55mm kit lenses in that price range, plus a 24mm-85mm zoom. Canon offers several choices, including the most popular starter lens Canon offers for the T1i, which is shown in Figure 6.2. Canon's best-bet first lenses are as follows:

- **Canon EF-S 18-55mm f/3.5-5.6 IS Autofocus lens.** This lens has image stabilization that can counter camera shake by providing the vibration-stopping capabilities of a shutter speed four stops faster than the one you've dialed in. That is, with image stabilization activated, you can shoot at 1/30 second and eliminate camera shake as if you were using a shutter speed of 1/250th second. (At least, that's what Canon claims; I usually have slightly less impressive results.) Of course, IS doesn't freeze subject motion—that basketball player driving for a lay-up will still be blurry at 1/30th second, even though the effects of camera shake will be effectively nullified. But this lens is an all-around good choice if your budget is tight.

- **Canon EF-S 17-85mm f/4-5.6 IS USM Autofocus lens.** This lens is a very popular "basic" lens sold for the T1i. The allure here is the longer telephoto range, coupled with the built-in image stabilization, which allows you to shoot rock-solid photos at shutter speeds that are at least two or three notches slower than you'd need normally (say, 1/8th second instead of 1/30th or 1/60th second), as long as your

Figure 6.2
The Canon EF-S 18-55mm f/3.5-5.6 IS Autofocus lens ships as a basic kit lens for the Rebel T1i.

subject isn't moving. It also has a quiet, fast, reliable ultrasonic motor (more on that later, too). This is another lens designed for the 1.6X crop factor; all but one of the remaining lenses in this list can also be used on full-frame cameras. (I'll tell you why later in this chapter.) This lens is shown in Figure 6.3.

Figure 6.3
The Canon EF-S 17-85mm f/4-5.6 IS USM Auto-focus lens is another popular starter lens for the Rebel T1i.

- **Canon EF-S 18-200mm f/3.5-5.6 IS Autofocus lens.** This one, priced at about $600, has been wildly popular as a basic lens for the T1i, because it's light, compact, and covers a full range from true wide-angle to long telephoto. Image stabilization keeps your pictures sharp at the long end of the zoom range, allowing the longer shutter speeds that the f/5.6 maximum aperture demands at 200mm. Automatic panning detection turns the IS feature off when panning in both horizontal and vertical directions. A new "Super Spectra Coating" minimizes flare and ghosting, while optimizing color rendition. Can you tell that I like this lens?

- **Canon EF 55-200mm f/4.5-5.6 II USM Autofocus Lightweight Compact Telephoto Zoom lens.** If you bought the 18-55mm kit lens, this one picks up where that one leaves off, going from short telephoto to medium long (88mm-320mm full-frame equivalent). It features a desirable ultrasonic motor. Best of all, it's very affordable at around $225. If you can afford only two lenses, the 18-55mm and this one make a good basic set.

- **EF-S 55-250mm f/4-5.6 IS Telephoto Zoom lens.** This is an image-stabilized EF-S lens (which means it can't be used with Canon's 1.3X and 1.0X crop-factor pro cameras), providing the longest focal range in the EF-S range to date, and that 4-stop Image Stabilizer. Again, at about $250, it's more money than the older, non-stabilized EF version, but it's worth the extra cost.

- **Canon EF 24-85mm f/3.5-4.5 USM Autofocus Wide-Angle Telephoto Zoom lens.** If you can get by with normal focal length to medium telephoto range, Canon offers four affordable lenses, plus one more expensive killer lens that's worth the extra expenditure. All of them can be used on full-frame or cropped-frame digital Canons, which is why they include "wide angle" in their product names. They're really wide-angle lenses only when mounted on a full-frame camera. This one, priced in the $300 range, offers a useful range of focal lengths, extending from the equivalent of 38mm to 136mm.

- **Canon EF 28-105mm f/3.5-4.5 II USM Autofocus Wide-Angle Telephoto Zoom lens.** If you want to save about $100 and gain a little reach, this 45mm-168mm (equivalent lens) might be what you are looking for.

- **Canon EF 28-135mm f/3.5-5.6 IS USM Image-Stabilized Autofocus Wide-Angle Telephoto Zoom lens.** Image stabilization is especially useful at longer focal lengths, which makes this 45mm-216mm (equivalent) lens worth its $400-plus price tag. Several retailers are packing this lens with the T1i as a kit.

- **Canon EF 28-200mm f/3.5-5.6 USM Autofocus Wide-Angle Telephoto Zoom lens.** If you want one lens to do everything except wide-angle photography, this 7X zoom lens costs less than $400 and takes you from the equivalent of 45mm out to a long 320mm.

- **Canon Zoom Wide-Angle-Telephoto EF 24-70mm f/2.8L USM Autofocus lens.** I couldn't leave this premium lens out of the mix, even though it costs well over $1,000. As part of Canon's L-series (Luxury) lens line, it offers the best sharpness over its focal range than any of the other lenses in this list. Best of all, it's fast (for a zoom), with an f/.2.8 maximum aperture that *doesn't change* as you zoom out. Unlike the other lenses, which may offer only an f/5.6 maximum f/stop at their longest zoom setting, this is a *constant aperture* lens, which retains its maximum f/stop. The added sharpness, constant aperture, and ultra-smooth USM motor are what you're paying for with this lens.

What Lenses Can You Use?

The previous section helped you sort out what lens you need to buy with your T1i (assuming you already didn't own any Canon lenses). Now, you're probably wondering what lenses can be added to your growing collection (trust me, it will grow). You need to know which lenses are suitable and, most importantly, which lenses are fully compatible with your Rebel T1i.

With the Canon T1i, the compatibility issue is a simple one: It accepts any lens with the EF or EF-S designation, with full availability of all autofocus, autoaperture, autoexposure, and image-stabilization features (if present). It's comforting to know that any EF (for full-frame or cropped sensors) or EF-S (for cropped sensor cameras only) will work as designed with your camera. As I noted at the beginning of the chapter, that's more than 40 million lenses!

But wait, there's more. You can also attach Nikon F mount, Leica R, Olympus OM, and M42 ("Pentax screw mount") lenses with a simple adapter, if you don't mind losing automatic focus and aperture control. If you use one of these lenses, you'll need to focus manually (even if the lens operates in Autofocus mode on the camera it was designed for), and adjust the f/stop to the aperture you want to use to take the picture. That means that lenses that don't have an aperture ring (such as Nikon G-series lenses) must be used only at their maximum aperture. Because of these limitations, you probably won't want to make extensive use of "foreign" lenses on your T1i, but an adapter can help you when you really, really need to use a particular focal length but don't have a suitable Canon-compatible lens. For example, I occasionally use an older 400mm lens that was originally designed for the Nikon line on my T1i. The lens needs to be mounted on a tripod for steadiness, anyway, so its slower operation isn't a major pain. Another good match is the 105mm Micro-Nikkor I sometimes use with my Canon T1i, as I don't own a Canon macro lens with that focal length. Macro photos, too, are most often taken with the camera mounted on a tripod, and manual focus makes a lot of sense for fine-tuning focus and depth-of-field. Because of the contemplative nature of close-up photography, it's not much of an inconvenience to stop down to the taking aperture just before exposure.

The limitations on use of lenses within Canon's own product line (as well as lenses produced for earlier Canon SLRs by third-party vendors) are fairly clear-cut. The Rebel T1i cannot be used with any of Canon's earlier lens-mounting schemes for its film cameras, including the immediate predecessor to the EF mount, the FD mount (introduced with the Canon F1 in 1964 and used until the Canon T60 in 1990), FL (1964-1971), or the original Canon R mount (1959-1964). That's really all you need to know. While you'll find FD-to-EF adapters for about $40, you'll lose so many functions that it's rarely worth the bother.

WHY SO MANY LENS MOUNTS?

Four different lens mounts in 40-plus years might seem like a lot of different mounting systems, especially when compared to the Nikon F mount of 1959, which retained quite a bit of compatibility with that company's film and digital camera bodies during that same span. However, in digital photography terms, the EF mount itself is positively ancient, having remained reasonably stable for almost two decades. Lenses designed for the EF system work reliably with every EOS film and digital camera ever produced.

However, at the time, yet another lens mount switch, especially a change from the traditional breech system to a more conventional bayonet-type mount, was indeed a daring move by Canon. One of the reasons for staying with a particular lens type is to "lock" current users into a specific camera system. By introducing the EF mount, Canon in effect cut loose every photographer in its existing user base. If they chose to upgrade, they were free to choose another vendor's products and lenses. Only satisfaction with the previous Canon product line and the promise of the new system would keep them in the fold.

In retrospect, the switch to the EF mount seems like a very good idea, as the initial EOS film cameras can now be seen as the beginning of Canon's rise to eventually become the leader in film and (later) digital SLR cameras. By completely revamping its lens mounting system, the company was able to take advantage of the latest advances in technology without compromise.

For example, when the original EF bayonet mount was introduced in 1987, the system incorporated new autofocus technology (EF actually stands for "electro focus") in a more rugged and less complicated form. A tiny motor was built into the lens itself, eliminating the need for mechanical linkages with the camera. Instead, electrical contacts are used to send power and the required focusing information to the motor. That's a much more robust and resilient system that made it easier for Canon to design faster and more accurate autofocus mechanisms just by redesigning the lenses.

EF vs. EF-S

Today, in addition to its EF lenses, Canon offers lenses that use the EF-S (the S stands for "short back focus") mount, with the chief difference being (as you might expect) lens components that extend farther back into the camera body of some of Canon's latest digital cameras (specifically those with smaller than full-frame sensors), such as the T1i and other Rebels. As I'll explain next, this refinement allows designing more compact, less-expensive lenses especially for those cameras, but not for models like the EOS 5D, 1Ds Mark III, or 1D Mark III (even though the latter camera does have a sensor that is smaller than full frame).

Canon's EF-S lens mount variation was born in 2003, when the company virtually invented the consumer-oriented digital SLR category by introducing the original EOS 300D/Digital Rebel, a dSLR that cost less than $1,000 *with lens* at a time when all other interchangeable lens digital cameras (including the T1i's "grandparent," the original EOS 10D) were priced closer to $2,000 with a basic lens. Like the EOS 10D introduced earlier that same year, the Rebel featured a smaller than full-frame sensor with a 1.6X crop factor (Canon calls this format APS-C). But the Rebel accepted lenses that took advantage of the shorter mirror found in APS-C cameras, with elements of shorter focal length lenses (wide angles) that extended *into* the camera, space that was off limits in other models because the mirror passed through that territory as it flipped up to expose the shutter and sensor. (Canon even calls its flip-up reflector a "half mirror.")

In short (so to speak), the EF-S mount made it easier to design less-expensive wide-angle lenses that could be used *only* with 1.6X-crop cameras, and featured a simpler design and reduced coverage area suitable for those non-full-frame models. The new mount made it possible to produce lenses like the ultrawide EF-S 10-22mm f/3.5-4.5 USM lens, which has the equivalent field of view as a 16mm-35mm zoom on a full-frame camera. (See Figure 6.4.)

Figure 6.4
The EF-S 10-22mm ultrawide lens was made possible by the shorter back focus difference offered by the original Digital Rebel and subsequent Canon 1.6X "cropped sensor" models.

Suitable cameras for EF-S lenses include the entire Digital Rebel and Rebel lineup, the Canon EOS 20D/30D/40D/50D, and, today, the Rebel T1i. The EF-S lenses cannot be used on the EOS 10D, the 1D Mark II/N/Mark III (which have a 28.7mm × 19.1mm APS-H sensor with a 1.3X crop factor), or any of the full-frame digital or film EOS models. It's easy to tell an EF lens from an EF-S lens: The latter incorporate EF-S into their name! Plus, EF lenses have a raised red dot on the barrel that is used to align the lens with a matching dot on the camera when attaching the lens. EF-S lenses and compatible bodies use a white square instead. EF-S lenses also have a rubber ring at the attachment end that provides a bit of weather/dust sealing and protects the back components of the lens if a user attempts to mount it on a camera that is not EF-S compatible.

Ingredients of Canon's Alphanumeric Soup

The actual product names of individual Canon lenses are fairly easy to decipher; they'll include either the EF or EF-S designation, the focal length or focal length range of the lens, its maximum aperture, and some other information. Additional data may be engraved or painted on the barrel or ring surrounding the front element of the lens, as shown in Figure 6.5. Here's a decoding of what the individual designations mean:

- **EF/EF-S.** If the lens is marked EF, it can safely be used on any Canon EOS camera, film or digital. If it is an EF-S lens, it should be used only on an EF-S compatible camera, such as the Rebels, EOS 20D/30D/40D, and any newer APS-C cameras introduced after the publication of this book.

- **Focal length.** Given in millimeters or a millimeter range, such as *60mm* in the case of a popular Canon macro lens, or *17-55mm*, used to describe a medium-wide to short-telephoto zoom.

- **Maximum aperture.** The largest f/stop available with a particular lens is given in a string of numbers that might seem confusing at first glance. For example, you might see *1:1.8* for a fixed-focal length (prime) lens, and *1:4.5-5.6* for a zoom. The initial 1: signifies that the f/stop given is actually a ratio or fraction (in regular notation, f/ replaces the 1:), which is why a 1:2 (or f/2) aperture is larger than a 1:4 (or f/4) aperture—just as 1/2 is larger than 1/4. With most zoom lenses, the maximum aperture changes as the lens is zoomed to the telephoto position, so a range is given instead: 1:4.5-5.6. (Some zooms, called *constant aperture* lenses, keep the same maximum aperture throughout their range.)

- **Autofocus type.** Most newer Canon lenses that aren't of the bargain-basement type use Canon's *ultrasonic motor* autofocus system (more on that later) and are given the USM designation. If USM does not appear on the lens or its model name, the lens uses the less sophisticated AFD (arc-form drive) autofocus system or the micro-motor (MM) drive mechanism.

Figure 6.5 Most of the key specifications of the lens are marked on the ring around the front element.

- **Series.** Canon adds a Roman numeral to many of its products to represent an updated model with the same focal length or focal length range, so some lenses will have a II or III added to their name.

- **Pro quality.** Canon's more expensive lenses with more rugged construction and higher optical quality, intended for professional use, include the letter L (for "luxury") in their product name. You can further differentiate these lenses visually by a red ring around the lens barrel and the off-white color of the metal barrel itself in virtually all telephoto L-series lenses. (Some L-series lenses have shiny or textured black plastic exterior barrels.) Internally, every L lens includes at least one lens element that is built of ultra-low dispersion glass, is constructed of expensive fluorite crystal, or uses an expensive ground (not molded) aspheric (non-spherical) lens component.

- **Filter size.** You'll find the front lens filter thread diameter in millimeters included on the lens, preceded by a Ø symbol, as in Ø67 or Ø72.

- **Special-purpose lenses.** Some Canon lenses are designed for specific types of work, and they include appropriate designations in their names. For example, close-focusing lenses such as the Canon EF-S 60mm f/2.8 Macro USM lens incorporate the word *Macro* into their name. Lenses with perspective control features preface the lens name with T-S (for tilt-shift). Lenses with built-in image-stabilization features, such as the nifty EF 28-300mm f/3.5-5.6L IS USM Telephoto Zoom include *IS* in their product names.

SORTING THE MOTOR DRIVES

Incorporating the autofocus motor inside the lens was an innovative move by Canon, and this allowed the company to produce better and more sophisticated lenses as technology became available to upgrade the focusing system. As a result, you'll find four different types of motors in Canon-designed lenses, each with cost and practical considerations.

- **AFD (Arc-form drive)** and **Micromotor (MM)** drives are built around tiny versions of electromagnetic motors, which generally use gear trains to produce the motion needed to adjust the focus of the lens. Both are slow, noisy, and not particularly effective with larger lenses. Manual focus adjustments are possible only when the motor drive is disengaged.

- **Micromotor ultrasonic motor (USM)** drives use high-frequency vibration to produce the motion used to drive the gear train, resulting in a quieter operating system at a cost that's not much more than that of electromagnetic motor drives. With the exception of a couple lenses that have a slipping clutch mechanism, manual focus with this kind of system is possible only when the motor drive is switched off and the lens is set in Manual mode. This is the kind of USM system you'll find in lower-cost lenses.

- **Ring ultrasonic motor (USM)** drives, available in two different types (*electronic focus ring USM* and *ring USM*), also use high-frequency movement, but generate motion using a pair of vibrating metal rings to adjust focus. Both variations allow a feature called Full Time Manual (FTM) focus, which lets you make manual adjustments to the lens's focus even when the autofocus mechanism is engaged. With electronic focus ring USM, manual focus is possible only when the lens is mounted on the camera and the camera is turned on; the focus ring of lenses with ring USM can be turned at any time.

Your Second (and Third...) Lens

There are really only two advantages to owning just a single lens. One of them is creative. Keeping one set of optics mounted on your T1i all the time forces you to be especially imaginative in your approach to your subjects. I once visited Europe with only a single camera body and a 35mm f/2 lens. The experience was actually quite exciting, because I had to use a variety of techniques to allow that one lens to serve for landscapes, available light photos, action, close-ups, portraits, and other kinds of images. Canon makes an excellent 35mm f/2 lens (which focuses down to 9.6 inches) that's perfect for that kind of experiment; although, today, my personal choice would be the sublime (and expensive) Canon Wide-Angle EF 35mm f/1.4L USM Autofocus lens.

Of course, it's more likely that your "single" lens is actually a zoom, which is, in truth, many lenses in one, taking you from, say, 17mm to 85mm (or some other range) with a rapid twist of the zoom ring. You'll still find some creative challenges when you stick to a single zoom lens's focal lengths.

The second advantage of the unilens camera is only a marginal technical benefit since the introduction of automatic sensor cleaning. If you don't exchange lenses, the chances of dust and dirt getting inside your T1i and settling on the sensor is reduced (but *not* eliminated entirely). Although I've known some photographers who minimized the number of lens changes they made for this very reason, reducing the number of lenses you work with is not a productive or rewarding approach for most of us. The T1i's automatic sensor cleaning feature has made this "advantage" much less significant than it was in the past.

It's more likely that you'll succumb to the malady known as *Lens Lust*, which is defined as an incurable disease marked by a significant yen for newer, better, longer, faster, sharper, anything-er optics for your camera. (And, it must be noted, this disease can *cost* you significant yen—or dollars, or whatever currency you use.) In its worst manifestations, sufferers find themselves with lenses that have overlapping zoom ranges or capabilities, because one or the other offers a slight margin in performance or suitability for specific tasks. When you find yourself already lusting after a new lens before you've really had a chance to put your latest purchase to the test, you'll know the disease has reached the terminal phase.

What Lenses Can Do for You

A saner approach to expanding your lens collection is to consider what each of your options can do for you and then choose the type of lens that will really boost your creative opportunities.

Here's a general guide to the sort of capabilities you can gain by adding a lens to your repertoire.

- **Wider perspective.** Your 18-55mm f/3.5-5.6 or 17-85mm f/4-5.6 lens has served you well for moderate wide-angle shots. Now you find your back is up against a wall and you *can't* take a step backwards to take in more subject matter. Perhaps you're standing on the rim of the Grand Canyon, and you want to take in as much of the breathtaking view as you can. You might find yourself just behind the baseline at a high school basketball game and want an interesting shot with a little perspective distortion tossed in the mix. There's a lens out there that will provide you with what you need, such as the EF-S 10-22mm f/3.5-4.5 USM Zoom. If you want to stay in the sub-$600 price category, you'll need something like the Sigma Super Wide-Angle 10-20mm f/4-5.6 EX DC HSM Autofocus lens. The two lenses provide the equivalent of a 16mm to 32/35mm wide-angle view. For a distorted view, there is the Canon Fisheye EF 15mm f/2.8 Autofocus, with a similar lens available from Sigma, which offers an extra-wide circular fisheye, and the Sigma Fisheye 8mm f/3.5 EX DG Circular Fisheye. Your extra-wide choices may not be abundant, but they are there. Figure 6.6 shows the perspective you get from an ultrawide-angle lens.

- **Bring objects closer.** A long lens brings distant subjects closer to you, offers better control over depth-of-field, and avoids the perspective distortion that wide-angle lenses provide. They compress the apparent distance between objects in your frame. In the telephoto realm, Canon is second to none, with a dozen or more offerings in the sub-$600 range, including the Canon EF 100-300mm f/4.5-5.6 USM Autofocus and Canon EF 70-300mm f/4-5.6 IS USM Autofocus Telephoto Zoom lenses, and a broad array of zooms and fixed-focal length optics if you're willing to spend up to $1,000 or a bit more. Don't forget that the Rebel T1i's crop factor narrows the field of view of all these lenses, so your 70-300mm lens looks more like a 112mm-480mm zoom through the viewfinder. Figures 6.7 and 6.8 were taken from the same position as Figure 6.6, but with an 85mm and 500mm lens, respectively.

- **Bring your camera closer.** Macro lenses allow you to focus to within an inch or two of your subject. Canon's best close-up lenses are all fixed focal length optics in the 50mm to 180mm range (including the well-regarded Canon EF-S 60mm f/2.8 and Canon EF 100mm f/2.8 USM Macro Autofocus lenses). But you'll find macro zooms available from Sigma and others. They don't tend to focus quite as close, but they provide a bit of flexibility when you want to vary your subject distance (say, to avoid spooking a skittish creature).

Figure 6.6 An ultrawide-angle lens provided this view of Castle Rock in Sedona, Arizona.

Figure 6.7 This photo, taken from roughly the same distance, shows the view using a short telephoto lens.

Figure 6.8 A longer telephoto lens captured this closer view of the castle from approximately the same shooting position.

- **Look sharp.** Many lenses, particularly Canon's luxury "L" line, are prized for their sharpness and overall image quality. While your run-of-the-mill lens is likely to be plenty sharp for most applications, the very best optics are even better over their entire field of view (which means no fuzzy corners), are sharper at a wider range of focal lengths (in the case of zooms), and have better correction for various types of distortion. That's why the Canon EF 28-105mm f/3.5-4.5 II USM Zoom lens costs a couple hundred dollars, while the "similar" (in zoom range only) Canon EF 24-105mm f/4L IS USM Zoom is priced $1,000 higher.

- **More speed.** Your Canon EF 100-300mm f/4.5-5.6 Telephoto Zoom lens might have the perfect focal length and sharpness for sports photography, but the maximum aperture won't cut it for night baseball or football games, or, even, any sports shooting in daylight if the weather is cloudy or you need to use some ungodly fast shutter speed, such as 1/4,000th second. You might be happier with the Canon EF 100mm f/2 Medium Telephoto for close-range stuff, or even the pricier Canon EF 135mm f/2L. If money is no object, you can spring for Canon's 400mm f/2.8 and 600mm f/4 L-series lenses (both with image stabilization and priced in the $6,500-and-up stratosphere). Or, maybe you just need the speed and can benefit from an f/1.8 or f/1.4 lens in the 20mm-85mm range. They're all available in Canon mounts (there's even an 85mm f/1.2 and 50mm f/1.2 for the real speed demons). With any of these lenses you can continue photographing under the dimmest of lighting conditions without the need for a tripod or flash.

- **Special features.** Accessory lenses give you special features, such as tilt/shift capabilities to correct for perspective distortion in architectural shots. Canon offers three of these TS-E lenses in 24mm, 45mm, and 90mm focal lengths, at a little over $1,000 each. You'll also find macro lenses, including the MP-E 65mm f/2.8 1-5x macro photo lens, which shoots *only* in the 1X to 5X life-size range. If you want diffused images, check out the EF 135mm f/2.8 with two soft-focus settings. The fisheye lenses mentioned earlier, and all IS (image-stabilized) lenses also count as special-feature optics.

Zoom or Prime?

Zoom lenses have changed the way serious photographers take pictures. One of the reasons that I own 12 SLR film bodies is that in ancient times it was common to mount a different fixed focal length prime lens on various cameras and take pictures with two or three cameras around your neck (or tucked in a camera case) so you'd be ready to take a long shot or an intimate close-up or wide-angle view on a moment's notice, without the need to switch lenses. It made sense (at the time) to have a half dozen or so bodies (two to use, one in the shop, one in transit, and a couple backups). Zoom lenses of the time had a limited zoom range, were heavy, and not very sharp (especially when you tried to wield one of those monsters handheld).

That's all changed today. Lenses like the razor-sharp Canon EF 28-300mm f/3.5-5.6L IS USM can boast 10X or longer zoom ranges, in a package that's about 7-inches long, and while not petite at 3.7 pounds, quite usable handheld (especially with IS switched on). Although such a lens might seem expensive at $2,200-plus, it's actually much less costly than the six or so lenses it replaces.

When selecting between zoom and prime lenses, there are several considerations to ponder. Here's a checklist of the most important factors. I already mentioned image quality and maximum aperture earlier, but those aspects take on additional meaning when comparing zooms and primes.

■ **Logistics.** As prime lenses offer just a single focal length, you'll need more of them to encompass the full range offered by a single zoom. More lenses mean additional slots in your camera bag, and extra weight to carry. Just within Canon's line alone you can select from about a dozen general-purpose prime lenses in 28mm, 35mm, 50mm, 85mm, 100mm, 135mm, 200mm, and 300mm focal lengths, all of which are overlapped by the 28-300mm zoom I mentioned earlier. Even so, you might be willing to carry an extra prime lens or two in order to gain the speed or image quality that a particular lens offers.

■ **Image quality.** Prime lenses usually produce better image quality at their focal length than even the most sophisticated zoom lenses at the same magnification. Zoom lenses, with their shifting elements and f/stops that can vary from zoom position to zoom position, are in general more complex to design than fixed focal length lenses. That's not to say that the very best prime lenses can't be complicated as well. However, the exotic designs, aspheric elements, low-dispersion glass, and Canon's new diffraction optics (DO) technology (a three-layer diffraction grating to better control how light is captured by a lens) can be applied to improving the quality of the lens, rather than wasting a lot of it on compensating for problems caused by the zoom process itself.

- **Maximum aperture.** Because of the same design constraints, zoom lenses usually have smaller maximum apertures than prime lenses, and the most affordable zooms have a lens opening that grows effectively smaller as you zoom in. The difference in lens speed verges on the ridiculous at some focal lengths. For example, the 18mm-55mm basic zoom gives you a 55mm f/5.6 lens when zoomed all the way out, while prime lenses in that focal length commonly have f/1.8 or faster maximum apertures. Indeed, the fastest f/2, f/1.8, f1/4, and f/1.2 lenses are all primes, and if you require speed, a fixed focal length lens is what you should rely on. Figure 6.9 shows an image taken with a Canon 85mm f 1.8 Series EF USM Telephoto lens.

- **Speed.** Using prime lenses takes time and slows you down. It takes a few seconds to remove your current lens and mount a new one, and the more often you need to do that, the more time is wasted. If you choose not to swap lenses, when using a fixed focal length lens you'll still have to move closer or farther away from your subject to get the field of view you want. A zoom lens allows you to change magnifications and focal lengths with the twist of a ring and generally saves a great deal of time.

Categories of Lenses

Lenses can be categorized by their intended purpose—general photography, macro photography, and so forth—or by their focal length. The range of available focal lengths is usually divided into three main groups: wide-angle, normal, and telephoto. Prime lenses fall neatly into one of these classifications. Zooms can overlap designations, with a significant number falling into the catch-all wide-to-telephoto zoom range. This section provides more information about focal length ranges, and how they are used.

Any lens with an equivalent focal length of 10mm to 20mm is said to be an *ultrawide-angle lens*; from about 20mm to 40mm (equivalent) is said to be a *wide-angle lens*. *Normal lenses* have a focal length roughly equivalent to the diagonal of the film or sensor, in millimeters, and so fall into the range of about 45mm to 60mm (on a full-frame camera). *Telephoto lenses* usually fall into the 75mm and longer focal lengths, while those from about 300mm-400mm and longer often are referred to as *super-telephotos*.

Figure 6.9
An 85mm f/1.8 lens was perfect for this hand-held photo of a bluegrass musician.

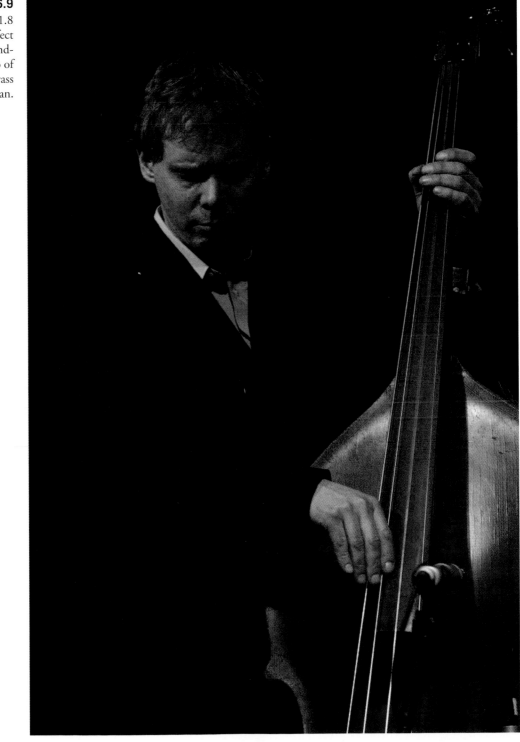

Using Wide-Angle and Wide-Zoom Lenses

To use wide-angle prime lenses and wide zooms, you need to understand how they affect your photography. Here's a quick summary of the things you need to know.

- **More depth-of-field.** Practically speaking, wide-angle lenses offer more depth-of-field at a particular subject distance and aperture. (But see the sidebar below for an important note.) You'll find that helpful when you want to maximize sharpness of a large zone, but not very useful when you'd rather isolate your subject using selective focus (telephoto lenses are better for that).

- **Stepping back.** Wide-angle lenses have the effect of making it seem that you are standing farther from your subject than you really are. They're helpful when you don't want to back up, or can't because there are impediments in your way.

- **Wider field of view.** While making your subject seem farther away, as implied above, a wide-angle lens also provides a larger field of view, including more of the subject in your photos. Table 6.1 shows the diagonal field of view offered by an assortment of lenses, taking into account the crop factor introduced by the Rebel T1i's smaller-than-full-frame sensor.

Table 6.1 Field of View at Various Focal Lengths

Diagonal Field of View	Focal Length at 1X Crop	Focal Length Needed to Produce Same Field of View at 1.6X Crop
107 degrees	16mm	10mm
94 degrees	20mm	12mm
84 degrees	24mm	15mm
75 degrees	28mm	18mm
63 degrees	35mm	22mm
47 degrees	50mm	31mm
28 degrees	85mm	53mm
18 degrees	135mm	85mm
12 degrees	200mm	125mm
8.2 degrees	300mm	188mm

- **More foreground.** As background objects retreat, more of the foreground is brought into view by a wide-angle lens. That gives you extra emphasis on the area that's closest to the camera. Photograph your home with a normal lens/normal zoom setting, and the front yard probably looks fairly conventional in your photo (that's why they're called "normal" lenses). Switch to a wider lens and you'll discover that your lawn now makes up much more of the photo. So, wide-angle lenses are great when you want to emphasize that lake in the foreground, but problematic when your intended subject is located farther in the distance.

- **Super-sized subjects.** The tendency of a wide-angle lens to emphasize objects in the foreground, while de-emphasizing objects in the background can lead to a kind of size distortion that may be more objectionable for some types of subjects than others. Shoot a bed of flowers up close with a wide angle, and you might like the distorted effect of the larger blossoms nearer the lens. Take a photo of a family member with the same lens from the same distance, and you're likely to get some complaints about that gigantic nose in the foreground.

- **Perspective distortion.** When you tilt the camera so the plane of the sensor is no longer perpendicular to the vertical plane of your subject, some parts of the subject are now closer to the sensor than they were before, while other parts are farther away. So, buildings, flagpoles, or NBA players appear to be falling backwards, as you can see in Figure 6.10. While this kind of apparent distortion (it's not caused by a defect in the lens) can happen with any lens, it's most apparent when a wide angle is used.

- **Steady cam.** You'll find that you can handhold a wide-angle lens at slower shutter speeds, without need for image stabilization, than you can with a telephoto lens. The reduced magnification of the wide-lens or wide-zoom setting doesn't emphasize camera shake like a telephoto lens does.

- **Interesting angles.** Many of the factors already listed combine to produce more interesting angles when shooting with wide-angle lenses. Raising or lowering a telephoto lens a few feet probably will have little effect on the appearance of the distant subjects you're shooting. The same change in elevation can produce a dramatic effect for the much-closer subjects typically captured with a wide-angle lens or wide-zoom setting.

Figure 6.10 Tilting the camera back produces this "falling back" look in architectural photos.

DOF IN DEPTH

The depth-of-field (DOF) advantage of wide-angle lenses is diminished when you enlarge your picture; believe it or not, a wide-angle image enlarged and cropped to provide the same subject size as a telephoto shot would have the *same* depth-of-field. Try it: take a wide-angle photo of a friend from a fair distance, and then zoom in to duplicate the picture in a telephoto image. Then, enlarge the wide shot so your friend is the same size in both. The wide photo will have the same DOF (and will have much less detail, too).

The crop factor strikes again! You can see from this table that wide-angle lenses provide a broader field of view, and that, because of the T1i's 1.6 crop factor, lenses must have a shorter focal length to provide the same field of view. If you like working with a 28mm lens with your full-frame camera, you'll need an 18mm lens for your Rebel T1i to get the same field of view. (Some focal lengths have been rounded slightly for simplification.)

Avoiding Potential Wide-Angle Problems

Wide-angle lenses have a few quirks that you'll want to keep in mind when shooting so you can avoid falling into some common traps. Here's a checklist of tips for avoiding common problems:

- **Symptom: converging lines.** Unless you want to use wildly diverging lines as a creative effect, it's a good idea to keep horizontal and vertical lines in landscapes, architecture, and other subjects carefully aligned with the sides, top, and bottom of the frame. That will help you avoid undesired perspective distortion. Sometimes it helps to shoot from a slightly elevated position so you don't have to tilt the camera up or down.

- **Symptom: color fringes around objects.** Lenses are often plagued with fringes of color around backlit objects, produced by *chromatic aberration*, which comes in two forms: *longitudinal/axial*, in which all the colors of light don't focus in the same plane; and *lateral/transverse*, in which the colors are shifted to one side. Axial chromatic aberration can be reduced by stopping down the lens, but transverse CA cannot. Both can be reduced by using lenses with low diffraction index glass (or UD elements, in Canon nomenclature) and by incorporating elements that cancel the chromatic aberration of other glass in the lens. For example, a strong positive lens made of low-dispersion crown glass (made of a soda-lime-silica composite) may be mated with a weaker negative lens made of high-dispersion flint glass, which contains lead.

- **Symptom: lines that bow outward.** Some wide-angle lenses cause straight lines to bow outwards, with the strongest effect at the edges. In fisheye (or *curvilinear*) lenses, this defect is a feature, as you can see in Figure 6.11. When distortion is not desired, you'll need to use a lens that has corrected barrel distortion. Manufacturers like Canon do their best to minimize or eliminate it (producing a *rectilinear* lens), often using *aspherical* lens elements (which are not cross-sections of a sphere). You can also minimize barrel distortion simply by framing your photo with some extra space all around, so the edges where the defect is most obvious can be cropped out of the picture.

- **Symptom: dark corners and shadows in flash photos.** The Canon EOS Rebel T1i's built-in electronic flash is designed to provide even coverage for lenses as wide as 17mm. If you use a wider lens, you can expect darkening, or *vignetting*, in the corners of the frame. At wider focal lengths, the lens hood of some lenses (my 17mm-85mm lens is a prime offender) can cast a semi-circular shadow in the lower portion of the frame when using the built-in flash. Sometimes removing the lens hood or zooming in a bit can eliminate the shadow. Mounting an external flash unit, such as the mighty Canon 580EX can solve both problems, as it has zoomable coverage up to 114 degrees with the included adapter, sufficient for a 9mm rectilinear lens (14mm equivalent). Its higher vantage point eliminates the problem of lens-hood shadow, too.

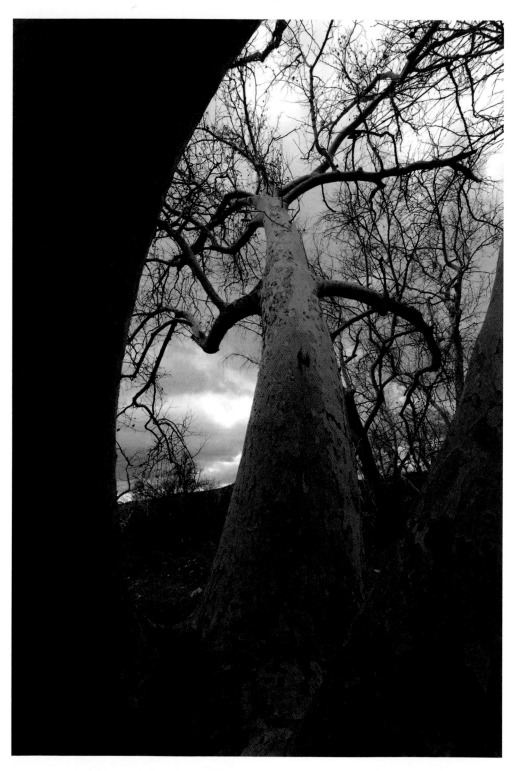

Figure 6.11
Many wide-angle lenses cause lines to bow outwards towards the edges of the image; with a fisheye lens, this tendency is considered an interesting feature.

- **Symptom: light and dark areas when using polarizing filter.** If you know that polarizers work best when the camera is pointed 90 degrees away from the sun and have the least effect when the camera is oriented 180 degrees from the sun, you know only half the story. With lenses having a focal length of 10mm to 18mm (the equivalent of 16mm-28mm), the angle of view (107 to 75 degrees diagonally, or 97 to 44 degrees horizontally) is extensive enough to cause problems. Think about it: when a 10mm lens is pointed at the proper 90-degree angle from the sun, objects at the edges of the frame will be oriented at 135 to 41 degrees, with only the center at exactly 90 degrees. Either edge will have much less of a polarized effect. The solution is to avoid using a polarizing filter with lenses having an actual focal length of less than 18mm (or 28mm equivalent).

Using Telephoto and Tele-Zoom Lenses

Telephoto lenses also can have a dramatic effect on your photography, and Canon is especially strong in the long-lens arena, with lots of choices in many focal lengths and zoom ranges. You should be able to find an affordable telephoto or tele-zoom to enhance your photography in several different ways. Here are the most important things you need to know. In the next section, I'll concentrate on telephoto considerations that can be problematic—and how to avoid those problems.

- **Selective focus.** Long lenses have reduced depth-of-field within the frame, allowing you to use selective focus to isolate your subject. You can open the lens up wide to create shallow depth-of-field, or close it down a bit to allow more to be in focus. The flip side of the coin is that when you *want* to make a range of objects sharp, you'll need to use a smaller f/stop to get the depth-of-field you need. Like fire, the depth-of-field of a telephoto lens can be friend or foe. Figure 6.12 shows a photo of a statue with an ugly background, so I photographed it using a short telephoto lens and wider f/stop to de-emphasize the other glassware in the background.

- **Getting closer.** Telephoto lenses bring you closer to wildlife, sports action, and candid subjects. No one wants to get a reputation as a surreptitious or "sneaky" photographer (except for paparazzi), but when applied to candids in an open and honest way, a long lens can help you capture memorable moments while retaining enough distance to stay out of the way of events as they transpire.

- **Reduced foreground/increased compression.** Telephoto lenses have the opposite effect of wide angles: they reduce the importance of things in the foreground by squeezing everything together. This compression even makes distant objects appear to be closer to subjects in the foreground and middle ranges. You can use this effect as a creative tool.

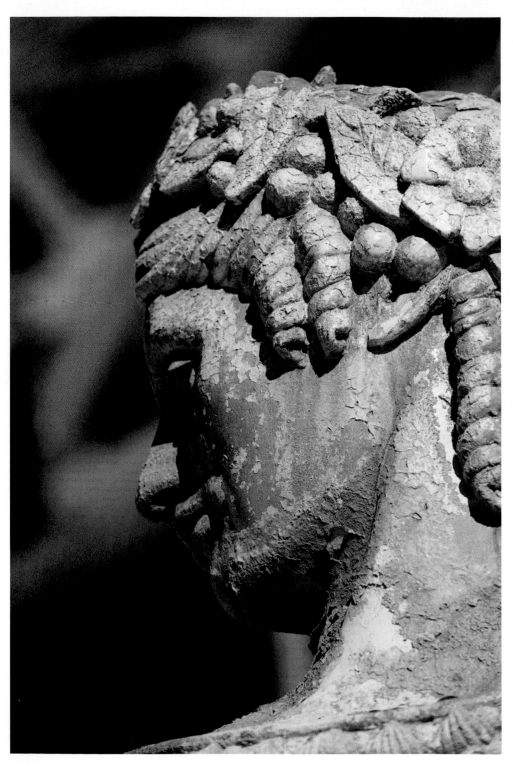

Figure 6.12
A wide f/stop
helped isolate
this statue from
its background.

- **Accentuates camera shakiness.** Telephoto focal lengths hit you with a double whammy in terms of camera/photographer shake. The lenses themselves are bulkier, more difficult to hold steady, and may even produce a barely perceptible see-saw rocking effect when you support them with one hand halfway down the lens barrel. Telephotos also magnify any camera shake. It's no wonder that image stabilization is popular in longer lenses.

- **Interesting angles require creativity.** Telephoto lenses require more imagination in selecting interesting angles, because the "angle" you do get on your subjects is so narrow. Moving from side to side or a bit higher or lower can make a dramatic difference in a wide-angle shot, but raising or lowering a telephoto lens a few feet probably will have little effect on the appearance of the distant subjects you're shooting.

Avoiding Telephoto Lens Problems

Many of the "problems" that telephoto lenses pose are really just challenges and not that difficult to overcome. Here is a list of the seven most common picture maladies and suggested solutions.

- **Symptom: flat faces in portraits.** Head-and-shoulders portraits of humans tend to be more flattering when a focal length of 50mm to 85mm is used. Longer focal lengths compress the distance between features like noses and ears, making the face look wider and flat. A wide-angle might make noses look huge and ears tiny when you fill the frame with a face. So stick with 50mm to 85mm focal lengths, going longer only when you're forced to shoot from a greater distance, and wider only when shooting three-quarters/full-length portraits, or group shots.

- **Symptom: blur due to camera shake.** Use a higher shutter speed (boosting ISO if necessary), consider an image-stabilized lens, or mount your camera on a tripod, monopod, or brace it with some other support. Of those three solutions, only the first will reduce blur caused by *subject* motion; an IS lens or tripod won't help you freeze a racecar in mid-lap.

- **Symptom: color fringes.** Chromatic aberration is the most pernicious optical problem found in telephoto lenses. There are others, including spherical aberration, astigmatism, coma, curvature of field, and similarly scary-sounding phenomena. The best solution for any of these is to use a better lens that offers the proper degree of correction, or stop down the lens to minimize the problem. But that's not always possible. Your second-best choice may be to correct the fringing in your favorite RAW conversion tool or image editor. Photoshop's Lens Correction filter (found in the Filter>Distort> menu) offers sliders that minimize both red/cyan and blue/yellow fringing.

- **Symptom: lines that curve inwards.** Pincushion distortion is found in many telephoto lenses. You might find after a bit of testing that it is worse at certain focal lengths with your particular zoom lens. Like chromatic aberration, it can be partially corrected using tools like Photoshop's Lens Correction filter.

- **Symptom: low contrast from haze or fog.** When you're photographing distant objects, a long lens shoots through a lot more atmosphere, which generally is muddied up with extra haze and fog. That dirt or moisture in the atmosphere can reduce contrast and mute colors. Some feel that a skylight or UV filter can help, but this practice is mostly a holdover from the film days. Digital sensors are not sensitive enough to UV light for a UV filter to have much effect. So you should be prepared to boost contrast and color saturation in your Picture Styles menu or image editor if necessary.

- **Symptom: low contrast from flare.** Lenses are furnished with lens hoods for a good reason: to reduce flare from bright light sources at the periphery of the picture area, or completely outside it. Because telephoto lenses often create images that are lower in contrast in the first place, you'll want to be especially careful to use a lens hood to prevent further effects on your image (or shade the front of the lens with your hand).

- **Symptom: dark flash photos.** Edge-to-edge flash coverage isn't a problem with telephoto lenses as it is with wide angles. The shooting distance is. A long lens might make a subject that's 50 feet away look as if it's right next to you, but your camera's flash isn't fooled. You'll need extra power for distant flash shots, and probably more power than your T1i's built-in flash provides. The shoe-mount Canon 580EX II Speedlite, for example, can automatically zoom its coverage down to that of a medium telephoto lens, providing a theoretical full-power shooting aperture of about f/8 at 50 feet and ISO 400. (Try *that* with the built-in flash!)

Telephotos and Bokeh

Bokeh describes the aesthetic qualities of the out-of-focus parts of an image and whether out-of-focus points of light—circles of confusion—are rendered as distracting fuzzy discs or smoothly fade into the background. *Boke* is a Japanese word for "blur," and the h was added to keep English speakers from rendering it monosyllabically to rhyme with *broke*. Although bokeh is visible in blurry portions of any image, it's of particular concern with telephoto lenses, which, thanks to the magic of reduced depth-of-field, produce more obviously out-of-focus areas.

Bokeh can vary from lens to lens, or even within a given lens depending on the f/stop in use. Bokeh becomes objectionable when the circles of confusion are evenly illuminated, making them stand out as distinct discs, or, worse, when these circles are darker in the center, producing an ugly "doughnut" effect. A lens defect called spherical aberration may produce out-of-focus discs that are brighter on the edges and darker in the center, because the lens doesn't focus light passing through the edges of the lens exactly as it does light going through the center. (Mirror or *catadioptric* lenses also produce this effect.)

Other kinds of spherical aberration generate circles of confusion that are brightest in the center and fade out at the edges, producing a smooth blending effect, as you can see at right in Figure 6.13. Ironically, when no spherical aberration is present at all, the discs are a uniform shade, which, while better than the doughnut effect, is not as pleasing as the bright center/dark edge rendition. The shape of the disc also comes into play, with round smooth circles considered the best, and nonagonal or some other polygon (determined by the shape of the lens diaphragm) considered less desirable.

If you plan to use selective focus a lot, you should investigate the bokeh characteristics of a particular lens before you buy. Canon user groups and forums will usually be full of comments and questions about bokeh, so the research is fairly easy.

Figure 6.13 Bokeh is less pleasing when the discs are prominent (left), and less obtrusive when they blend into the background (right).

Add-ons and Special Features

Once you've purchased your telephoto lens, you'll want to think about some appropriate accessories for it. There are some handy add-ons available that can be valuable. Here are a couple of them to think about.

Lens Hoods

Lens hoods are an important accessory for all lenses, but they're especially valuable with telephotos. As I mentioned earlier, lens hoods do a good job of preserving image contrast by keeping bright light sources outside the field of view from striking the lens and, potentially, bouncing around inside that long tube to generate flare that, when coupled with atmospheric haze, can rob your image of detail and snap. In addition, lens hoods serve as valuable protection for that large, vulnerable, front lens element. It's easy to forget that you've got that long tube sticking out in front of your camera and accidentally whack the front of your lens into something. It's cheaper to replace a lens hood than it is to have a lens repaired, so you might find that a good hood is valuable protection for your prized optics.

When choosing a lens hood, it's important to have the right hood for the lens, usually the one offered for that lens by Canon or the third-party manufacturer. You want a hood that blocks precisely the right amount of light: neither too much light nor too little. A hood with a front diameter that is too small can show up in your pictures as vignetting. A hood that has a front diameter that's too large isn't stopping all the light it should. Generic lens hoods may not do the job.

When your telephoto is a zoom lens, it's even more important to get the right hood, because you need one that does what it is supposed to at both the wide-angle and telephoto ends of the zoom range. Lens hoods may be cylindrical, rectangular (shaped like the image frame), or petal shaped (that is, cylindrical, but with cut-out areas at the corners which correspond to the actual image area). Lens hoods should be mounted in the correct orientation (a bayonet mount for the hood usually takes care of this).

Telephoto Extenders

Telephoto extenders (often called teleconverters outside the Canon world) multiply the actual focal length of your lens, giving you a longer telephoto for much less than the price of a lens with that actual focal length. These extenders fit between the lens and your camera and contain optical elements that magnify the image produced by the lens. Available in 1.4X and 2.0X configurations from Canon, an extender transforms, say, a 200mm lens into a 280mm or 400mm optic, respectively. Given the T1i's crop factor,

Figure 6.14
Telephoto extenders multiply the true focal length of your lenses—but at a cost of some sharpness and aperture speed.

your 200mm lens now has the same field of view as a 448mm or 640mm lens on a full-frame camera. At around $300 each, they're quite a bargain, aren't they? You can also find less expensive telephoto extenders, like the one shown in Figure 6.14, from third-party suppliers.

Actually, there are some downsides. While extenders retain the closest focusing distance of your original lens, autofocus is maintained only if the lens's original maximum aperture is f/4 or larger (for the 1.4X extender) or f/2.8 or larger (for the 2X extender). The components reduce the effective aperture of any lens they are used with, by one f/stop with the 1.4X extender, and 2 f/stops with the 2X extender. So, your EF 200mm f/2.8L II USM becomes a 280mm f/4 or 400mm f/5.6 lens. Although Canon extenders are precision optical devices, they do cost you a little sharpness, but that improves when you reduce the aperture by a stop or two. Each of the extenders is compatible only with a particular set of lenses of 135mm focal length or greater, so you'll want to check Canon's compatibility chart to see if the component can be used with the lens you want to attach to it.

If your lenses are compatible and you're shooting under bright lighting conditions, the Canon Extender EF 1.4x II and Canon Extender EF 2x II make handy accessories.

Macro Focusing

Some telephotos and telephoto zooms available for the Rebel T1i have particularly close focusing capabilities, making them *macro* lenses. Of course, the object is not necessarily to get close (get too close and you'll find it difficult to light your subject). What you're really looking for in a macro lens is to magnify the apparent size of the subject in the final image. Camera-to-subject distance is most important when you want to back up farther from your subject (say, to avoid spooking skittish insects or small animals). In that case, you'll want a macro lens with a longer focal length to allow that distance while retaining the desired magnification.

Canon makes 50mm, 60mm, 65mm, 100mm, and 180mm lenses with official macro designations. You'll also find macro lenses, macro zooms, and other close-focusing lenses available from Sigma, Tamron, and Tokina. If you want to focus closer with a macro lens, or any other lens, you can add an accessory called an *extension tube*, like the one shown in Figure 6.15. These add-ons move the lens farther from the focal plane, allowing it to focus more closely. Canon also sells add-on close-up lenses, which look like filters, and allow lenses to focus more closely.

Figure 6.15 Extension tubes enable any lens to focus more closely to the subject.

Image Stabilization

Canon has a burgeoning line of more than a dozen lenses with built-in image stabilization (IS) capabilities. This feature uses lens elements that are shifted internally in response to the motion of the lens during handheld photography, countering the shakiness the camera and photographer produce and which telephoto lenses magnify. However, IS is not limited to long lenses; the feature works like a champ at the 17mm zoom position of Canon's EF-S 17-85mm f4-5.6 IS USM and EF-S 17-55 f/2.8 IS USM lenses. Other Canon IS lenses provide stabilization with zooms that are as wide as 24-28mm.

Image stabilization provides you with camera steadiness that's the equivalent of at least two or three shutter speed increments. (Canon claims four, which I feel may be optimistic.) This extra margin can be invaluable when you're shooting under dim lighting conditions or handholding a long lens for, say, wildlife photography. Perhaps that shot of a foraging deer calls for a shutter speed of 1/1,000th second at f/5.6 with your EF 100-400mm f/4.5-5.6L IS USM lens. Relax. You can shoot at 1/250th second at f/11 and get virtually the same results, as long as the deer doesn't decide to bound off.

Or, maybe you're shooting a high school play without a tripod or monopod, and you'd really, really like to use 1/15th second at f/4. Assuming the actors aren't flitting around the stage at high speed, your 17mm-85mm IS lens can grab the shot for you at its wide-angle position. However, keep these facts in mind:

- **IS doesn't stop action.** Unfortunately, no IS lens is a panacea to replace the action-stopping capabilities of a higher shutter speed. Image stabilization applies only to camera shake. You still need a fast shutter speed to freeze action. IS works great in low light, when you're using long lenses, and for macro photography. It's not always the best choice for action photography, unless there's enough light to allow a sufficiently high shutter speed. If so, IS can make your shot even sharper.

- **IS slows you down.** The process of adjusting the lens elements takes time, just as autofocus does, so you might find that IS adds to the lag between when you press the shutter and when the picture is actually taken. That's another reason why image stabilization might not be a good choice for sports.

- **Use when appropriate.** Some IS lenses produce worse results if you use them while you're panning, although newer Canon IS lenses have a mode that works fine when the camera is deliberately moved from side to side during exposure. Older lenses can confuse the motion with camera shake and overcompensate. You might want to switch off IS when panning or when your camera is mounted on a tripod.

- **Do you need IS at all?** Remember that an inexpensive monopod might be able to provide the same additional steadiness as an IS lens, at a much lower cost. If you're out in the field shooting wild animals or flowers and think a tripod isn't practical, try a monopod first.

IMAGE STABILIZATION: IN THE CAMERA OR IN THE LENS?

Sony's acquisition of Konica Minolta's dSLR assets and the introduction of an improved in-camera image-stabilization system has revised an old debate about whether IS belongs in the camera or in the lens. Perhaps it's my Canon bias showing, but I am quite happy not to have image stabilization available in the body itself. Here are some reasons:

■ Should in-camera IS fail, you have to send the whole camera in for repair, and camera repairs are generally more expensive than lens repairs. I like being able to simply switch to another lens if I have an IS problem.

■ IS in the camera doesn't steady your view in the viewfinder, whereas an IS lens shows you a steadied image as you shoot.

■ You're stuck with the IS system built into your camera. If an improved system is incorporated into a lens and the improvements are important to you, just trade in your old lens for the new one.

■ Optimized stabilization. Canon claims that it is able to produce the best possible image stabilization for each lens it introduces, something that would not be possible if a "one size fits all lenses" stabilization scheme had to be built into the camera.

7

Making Light Work for You

Successful photographers and artists have an intimate understanding of the importance of light in shaping an image. Rembrandt was a master of using light to create moods and reveal the character of his subjects. Artist Thomas Kinkade's official tagline is "Painter of Light." The late Dean Collins, co-founder of Finelight Studios, revolutionized how a whole generation of photographers learned and used lighting. I recently attended a seminar called "Captivated by the Light," run by photo guru Ed Pierce. It's impossible to underestimate how the use of light adds to—and how misuse can detract from—your photographs.

All forms of visual art use light to shape the finished product. Sculptors don't have control over the light used to illuminate their finished work, so they must create shapes using planes and curved surfaces so that the form envisioned by the artist comes to life from a variety of viewing and lighting angles. Painters, in contrast, have absolute control over both shape and light in their work, as well as the viewing angle, so they can use both the contours of their two-dimensional subjects and the qualities of the "light" they use to illuminate those subjects to evoke the image they want to produce.

Photography is a third form of art. The photographer may have little or no control over the subject (other than posing human subjects) but can often adjust both viewing angle *and* the nature of the light source to create a particular compelling image. The direction and intensity of the light sources create the shapes and textures that we see. The distribution and proportions determine the contrast and tonal values: whether the image is stark or high key, or muted and low in contrast. The colors of the light (because even "white" light has a color balance that the sensor can detect), and how much of those colors the subject reflects or absorbs, paint the hues visible in the image.

As a Rebel T1i photographer, you must learn to be a painter and sculptor of light if you want to move from *taking* a picture to *making* a photograph. This chapter provides an introduction to using the two main types of illumination: *continuous* lighting (such as daylight, incandescent, or fluorescent sources) and the brief, but brilliant snippets of light we call *electronic flash*.

Continuous Illumination versus Electronic Flash

Continuous lighting is exactly what you might think: uninterrupted illumination that is available all the time during a shooting session. Daylight, moonlight, and the artificial lighting encountered both indoors and outdoors count as continuous light sources (although all of them can be "interrupted" by passing clouds, solar eclipses, a blown fuse, or simply by switching a lamp off). Indoor continuous illumination includes both the lights that are there already (such as incandescent lamps or overhead fluorescent lights indoors) and fixtures you supply yourself, including photoflood lamps or reflectors used to bounce existing light onto your subject.

The surge of light we call electronic flash is produced by a burst of photons generated by an electrical charge that is accumulated in a component called a *capacitor* and then directed through a glass tube containing xenon gas, which absorbs the energy and emits the brief flash. Electronic flash is notable because it can be much more intense than continuous lighting, lasts only a brief moment, and can be much more portable than supplementary incandescent sources. It's a light source you can carry with you and use anywhere.

Indeed, your Rebel T1i has a flip-up electronic flash unit built in, as shown in Figure 7.1. But you can also use an external flash, either mounted on the T1i's accessory shoe or used off-camera and linked with a cable or triggered by a slave light (which sets off a flash when it senses the firing of another unit). Studio flash units are electronic flash, too, and aren't limited to "professional" shooters, as there are economical "monolight" (one-piece flash/power supply) units available in the $200 price range. You can buy a couple to store in a closet and use to set up a home studio, or use as supplementary lighting when traveling away from home.

There are advantages and disadvantages to each type of illumination. Here's a quick checklist of pros and cons:

■ **Lighting preview—Pro: continuous lighting.** With continuous lighting, you always know exactly what kind of lighting effect you're going to get and, if multiple lights are used, how they will interact with each other, as you can see in Figure 7.2. With electronic flash, the general effect you're going to see may be a mystery until you've built some experience, and you may need to review a shot on the LCD, make some adjustments, and then reshoot to get the look you want. (In this sense, a digital camera's review capabilities replace the Polaroid test shots pro photographers relied on in decades past.)

Figure 7.1
One form of light that's always available is the flip-up flash on your Rebel T1i.

Figure 7.2
With continuous lighting, you always know the effect you're going to get.

- **Lighting preview—Con: electronic flash.** While some external flash have a modeling light function (consisting of a series of low-powered bursts that flash for a period of time), your T1i lacks such a capability in its internal flash, and, in any case, this feature is no substitute for continuous illumination, or an always-on modeling lamp like that found in studio flash. As the number of flash units increases, lighting previews, especially if you want to see the proportions of illumination provided by each flash, grow more complex.

- **Exposure calculation—Pro: continuous lighting.** Your T1i has no problem calculating exposure for continuous lighting, because it remains constant and can be measured through a sensor that interprets the light reaching the viewfinder. The amount of light available just before the exposure will, in almost all cases, be the same amount of light present when the shutter is released. The T1i's Spot metering mode can be used to measure and compare the proportions of light in the highlights and shadows, so you can make an adjustment (such as using more or less fill light) if necessary. You can even use a handheld light meter to measure the light yourself and set the exposure in Manual mode.

- **Exposure calculation—Con: electronic flash.** Electronic flash illumination doesn't exist until the flash fires, and so can't be measured by the T1i's exposure sensor when the mirror is flipped up during the exposure. Instead, the light must be measured by interpreting the intensity of a preflash triggered an instant before the main flash, as it is reflected back to the camera and through the lens. An alternative is to use a sensor built into the flash itself and measure reflected light that has not traveled through the lens. If you have a do-it-yourself bent, there are handheld flash meters, too, including models that measure both flash and continuous light.

- **Evenness of illumination—Pro/con: continuous lighting.** Of continuous light sources, daylight, in particular, provides illumination that tends to fill an image completely, lighting up the foreground, background, and your subject almost equally. Shadows do come into play, of course, so you might need to use reflectors or fill-in light sources to even out the illumination further, but barring objects that block large sections of your image from daylight, the light is spread fairly evenly. Indoors, however, continuous lighting is commonly less evenly distributed. The average living room, for example, has hot spots and dark corners. But on the plus side, you can *see* this uneven illumination and compensate with additional lamps.

- **Evenness of illumination—Con: electronic flash.** Electronic flash units (like continuous light sources such as lamps that don't have the advantage of being located 93 million miles from the subject) suffer from the effects of their proximity. The *inverse square law*, first applied to both gravity and light by Sir Isaac Newton, dictates that as a light source's distance increases from the subject, the amount of light reaching the subject falls off proportionately to the square of the distance. In plain

English, that means that a flash or lamp that's eight feet away from a subject provides only one-quarter as much illumination as a source that's four feet away (rather than half as much). (See Figure 7.3) This translates into relatively shallow "depth-of-light."

Figure 7.3

A light source that is twice as far away provides only one-quarter as much illumination.

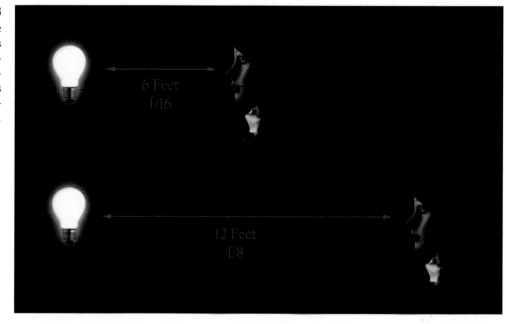

- **Action stopping—Con: continuous lighting.** Action stopping with continuous light sources is completely dependent on the shutter speed you've dialed in on the camera. And the speeds available are dependent on the amount of light available and your ISO sensitivity setting. Outdoors in daylight, there will probably be enough sunlight to let you shoot at 1/2,000th second and f/6.3 with a non-grainy sensitivity setting of ISO 400. That's a fairly useful combination of settings if you're not using a super-telephoto with a small maximum aperture. But inside, the reduced illumination quickly has you pushing your Rebel T1i to its limits. For example, if you're shooting indoor sports, there probably won't be enough available light to allow you to use a 1/2,000th second shutter speed (although I routinely shoot indoor basketball with my T1i at ISO 1600 and 1/500th second at f/4). In many indoor sports situations, you may find yourself limited to 1/500 second or slower.

- **Action stopping—Pro: electronic flash.** When it comes to the ability to freeze moving objects in their tracks, the advantage goes to electronic flash. The brief duration of electronic flash serves as a very high "shutter speed" when the flash is the main or only source of illumination for the photo. Your Rebel T1i's shutter speed may be set for 1/200th second during a flash exposure, but if the flash illumination predominates, the *effective* exposure time will be the 1/1,000th to 1/50,000th second or less duration of the flash, because the flash unit reduces the amount of light released by cutting short the duration of the flash. Figure 7.4 shows an eye-catching "hammer breaks bulb" photo by Cleveland photographer Kris Bosworth, who reports that syncing the flash with the event was the trickiest part of the whole experiment. The only fly in the ointment is that, if the ambient light is strong enough, it may produce a secondary, "ghost" exposure, as I'll explain later in this chapter.

Figure 7.4
A switch that was closed by the impact of the hammer on the bulb triggered the electronic flash that froze this action.

- **Cost—Pro: continuous lighting.** Incandescent or fluorescent lamps are generally much less expensive than electronic flash units, which can easily cost several hundred dollars. I've used everything from desktop hi-intensity lamps to reflector floodlights for continuous illumination at very little cost. There are lamps made especially for photographic purposes, too, priced up to $50 or so. Maintenance is economical, too; many incandescent or fluorescents use bulbs that cost only a few dollars.

- **Cost—Con: electronic flash.** Electronic flash units aren't particularly cheap. The lowest-cost dedicated flash designed specifically for the Canon dSLRs is about $110. Such units are limited in features, however, and intended for those with entry-level cameras. Plan to spend some money to get the features that a sophisticated electronic flash offers.

- **Flexibility—Con: continuous lighting.** Because incandescent and fluorescent lamps are not as bright as electronic flash, the slower shutter speeds required (see "Action Stopping," above) mean that you may have to use a tripod more often, especially when shooting portraits. The incandescent variety of continuous lighting gets hot, especially in the studio, and the side effects range from discomfort (for your human models) to disintegration (if you happen to be shooting perishable foods like ice cream). The heat also makes it more difficult to add filtration to incandescent sources.

- **Flexibility—Pro: electronic flash.** Electronic flash's action-freezing power allows you to work without a tripod in the studio (and elsewhere), adding flexibility and speed when choosing angles and positions. Flash units can be easily filtered, and, because the filtration is placed over the light source rather than the lens, you don't need to use high quality filter material. For example, a couple sheets of unexposed, processed Ektachrome film can make a dandy infrared-pass filter for your flash unit. Roscoe or Lee lighting gels, which may be too flimsy to use in front of the lens, can be mounted or taped in front of your flash with ease.

Continuous Lighting Basics

While continuous lighting and its effects are generally much easier to visualize and use than electronic flash, there are some factors you need to take into account, particularly the color temperature of the light. (Color temperature concerns aren't exclusive to continuous light sources, of course, but the variations tend to be more extreme and less predictable than those of electronic flash.)

Color temperature, in practical terms, is how "bluish" or how "reddish" the light appears to be to the digital camera's sensor. Indoor illumination is quite warm, comparatively, and appears reddish to the sensor. Daylight, in contrast, seems much bluer to the sensor. Our eyes (our brains, actually) are quite adaptable to these variations, so white objects don't appear to have an orange tinge when viewed indoors, nor do they seem excessively blue outdoors in full daylight. Yet, these color temperature variations are real and the sensor is not fooled. To capture the most accurate colors, we need to take the color temperature into account in setting the color balance (or *white balance*) of the T1i—either automatically using the camera's smarts, or manually, using our own knowledge and experience.

Color temperature can be confusing, because of a seeming contradiction in how color temperatures are named: warmer (more reddish) color temperatures (measured in degrees Kelvin) are the *lower* numbers, while cooler (bluer) color temperatures are *higher* numbers. It might not make sense to say that 3,400K is warmer than 6,000K, but that's the way it is. If it helps, think of a glowing red ember contrasted with a white-hot welder's torch, rather than fire and ice.

The confusion comes from physics. Scientists calculate color temperature from the light emitted by a mythical object called a black body radiator, which absorbs all the radiant energy that strikes it, and reflects none at all. Such a black body not only *absorbs* light perfectly, but it *emits* it perfectly when heated (and since nothing in the universe is perfect, that makes it mythical).

At a particular physical temperature, this imaginary object always emits light of the same wavelength or color. That makes it possible to define color temperature in terms of actual temperature in degrees on the Kelvin scale that scientists use. Incandescent light, for example, typically has a color temperature of 3,200K to 3,400K. Daylight might range from 5,500K to 6,000K. Each type of illumination we use for photography has its own color temperature range—with some cautions. The next sections will summarize everything you need to know about the qualities of these light sources.

Daylight

Daylight is produced by the sun, and so is moonlight (which is just reflected sunlight). Daylight is present, of course, even when you can't see the sun. When sunlight is direct, it can be bright and harsh. If daylight is diffused by clouds, softened by bouncing off objects such as walls or your photo reflectors, or filtered by shade, it can be much dimmer and less contrasty.

Daylight's color temperature can vary quite widely. It is highest (most blue) at noon when the sun is directly overhead because the light is traveling through a minimum amount of the filtering layer we call the atmosphere. The color temperature at high noon may be 6,000K. At other times of day, the sun is lower in the sky and the particles in the air provide a filtering effect that warms the illumination to about 5,500K for most of the day. Starting an hour before dusk and for an hour after sunrise, the warm appearance of the sunlight is even visible to our eyes when the color temperature may dip to 5,000-4,500K, as shown in Figure 7.5.

Figure 7.5 At dawn and dusk, the color temperature of daylight may dip as low as 4,500K.

Because you'll be taking so many photos in daylight, you'll want to learn how to use or compensate for the brightness and contrast of sunlight, as well as how to deal with its color temperature. I'll provide some hints later in this chapter.

Incandescent/Tungsten Light

The term incandescent or tungsten illumination is usually applied to the direct descendents of Thomas Edison's original electric lamp. Such lights consist of a glass bulb that contains a vacuum, or is filled with a halogen gas, and contains a tungsten filament that is heated by an electrical current, producing photons and heat. Tungsten-halogen lamps are a variation on the basic light bulb, using a more rugged (and longer-lasting) filament that can be heated to a higher temperature, housed in a thicker glass or quartz envelope, and filled with iodine or bromine ("halogen") gases. The higher temperature allows tungsten-halogen (or quartz-halogen/quartz-iodine, depending on their construction) lamps to burn "hotter" and whiter. Although popular for automobile headlamps today, they've also been popular for photographic illumination.

Although incandescent illumination isn't a perfect black body radiator, it's close enough that the color temperature of such lamps can be precisely calculated and used for photography without concerns about color variation (at least, until the very end of the lamp's life).

The other qualities of this type of lighting, such as contrast, are dependent on the distance of the lamp from the subject, type of reflectors used, and other factors that I'll explain later in this chapter.

Fluorescent Light/Other Light Sources

Fluorescent light has some advantages in terms of illumination, but some disadvantages from a photographic standpoint. This type of lamp generates light through an electro-chemical reaction that emits most of its energy as visible light, rather than heat, which is why the bulbs don't get as hot. The type of light produced varies depending on the phosphor coatings and type of gas in the tube. So, the illumination fluorescent bulbs produce can vary widely in its characteristics.

That's not great news for photographers. Different types of lamps have different "color temperatures" that can't be precisely measured in degrees Kelvin, because the light isn't produced by heating. Worse, fluorescent lamps have a discontinuous spectrum of light that can have some colors missing entirely. A particular type of tube can lack certain shades of red or other colors (see Figure 7.6), which is why fluorescent lamps and other

Figure 7.6
The fluorescent lighting in this gym added a distinct greenish cast to the image.

alternative technologies such as sodium-vapor illumination can produce ghastly look-ing human skin tones. Their spectra can lack the reddish tones we associate with healthy skin and emphasize the blues and greens popular in horror movies.

Adjusting White Balance

I showed you how to adjust white balance in Chapter 3, using the T1i's built-in presets, white balance shift capabilities, and white balance bracketing (there's more on bracket-ing in Chapter 4, too).

In most cases, however, the Rebel T1i will do a good job of calculating white balance for you, so Auto can be used as your choice most of the time. Use the preset values or set a custom white balance that matches the current shooting conditions when you need to. The only really problematic light sources are likely to be fluorescents. Vendors, such as GE and Sylvania, may actually provide a figure known as the *color rendering index* (or CRI), which is a measure of how accurately a particular light source represents stan-dard colors, using a scale of 0 (some sodium-vapor lamps) to 100 (daylight and most incandescent lamps). Daylight fluorescents and deluxe cool white fluorescents might have a CRI of about 79 to 95, which is perfectly acceptable for most photographic appli-cations. Warm white fluorescents might have a CRI of 55. White deluxe mercury vapor lights are less suitable with a CRI of 45, while low-pressure sodium lamps can vary from CRI 0-18.

Remember that if you shoot RAW, you can specify the white balance of your image when you import it into Photoshop, Photoshop Elements, or another image editor using your preferred RAW converter. While color-balancing filters that fit on the front of the lens exist, they are primarily useful for film cameras, because film's color balance can't be tweaked as extensively as that of a sensor.

Electronic Flash Basics

Until you delve into the situation deeply enough, it might appear that serious photog-raphers have a love/hate relationship with electronic flash. You'll often hear that flash photography is less natural looking, and that the built-in flash in most cameras should never be used as the primary source of illumination because it provides a harsh, garish look. Indeed, most "pro" cameras like the Canon EOS 1D Mark III and 1Ds Mark III don't have a built-in flash at all. Available ("continuous") lighting is praised, and built-in flash photography seems to be roundly denounced.

In truth, however, the bias is against *bad* flash photography. Indeed, flash has become the studio light source of choice for pro photographers, because it's more intense (and its intensity can be varied to order by the photographer), freezes action, frees you from using a tripod (unless you want to use one to lock down a composition), and has a snappy, consistent light quality that matches daylight. (While color balance changes as the flash duration shortens, some Canon flash units can communicate to the camera the exact white balance provided for that shot.) And even pros will cede that the built-in flash of the Canon EOS Rebel T1i has some important uses as an adjunct to existing light, particularly to fill in dark shadows.

But electronic flash isn't as inherently easy to use as continuous lighting. As I noted earlier, electronic flash units are more expensive, don't show you exactly what the lighting effect will be (unless you use a second source called a *modeling light* for a preview), and the exposure of electronic flash units is more difficult to calculate accurately.

How Electronic Flash Works

The bursts of light we call electronic flash are produced by a flash of photons generated by an electrical charge that is accumulated in a component called a *capacitor*, and are then directed through a glass tube containing xenon gas, which absorbs the energy and emits the brief flash. For the pop-up flash built into the Rebel T1i, the full burst of light lasts about 1/1,000th second and provides enough illumination to shoot a subject 10 feet away at f/4 using the ISO 100 setting. In a more typical situation, you'd use ISO 200, f/5.6 to f/8 and photograph something 8 to 10 feet away. As you can see, the built-in flash is somewhat limited in range; you'll see why external flash units are often a good idea later in this chapter.

An electronic flash (whether built in or connected to the Rebel T1i through a cable plugged into a hot shoe adapter) is triggered at the instant of exposure, during a period when the sensor is fully exposed by the shutter. As I mentioned earlier in this book, the T1i has a vertically traveling shutter that consists of two curtains. The first curtain opens and moves to the opposite side of the frame, at which point the shutter is completely open. The flash can be triggered at this point (so-called *first-curtain sync*), making the flash exposure. Then, after a delay that can vary from 30 seconds to 1/200th second (with the Rebel T1i; other cameras may sync at a faster or slower speed), a second curtain begins moving across the sensor plane, covering up the sensor again. If the flash is triggered just before the second curtain starts to close, then *second-curtain sync* is used. In both cases, though, a shutter speed of 1/200th second is the maximum that can be used to take a photo.

If you happen to try to set the T1i's shutter to a faster speed in Tv or M mode, the camera will automatically adjust the shutter speed down to 1/200th second when using flash. In Av, P, or any of the Basic Zone modes, the T1i will never select a shutter speed higher than 1/200th second when using flash. Actually, in P mode, shutter speed is automatically set between 1/60th and 1/200th second when using flash.

Figure 7.7 illustrates how this works, with a fanciful illustration of a generic shutter (your T1i's shutter does *not* look like this, and some vertically traveling shutters move bottom to top rather than the top-to-bottom motion shown). Both curtains are tightly

Figure 7.7
A focal plane shutter has two curtains, the lower, or front curtain, and an upper, second curtain.

closed at upper left. At upper right, the first curtain begins to move downwards, starting to expose a narrow slit that reveals the sensor behind the shutter. At lower left, the first curtain moves downwards farther until, as you can see at lower right in the figure, the sensor is fully exposed.

When first-curtain sync is used, the flash is triggered at the instant that the sensor is completely exposed. The shutter then remains open for an additional length of time (from 30 seconds to 1/200th second), and the second curtain begins to move downward, covering the sensor once more. When second-curtain sync is activated, the flash is triggered *after* the main exposure is over, just before the second curtain begins to move downward.

Ghost Images

The difference between triggering the flash when the shutter just opens, or just when it begins to close might not seem like much. But whether you use first-curtain sync (the default setting) or second-curtain sync (an optional setting) can make a significant difference to your photograph *if the ambient light in your scene also contributes to the image.*

At faster shutter speeds, particularly 1/200th second, there isn't much time for the ambient light to register, unless it is very bright. It's likely that the electronic flash will provide almost all the illumination, so first-curtain sync or second-curtain sync isn't very important. However, at slower shutter speeds, or with very bright ambient light levels, there is a significant difference, particularly if your subject is moving, or the camera isn't steady.

In any of those situations, the ambient light will register as a second image accompanying the flash exposure, and if there is movement (camera or subject), that additional image will not be in the same place as the flash exposure. It will show as a ghost image and, if the movement is significant enough, as a blurred ghost image trailing in front of or behind your subject in the direction of the movement.

As I noted, when you're using first-curtain sync, the flash's main burst goes off the instant the shutter opens fully (a pre-flash used to measure exposure in auto flash modes fires *before* the shutter opens). This produces an image of the subject on the sensor. Then, the shutter remains open for an additional period (30 seconds to 1/200th second, as I said). If your subject is moving, say, towards the right side of the frame, the ghost image produced by the ambient light will produce a blur on the right side of the original subject image, making it look as if your sharp (flash-produced) image is chasing the ghost. For those of us who grew up with lightning-fast superheroes who always left a ghost trail *behind them*, that looks unnatural (see Figure 7.8).

So, Canon uses second-curtain sync to remedy the situation. In that mode, the shutter opens, as before. The shutter remains open for its designated duration, and the ghost image forms. If your subject moves from the left side of the frame to the right side, the ghost will move from left to right, too. *Then*, about 1.5 milliseconds before the second shutter curtain closes, the flash is triggered, producing a nice, sharp flash image *ahead* of the ghost image. Voilà! We have monsieur *Speed Racer* outdriving his own trailing image.

Figure 7.8 First-curtain sync produces an image that trails in front of the flash exposure (top), while second-curtain sync creates a more "natural looking" trail behind the flash image.

Avoiding Sync Speed Problems

Using a shutter speed faster than 1/200th second can cause problems. Triggering the electronic flash only when the shutter is completely open makes a lot of sense if you think about what's going on. To obtain shutter speeds faster than 1/200th second, the T1i exposes only part of the sensor at one time, by starting the second curtain on its journey before the first curtain has completely opened, as shown in Figure 7.9. That effectively provides a briefer exposure as the open slit between the blades of the shutter passes over the surface of the sensor. If the flash were to fire during the time when the first and second curtains partially obscured the sensor, only the slit that was actually open would be exposed.

Figure 7.9 A closed shutter (left); partially open shutter as the first curtain begins to move downwards (middle); only part of the sensor is exposed as the slit moves (right).

You'd end up with only a narrow band, representing the portion of the sensor that was exposed when the picture is taken. For shutter speeds *faster* than 1/200th second, the second curtain begins moving *before* the first curtain reaches the top of the frame. As a result, a moving slit, the distance between the first and second curtains, exposes one portion of the sensor at a time as it moves from the bottom to the top. Figure 7.9 shows three views of our typical (but imaginary) focal plane shutter. At left is pictured the closed shutter; in the middle version you can see the first curtain has moved up about 1/4 of the distance to the top; and in the right-hand version, the second curtain has started to "chase" the first curtain across the frame towards the top.

If the flash is triggered while this slit is moving, only the exposed portion of the sensor will receive any illumination. You end up with a photo like the one shown in Figure 7.10. Note that a band across the top of the image is black. That's a shadow of the second shutter curtain, which had started to move when the flash was triggered. Sharp-eyed readers will wonder why the black band is at the *bottom* of the frame rather than at the top, where the second curtain begins its journey. The answer is simple: your lens flips the image upside down and forms it on the sensor in a reversed position. You never notice that, because the camera is smart enough to show you the pixels that make up your photo in their proper orientation during picture review. But this image flip is why, if your sensor gets dirty and you detect a spot of dust in the upper half of a test photo, if cleaning manually, you need to look for the speck in the *bottom* half of the sensor.

Figure 7.10
If a shutter speed faster than 1/200th second is used, you can end up photographing only a portion of the image.

I generally end up with sync speed problems only when shooting in the studio, using studio flash units rather than my T1i's built-in flash or a Canon dedicated Speedlight. That's because if you're using either type of "smart" flash, the camera knows that a strobe is attached, and remedies any unintentional goof in shutter speed settings. If you happen to set the T1i's shutter to a faster speed in Tv or M mode, the camera will automatically adjust the shutter speed down to 1/200th second. In Av, P, or any of the Basic Zone modes, where the T1i selects the shutter speed, it will never choose a shutter speed higher than 1/200th second when using flash. In P mode, shutter speed is automatically set between 1/60th to 1/200th second when using flash.

But when using a non-dedicated flash, such as a studio unit plugged into the T1i's hot shoe connector, the camera has no way of knowing that a flash is connected, so shutter speeds faster than 1/200th second can be set inadvertently. Note that the T1i can use a feature called *high-speed sync* that allows shutter speeds faster than 1/200th second with certain external dedicated Canon flash units. When using high-speed sync, the flash fires a continuous serious of bursts at reduced power for the entire duration of the exposure, so that the illumination is able to expose the sensor as the slit moves. High-speed sync is set using the controls that adjust the compatible external flash.

Determining Exposure

Calculating the proper exposure for an electronic flash photograph is a bit more complicated than determining the settings by continuous light. The right exposure isn't simply a function of how far away your subject is (which the T1i can figure out based on the autofocus distance that's locked in just prior to taking the picture). Various objects reflect more or less light at the same distance so, obviously, the camera needs to measure the amount of light reflected back and through the lens. Yet, as the flash itself isn't available for measuring until it's triggered, the T1i has nothing to measure.

The solution is to fire the flash twice. The initial shot is a preflash that can be analyzed, then followed by a main flash that's given exactly the calculated intensity needed to provide a correct exposure. As a result, the primary flash may be longer for distant objects and shorter for closer subjects, depending on the required intensity for exposure. This through-the-lens evaluative flash exposure system is called E-TTL II, and it operates whenever the pop-up internal flash is used, or if you have attached a Canon dedicated flash unit to the T1i.

Guide Numbers

Guide numbers, usually abbreviated GN, are a way of specifying the power of an electronic flash in a way that can be used to determine the right f/stop to use at a particular shooting distance and ISO setting. In fact, before automatic flash units became prevalent, the GN was actually used to do just that. A GN is usually given as a pair of numbers for both feet and meters that represent the range at ISO 100. For example, the Rebel T1i's built-in flash has a GN of 13/43 (meters/feet) at ISO 100. To calculate the right exposure at that ISO setting, you'd divide the guide number by the distance to arrive at the appropriate f/stop.

Using the T1i's built-in flash as an example, at ISO 100 with its GN of 43, if you wanted to shoot a subject at a distance of 10 feet, you'd use f/4.3 (43 divided by 10; round to f/4 for simplicity's sake). At 8 feet, an f/stop of f/5.4 (round up to f/5.6) would be used. Some quick mental calculations with the GN will give you any particular electronic flash's range. You can easily see that the built-in flash would begin to peter out at about 15 feet, where you'd need an aperture of f/2.8 at ISO 100. Of course, in the real world you'd probably bump the sensitivity up to a setting of ISO 400 so you could use a more practical f/5.6 at that distance.

Today, guide numbers are most useful for comparing the power of various flash units. You don't need to be a math genius to see that an electronic flash with a GN of, say, 165 would be *a lot* more powerful than your built-in flash (at ISO 100, you could use f/11 instead of f/2.8 at 15 feet).

Using the Built-In Flash

The Canon EOS Rebel T1i's built-in flash is a handy accessory because it is available as required, without the need to carry an external flash around with you constantly. This section explains how to use the flip-up flash in the various Basic Zone and Creative Zone modes.

Basic Zone Flash

When the T1i is set to one of the Basic Zone modes (except for Landscape, Sports, or Flash Off modes), the built-in flash will pop up when needed to provide extra illumination in low-light situations, or when your subject matter is backlit and could benefit from some fill flash. The flash doesn't pop up in Landscape mode because the flash doesn't have enough reach to have much effect for pictures of distant vistas in any case; nor does the flash pop up automatically in Sports mode, because you'll often want to use shutter speeds faster than 1/200th second and/or be shooting subjects that are out of flash range. Pop-up flash is disabled in Flash Off mode for obvious reasons. When using the Basic Zone modes, the flash can't be popped up manually; it will flip into place only when the T1i decides you need it.

If you happen to be shooting a landscape photo and do want to use flash (say, to add some illumination to a subject that's closer to the camera), or you want flash with your sports photos, or you *don't* want the flash popping up all the time when using one of the other Basic Zone modes, switch to an appropriate Creative Zone mode and use that instead.

Creative Zone Flash

When you're using a Creative Zone mode, you'll have to judge for yourself when flash might be useful, and flip it up yourself by pressing the Flash button on the side of the pentaprism. The behavior of the internal flash varies, depending on which Creative Zone mode you're using.

- **P/A-DEP.** In these modes, the T1i fully automates the exposure process, giving you subtle fill flash effects in daylight, and fully illuminating your subject under dimmer lighting conditions. The camera selects a shutter speed from 1/60th to 1/200th second and sets an appropriate aperture.

- **Av.** In Aperture Priority mode, you set the aperture as always, and the T1i chooses a shutter speed from 30 seconds to 1/200th second. Use this mode with care, because if the camera detects a dark background, it will use the flash to expose the main subject in the foreground, and then leave the shutter open long enough to allow the background to be exposed correctly, too. If you're not using an image-stabilized lens, you can end up with blurry ghost images even of non-moving subjects at exposures longer than 1/30th second, and if your camera is not mounted on a tripod, you'll see these blurs at exposures longer than about 1/8th second even if you are using IS.

- **Tv.** When using flash in Tv mode, you set the shutter speed from 30 seconds to 1/200th second, and the T1i will choose the correct aperture for the correct flash exposure. If you accidentally set the shutter speed higher than 1/200th second, the camera will reduce it to 1/200th second when you're using the flash.

- **M.** In Manual mode, you select both shutter speed (30 seconds to 1/200th second) and aperture. The camera will adjust the shutter speed to 1/200th second if you try to use a faster speed with flash. The E-TTL II system will provide the correct amount of exposure for your main subject at the aperture you've chosen (if the subject is within the flash's range, of course).

When using Creative Zone modes (or any Basic Zone mode in which flash is used), if Red-Eye Reduction is turned on in the Shooting menu (as described in Chapter 3), the red-eye reduction lamp will illuminate for about 1.5 seconds when you press down the shutter release halfway, theoretically causing your subjects' irises to contract (if they are looking toward the camera), and thereby reducing the red-eye effect in your photograph.

Flash Range

The illumination of the T1i's built-in flash varies with distance, focal length, and ISO sensitivity setting.

- **Distance.** The farther away your subject is from the camera, the greater the light fall-off, thanks to the inverse square law discussed earlier. Keep in mind that a subject that's twice as far away receives only one-quarter as much light, which is two f/stops' worth.

- **Focal length.** The built-in flash "covers" only a limited angle of view, which doesn't change, but which is sufficient for most lenses, including the 18-55mm kit lens. With lenses wider than 18mm, however, , the frame may not be covered fully, and you'll experience dark areas, especially in the corners. As you zoom in using longer focal lengths, some of the illumination is outside the area of view and is "wasted." (This phenomenon is why some external flash units, such as the 580EX II, "zoom" to match the zoom setting of your lens to concentrate the available flash burst onto the actual subject area.)

- **ISO setting.** The higher the ISO sensitivity, the more photons captured by the sensor. So, doubling the sensitivity from ISO 100 to 200 produces the same effect as, say, opening up your lens from f/8 to f/5.6.

Flash Control Menus

I first described the Flash Control menus in Chapter 3, but am going to recap the information here. This multi-level menu entry includes five settings for controlling the Canon EOS Rebel T1i's built-in, pop-up electronic flash unit, as well as dedicated Canon Speedlites you can attach to the camera (see Figure 7.11).

Figure 7.11
The Flash Control menu entry has five setting sub-menus.

Flash Firing

Use this option to enable or disable the built-in or accessory electronic flash in Creative Zone modes. When disabled, the flash cannot fire even if you accidentally elevate it, or have an accessory flash attached and turned on when using Creative Zone modes.

There are several situations in which you might prefer to totally disable the T1i's built-in and accessory flash. Flash might be a no-no when shooting in sensitive environments, such as concerts, in museums, or during religious ceremonies. You might also want to disable the flash when you want to use the AF-assist beam to help in autofocusing, but do not want the flash to fire.

Built-in Flash Function Setting

There are three choices for this menu choice. (The Flash mode entry is grayed out and cannot be selected, as the built-in flash mode is fixed at the E-TTL II setting):

- **Shutter sync.** You can choose 1st Curtain sync, which fires the flash as soon as the shutter is completely open (this is the default mode). Alternatively, you can select 2nd Curtain sync, which fires a pre-flash used to measure exposure as soon as the shutter release is pressed down all the way, but before the shutter opens, and then triggers a second flash at the end of the exposure, just before the shutter starts to close. This action allows photographing a blurred trail of light of moving objects with sharp flash exposures at the beginning and the end of the exposure, as I described earlier in this chapter.

- **Flash exp. comp.** This is an alternate method of setting flash exposure compensation. Select with the Set button, then dial in the amount of flash EV compensation you want using the left/right cross keys. The EV that was in force prior to your adjustment is shown with a blue indicator. Press Set again to confirm your change, and then press the Menu button to exit.

- **E-TTL II.** You can choose Evaluative or Average metering modes for the electronic flash exposure meter. Evaluative looks at selected areas in the scene to calculate exposure, while Average calculates flash exposure by reading the entire scene.

External Flash Function Setting

This menu is available only when you have a compatible dedicated Canon Speedlite electronic flash attached and switched on. The settings available are shown in Figure 7.12. If you press the DISP button while adjusting flash settings, both the changes made to the settings of an attached external flash and to the built-in flash will be cleared.

- **Flash mode.** This entry allows you to set the flash mode for the external flash, from E-TTL II, A-TTL, or TTL. All three provide through-the-lens flash metering, but with different degrees of sophistication. E-TTL (Evaluative Through-the-Lens) uses a preflash just prior to taking the picture to allow the camera's metering sensor to read the flash exposure and compare it with ambient light to provide the best exposure. A-TTL (Advanced Through-the-Lens) metering is an earlier system used with

Figure 7.12
External flash units can be controlled from the Canon EOS Rebel T1i using this menu.

some Canon speedlights to read illumination through the lens, but concentrate sensitivity on the active focus point, also using a preflash. The TTL (Through-the-Lens) system is a less sophisticated flash exposure control system used by some flash units. It doesn't use a preflash. You should always choose E-TTL if your flash supports it, or select one of the other systems compatible with the Speedlite you are using.

- **Shutter sync.** As with the T1i's internal flash, you can choose 1st Curtain sync, which fires the flash as soon as the shutter is completely open (this is the default mode). Alternatively, you can select 2nd Curtain sync, which fires the flash as soon as the shutter opens, and then triggers a second flash at the end of the exposure, just before the shutter starts to close.

- **FEB.** Flash Exposure Bracketing (FEB) operates similarly to ordinary exposure bracketing, providing a series of different exposures to improve your chances of getting the exact right exposure, or to provide alternative renditions for creative purposes.

- **Flash exposure compensation.** You can adjust flash exposure using a menu here. Select this option with the Set button, then dial in the amount of flash EV compensation you want using the cross keys. The EV that was in place before you started to make your adjustment is shown as a blue indicator, so you can return to that value quickly. Press Set again to confirm your change, then press the Menu button twice to exit.

- **E-TTL II.** You can choose Evaluative (Matrix) or Average metering modes for the electronic flash exposure meter. Evaluative looks at selected areas in the scene to calculate exposure, while Average calculates flash exposure by reading the entire scene.

- **Zoom.** Some flash units can vary their coverage to better match the field of view of your lens at a particular focal length. You can allow the external flash to zoom automatically, based on information provided, or manually, using a zoom button on the flash itself.

External Flash Custom Function Setting

Many external Speedlites from Canon include their own list of Custom Functions, which can be used to specify things like flash metering mode and flash bracketing sequences, as well as more sophisticated features, such as modeling light/flash (if available), use of external power sources (if attached), and functions of any slave unit attached to the external flash. This menu entry allows you to set an external flash unit's Custom Functions from your T1i's menu.

Clear External Flash Custom Function Setting

This entry allows you to zero-out any changes you've made to your external flash's Custom Functions, and return them to their factory default settings.

Using FE Lock and Flash Exposure Compensation

If you want to lock flash exposure for a subject that is not centered in the frame, you can use the FE Lock button (*) to lock in a specific flash exposure, although the procedure is made tricky because of the sequence of steps that the T1i requires. Depress and hold the shutter button halfway to lock in focus, then center the viewfinder on the subject you want to correctly expose, and press the * button. (It's quite difficult to hold the camera, hold the shutter release down halfway, and then press the * button. To make things more interesting, Canon also recommends that you look into the viewfinder to make sure the Flash Ready icon is still lit while doing this.) If you're successful, the pre-flash fires and calculates exposure, displaying the FEL (flash exposure lock) message in the viewfinder. Then, recompose your photo and press the shutter down the rest of the way to take the photo.

You can also manually add or subtract exposure to the flash exposure calculated by the T1i. Just press the Choose the Flash Control entry in Shooting 1 menu, choose Built-in Flash, then the Built-in Flash function, and choose Select Flash Exp. Comp. Then use the left/right cross keys to enter flash exposure compensation plus or minus two f/stops. The exposure index scale on the LCD and in the viewfinder will indicate the change you've made, and a flash exposure compensation icon will appear to warn you that an adjustment has been made. As with non-flash exposure compensation, the compensation you make remains in effect for the pictures that follow, and even when you've turned the camera off, remember to cancel the flash exposure compensation adjustment by reversing the steps used to set it when you're done using it.

Using External Electronic Flash

Canon offers a broad range of accessory electronic flash units for the Rebel T1i. They can be mounted to the flash accessory shoe, or used off-camera with a dedicated cord that plugs into the flash shoe to maintain full communications with the camera for all special features. They range from the Speedlite 580EX II (see Figure 7.13), which can correctly expose subjects up to 24 feet away at f/11 and ISO 200, to the 220EX, which is good out to 9 feet at f/11 and ISO 200. (You'll get greater ranges at even higher ISO settings, of course.) There are also two electronic flash units specifically for specialized close-up flash photography.

Speedlite 580EX II

This flagship of the Canon accessory flash line is the most powerful unit the company offers, with a GN of 190, and a manual/automatic zoom flash head that covers the full frame of lenses from 24mm wide angle to 105mm telephoto. (There's a flip-down wide-angle diffuser that spreads the flash to cover a 14mm lens's field of view, too.) All angle specifications given by Canon refer to full-frame sensors, but this flash unit automatically converts its field of view coverage to accommodate the crop factor of the Rebel T1i

Figure 7.13
The Canon
Speedlite
580EX II is the
most powerful
shoe-mount
flash Canon
offers.

and the other 1.6X crop Canon dSLRs. Compared to the 580 EX it replaces, the Mark II model recycles (inaudibly—no more hum!) 20 percent faster, and has improved dust- and water-resistance so you can use it in harsher environments.

The unit offers full-swivel, 180 degrees in either direction, and has its own built-in AF assist beam and an exposure system that's compatible with the nine focus points of the T1i. Powered by economical AA-size batteries, the unit recycles in 0.1 to 6 seconds, and can squeeze 100 to 700 flashes from a set of alkaline batteries.

The 580EX II automatically communicates white balance information to your camera, allowing it to adjust WB to match the flash output. You can even simulate a modeling light effect: When you press the Depth-of-Field Preview button on the T1i, the 580EX II emits a one-second burst of light that allows you to judge the flash effect. If you're using multiple flash units with Canon's wireless E-TTL system, this model can serve as a master flash that controls the slave units you've set up (more about this later) or function as a slave itself.

It's easy to access all the features of this unit because it has a large backlit LCD panel on the back that provides information about all flash settings. There are 14 Custom

Functions that can be controlled from the flash. These functions are (the first setting is the default value) as follows:

C.Fn 01   Automatic cancellation of Flash Exposure Bracketing (Enable/Disable)

C.Fn 02   Flash Exposure Bracketing Sequence (Metered > Decreased > Increased Exposure or Decreased > Metered > Increased Exposure)

C.Fn 03   Flash metering exposure (E-TTL II/E-TTL)

C.Fn 04   Slave unit's auto power off time (60 minutes/10 minutes)

C.Fn 05   Cancellation of slave unit auto power off by master unit (Within 1 hour/Within 8 Hours)

C.Fn 06   Modeling Flash (Enable/Disable)

C.Fn 07   Flash recycling on external power (Use internal and external power/Use only external power)

C.Fn 08   Quick Flash with continuous shooting (Disable/Enable)

C.Fn 09   Test firing with autoflash power level (1/32 power/full power)

C.Fn 10   Modeling flash triggered by test firing button (Disable/Enable)

C.Fn 11   Auto setting of flash coverage to match image size (Enable/Disable)

C.Fn 12   AF-assist beam OFF (Disable/Enable)

C.Fn 13   Flash Exposure Compensation setting button (Flash unit Select/Set with Select Dial/Select Dial only)

C.Fn 14   Auto Power Off (On/Off)

Speedlite 430EX II

This less pricey electronic flash has a GN of 141, with automatic and manual zoom coverage from 24mm to 105mm, and the same wide-angle pullout panel found on the 580EX II that covers the area of a 14mm lens on a full-frame camera, and automatic conversion to the cropped frame area of the T1i and other 1.6X crop Canon dSLRs. The 430EX also communicates white balance information with the camera, and has its own AF assist beam. Compatible with Canon's wireless E-TTL system, it makes a good slave unit, but cannot serve as a master flash. It, too, uses AA batteries, and offers recycle times of 0.1 to 3.7 seconds for 200 to 1,400 flashes, depending on subject distance.

Speedlite 270EX

This newest Canon Speedlite (with a GN of 72) is small enough at five ounces to fit in a pocket, and, instead of zooming, uses two fixed coverage levels for 28mm and 50mm focal length lenses. It offers bounce-lighting capabilities, and uses two AA batteries, which provide enough power to recycle the unit in four seconds between flashes. Like its "big brothers," the 270X communicates white balance information to the camera and includes a built-in AF assist beam.

Speedlite 220EX

This most basic Canon Speedlight offers automatic operation only, and none of the fancy features of its more expensive siblings. Its 72 guide number is a little beefier than the T1i's built-in flash, making it a good choice as a low-power auxiliary flash unit. It lacks a zoomable flash head and offers fixed coverage equivalent to the field of view of a 28mm full-frame lens. Expect 250 to 1,700 flashes from a set of four AA batteries and recycle times of 0.1 to 4.5 seconds. The built-in AF assist beam is linked to the center focusing point of the T1i only.

More Advanced Lighting Techniques

As you advance in your Canon EOS Rebel T1i photography, you'll want to learn more sophisticated lighting techniques, using more than just straight-on flash, or using just a single flash unit. Entire books have been written on lighting techniques, and I've written multiple chapters on them in books of my own, including *David Busch's Quick Snap Guide to Lighting*. I'm going to provide a quick introduction to some of the techniques you should be considering.

Diffusing and Softening the Light

Direct light can be harsh and glaring, especially if you're using the flash built into your camera, or an auxiliary flash mounted in the hot shoe and pointed directly at your subject. The first thing you should do is stop using direct light (unless you're looking for a stark, contrasty appearance as a creative effect). There are a number of simple things you can do with both continuous and flash illumination.

- **Use window light.** Light coming in a window can be soft and flattering, and a good choice for human subjects. Move your subject close enough to the window that its light provides the primary source of illumination. You might want to turn off other lights in the room, particularly to avoid mixing daylight and incandescent light. (See Figure 7.14.)

- **Use fill light.** Your T1i's built-in flash makes a perfect fill-in light for the shadows, brightening inky depths with a kicker of illumination. (See Figure 7.15.)

- **Bounce the light.** External electronic flash units mounted on the T1i usually have a swivel that allows them to be pointed up at a ceiling for a bounce light effect. You can also bounce the light off a wall. You'll want the ceiling or wall to be white or have a neutral gray color to avoid a color cast.

Figure 7.14 Window light makes the perfect diffuse illumination for informal soft-focus portraits like this one.

Figure 7.15 Fill flash brightened the shadows of this shot taken in the shade of a tree.

- **Use reflectors.** Another way to bounce the light is to use reflectors or umbrellas that you can position yourself to provide a greater degree of control over the quantity and direction of the bounced light. Good reflectors can be pieces of foamboard, Mylar, or a reflective disk held in place by a clamp and stand. Although some expensive umbrellas and reflectors are available, spending a lot isn't necessary. A simple piece of white foamboard does the job beautifully. Umbrellas have the advantage of being compact and foldable, while providing a soft, even kind of light. They're relatively cheap, too, with a good 40-inch umbrella available for as little as $20.

- **Use diffusers.** Sto-Fen and some other vendors offer clip-on diffusers like the one shown in Figures 7.16 and 7.17, that fit over your electronic flash head and provide a soft, flattering light. These add-ons are more portable than umbrellas and other reflectors, yet provide a nice diffuse lighting effect.

Figure 7.16 The Sto-Fen OmniBounce is a clip-on diffuser that softens the light of an external flash unit.

Figure 7.17 Softboxes use Velcro strips to attach them to third-party flash units (like the one shown) or any Canon external flash.

Using Multiple Light Sources

Once you gain control over the qualities and effects you get with a single light source, you'll want to graduate to using multiple light sources. Using several lights allows you to shape and mold the illumination of your subjects to provide a variety of effects, from backlighting to side lighting to more formal portrait lighting. You can start simply with several incandescent light sources, bounced off umbrellas or reflectors that you construct. Or you can use more flexible multiple electronic flash setups.

Effective lighting is the one element that differentiates great photography from candid or snapshot shooting. Lighting can make a mundane subject look a little more glamorous—make subjects appear to be soft when you want a soft look, or bright and sparkly when you want a vivid look, or strong and dramatic if that's what you desire. As you might guess, having control over your lighting means that you probably can't use the lights that are already in the room. You'll need separate, discrete lighting fixtures that can be moved, aimed, brightened, and dimmed on command.

Selecting your lighting gear will depend on the type of photography you do, and the budget you have to support it. It's entirely possible for a beginning T1i photographer to create a basic, inexpensive lighting system capable of delivering high-quality results for a few hundred dollars, just as you can spend megabucks ($1,000 and up) for a sophisticated lighting system.

Basic Flash Setups

If you want to use multiple electronic flash units, the Canon Speedlites described earlier will serve admirably. The two higher-end models can be used with Canon's wireless

E-TTL feature, which allows you to set up to three separate groups of flash units (several flashes can be included in each group) and trigger them using a master flash (such as the 580EX II) and the camera. Just set up one master unit (there's a switch on the unit's foot that sets it for master mode) and arrange the compatible slave units around your subject. You can set the relative power of each unit separately, thereby controlling how much of the scene's illumination comes from the main flash, and how much from the auxiliary flash units, which can be used as fill flash, background lights, or, if you're careful, to illuminate the hair of portrait subjects.

Studio Flash

If you're serious about using multiple flash units, a studio flash setup might be more practical. The traditional studio flash is a multi-part unit, consisting of a flash head that mounts on your light stand, and is tethered to an AC (or sometimes battery) power supply. A single power supply can feed two or more flash heads at a time, with separate control over the output of each head.

When they are operating off AC power, studio flash don't have to be frugal with the juice, and are often powerful enough to illuminate very large subjects or to supply lots and lots of light to smaller subjects. The output of such units is measured in watt seconds (ws), so you could purchase a 200ws, 400ws, or 800ws unit, and a power pack to match.

Their advantages include greater power output, much faster recycling, built-in modeling lamps, multiple power levels, and ruggedness that can stand up to transport, because many photographers pack up these kits and tote them around as location lighting rigs. Studio lighting kits can range in price from a few hundred dollars for a set of lights, stands, and reflectors, to thousands for a high-end lighting system complete with all the necessary accessories.

A more practical choice these days are *monolights* (see Figure 7.18), which are "all-in-one" studio lights that sell for about $200-$400. They have the flash tube, modeling light, and power supply built into a single unit that can be mounted on a light stand. Monolights are available in AC-only and battery-pack versions, although an external battery eliminates some of the advantages of having a flash with everything in one unit. They are very portable, because all you need is a case for the monolight itself, plus the stands and other accessories you want to carry along. Because these units are so popular with photographers who are not full-time professionals, the lower-cost monolights are often designed more for lighter duty than professional studio flash. That doesn't mean they aren't rugged; you'll just need to handle them with a little more care, and, perhaps, not expect them to be used eight hours a day for weeks on end. In most other respects, however, monolights are the equal of traditional studio flash units in terms of fast recycling, built-in modeling lamps, adjustable power, and so forth.

Figure 7.18
All-in-one "monolights" contain flash, power supply, and a modeling light in one compact package (umbrella not included).

Connecting Multiple Units to Your Canon EOS Rebel T1i

Non-dedicated electronic flash units can't use the automated E-TTL II features of your Rebel T1i; you'll need to calculate exposure manually, through test shots evaluated on your camera's LCD, or by using an electronic flash meter. Moreover, you don't have to connect them to the accessory shoe on top of the camera. Instead, you can use an adapter in the hot shoe to provide a PC/X connector, and use a shutter speed of 1/60th second or slower.

You should be aware that older electronic flash units sometimes use a triggering voltage that is too much for your T1i to handle. You can actually damage the camera's electronics if the voltage is too high. You won't need to worry about this if you purchase brand new units from Alien Bees, Adorama, or other vendors. But if you must connect an external flash with an unknown triggering voltage, I recommend using a Wein Safe Sync (see Figure 7.19), which isolates the flash's voltage from the camera triggering circuit, and provides a PC/X adapter for plugging in non-dedicated flash units.

Another safe way to connect external cameras is through a radio-control device, such as the transmitter/receiver set shown in Figure 7.20. It piggybacks onto the PC/X adapter you've fastened to your hot shoe, and plugs into your adaptor's PC/X connector. It transmits a signal to a matching receiver that's connected to your flash unit. The receiver has

Figure 7.19 A voltage isolator can prevent frying your T1i's flash circuits if you use an older electronic flash, and it provides a PC/X connector, which the Rebel T1i lacks.

Figure 7.20 A radio-control device frees you from a sync cord tether between your flash and camera.

both a PC connector of its own as well as a "monoplug" connector (it looks like a headphone plug) that links to a matching port on compatible flash units.

Finally, some flash units have an optical slave trigger built in, or can be fitted with one, so that they fire automatically when another flash, including your camera's built-in unit, fires.

Other Lighting Accessories

Once you start working with light, you'll find there are plenty of useful accessories that can help you. Here are some of the most popular that you might want to consider.

Soft Boxes

Soft boxes are large square or rectangular devices that may resemble a square umbrella with a front cover, and produce a similar lighting effect. They can extend from a few feet square to massive boxes that stand five or six feet tall—virtually a wall of light. With a flash unit or two inside a soft box, you have a large, semi-directional light source that's very diffuse and very flattering for portraiture and other people photography.

Soft boxes are also handy for photographing shiny objects. They not only provide a soft light, but if the box itself happens to reflect in the subject (say you're photographing a chromium toaster), the box will provide an interesting highlight that's indistinct and not distracting.

You can buy soft boxes (like the one shown in Figure 7.21) or make your own. Some lengths of friction-fit plastic pipe and a lot of muslin cut and sewed just so may be all that you need.

Figure 7.21
Softboxes pro-
vide an even,
diffuse light
source.

Light Stands

Both electronic flash and incandescent lamps can benefit from light stands. These are lightweight, tripod-like devices (but without a swiveling or tilting head) that can be set on the floor, tabletops, or other elevated surfaces and positioned as needed. Light stands should be strong enough to support an external lighting unit, up to and including a rel- atively heavy flash with soft box or umbrella reflectors. You want the supports to be capable of raising the lights high enough to be effective. Look for light stands capable of extending six to seven feet high. The nine-foot units usually have larger, steadier bases, and extend high enough that you can use them as background supports. You'll be using these stands for a lifetime, so invest in good ones. I bought the light stand shown in Figure 7.22 when I was in college, and I have been using it for decades.

Backgrounds

Backgrounds can be backdrops of cloth, sheets of muslin you've painted yourself using a sponge dipped in paint, rolls of seamless paper, or any other suitable surface your mind can dream up. Backgrounds provide a complementary and non-distracting area behind subjects (especially portraits) and can be lit separately to provide contrast and separation that outlines the subject, or which helps set a mood.

I like to use plain-colored backgrounds for portraits, and white seamless backgrounds for product photography. You can usually construct these yourself from cheap materials and tape them up on the wall behind your subject, or mount them on a pole stretched between a pair of light stands.

Snoots and Barn Doors

These fit over the flash unit and direct the light at your subject. Snoots are excellent for converting a flash unit into a hair light, while barn doors give you enough control over the illumination by opening and closing their flaps that you can use another flash as a background light, with the capability of feathering the light exactly where you want it on the background. A barndoor unit is shown in Figure 7.23.

Figure 7.22 Light stands can hold lights, umbrellas, backdrops, and other equipment.

Figure 7.23 Snoots and barn doors allow you to modulate the light from a flash or lamp, and they are especially useful for hair lights and background lights.

Downloading and Editing Your Images

Taking the picture is only half the work and, in some cases, only half the fun. After you've captured some great images and have them safely stored on your Canon EOS Rebel T1i's memory card, you'll need to transfer them from your camera and memory card to your computer, where they can be organized, fine-tuned in an image editor, and prepared for web display, printing, or some other final destination.

Fortunately, there are lots of software utilities and applications to help you do all these things. This chapter will introduce you to a few of them.

What's in the Box?

Your Canon EOS Rebel T1i came with software programs on CD for both Windows PCs and Macs. Pop the CD into your computer and it will self-install a selection of these useful applications and utilities. Manuals for all these programs are included on CD, too, but here's a summary of what you get on the EOS Digital Solutions disk:

Picture Style Editor

The Picture Style Editor, shown in Figure 8.1, allows you to create your own custom Picture Styles, or edit existing styles, including the Standard, Landscape, Faithful, and other predefined settings already present in your Rebel T1i. You can change sharpness, contrast, color saturation, and color tone—and a lot more—and then save the modifications as a .PF2 file that can be uploaded to the camera, or used by Digital Photo Professional (described later in this chapter) to modify a RAW image as it is imported.

Figure 8.1 The new Picture Style Editor lets you create your own Picture Styles for use by the T1i or Digital Photo Professional when importing image files.

You can define your own color response using a color picker in a sample RAW photograph to choose a specific hue, which you can then modify using hue/saturation/luminance adjustments. The range of adjacent colors affected by your new settings can also be specified. Before/after views let you compare the Picture Style settings you've entered with standard settings using a sample image you upload.

Among the most valuable features of the Canon EOS Rebel T1i is its compatibility with Canon's Picture Style Editor (PSE, not to be confused with the "other" PSE—Adobe Photoshop Elements) software. With PSE, shooters can actually design the look of their photographs by inputting their own preferred style, color, and tone curves. The Rebel T1i also ships with the latest versions of Canon's powerful software applications, including Digital Photo Professional and EOS Utility, which now support the camera's Remote Live View and Dust Delete Data functions, as well as incorporating a broad range of additional improvements designed to enhance image quality and speed up workflow. Also included are ZoomBrowser EX and ImageBrowser for easy browsing, viewing, printing, and archiving with compatible computer operating systems, including Microsoft Windows Vista and Windows XP, as well as Mac OS X.

EOS Utility

Both Windows and Mac versions are provided for this useful program. It serves as command center for several functions, all available from the main control panel, shown in Figure 8.2. It includes an image downloading module that previews the images in your T1i, and can automatically copy them from the camera to either Digital Photo Professional or ZoomBrowser EX (see Figure 8.3).

Figure 8.2
The EOS Utility has a settings/remote shooting function that allows you to control a T1i connected to your computer with the USB cable.

Figure 8.3
The download utility allows transfer of photos from your camera or memory card to Digital Photo Professional or ZoomBrowser EX.

It also includes a camera settings/remote shooting module that allows you to link your computer with the T1i and use a dialog box (see Figure 8.4) to change camera settings and to control the camera for remote shooting. You can have access to many of the T1i's menus right from the software (see Figure 8.5). The settings feature is especially useful for changing Picture Styles quickly, while you'll find the remote shooting capabilities useful when you want to program a delay before the camera takes a picture, or do some interval (time-lapse) shooting. The updated version of the utility (Version 2.1 and later) supports the T1i's Live View and Dust Delete Data functions. It includes many preferences you can use to tailor its operation (see Figure 8.6).

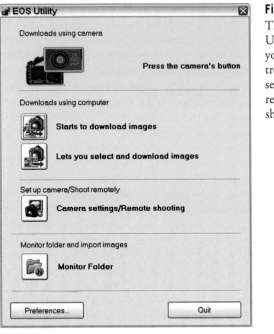

Figure 8.4
The EOS Utility gives you direct control of camera settings for remote shooting.

Figure 8.5
You can access many of the Rebel T1i's menu settings from your computer.

Figure 8.6 The EOS Utility five tabs' worth of preferences for modifying how it behaves.

ZoomBrowser/ImageBrowser

This is an image viewing and editing application for Windows PCs (the equivalent program for Macs is called ImageBrowser and performs the same functions). You can organize, sort, classify, and rename files, and convert JPEG files in batches. This utility is especially useful for printing index sheets of groups of images (see Figure 8.7). It can also prepare images for e-mailing. It works with RAW Image Task for converting CR2 files to some other format, and it can be used to select images for merging using PhotoStitch.

The simple image editing facilities of ZoomBrowser allow red-eye correction, brightness/contrast and color correction, manipulating sharpness, trimming photos, and a few other functions. For more complex editing, you can transfer images directly from this application to Photoshop or another image editor.

PhotoStitch

This Windows/Mac utility allows you to take several JPEG images and combine them to create a panorama in a single new file. You can choose the images to be merged in ZoomBrowser and then transfer them to PhotoStitch, or operate the utility as a stand-alone module and select the images using the standard File > Open commands (see Figure 8.8).

Figure 8.7
ZoomBrowser allows organizing your images and performing simple fixes.

Figure 8.8
Panoramas are easy to create with PhotoStitch.

Digital Photo Professional

While far from a Photoshop replacement, Digital Photo Professional is a useful image editing program that helps you organize, trim, correct, and print images. You can make RAW adjustments, correct tonal curves, color tone, color saturation, sharpness, as well as brightness and contrast. Especially handy are the "recipes" that can be developed and saved so that a given set of corrections can be kept separate from the file itself, and, if desired, applied to other images (see Figure 8.9).

Figure 8.9 Digital Photo Professional will never replace Photoshop, but it has some basic image editing features.

Transferring Your Photos

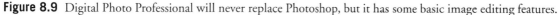

While it's rewarding to capture some great images and have them ensconced in your camera, eventually you'll be transferring them to your laptop or PC, whether you're using a Windows or Macintosh machine. You have three options for image transfer: direct transfer over a USB cable, automated transfer using a card reader and transfer software such as the EOS Utility or Adobe Photoshop Elements Photo Downloader, or manual transfer using drag and drop from a memory card inserted in a card reader.

Direct-Direct Transfer/Indirect-Direct Transfer

There are some advantages to transferring photos directly from your T1i to a computer. The destination computer doesn't need to have a card reader; all it requires is a USB port. So, if you have the USB cable that came with your camera, you can transfer photos to any computer that has the Canon utility software installed. However, direct transfer uses your T1i's internal battery power, while removing the card and transferring the photos with a card reader installed on the destination computer does not.

You can select which images are transferred to the computer, or transfer all the images, both RAW and JPEG, that are on the memory card. Canon gives you two different methods, one using the camera to direct the transfer process (I call this Direct-Direct Transfer), and one using both the camera and software on your computer to manage the transfer (I call this Indirect-Direct Transfer—for no good reason). Both methods require that you install the software furnished with the T1i, including the EOS Utility and Digital Photo Professional. The CD bundled with your camera has versions of each for both Macintosh and Windows.

Direct-Direct Transfer

With this option, you don't have to fiddle with the software on your computer. The camera does all the work (so don't look for options on your computer!). You lose the ability to customize your transfer (say, to rename the files as they are deposited on your computer), but the process is fast and easy. Just follow these steps:

1. Connect the USB cable to the USB terminal on the left side of the T1i (under the rubber cover, as seen from shooting position), and plug the other end into a USB port on the destination computer (which you have cleverly turned on in anticipation of this transfer).

2. Turn on the T1i. The Direct Transfer screen shown in Figure 8.10 will appear on the camera's LCD screen, and the blue transfer LED located to the right of the Print/Share button on the back of the camera will illuminate. The EOS Utility screen will pop up on your computer display.

3. Choose one of these options:

   - **All Images** to transfer all images on the memory card.
   - **New Images** to transfer only images that haven't already been transferred.
   - **Transfer Order Images** to transfer images that have already been marked as described in the next section.
   - **Select and Transfer** if you'd like to choose specific images to be transferred. (This option is not selectable until you've marked at least some images for transfer, as described in the next section.)
   - **Wallpaper** to create a copy of an image that can be used as wallpaper on the desktop of your computer.

Figure 8.10
You can trans-
fer images
directly from
your camera to
the computer
using the T1i
as the
controller.

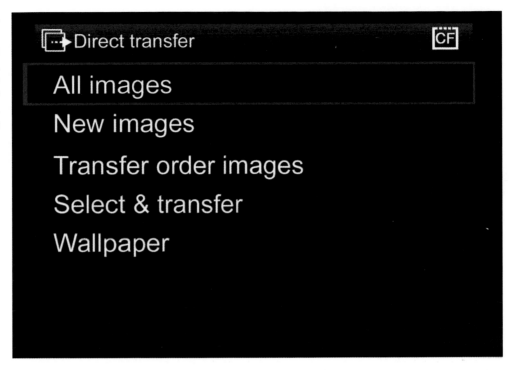

4. Press Set or the Print/Share button (illuminated with that blue LED) to start the transfer.

5. Press the Menu button when finished to exit.

Your photos will be transferred automatically, and Digital Photo Professional will open to display thumbnails of the images.

Indirect-Direct Transfer

You can also use a combination of camera selections and the EOS Utility software included with your camera to transfer photos. This option allows you to choose which images to transfer, and to apply various preferences to the process, such as renaming the files to reflect their content.

Follow these steps to transfer your photos using this method:

1. Press the Menu button and select Transfer Order Selection in the Playback menu. Press Set. You'll see a screen like the one in Figure 8.11.

2. Use the cross keys to select either All Image (if you want to transfer every image), Sel. Image (if you want to transfer the selected images), or By Folder to choose a specific folder of images on your memory card. Press Set.

Figure 8.11
Choose to
select images
for transfer,
transfer by
folder, or trans-
fer all images.

3a. If you've chosen All Image, choose Mark All on Card to select all the images, or Clear All on Card to unmark all the images, and press Set. Then press the Menu button to exit this selection screen and store your choice to the memory card. Continue with Step 4.

3b. If you've selected Sel. Image, the transfer image selection screen appears. Use the cross keys to scroll through the available images. Press the Thumbnail/Zoom Out and Zoom In buttons to alternate between a three-image and single-image view. When an image you want to transfer is highlighted, press the Set button to add a check mark to the box in the image. If you change your mind, press Set again to unmark the image. Choose all the images you want to transfer, and press Menu to exit this selection screen, and Menu again to store your choices on the memory card. Continue with Step 4.

3c. If you selected By Folder, the screen shown in Figure 8.12 appears. Choose either Mark All in Folder to choose a specific folder on your memory card, or Clear All in Folder to unmark images. Then press Set. You'll then see a folder selection screen like the one in Figure 8.13. It shows a list of folders on your memory card, with thumbnails of the first and last images in the folder provided for the highlighted folder name. Choose the folder you want to transfer, and press Set. Press the Menu button again to store your choices on the memory card and continue with Step 4.

Figure 8.12
Mark or clear
all images in a
specific folder
for transfer.

Figure 8.13
Select the
folder contain-
ing the images
you want to
transfer.

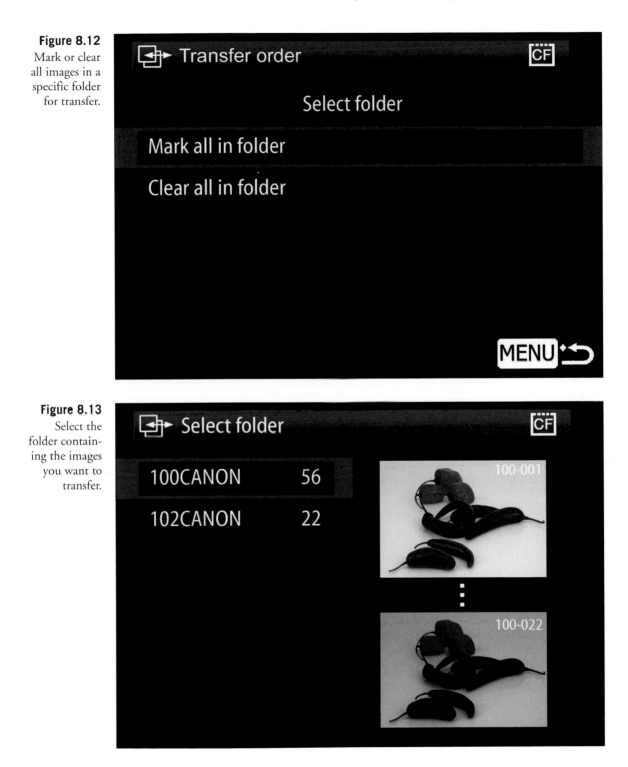

4. Connect the USB cable to the DIGITAL terminal on the left side of the T1i (under the rubber cover) and plug the other end into a USB port on the destination computer.

5. Turn on the T1i. The EOS Utility will appear, ready to download your photos. (If you have another program installed that also has a transfer utility, such as Adobe Photoshop Elements 7.0's Photo Downloader, it may pop up as well. Close that window if you want to use the EOS Utility.)

6. Use the controls within the EOS Utility to activate the transfer process.

Using a Card Reader and Software

You can also use a memory card reader and software to transfer photos and automate the process using the EOS Utility, Photoshop Elements' Photo Downloader, or the downloading program supplied with some other third-party applications. This method is more frugal in its use of your T1i's battery and can be faster if you have a speedy USB 2.0 or FireWire card reader attached to an appropriate port.

The installed software automatically remains in memory as you work, and it recognizes when a memory card is inserted in your card reader; you don't have to launch it yourself. With Photoshop Elements's Photo Downloader, you can click Get Photos to begin the transfer of all images immediately or choose Advanced Dialog to produce a dialog box like the one shown in Figure 8.14, and then select which images to download from the memory card by marking them with a check. You can select the photos you want to transfer, plus options such as Automatically Fix Red Eyes. Start the download, and a confirmation dialog box like the one in Figure 8.15 shows the progress.

Figure 8.14
With Advanced view activated, Photoshop Elements' Photo Downloader allows you to select the photos you want to copy to your computer and apply some options such as new filenames or red-eye fixes automatically.

Figure 8.15
The Photo Downloader's confirmation dialog box shows the progress as images are transferred.

Dragging and Dropping

The final way to move photos from your memory card to your computer is the old-fashioned way: manually dragging and dropping the files from one window on your computer to another. The procedure works pretty much the same whether you're using a Mac or a PC.

1. Remove the memory card from the Rebel T1i and insert it in your memory card reader.

2. Using Windows Explorer, My Computer, or your Mac desktop, open the icon representing the memory card, which appears on your desktop as just another disk drive.

3. Open a second window representing the folder on your computer that you want to use as the destination for the files you are copying or moving.

4. Drag and drop the files from the memory card window to the folder on your computer. You can select individual files, press Ctrl/Command+A to select all the files, or Ctrl/Command+click to select multiple files.

Editing Your Photos

Image manipulation tasks fall into several categories. You might want to fine-tune your images, retouch them, change color balance, composite several images together, and perform other tasks we know as image editing, with a program like Adobe Photoshop, Photoshop Elements, or Corel Photo Paint.

You might want to play with the settings in RAW files, too, as you import them from their .CR2 state into an image editor. There are specialized tools expressly for tweaking RAW files, ranging from Canon's own Digital Photo Professional to Adobe Camera Raw, and PhaseOne's Capture One Pro (C1 Pro). A third type of manipulation is the specialized task of noise reduction, which can be performed within Photoshop, Adobe Camera Raw, or tools like Bibble Professional. There are also specialized tools just for noise reduction, such as Noise Ninja (also included with Bibble) and Neat Image.

Each of these utilities and applications deserves a chapter of its own, so I'm simply going to enumerate some of the most popular image editing and RAW conversion programs here and tell you a little about what they do.

Image Editors

Image editors are general-purpose photo-editing applications that can do color correction, tonal modifications, retouching, combining of several images into one, and usually include tools for working with RAW files and reducing noise. So, you'll find programs like those listed here good for all-around image manipulation. The leading programs are:

Adobe Photoshop/Photoshop Elements. Photoshop is the serious photographer's number one choice for image editing, and Elements is an excellent option for those who need most of Photoshop's power, but not all of its professional-level features. Unfortunately, Adobe's releases of Elements for the Macintosh tend to lag behind the Windows versions. Both editors use the latest version of Adobe's Camera Raw plug-in, which makes it easy to adjust things like color space profiles, color depth (either 8 bits or 16 bits per color channel), image resolution, white balance, exposure, shadows, brightness, sharpness, luminance, and noise reduction. One plus with the Adobe products is that they are available in identical versions for both Windows and Macs (eventually!).

Corel Photo Paint. This is the image-editing program that is included in the popular CorelDRAW Graphics suite. Although a Mac version was available in the past, this is primarily a Windows application today. It's a full-featured photo retouching and image-editing program with selection, retouching, and painting tools for manual image manipulations, and it also includes convenient automated commands for a few common tasks, such as red-eye removal. Photo Paint accepts Photoshop plug-ins to expand its assortment of filters and special effects.

Corel Paint Shop Pro. This is a general-purpose Windows-only image editor that has gained a reputation as the "poor person's Photoshop" for providing a substantial portion of Photoshop's capabilities at a fraction of the cost. It includes a nifty set of wizard-like commands that automate common tasks, such as removing red eye and scratches, as well as filters and effects, which can be expanded with other Photoshop plug-ins.

Corel Painter. Here's another image-editing program from Corel for both Mac and Windows. This one's strength is in mimicking natural media, such as charcoal, pastels, and various kinds of paint. Painter includes a basic assortment of tools that you can use to edit existing images, but the program is really designed for artists to use in creating original illustrations. As a photographer, you might prefer another image editor, but if you like to paint on top of your photographic images, nothing else really does the job of Painter.

Corel PhotoImpact. Corel finally brought one of the last remaining non-Adobe image editors into its fold when it acquired PhotoImpact. This is a general-purpose photo-editing program for Windows with a huge assortment of brushes for painting, retouching, and cloning, in addition to the usual selection, cropping, and fill tools. If you frequently find yourself performing the same image manipulations on a number of files, you'll appreciate PhotoImpact's batch operations. Using this feature, you can select multiple image files and then apply any one of a long list of filters, enhancements, or auto-process commands to all the selected files.

RAW Utilities

Your software choices for manipulating RAW files are broader than you might think. Camera vendors always supply a utility to read their cameras' own RAW files, but sometimes, particularly with those point-and-shoot cameras that can produce RAW files, the options are fairly limited. Most Canon dSLR users have gone beyond the Canon File View Utility to something better from third parties, such as Capture1. Other vendors, such as Nikon (with its Nikon Capture), offer RAW file handling that is much more flexible and powerful.

Because in the past digital camera vendors offered RAW converters that weren't very good (Canon's File View Utility comes to mind), there is a lively market for third-party RAW utilities available at extra cost. However, the EOS Utility and Digital Photo Professional do a good job and may be all that you need.

The third-party solutions are usually available as standalone applications (often for both Windows and Macintosh platforms), as Photoshop-compatible plug-ins, or both. Because the RAW plug-ins displace Photoshop's own RAW converter, I tend to prefer to use most RAW utilities in standalone mode. That way, if I choose to open a file directly in Photoshop, it automatically opens using Photoshop's fast and easy-to-use Adobe Camera Raw (ACR) plug-in. If I have more time or need the capabilities of another converter, I can load that, open the file, and make my corrections there. Most are able to transfer the processed file directly to Photoshop even if you aren't using plug-in mode.

This section provides a quick overview of the range of RAW file handlers, so you can get a better idea of the kinds of information available with particular applications. I'm going to include both high-end and low-end RAW browsers so you can see just what is available.

Digital Photo Professional

Digital Photo Professional, introduced earlier in this chapter, is preferred by many for Canon dSLR cameras like the Rebel T1i.

DPP offers much higher-speed processing of RAW images than was available with the late, not lamented, sluggardly File Viewer Utility (as much as six times faster). Canon says this utility rivals third-party standalone and plug-in RAW converters in speed and features. It supports both Canon's original CRW format and the newer CR2 RAW format used by the T1i, along with TIFF, Exif TIFF, and JPEG.

You can save settings that include multiple adjustments and apply them to other images, and use the clever comparison mode to compare your original and edited versions of an image either side by side or within a single split image. The utility allows easy adjustment of color channels, tone curves, exposure compensation, white balance, dynamic range, brightness, contrast, color saturation, ICC Profile embedding, and assignment of monitor profiles. A new feature is the ability to continue editing images while batches of previously adjusted RAW files are rendered and saved in the background.

IrfanView

At the low (free) end of the price scale is IrfanView, a Windows freeware program you can download at www.irfanview.com. It can read many common RAW photo formats. It's a quick way to view RAW files (just drag and drop to the IrfanView window) and make fast changes to the unprocessed file. You can crop, rotate, or correct your image, and do some cool things like swap the colors around (red for blue, blue for green, and so forth) to create false color pictures.

The price is right, and IrfanView has some valuable capabilities. Check out www.irfanview.com.

Phase One Capture One Pro (C1 Pro)

If there is a Cadillac of RAW converters for Nikon and Canon digital SLR cameras, C1 Pro has to be it. This premium-priced program does everything, does it well, and does it quickly. If you can't justify the price tag of this professional-level software, there are "lite" versions for serious amateurs and cash-challenged professionals called Capture One dSLR and Capture One dSLR SE.

Aimed at photographers with high-volume needs (that would include school and portrait photographers, as well as busy commercial photographers), C1 Pro is available for both Windows and Mac OS X, and supports a broad range of Canon digital cameras. Phase One is a leading supplier of megabucks digital camera backs for medium and larger format cameras, so they really understand the needs of photographers.

The latest features include individual noise reduction controls for each image, automatic levels adjustment, a "quick develop" option that allows speedy conversion from RAW to TIFF or JPEG formats, dual-image side-by-side views for comparison purposes, and helpful grids and guides that can be superimposed over an image. Photographers concerned about copyright protection will appreciate the ability to add watermarks to the output images. See www.phaseone.com.

Bibble Pro

One of my personal favorites among third-party RAW converters is Bibble Pro, which just came out with a new version as I was writing this book. It supports one of the broadest ranges of RAW file formats available (which can be handy if you find yourself with the need to convert a file from a friend or colleague's non-Canon camera), including NEF files from Nikon D1, D1x/h, D2H, D100; .CRW files from the Canon C30/D60/10D/300D; .CR2 files from the Canon EOS Rebel T1i and other newer models; .ORF files from the Olympus E10/E20/E1/C5050/C5060; .DCR files from the Kodak 720x/760/14n; .RAF files from the Fuji S2Pro; .PEF files from Pentax ISTD; .MRW files from the Minolta Maxxum; and .TIF from Canon 1D/1DS.

The utility supports lots of different platforms, too. It's available for Windows, Mac OS X, and, believe it or not, Linux.

Bibble works fast because it offers instantaneous previews and real-time feedback as changes are made. That's important when you have to convert many images in a short time. Bibble's batch-processing capabilities also let you convert large numbers of files using settings you specify without further intervention.

Its customizable interface lets you organize and edit images quickly and then output them in a variety of formats, including 16-bit TIFF and PNG. You can even create a web gallery from within Bibble. I often find myself disliking the generic filenames applied to digital images by cameras, so I really like Bibble's ability to rename batches of files using new names that you specify.

Bibble is fully color managed, which means it can support all the popular color spaces (Adobe sRGB and so forth) and use custom profiles generated by third-party color-management software. There are two editions of Bibble, a Pro version and a Lite version. Because the Pro version is reasonably priced at $129, I don't really see the need to save $60 with the Lite edition, which lacks the top-line's options for tethered shooting, embedding IPTC-compatible captions in images, and can also be used as a Photoshop plug-in (if you prefer not to work with the application in its standalone mode). Bibble Pro now incorporates Noise Ninja technology, so you can get double-duty from this valuable application. See www.bibblelabs.com.

BreezeBrowser

BreezeBrowser was long the RAW converter of choice for Canon dSLR owners who run Windows and who were dissatisfied with Canon's lame antique File Viewer Utility. It works quickly and has lots of options for converting CRW and CR2 files to other formats. You can choose to show highlights that will be blown out in your finished photo as flashing areas (so they can be more easily identified and corrected), use histograms to correct tones, add color profiles, auto rotate images, and adjust all those RAW image parameters, such as white balance, color space, saturation, contrast, sharpening, color tone, EV compensation, and other settings.

You can also control noise reduction (choosing from low, normal, or high reduction), evaluate your changes in the live preview, and then save the file as a compressed JPEG or as either an 8-bit or 16-bit TIFF file. BreezeBrowser can also create HTML web galleries directly from your selection of images. See www.breezesys.com.

Adobe Photoshop

The latest version of Photoshop includes a built-in RAW plug-in that is compatible with the proprietary formats of a growing number of digital cameras, both new and old. This plug-in also works with Photoshop Elements.

To open a RAW image in Photoshop, just follow these steps (Elements users can use much the same workflow, although fewer settings are available):

1. Transfer the RAW images from your camera to your computer's hard drive.

2. In Photoshop, choose Open from the File menu, or use Bridge.

3. Select a RAW image file. The Adobe Camera Raw plug-in will pop up, showing a preview of the image, like the one shown in Figure 8.16.

Figure 8.16 The basic ACR dialog box looks like this when processing a single image.

4. If you like, use one of the tools found in the toolbar at the top left of the dialog box. From left to right, they are:

- **Zoom.** Operates just like the Zoom tool in Photoshop.

- **Hand.** Use like the Hand tool in Photoshop.

- **White Balance.** Click an area in the image that should be neutral gray or white to set the white balance quickly.

- **Color Sampler.** Use to determine the RGB values of areas you click with this eyedropper.

- **Crop.** Pre-crops the image so that only the portion you specify is imported into Photoshop. This option saves time when you want to work on a section of a large image, and you don't need the entire file.

- **Straighten.** Drag in the preview image to define what should be a horizontal or vertical line, and ACR will realign the image to straighten it.

- **Retouch.** Used to heal or clone areas you define.

- **Red-Eye Removal.** Quickly zap red pupils in your human subjects.

- **ACR Preferences.** Produces a dialog box of Adobe Camera Raw preferences.

- **Rotate Counterclockwise.** Rotates counterclockwise in 90-degree increments with a click.

- **Rotate Clockwise.** Rotates clockwise in 90-degree increments with a click.

5. Using the Basic tab, you can have ACR show you red and blue highlights in the preview that indicate shadow areas that are clipped (too dark to show detail) and light areas that are blown out (too bright). Click the triangles in the upper-left corner of the histogram display (shadow clipping) and upper-right corner (highlight clipping) to toggle these indicators on or off.

6. Also in the Basic tab you can choose white balance, either from the drop-down list or by setting a color temperature and green/magenta color bias (tint) using the sliders.

7. Other sliders are available to control exposure, recovery, fill light, blacks, brightness, contrast, vibrance, and saturation. A checkbox can be marked to convert the image to grayscale.

8. Make other adjustments (described in more detail below).

9. ACR makes automatic adjustments for you. You can click Default and make the changes for yourself, or click the Auto link (located just above the Exposure slider) to reapply the automatic adjustments after you've made your own modifications.

10. If you've marked more than one image to be opened, the additional images appear in a "filmstrip" at the left side of the screen. You can click on each thumbnail in the filmstrip in turn and apply different settings to each.

11. Click Open Image/Open Image(s) into Photoshop using the settings you've made, or click Save Image at the bottom left to save the settings you've made without opening the file.

The Basic tab is displayed by default when the ACR dialog box opens, and it includes most of the sliders and controls you'll need to fine-tune your image as you import it into Photoshop. These include:

- **White Balance.** Leave it As Shot or change to a value such as Daylight, Cloudy, Shade, Tungsten, Fluorescent, or Flash. If you like, you can set a custom white balance using the Temperature and Tint sliders.

- **Exposure.** This slider adjusts the overall brightness and darkness of the image.

- **Recovery.** Restores detail in the red, green, and blue color channels.

- **Fill Light.** Reconstructs detail in shadows.

- **Blacks.** Increases the number of tones represented as black in the final image, emphasizing tones in the shadow areas of the image.

- **Brightness.** This slider adjusts the brightness and darkness of an image.

- **Contrast.** Manipulates the contrast of the midtones of your image.

- **Convert to Grayscale.** Mark this box to convert the image to black and white.

- **Vibrance.** Prevents over-saturation when enriching the colors of an image.

- **Saturation.** Manipulates the richness of all colors equally, from zero saturation (gray/black, no color) at the −100 setting to double the usual saturation at the +100 setting.

Additional controls are available on the Tone Curve, Detail, HSL/Grayscale, Split Toning, Lens Corrections, Camera Calibration, and Presets tabs, shown in Figure 8.17. The Tone Curve tab can change the tonal values of your image. The Detail tab lets you adjust sharpness, luminance smoothing, and apply color noise reduction. The HSL/Grayscale tab offers controls for adjusting hue, saturation, and lightness and converting an image to black and white. Split Toning helps you colorize an image with sepia or cyanotype (blue) shades. The Lens Corrections tab has sliders to adjust for chromatic aberrations and vignetting. The Camera Calibration tab provides a way for calibrating the color corrections made in the Camera Raw plug-in. The Presets tab (not shown) is used to load settings you've stored for reuse.

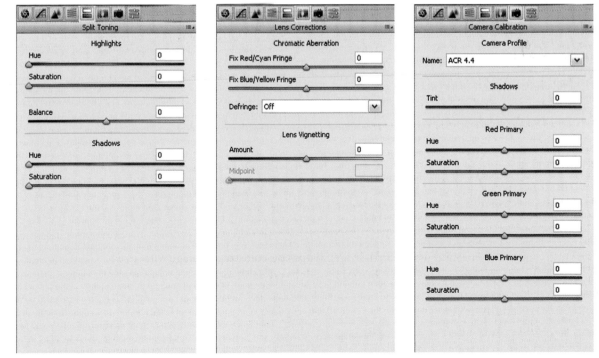

Figure 8.17 More controls are available within the additional tabbed dialog boxes in Adobe Camera Raw.

Canon EOS Rebel T1i/500D: Troubleshooting and Prevention

One of the nice things about modern electronic cameras like the Canon EOS Rebel T1i is that they have fewer mechanical moving parts to fail, so they are less likely to "wear out." No film transport mechanism, no wind lever or motor drive, no complicated mechanical linkages from camera to lens to physically stop down the lens aperture. Instead, tiny, reliable motors are built into each lens (and you lose the use of only that lens should something fail), and one of the few major moving parts in the camera itself is a lightweight mirror (its small size one of the advantages of the T1i's 1.6X crop factor) that flips up and down with each shot.

Of course, the camera also has a moving shutter that can fail, but the shutter is built rugged enough that you can expect it to last 100,000 shutter cycles or more. Unless you're shooting sports in Continuous mode day in and day out, the shutter on your T1i is likely to last as long as you expect to use the camera.

The only other things on the camera that move are switches, dials, buttons, the flip-up electronic flash, and the door that slides open to allow you to remove and insert the memory card. Unless you're extraordinarily clumsy or unlucky and manage to give your built-in flash a good whack while it is in use, there's not a lot that can go wrong mechanically with your Rebel T1i.

On the other hand, one of the chief drawbacks of modern electronic cameras is that they are modern *electronic* cameras. Your T1i is fully dependent on two different batteries. Without them, the camera can't be used. There are numerous other electrical and electronic connections in the camera (many connected to those mechanical switches and dials), and components like the color LCD and top panel status LCD that can potentially fail or suffer damage. The camera also relies on its "operating system," or *firmware*, which can be plagued by bugs that cause unexpected behavior. Luckily, electronic components are generally more reliable and trouble-free, especially when compared to their mechanical counterparts from the pre-electronic film camera days. (Film cameras of the last 10 to 20 years have had almost as many electronic features as digital cameras, but, believe it or not, there were whole generations of film cameras that had *no* electronics or batteries.)

Digital cameras have problems unique to their breed, too; the most troublesome being the need to clean the sensor of dust and grime periodically. This chapter will show you how to diagnose problems, fix some common ills, and, importantly, learn how to avoid them in the future.

Update Your Firmware

As I said, the firmware in your Rebel T1i is the camera's operating system, which handles everything from menu display (including fonts, colors, and the actual entries themselves), what languages are available, and even support for specific devices and features. Upgrading the firmware to a new version makes it possible to add new features while fixing some of the bugs that sneak in. For example, a firmware update for the 20D added the ability to use the WFT-E1 wireless file transmitter.

Sometimes firmware updates happen during product development; I received my Rebel T1i a few weeks after it was introduced, and it already had firmware Version 1.0.4 installed. Official firmware for your T1i is given a version number that you can view by turning the power on, pressing the Menu button, and scrolling to Firmware Ver. x.x.x in the Setup 3 menu. As I write this, the current version is 1.0.9, shown in Figure 9.1. The first number in the string represents the major release number, while the second and third represent less significant upgrades and minor tweaks, respectively. Theoretically, a camera should have a firmware version number of 1.0.0 when it is introduced, but vendors have been known to do some minor fixes during testing and unveil a camera with a 1.0.1 firmware designation (or even 1.0.9 in the case of the T1i). If a given model is available long enough, as the EOS 20D was, it can evolve into significant upgrades, such as 2.0.3.

Oddly enough, sometimes an update is so minor that it doesn't earn an upgraded number. When Canon introduced firmware version 1.0.4 for an earlier model, it discovered that some of the characters for Simplified Chinese and Traditional Chinese languages

Figure 9.1
You can view
the current
firmware ver-
sion in the
Setup 3 menu.

caused problems when displayed on the LCD monitor, and issued a *new* Version 1.0.4. It recommended installing this fixed firmware for anyone experiencing the problem, even if the user had already upgraded to Version 1.0.4.

Firmware upgrades are used most frequently to fix bugs in the software, and much less frequently to add or enhance features. For example, previous firmware upgrades for Canon cameras have mended things like incorrect color temperature reporting when using specific Canon Speedlites, or problems communicating with memory cards under certain conditions. The exact changes made to the firmware are generally spelled out in the firmware release announcement. You can examine the remedies provided and decide if a given firmware patch is important to you. If not, you can usually safely wait a while before going through the bother of upgrading your firmware—at least long enough for the early adopters to report whether the bug fixes have introduced new bugs of their own. Each new firmware release incorporates the changes from previous releases, so if you skip a minor upgrade you should have no problems.

Upgrading Your Firmware

If you're computer savvy, you might wonder how your Rebel T1i is able to overwrite its own operating system—that is, how can the existing firmware be used to load the new version on top of itself? It's a little like lifting yourself by reaching down and pulling up on your bootstraps. Not ironically, that's almost exactly what happens: At your command (when you start the upgrade process), the T1i shifts into a special mode in which it is no longer operating from its firmware but, rather, from a small piece of software called a *bootstrap loader*—a separate, protected software program that functions only at startup or when upgrading firmware. The loader's function is to look for firmware to launch or, when directed, to copy new firmware from a memory card to the internal memory space where the old firmware is located. Once the new firmware has replaced the old, you can turn your camera off and then on again, and the updated operating system will be loaded.

Because the loader software is small in size and limited in function, there are some restrictions on what it can do. For example, the loader software isn't set up to go hunting through your memory card for the firmware file. It looks only in the top or root directory of your card, so that's where you must copy the firmware you download. Once you've determined that a new firmware update is available for your camera and that you want to install it, just follow these steps. (If you chicken out, any Canon Service Center can install the firmware upgrade for you.)

WARNING

Use a fully charged battery or Canon's optional ACK-E5 AC adapter kit to ensure that you'll have enough power to operate the camera for the entire upgrade. Moreover, you should not turn off the camera while your old firmware is being overwritten. Don't open the memory card door or do anything else that might disrupt operation of the T1i while the firmware is being installed.

---

1. Download the firmware from Canon (you'll find it in the Downloads section of the Support portion of Canon's website) and place it on your computer's hard drive. The firmware is contained in a self-extracting file for either Windows or Mac OS. It will have a name such as T1i00110.fir.

2. In your camera, format a memory card to ensure that the proper file system has been formatted onto the card. Choose Format from the Setup 1 menu, and initialize the card (make sure you don't have images you want to keep before you do this!).

3. You can copy the upgrade software to the card either using a memory card reader or by connecting the camera to your computer with a USB cable and using the EOS Utility application furnished with your camera.

4. Insert the memory card in the camera and then turn on the camera Press Menu and scroll to Firmware Ver. x.x.x in the Setup 3 menu and press the Set button. Choose OK and press the Set button to begin loading the update program.

5. A final confirmation screen will appear. Press Set to confirm. The firmware will be updated.

6. When you see the completion screen, press the Set button to complete the process.

7. Turn off the Rebel T1i, and remove the AC adapter, if used. Then turn the camera on to boot up your camera with the new firmware update.

8. Be sure to reformat the card before returning it to regular use to remove the firmware software.

Protect Your LCD

The three-inch color LCD on the back of your Rebel T1i almost seems like a target for banging, scratching, and other abuse. Fortunately, it's quite rugged, and a few errant knocks are unlikely to shatter the protective cover over the LCD, and scratches won't easily mar its surface. However, if you want to be on the safe side, there are a number of protective products you can purchase to keep your LCD safe—and, in some cases, make it a little easier to view. Here's a quick overview of your options.

- **Plastic overlays.** The simplest solution (although not always the cheapest) is to apply a plastic overlay sheet or "skin" cut to fit your LCD. These adhere either by static electricity or through a light adhesive coating that's even less clingy than stick-it notes. You can cut down overlays made for PDAs (although these can be pricey at up to $19.95 for a set of several sheets), or purchase overlays sold specifically for digital cameras. Vendors such as Hoodman (www.hoodmanusa.com) offer overlays of this type. These products will do a good job of shielding your T1i's LCD screen from scratches and minor impacts, but will not offer much protection from a good whack.

- **Acrylic/glass shields.** These scratch-resistant acrylic or glass panels, laser cut to fit your camera perfectly, are my choice as the best protection solution, and what I use on my own T1i. At about $10 each, they also happen to be the least expensive option as well. I prefer the GGS glass overlays, shown in Figure 9.2, available on eBay and from other sources. They attach using sticky adhesive that's already applied to the edges, and which holds the panel flush and tight, but which allow the shield to be pried off and the adhesive removed easily if you want to remove or replace it. They don't attenuate your view of the LCD and are non-reflective enough for use under a variety of lighting conditions. If your shield isn't designed specifically for the T1i, it may block the Display Off sensor under the viewfinder, so check that out before you attach one to your LCD.

- **Flip-up hoods.** These protectors slip on using the flanges around your T1i's eyepiece, and provide a cover that completely shields the LCD, but unfolds to provide a three-sided hood that allows viewing the LCD while minimizing the extraneous light falling on it and reducing contrast. They're sold for about $40 by Delkin and Hoodman. If you want to completely protect your LCD from hard knocks and need to view the screen outdoors in bright sunlight, there is nothing better. However, I have a couple problems with these devices. First, with the cover closed, you can't peek down after taking a shot to see what your image looks like during picture review. You must open the cap each time you want to look at the LCD. Moreover, with the hood unfolded, it's difficult to look through the viewfinder: Don't count on being able to use the viewfinder *and* the LCD at the same time with one of these hoods in place.

- **Magnifiers.** If you look hard enough, you should be able to find an LCD magnifier that fits over the monitor panel and provides a 2X magnification. These often strap on clumsily, and serve better as a way to get an enlarged view of the LCD than as protection. Hoodman and other suppliers offer these specialized devices.

Figure 9.2
A tough tempered glass shield can protect your LCD from scratches.

Troubleshooting Memory Cards

Sometimes good memory cards go bad. Sometimes good photographers can treat their memory cards badly. It's possible that a memory card that works fine in one camera won't be recognized when inserted into another. In the worst case, you can have a card full of important photos and find that the card seems to be corrupted and you can't access any of them. Don't panic! If these scenarios sound horrific to you, there are lots of things you can do to prevent them from happening, and a variety of remedies available if they do occur. You'll want to take some time—before disaster strikes—to consider your options.

All Your Eggs in One Basket?

The debate about whether it's better to use one large memory card or several smaller ones has been going on since even before there were memory cards. I can remember when computer users wondered whether it was smarter to install a pair of 200MB (not *gigabyte*) hard drives in their computer, or if they should go for one of those new-fangled 500MB models. By the same token, a few years ago the user groups were full of proponents who insisted that you ought to use 128MB memory cards rather than the huge 512MB versions. Today, most of the arguments involve 4GB cards versus 2GB cards or 4GB cards versus 8GB cards, and I expect that as prices for 16GB memory cards continue to drop, they'll find their way into the debate as well.

Why all the fuss? Are 4GB memory cards more likely to fail than 2GB cards? Are you risking all your photos if you trust your images to a larger card? Isn't it better to use several smaller cards, so that if one fails you lose only half as many photos? Or, isn't it wiser to put all your photos onto one larger card, because the more cards you use, the better your odds of misplacing or damaging one and losing at least some pictures?

In the end, the "eggs in one basket" argument boils down to statistics, and how you happen to use your T1i. The rationales can go both ways. If you have multiple smaller cards, you do increase your chances of something happening to one of them, so, arguably, you might be boosting the odds of losing some pictures. If all your images are important, the fact that you've lost 100 rather than 200 pictures isn't very comforting.

Also consider that the eggs/basket scenario assumes that the cards that are lost or damaged are always full. It's actually likely that your 4GB card might suffer a mishap when it's less than half-full (indeed, it's more likely that a large card won't be completely filled before it's offloaded to a computer), so you really might not lose any more shots with a single 4GB card than with multiple 2GB cards.

If you shoot photojournalist-type pictures, you probably change memory cards when they're less than completely full in order to avoid the need to do so at a crucial moment. (When I shoot sports, my cards rarely reach 80 to 90 percent of capacity before I change them.) Using multiple smaller cards means you have to change them that more often, which can be a real pain when you're taking a lot of photos. As an example, if you use 1GB memory cards with a Rebel T1i and shoot RAW+JPEG FINE, you may get only a couple dozen pictures on the card—about the capacity of a 36-exposure roll of film (remember those?). In my book, I prefer keeping all my eggs in one basket, and then making very sure that nothing happens to that basket.

There is only one really good reason to justify limiting yourself to smaller memory cards when larger ones can be purchased at the same cost per-gigabyte. That is when every single picture is precious to you, and the loss of any of them would be a disaster. If you're a wedding photographer, for example, and unlikely to be able to restage the nuptials if a memory card goes bad, you'll probably want to shoot no more pictures than you can afford to lose on a single card, and have an assistant ready to copy each card removed from the camera onto a backup hard drive or DVD onsite.

To be even safer, you'd want to alternate cameras or have a second photographer at least partially duplicating your coverage so your shots are distributed over several memory cards simultaneously. (Strictly speaking, the safest route of all is to buy one of the wireless-enabled Eye-Fi SD cards that can transmit directly to your computer over a network. [Check out www.eye.fi—no .com in the URL!]) These cards can beam the images over to a computer as you shoot them.

If none of these options are available to you, consider *interleaving* your shots. Say you don't shoot weddings, but you do go on vacation from time to time. Take 50 or so pictures on one card, or whatever number of images might fill about 25 percent of its capacity. Then, replace it with a different card and shoot about 25 percent of that card's available space. Repeat these steps with diligence (you'd have to be determined to go through this inconvenience), and, if you use four or more memory cards, you'll find your pictures from each location scattered among the different memory cards. If you lose or damage one, you'll still have *some* pictures from all the various stops on your trip on the other cards. That's more work than I like to do (I usually tote around a portable hard disk and copy the files to the drive as I go), but it's an option.

What Can Go Wrong?

There are lots of things that can go wrong with your memory card, but the ones that aren't caused by human stupidity are statistically very rare. Yes, a memory card's internal bit bin or controller can suddenly fail due to a manufacturing error or some inexplicable event caused by old age. However, if your memory card works for the first week or two that you own it, it should work forever. There's really not a lot that can wear out.

The typical memory card is rated for a Mean Time Between Failures of 1,000,000 hours of use. That's constant use 24/7 for more than 100 years! According to the manufacturers, they are good for 10,000 insertions in your camera, and should be able to retain their data (and that's without an external power source) for something on the order of

11 years. Of course, with the millions of memory cards in use, there are bound to be a few lemons here or there.

Given the reliability of solid-state memory, compared to magnetic memory, though, it's more likely that your memory card problems will stem from something that you do. Although they're not as tiny as the xD cards a few other digital SLRs use, Secure Digital memory cards are still small and easy to misplace if you're not careful. For that reason, it's a good idea to keep them in their original cases or a "card safe" offered by Gepe (www.gepecardsafe.com), Pelican (www.pelican.com), and others. Always placing your memory card in a case can provide protection from the second-most common mishap that befalls memory cards: the household laundry. If you slip a memory card in a pocket, rather than a case or your camera bag often enough, sooner or later it's going to end up in the washing machine and probably the clothes dryer, too. There are plenty of reports of relieved digital camera owners who've laundered their memory cards and found they still worked fine, but it's not uncommon for such mistreatment to do some damage.

Memory cards can also be stomped on, accidentally bent, dropped into the ocean, chewed by pets, and otherwise rendered unusable in myriad ways. It's also remotely possible to force a card into your T1i's memory card slot incorrectly if you're diligent enough, doing little damage to the card itself, but possibly damaging the camera internally, eliminating its ability to read or write to any memory card. I've never heard of this happening with a camera using SD cards, but don't discount the ingenuity of a determined fumble-fingers.

Or, if the card is formatted in your computer with a memory card reader, your T1i may fail to recognize it. Occasionally, I've found that a memory card used in one camera would fail if used in a different camera (until I reformatted it in Windows, and then again in the camera). Every once in awhile, a card goes completely bad and—seemingly—can't be salvaged.

Another way to lose images is to do commonplace things with your memory card at an inopportune time. If you remove the card from the T1i while the camera is writing images to the card, you'll lose any photos in the buffer and may damage the file structure of the card, making it difficult or impossible to retrieve the other pictures you've taken. The same thing can happen if you remove the memory card from your computer's card reader while the computer is writing to the card (say, to erase files you've already moved to your computer). You can avoid this by *not* using your computer to erase files on a memory card but, instead, always reformatting the card in your T1i before you use it again.

What Can You Do?

Pay attention: If you're having problems, the *first* thing you should do is *stop* using that memory card. Don't take any more pictures. Don't do anything with the card until you've figured out what's wrong. Your second line of defense (your first line is to be sufficiently careful with your cards that you avoid problems in the first place) is to *do no harm* that hasn't already been done. Read the rest of this section and then, if necessary, decide on a course of action (such as using a data recovery service or software described later) before you risk damaging the data on your card further.

Now that you've calmed down, the first thing to check is whether you've actually inserted a card in the camera. If you've set the camera in the Shooting menu so that Shoot w/o card has been turned on, it's entirely possible (although not particularly plausible) that you've been snapping away with no memory card to store the pictures to, which can lead to massive disappointment later on. Of course, the No memory card message appears on the LCD when the camera is powered up, and it is superimposed on the review image after every shot, but maybe you're inattentive, aren't using picture review, or have purchased one of those LCD fold-up hoods mentioned earlier in this chapter. You can avoid all this by turning the Shoot w/o card feature off and leaving it off.

Things get more exciting when the card itself is put in jeopardy. If you lose a card, there's not a lot you can do other than take a picture of a similar card and print up some Have You Seen This Lost Flash Memory? flyers to post on utility poles all around town.

If all you care about is reusing the card, and have resigned yourself to losing the pictures, try reformatting the card in your camera. You may find that reformatting removes the corrupted data and restores your card to health. Sometimes I've had success reformatting a card in my computer using a memory card reader (this is normally a no-no because your operating system doesn't understand the needs of your T1i), and *then* reformatting again in the camera.

If your memory card is not behaving properly, and you *do* want to recover your images, things get a little more complicated. If your pictures are very valuable, either to you or to others (for example, a wedding), you can always turn to professional data recovery firms. Be prepared to pay hundreds of dollars to get your pictures back, but these pros often do an amazing job. You wouldn't want them working on your memory card on

THE ULTIMATE IRONY

I recently purchased an 8GB Kingston memory card that was furnished with some nifty OnTrack data recovery software. The first thing I did was format the card to make sure it was OK. Then I hunted around for the free software, only to discover it was preloaded onto the memory card. I was supposed to copy the software to my computer before using the memory card for the first time.

Fortunately, I had the OnTrack software that would reverse my dumb move, so I could retrieve the software. No, wait. I *didn't* have the software I needed to recover the software I erased. I'd reformatted it to oblivion. Chalk this one up as either the ultimate irony or Stupid Author Trick #523.

behalf of the police if you'd tried to erase some incriminating pictures. There are many firms of this type, and I've never used them myself, so I can't offer a recommendation. Use a Google search to turn up a ton of them.

A more reasonable approach is to try special data recovery software you can install on your computer and attempt to resurrect your "lost" images yourself. They may not actually be gone completely. Perhaps your memory card's "table of contents" is jumbled, or only a few pictures are damaged in such a way that your camera and computer can't read some or any of the pictures on the card. Some of the available software was written specifically to reconstruct lost pictures, while other utilities are more general-purpose applications that can be used with any media, including floppy disks and hard disk drives. They have names like OnTrack, Photo Rescue 2, Digital Image Recovery, MediaRecover, Image Recall, and the aptly named Recover My Photos. You'll find a comprehensive list and links, as well as some picture-recovery tips at www.ultimateslr.com/memory-card-recovery.php.

DIMINISHING RETURNS

Usually, once you've recovered any images on a memory card, reformatted it, and returned it to service, it will function reliably for the rest of its useful life. However, if you find a particular card going bad more than once, you'll almost certainly want to stop using it forever. See if you can get it replaced by the manufacturer, if you can, but, in the case of memory card failures, the third time is never the charm.

Clean Your Sensor

There's no avoiding dust. No matter how careful you are, some of it is going to settle on your camera and on the mounts of your lenses, eventually making its way inside your camera to settle in the mirror chamber. As you take photos, the mirror flipping up and down causes the dust to become airborne and eventually make its way past the shutter curtain to come to rest on the anti-aliasing filter atop your sensor. There, dust and particles can show up in every single picture you take at a small enough aperture to bring the foreign matter into sharp focus. No matter how careful you are and how cleanly you work, eventually you will get some of this dust on your camera's sensor. Some say that CMOS sensors, like the one found in the Rebel T1i, "attract" less dust than CCD sensors found in cameras from other vendors. But even the cleanest-working photographers using Canon cameras are far from immune.

Fortunately, one of the Rebel T1i's most useful new features is the automatic sensor cleaning system that reduces or eliminates the need to clean your camera's sensor manually. As I mentioned in Chapter 3, Canon has applied anti-static coatings to the sensor and other portions of the camera body interior to counter charge build-ups that attract dust. A separate filter over the sensor vibrates ultrasonically each time the T1i is powered on or off, shaking loose any dust.

Although the automatic sensor cleaning feature operates when you power the camera up or turn it off, you can activate it at any time. Choose Sensor Cleaning from the Setup 2 menu, and select Clean Now. If you'd rather turn the feature on or off, choose Auto Cleaning instead, and then choose either Enable or Disable with the cross keys. Press Set, then press the Menu button to return to the Setup 2 menu. (See Figure 9.3.)

Figure 9.3
You can activate automatic sensor cleaning immediately or enable/disable the feature.

If some dust does collect on your sensor, you can often map it out of your images (making it invisible) using software techniques with the Dust Delete Data feature in the Shooting 2 menu. Operation of this feature is described in Chapter 3. Of course, even with the Rebel T1i's automatic sensor cleaning/dust resistance features, you may still be required to manually clean your sensor from time to time. This section explains the phenomenon and provides some tips on minimizing dust and eliminating it when it begins to affect your shots. I also cover this subject in my book *Digital SLR Pro Secrets*, with complete instructions for constructing your own sensor cleaning tools. However, I'll provide a condensed version of some of the information in that book, because sensor dust and sensor cleaning are two of the most contentious subjects Canon EOS Rebel T1i owners have to deal with.

Dust the FAQs, Ma'am.

Here are some of the most frequently asked questions about sensor dust issues.

Q. I see tiny specks in my viewfinder. Do I have dust on my sensor?

A. If you see sharp, well-defined specks, they are clinging to the underside of your focus screen and not on your sensor. They have absolutely no effect on your photographs, and are merely annoying or distracting.

Q. I can see dust on my mirror. How can I remove it?

A. Like focus-screen dust, any artifacts that have settled on your mirror won't affect your photos. You can often remove dust on the mirror or focus screen with a bulb air blower, which will loosen it and whisk it away. Stubborn dust on the focus screen can sometimes be gently flicked away with a soft brush designed for cleaning lenses. I don't recommend brushing the mirror or touching it in any way. The mirror is a special front-surface-silvered optical device (unlike conventional mirrors, which are silvered on the back side of a piece of glass or plastic) and can be easily scratched. If you can't blow off mirror dust, it's best to just forget about it. You can't see it in the viewfinder, anyway.

Q. I see a bright spot in the same place in all of my photos. Is that sensor dust?

A. You've probably got either a "hot" pixel or one that is permanently "stuck" due to a defect in the sensor. A hot pixel is one that shows up as a bright spot only during long exposures as the sensor warms. A pixel stuck in the "on" position always appears in the image. Both show up as bright red, green, or blue pixels, usually surrounded by a small cluster of other improperly illuminated pixels, caused by the camera's interpolating the hot or stuck pixel into its surroundings, as shown in Figure 9.4. A stuck pixel can also be permanently dark. Either kind is likely to show up when they contrast with plain, evenly colored areas of your image.

Figure 9.4

A stuck pixel is surrounded by improperly interpolated pixels created by the T1i's demosaicing algorithm.

Finding one or two hot or stuck pixels in your sensor is unfortunately fairly common. They can be "removed" by telling the T1i to ignore them through a simple process called *pixel mapping*. If the bad pixels become bothersome, Canon can remap your sensor's pixels with a quick trip to a service center.

Bad pixels can also show up on your camera's color LCD panel, but, unless they are abundant, the wisest course is to just ignore them.

Q. I see an irregular out-of-focus blob in the same place in my photos. Is that sensor dust?

A. Yes. Sensor contaminants can take the form of tiny spots, larger blobs, or even curvy lines if they are caused by minuscule fibers that have settled on the sensor. They'll appear out of focus because they aren't actually on the sensor surface but, rather, a fraction of a millimeter above it on the filter that covers the sensor. The smaller the f/stop used, the more in-focus the dust becomes. At large apertures, it may not be visible at all.

Q. I never see any dust on my sensor. What's all the fuss about?

A. Those who never have dust problems with their Rebel T1i fall into one of four categories: those for whom the camera's automatic dust removal features are working well; those who seldom change their lenses and have clean working habits that minimize the amount of dust that invades their cameras in the first place; those who simply don't notice the dust (often because they don't shoot many macro photos or other pictures using the small f/stops that make dust evident in their images); and those who are very, very lucky.

Identifying and Dealing with Dust

Sensor dust is less of a problem than it might be because it shows up only under certain circumstances. Indeed, you might have dust on your sensor right now and not be aware of it. The dust doesn't actually settle on the sensor itself, but, rather, on a protective filter a very tiny distance above the sensor, subjecting it to the phenomenon of *depth-of-focus*. Depth-of-focus is the distance the focal plane can be moved and still render an object in sharp focus. At f/2.8 to f/5.6 or even smaller, sensor dust, particularly if small, is likely to be outside the range of depth-of-focus and blur into an unnoticeable dot.

However, if you're shooting at f/16 to f/22 or smaller, those dust motes suddenly pop into focus. Forget about trying to spot them by peering directly at your sensor with the shutter open and the lens removed. The period at the end of this sentence, about .33mm in diameter, could block a group of pixels measuring 40×40 pixels (160 pixels in all!). Dust spots that are even smaller than that can easily show up in your images if you're shooting large, empty areas that are light colored. Dust motes are most likely to show up in the sky, as in Figure 9.5, or in white backgrounds of your seamless product shots and are less likely to be a problem in images that contain lots of dark areas and detail.

Figure 9.5
Only the dust
spots in the sky
are apparent in
this shot.

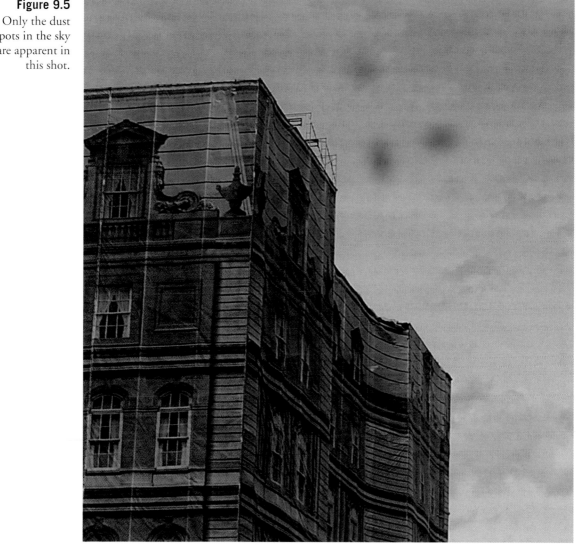

To see if you have dust on your sensor, take a few test shots of a plain, blank surface (such as a piece of paper or a cloudless sky) at small f/stops, such as f/22, and a few wide open. Open Photoshop, copy several shots into a single document in separate layers, then flip back and forth between layers to see if any spots you see are present in all layers. You may have to boost contrast and sharpness to make the dust easier to spot.

Avoiding Dust

Of course, the easiest way to protect your sensor from dust is to prevent it from settling on the sensor in the first place. Some Canon lenses come with rubberized seals around the lens mounts that help keep dust from infiltrating, but you'll find that dust will still find a way to get inside. Here are my stock tips for eliminating the problem before it begins.

■ **Clean environment.** Avoid working in dusty areas if you can do so. Hah! Serious photographers will take this one with a grain of salt, because it usually makes sense to go where the pictures are. Only a few of us are so paranoid about sensor dust (considering that it is so easily removed) that we'll avoid moderately grimy locations just to protect something that is, when you get down to it, just a tool. If you find a great picture opportunity at a raging fire, during a sandstorm, or while surrounded by dust clouds, you might hesitate to take the picture, but, with a little caution (don't remove your lens in these situations, and clean the camera afterwards!) you can still shoot. However, it still makes sense to store your camera in a clean environment. One place cameras and lenses pick up a lot of dust is inside a camera bag. Clean your bag from time to time, and you can avoid problems.

■ **Clean lenses.** There are a few paranoid types that avoid swapping lenses in order to minimize the chance of dust getting inside their cameras. It makes more sense just to use a blower or brush to dust off the rear lens mount of the replacement lens first, so you won't be introducing dust into your camera simply by attaching a new, dusty lens. Do this before you remove the lens from your camera, and then avoid stirring up dust before making the exchange.

■ **Work fast.** Minimize the time your camera is lens-less and exposed to dust. That means having your replacement lens ready and dusted off, and a place to set down the old lens as soon as it is removed, so you can quickly attach the new lens.

■ **Let gravity help you.** Face the camera downward when the lens is detached so any dust in the mirror box will tend to fall away from the sensor. Turn your back to any breezes, indoor forced air vents, fans, or other sources of dust to minimize infiltration.

■ **Protect the lens you just removed.** Once you've attached the new lens, quickly put the end cap on the one you just removed to reduce the dust that might fall on it.

■ **Clean out the vestibule.** From time to time, remove the lens while in a relatively dust-free environment and use a blower bulb like the one shown in Figure 9.6 (*not* compressed air or a vacuum hose) to clean out the mirror box area. A blower bulb is generally safer than a can of compressed air, or a strong positive/negative airflow, which can tend to drive dust farther into nooks and crannies.

Figure 9.6

Use a robust air bulb to clean your sensor.

- **Be prepared.** If you're embarking on an important shooting session, it's a good idea to clean your sensor *now*, rather than coming home with hundreds or thousands of images with dust spots caused by flecks that were sitting on your sensor before you even started. Before I left on my recent trip to Spain, I put both cameras I was taking through a rigid cleaning regimen, figuring they could remain dust-free for a measly 10 days. I even left my bulky blower bulb at home. It was a big mistake, but my intentions were good. I now have a smaller version of the Giottos Rocket Blower, and *that* goes with me everywhere.

- **Clone out existing spots in your image editor.** Photoshop and other editors have a Clone tool or Healing Brush you can use to copy pixels from surrounding areas over the dust spot or dead pixel. This process can be tedious, especially if you have lots of dust spots and/or lots of images to be corrected. The advantage is that this sort of manual fix-it probably will do the least damage to the rest of your photo. Only the cloned pixels will be affected.

- **Use filtration in your image editor.** A semi-smart filter like Photoshop's Dust & Scratches filter can remove dust and other artifacts by selectively blurring areas that the plug-in decides represent dust spots. This method can work well if you have many dust spots because you won't need to patch them manually. However, any automated method like this has the possibility of blurring areas of your image that you didn't intend to soften.

Sensor Cleaning

Those new to the concept of sensor dust actually hesitate before deciding to clean their cameras themselves. Isn't it a better idea to pack up your T1i and send it to a Canon service center so their crack technical staff can do the job for you? Or, at the very least, shouldn't you let the friendly folks at your local camera store do it?

Of course, if you choose to let someone else clean your sensor, they will be using methods that are more or less identical to the techniques you would use yourself. None of these techniques are difficult, and the only difference between their cleaning and your cleaning is that they might have done it dozens or hundreds of times. If you're careful, you can do just as good a job.

Of course vendors like Canon won't tell you this, but it's not because they don't trust you. It's not that difficult for a real goofball to mess up his camera by hurrying or taking a shortcut. Perhaps the person uses the "Bulb" method of holding the shutter open and a finger slips, allowing the shutter curtain to close on top of a sensor cleaning brush. Or, someone tries to clean the sensor using masking tape, and ends up with goo all over its surface. If Canon recommended *any* method that's mildly risky, someone would do it wrong, and then the company would face lawsuits from those who'd contend they did it exactly in the way the vendor suggested, so the ruined camera is not their fault.

If you visit Canon's website, you'll find this recommendation: "If the image sensor needs cleaning, we recommend having it cleaned at a Canon service center, as it is a very delicate component."

You can see that vendors like Canon tend to be conservative in their recommendations, and, in doing so, make it seem as if sensor cleaning is more daunting and dangerous than it really is. Some vendors recommend only dust-off cleaning, through the use of reasonably gentle blasts of air, while condemning more serious scrubbing with swabs and cleaning fluids. However, these cleaning kits for the exact types of cleaning they recommended against are for sale in Japan only, where, apparently, your average photographer is more dexterous than those of us in the rest of the world. These kits are similar to those used by official repair staff to clean your sensor if you decide to send your camera in for a dust-up.

As I noted, sensors can be affected by dust particles that are much smaller than you might be able to spot visually on the surface of your lens. The filters that cover sensors tend to be fairly hard compared to optical glass. Cleaning the 22.2mm × 14.8mm sensor in your Canon T1i within the tight confines of the mirror box can call for a steady hand and careful touch. If your sensor's filter becomes scratched through inept cleaning, you can't simply remove it yourself and replace it with a new one.

There are four basic kinds of cleaning processes that can be used to remove dusty and sticky stuff that settles on your dSLR's sensor. All of these must be performed with the shutter locked open. I'll describe these methods and provide instructions for locking the shutter later in this section.

- **Air cleaning.** This process involves squirting blasts of air inside your camera with the shutter locked open. This works well for dust that's not clinging stubbornly to your sensor.

- **Brushing.** A soft, very fine brush is passed across the surface of the sensor's filter, dislodging mildly persistent dust particles and sweeping them off the imager.

- **Liquid cleaning.** A soft swab dipped in a cleaning solution such as ethanol is used to wipe the sensor filter, removing more obstinate particles.

- **Tape cleaning.** There are some who get good results by applying a special form of tape to the surface of their sensor. When the tape is peeled off, all the dust goes with it. Supposedly. I'd be remiss if I didn't point out right now that this form of cleaning is somewhat controversial; the other three methods are much more widely accepted. Now that Canon has equipped the front-sensor filter with a special anti-dust coating, I wouldn't chance damaging that coating by using any kind of adhesive tape.

Placing the Shutter in the Locked and Fully Upright Position for Landing

Make sure you're using a fully charged battery or the optional AC Adapter Kit ACK-E5.

1. Remove the lens from the camera and then turn on the camera.

2. Set the Rebel T1i to any one of the Creative Zone exposure modes. The shutter cannot be locked open in any of the Basic Zone modes.

3. You'll find the Clean Manually menu choice in the Setup 2 menu under Sensor Cleaning. Press the Set button.

4. Select OK and press Set again. The mirror will flip up and the shutter will open.

5. Use one of the methods described below to remove dust and grime from your sensor. Be careful not to accidentally switch the power off or open the memory card or battery compartment doors as you work. If that happens, the shutter may be damaged if it closes on your cleaning tool.

6. When you're finished, turn the power off, replace your lens, and switch your camera back on.

Air Cleaning

Your first attempts at cleaning your sensor should always involve gentle blasts of air. Many times, you'll be able to dislodge dust spots, which will fall off the sensor and, with luck, out of the mirror box. Attempt one of the other methods only when you've already tried air cleaning and it didn't remove all the dust.

Here are some tips for doing air cleaning:

- **Use a clean, powerful air bulb.** Your best bet is bulb cleaners designed for the job, like the one shown in Figure 9.6. Smaller bulbs, like those air bulbs with a brush attached sometimes sold for lens cleaning or weak nasal aspirators may not provide sufficient air or a strong enough blast to do much good.

- **Hold the Rebel T1i upside down.** Then look up into the mirror box as you squirt your air blasts, increasing the odds that gravity will help pull the expelled dust downward, away from the sensor. You may have to use some imagination in positioning yourself. (And don't let dust fall into your eye!)

- **Never use air canisters.** The propellant inside these cans can permanently coat your sensor if you tilt the can while spraying. It's not worth taking a chance.

- **Avoid air compressors.** Super-strong blasts of air are likely to force dust under the sensor filter.

Brush Cleaning

If your dust is a little more stubborn and can't be dislodged by air alone, you may want to try a brush, charged with static electricity, which can pick off dust spots by electrical attraction. One good, but expensive, option is the Sensor Brush sold at www.visible-dust.com. A cheaper version can be purchased at www.copperhillimages.com. You need a brush about 16mm wide, like the one shown in Figure 9.7, which can be stroked across the long dimension of your T1i's sensor.

Figure 9.7
A proper brush is required for dusting off your sensor.

Ordinary artist's brushes are much too coarse and stiff and have fibers that are tangled or can come loose and settle on your sensor. A good sensor brush's fibers are resilient and described as "thinner than a human hair." Moreover, the brush has a wooden handle that reduces the risk of static sparks. Check out my *Digital SLR Pro Secrets* book if you want to make a sensor brush (or sensor swabs) yourself.

Brush cleaning is done with a dry brush by gently swiping the surface of the sensor filter with the tip. The dust particles are attracted to the brush particles and cling to them. You should clean the brush with compressed air before and after each use, and store it in an appropriate air-tight container between applications to keep it clean and dust-free. Although these special brushes are expensive, one should last you a long time.

Liquid Cleaning

Unfortunately, you'll often encounter really stubborn dust spots that can't be removed with a blast of air or flick of a brush. These spots may be combined with some grease or a liquid that causes them to stick to the sensor filter's surface. In such cases, liquid cleaning with a swab may be necessary. During my first clumsy attempts to clean my own sensor, I accidentally got my blower bulb tip too close to the sensor, and some sort of deposit from the tip of the bulb ended up on the sensor. I panicked until I discovered that liquid cleaning did a good job of removing whatever it was that took up residence on my sensor.

You can make your own swabs out of pieces of plastic (some use fast food restaurant knives, with the tip cut at an angle to the proper size) covered with a soft cloth or Pec-Pad, as shown in Figures 9.8 and 9.9. However, if you've got the bucks to spend, you can't go wrong with good-quality commercial sensor cleaning swabs, such as those sold by Photographic Solutions, Inc. (www.photosol.com/swabproduct.htm).

You want a sturdy swab that won't bend or break so you can apply gentle pressure to the swab as you wipe the sensor surface. Use the swab with methanol (as pure as you can get it, particularly medical grade; other ingredients can leave a residue), or the Eclipse solution also sold by Photographic Solutions. Eclipse (see Figure 9.10) is actu-

Figure 9.8
You can make your own sensor swab from a plastic knife that's been truncated.

Figure 9.9 Carefully wrap a Pec-Pad around the swab.

Figure 9.10 Pure Eclipse solution makes the best sensor cleaning liquid.

ally quite a bit purer than even medical-grade methanol. A couple drops of solution should be enough, unless you have a spot that's extremely difficult to remove. In that case, you may need to use extra solution on the swab to help "soak" the dirt off.

Once you overcome your nervousness at touching your T1i's sensor, the process is easy. You'll wipe continuously with the swab in one direction, then flip it over and wipe in the other direction. Figure 9.11 shows a swab being lowered past the lens mount down to the sensor. You need to completely wipe the entire surface; otherwise, you may end up depositing the dust you collect at the far end of your stroke. Wipe; don't rub.

Figure 9.11
Carefully swab off the dust.

Tape Cleaning

There are people who absolutely swear by the tape method of sensor cleaning. The concept seems totally wacky, and I have never tried it personally, so I can't say with certainty that it either does or does not work. In the interest of completeness, I'm including it here. I can't give you a recommendation, so if you have problems, please don't blame me. The Rebel T1i is still too new to have generated any reports of users accidentally damaging the anti-dust coating on the sensor filter using this method.

Tape cleaning works by applying a layer of Scotch Brand Magic Tape to the sensor. This is a minimally sticky tape that some of the tape-cleaning proponents claim contains no adhesive. I did check this out with 3M, and can say that Magic Tape certainly *does* contain an adhesive. The question is whether the adhesive comes off when you peel back the tape, taking any dust spots on your sensor with it. The folks who love this method claim there is no residue. There have been reports from those who don't like the method that residue is left behind. This is all anecdotal evidence, so you're pretty much on your own in making the decision whether to try out the tape cleaning method.

Checking Your Work

If you want a close-up look at your sensor to make sure the dust has been removed, you can pay $50-$100 for a special sensor "microscope" with an illuminator, like the one shown in Figure 9.12. I use such a device when I'm close to home, but it's too bulky

Figure 9.12
A special "sensorscope" viewer can help detect any remaining dust on your sensor.

and too expensive to tuck a sensorscope into every camera bag I own. Instead, I have four or five plain old Carson MiniBrite PO-25 illuminated 3X magnifiers (less than $10), as seen in Figure 9.13. (Older packaging and ads may call this a 2X magnifier, but it's actually a 3X unit.) It has a built-in LED and, held a few inches from the lens mount with the lens removed from your T1i, provides a sharp, close-up view of the sensor, with enough contrast to reveal any dust that remains.

Figure 9.13
An illuminated magnifier like this Carson MiniBrite PO-25 is an inexpensive substitute 'scope that costs less than $10.

Glossary

Here are some terms you might encounter while reading this book or working with your Canon EOS Rebel T1i.

additive primary colors The red, green, and blue hues that are used alone or in combinations to create all other colors that you capture with a digital camera, view on a computer monitor, or work with in an image-editing program, such as Photoshop. *See also* CMYK color model.

A-DEP A Creative Zone mode that analyzes your scene and attempts to choose an f/stop and focus distance that will allow all the important subjects to be in sharp focus.

Adobe RGB One of two color space choices offered by the Canon EOS Rebel T1i. Adobe RGB is an expanded color space useful for commercial and professional printing, and it can reproduce a larger number of colors. Canon recommends against using this color space if your images will be displayed primarily on your computer screen or output by your personal printer. *See also* sRGB.

AEB Automatic exposure bracketing takes a series of pictures at different exposure increments to improve the chances of producing one picture that is perfectly exposed.

ambient lighting Diffuse, non-directional lighting that doesn't appear to come from a specific source but, rather, bounces off walls, ceilings, and other objects in the scene when a picture is taken.

analog/digital converter The Canon DIGIC 4 imaging processor built into the T1i to convert the analog information captured by the camera's sensor into digital bits that can be stored as an image bitmap.

angle of view The area of a scene that a lens can capture, determined by the focal length of the lens. Lenses with a shorter focal length have a wider angle of view than lenses with a longer focal length.

anti-alias A process that smoothes the look of rough edges in images (called *jaggies* or *staircasing*) by adding partially transparent pixels along the boundaries of diagonal lines that are merged into a smoother line by our eyes. *See also* jaggies.

Aperture Preferred A camera setting that allows you to specify the lens opening or f/stop that you want to use, with the camera selecting the required shutter speed automatically based on its light-meter reading. This setting is represented by the abbreviation Av on the T1i's Mode dial. *See also* Shutter Preferred.

artifact A type of noise in an image, or an unintentional image component produced in error by a digital camera during processing, usually caused by the JPEG compression process in digital cameras.

aspect ratio The proportions of an image as printed, displayed on a monitor, or captured by a digital camera.

autofocus A camera setting that allows the Canon EOS Rebel T1i to choose the correct focus distance for you, based on the contrast of an image (the image will be at maximum contrast when in sharp focus). The camera can be set for One Shot (generically known as *Single Autofocus*, in which the lens is not focused until the shutter release is partially depressed), AI Servo (known as *Continuous Autofocus*, in which the lens refocuses constantly as you frame and reframe the image), or AI AF, which allows the camera to switch back and forth between One Shot and AI Servo based on subject movement.

backlighting A lighting effect produced when the main light source is located behind the subject. Backlighting can be used to create a silhouette effect, or to illuminate translucent objects. *See also* front lighting and side lighting.

barrel distortion A lens defect that causes straight lines at the top or side edges of an image to bow outward into a barrel shape. *See also* pincushion distortion.

Basic Zone modes The EOS T1i's automated shooting modes, such as Landscape and Sports, that select lens opening, shutter speed, exposure, and other parameters for you.

blooming An image distortion caused when a photosite in an image sensor has absorbed all the photons it can handle so that additional photons reaching that pixel overflow to affect surrounding pixels, producing unwanted brightness and overexposure around the edges of objects.

blur To soften an image or part of an image by throwing it out of focus, or by allowing it to become soft due to subject or camera motion. Blur can also be applied in an image-editing program.

bokeh A term derived from the Japanese word for blur, which describes the aesthetic qualities of the out-of-focus parts of an image. Some lenses produce "good" bokeh and others offer "bad" bokeh. Some lenses produce uniformly illuminated out-of-focus discs. Others produce a disc that has a bright edge and a dark center, producing a "doughnut" effect, which is the worst from a bokeh standpoint. Lenses that generate a bright center that fades to a darker edge are favored, because their bokeh allows the circle of confusion to blend more smoothly with the surroundings. The bokeh characteristics of a lens are most important when you're using selective focus (say, when shooting a portrait) to deemphasize the background, or when shallow depth-of-field is a given because you're working with a macro lens, a long telephoto, or a wide-open aperture. *See also* circle of confusion.

bounce lighting Light bounced off a reflector, including ceiling and walls, to provide a soft, natural-looking light.

bracketing Taking a series of photographs of the same subject at different settings, including exposure and white balance, to help ensure that one setting will be the correct one. The Canon EOS Rebel T1i allows you to choose the order in which bracketed settings are applied, or bracket sequence.

buffer The digital camera's internal memory where an image is stored immediately after it is taken until it can be written to the camera's non-volatile (semi-permanent) memory or a memory card.

burst mode The digital camera's equivalent of the film camera's motor drive, used to take multiple shots within a short period of time, with each shot stored in a memory buffer temporarily before writing it to the media.

calibration A process used to correct for the differences in the output of a printer or monitor when compared to the original image. Once you've calibrated your scanner, monitor, and/or your image editor, the images you see on the screen more closely represent what you'll get from your printer, even though calibration is never perfect.

Camera Raw A plug-in included with Photoshop and Photoshop Elements that can manipulate the unprocessed images captured by digital cameras, such as the Canon EOS Rebel T1i's .CR2 files. The latest versions of this module can also work with JPEG and TIFF images.

camera shake Movement of the camera, aggravated by slower shutter speeds, which produces a blurred image. You can minimize camera shake by using a lens with built-in image stabilization.

CCD *See* charge-coupled device (CCD).

center-weighted meter A light-measuring device that emphasizes the area in the middle of the frame when calculating the correct exposure for an image. *See also* spot meter.

charge-coupled device (CCD) A type of solid-state sensor that captures the image used in scanners and digital cameras. *See also* complementary metal oxide semiconductor (CMOS).

chromatic aberration An image defect, often seen as green or purple fringing around the edges of an object, caused by a lens failing to focus all colors of a light source at the same point. *See also* fringing.

circle of confusion A term applied to the fuzzy discs produced when a point of light is out of focus. The circle of confusion is not a fixed size. The viewing distance and amount of enlargement of the image determine whether we see a particular spot on the image as a point or as a disc. *See also* bokeh.

close-up lens A lens add-on that allows you to take pictures at a distance that is less than the closest-focusing distance of the lens alone.

CMOS *See* complementary metal-oxide semiconductor (CMOS).

CMYK color model A way of defining all possible colors in percentages of cyan, magenta, yellow, and frequently, black. (K represents black, to differentiate it from blue in the RGB color model.) Black is added to improve rendition of shadow detail. CMYK is commonly used for printing (both on press and with your inkjet or laser color printer).

color correction Changing the relative amounts of color in an image to produce a desired effect, typically a more accurate representation of those colors. Color correction can fix faulty color balance in the original image, or compensate for the deficiencies of the inks used to reproduce the image.

complementary metal-oxide semiconductor (CMOS) A method for manufacturing a type of solid-state sensor that captures an image; used in scanners and digital cameras such as those from Canon, including the EOS Rebel T1i.

compression Reducing the size of a file by encoding using fewer bits of information to represent the original. Some compression schemes, such as JPEG, operate by discarding some image information, while others, such as RAW, preserve all the detail in the original, discarding only redundant data.

Continuous Autofocus An automatic focusing setting (AI Servo) in which the camera constantly refocuses the image as you frame the picture. This setting is often the best choice for moving subjects.

contrast The range between the lightest and darkest tones in an image. A high-contrast image is one in which the shades fall at the extremes of the range between white and black. In a low-contrast image, the tones are closer together.

Creative Zone modes The EOS T1i's semi-automated and manual shooting modes, including A-DEP, Program, Aperture Priority, Shutter Priority, and Manual, that allow you to select shutter speed and/or aperture yourself, with the camera calculating the proper exposure based on those parameters.

Custom Functions A group of 13 different settings you can make to specify how the EOS T1i behaves, such as the function of certain controls, electronic flash features, and other customizable attributes.

dedicated flash An electronic flash unit, such as the Canon 580EX II Speedlight, designed to work with the automatic exposure features of a specific camera.

depth-of-field A distance range in a photograph in which all included portions of an image are at least acceptably sharp. With the Canon EOS Rebel T1i, you can see the available depth-of-field at the taking aperture by pressing the Depth-of-Field Preview button, or estimate the range by viewing the depth-of-field scale found on many lenses.

diaphragm An adjustable component, similar to the iris in the human eye, that can open and close to provide specific-sized lens openings, or f/stops, and thus control the amount of light reaching the sensor or film.

diffuse lighting Soft, low-contrast lighting.

digital processing chip A solid-state device found in digital cameras (such as the EOS T1i's DIGIC 4 module) that's in charge of applying the image algorithms to the raw picture data prior to storage on the memory card.

diopter A value used to represent the magnification power of a lens, calculated as the reciprocal of a lens's focal length (in meters). Diopters are most often used to represent the optical correction used in a viewfinder to adjust for limitations of the photographer's eyesight, and to describe the magnification of a close-up lens attachment.

equivalent focal length A digital camera's focal length translated into the corresponding values for a 35mm film camera. This value can be calculated for lenses used with the Canon EOS Rebel T1i by multiplying by 1.6.

Evaluative metering One system of exposure calculation used by the EOS T1i that looks at many different segments of an image to determine the brightest and darkest portions.

exchangeable image file format (Exif) Developed to standardize the exchange of image data between hardware devices and software. A variation on JPEG, Exif is used by most digital cameras, and includes information such as the date and time a photo was taken, the camera settings, resolution, amount of compression, and other data.

Exif *See* exchangeable image file format (Exif).

exposure The amount of light allowed to reach the film or sensor, determined by the intensity of the light, the amount admitted by the iris of the lens, the length of time determined by the shutter speed, and the ISO sensitivity setting for the sensor.

exposure values (EV) EV settings are a way of adding or decreasing exposure without the need to reference f/stops or shutter speeds. For example, if you tell your camera to add +1EV, it will provide twice as much exposure by using a larger f/stop, slower shutter speed, or both.

fill lighting In photography, lighting is used to illuminate shadows. Reflectors or additional incandescent lighting or electronic flash can be used to brighten shadows. One common technique for outdoors is to use the camera's flash as a fill.

filter In photography, a device that fits over the lens, changing the light in some way. In image editing, a feature that changes the pixels in an image to produce blurring, sharpening, and other special effects. Photoshop includes several interesting filter effects, including Lens Blur and Photo Filters.

flash sync The timing mechanism that ensures that an internal or external electronic flash fires at the correct time during the exposure cycle. A digital SLR's flash sync speed is the highest shutter speed that can be used with flash, ordinarily 1/200th of a second with the Canon EOS Rebel T1i. *See also* front-curtain sync and rear-curtain sync.

focal length The distance between the film and the optical center of the lens when the lens is focused on infinity, usually measured in millimeters.

focal plane A line, perpendicular to the optical access, that passes through the focal point forming a plane of sharp focus when the lens is set at infinity. A focal plane indicator is etched into the Canon EOS Rebel T1i at the left side of the pentaprism.

focus tracking The ability of the automatic focus feature of a camera to change focus as the distance between the subject and the camera changes. One type of focus tracking is *predictive,* in which the mechanism anticipates the motion of the object being focused on, and adjusts the focus to suit.

format To erase a memory card and prepare it to accept files.

fringing A chromatic aberration that produces fringes of color around the edges of subjects, caused by a lens's inability to focus the various wavelengths of light onto the same spot. Purple fringing is especially troublesome with backlit images.

front-curtain sync (first-curtain sync) The default kind of electronic flash synchronization technique, originally associated with focal plane shutters, which consists of a traveling set of curtains, including a *front curtain* (1st Curtain in the T1i's menus), which opens to reveal the film or sensor, and a *rear curtain* (2nd Curtain in the T1i's menus), which follows at a distance determined by shutter speed to conceal the film or sensor at the conclusion of the exposure. For a flash picture to be taken, the entire sensor must be exposed at one time to the brief flash exposure, so the image is exposed after the front curtain has reached the other side of the focal plane, but before the rear curtain begins to move. Front-curtain sync causes the flash to fire at the beginning of this period when the shutter is completely open, in the instant that the first curtain of the focal plane shutter finishes its movement across the film or sensor plane. With slow shutter speeds, this feature can create a blur effect from the ambient light, showing as patterns that follow a moving subject, with the subject shown sharply frozen at the beginning of the blur trail. *See also* rear-curtain sync.

front lighting Illumination that comes from the direction of the camera. *See also* backlighting and side lighting.

f/stop The relative size of the lens aperture, which helps determine both exposure and depth-of-field. The larger the f/stop number, the smaller the f/stop itself.

graduated filter A lens attachment with variable density or color from one edge to another. A graduated neutral density filter, for example, can be oriented so the neutral density portion is concentrated at the top of the lens's view with the less dense or clear portion at the bottom, thus reducing the amount of light from a very bright sky while not interfering with the exposure of the landscape in the foreground. Graduated filters can also be split into several color sections to provide a color gradient between portions of the image.

gray card A piece of cardboard or other material with a standardized 18-percent reflectance. Gray cards can be used as a reference for determining correct exposure or for setting white balance.

HDMI (High Definition Multimedia Interface) An interface for transmitting audio and video information between a source, such as a digital camera or television tuner, to an output device, such as a high definition television (HDTV) monitor.

high contrast A wide range of density in a print, negative, or other image.

highlights The brightest parts of an image containing detail.

histogram A kind of chart showing the relationship of tones in an image using a series of 256 vertical bars, one for each brightness level. A histogram chart, such as the one the Canon EOS Rebel T1i can display during picture review, typically looks like a curve with one or more slopes and peaks, depending on how many highlight, midtone, and shadow tones are present in the image. The T1i can also display separate histograms for the red, green, and blue channels of an image.

hot shoe A mount on top of a camera used to hold an electronic flash, while providing an electrical connection between the flash and the camera.

hyperfocal distance A point of focus where everything from half that distance to infinity appears to be acceptably sharp. For example, if your lens has a hyperfocal distance of four feet, everything from two feet to infinity would be sharp. The hyperfocal distance varies by the lens and the aperture in use. If you know you'll be making a grab shot without warning, sometimes it is useful to turn off your camera's automatic focus, and set the lens to infinity, or, better yet, the hyperfocal distance. Then, you can snap off a quick picture without having to wait for the lag that occurs with most digital cameras as their autofocus locks in.

image rotation A feature that senses whether a picture was taken in horizontal or vertical orientation. That information is embedded in the picture file so that the camera and compatible software applications can automatically display the image in the correct orientation.

image stabilization A technology that compensates for camera shake, usually by adjusting the position of the camera sensor (with some vendors) or, in the case of Canon, lens elements that shift in response to movements of the camera.

incident light Light measured as it falls on a surface, as opposed to light reflected from that surface.

International Organization for Standardization (ISO) A governing body that provides standards used to represent film speed, or the equivalent sensitivity of a digital camera's sensor. Digital camera sensitivity is expressed in ISO settings.

interpolation A technique digital cameras, scanners, and image editors use to create new pixels required whenever you resize or change the resolution of an image based on the values of surrounding pixels. Devices such as scanners and digital cameras can use interpolation to create pixels in addition to those actually captured, thereby increasing the apparent resolution or color information in an image.

ISO *See* International Organization for Standardization (ISO).

jaggies Staircasing effect of lines, most easily seen at large magnifications that are not perfectly horizontal or vertical, caused by pixels that are too large to represent the line accurately. *See also* anti-alias.

JPEG Short for Joint Photographic Experts Group. A file "lossy" format that supports 24-bit color and reduces file sizes by selectively discarding image data. Digital cameras generally use JPEG compression to pack more images onto memory cards. You can select how much compression is used (and, therefore, how much information is thrown away) by selecting from among the High, Medium, and Low quality settings offered by your camera. *See also* RAW.

Kelvin (K) A unit of measure based on the absolute temperature scale in which absolute zero is zero; it's used to describe the color of continuous-spectrum light sources and applied when setting white balance. For example, daylight has a color temperature of about 5,500K, and a tungsten lamp has a temperature of about 3,400K.

lag time The interval between when the shutter is pressed and when the picture is actually taken. During that span, the camera may be automatically focusing and calculating exposure. With digital SLRs like the Canon EOS Rebel T1i, lag time is generally very short; with non-dSLRs, the elapsed time easily can be one second or more.

latitude The range of camera exposure that produces acceptable images with a particular digital sensor or film.

lens flare A feature of conventional photography that is both a bane and a creative outlet. It is an effect produced by the reflection of light internally among elements of an optical lens. Bright light sources within or just outside the field of view cause lens flare. Flare can be reduced by the use of coatings on the lens elements or with the use of lens hoods. Photographers sometimes use the effect as a creative technique, and Photoshop includes a filter that lets you add lens flare at your whim.

lighting ratio   The proportional relationship between the amount of light falling on the subject from the main light and other lights, expressed in a ratio, such as 3:1.

Live View   The ability of some Canon cameras, including the T1i, to provide a real-time preview image, as seen by the sensor, on the rear-panel color LCD, achieved by flipping up the mirror and opening the shutter.

lossless compression   An image-compression scheme, such as TIFF, that preserves all image detail. When the image is decompressed, it is identical to the original version.

lossy compression   An image-compression scheme, such as JPEG, that creates smaller files by discarding image information, which can affect image quality.

macro lens   A lens that provides continuous focusing from infinity to extreme close-ups, often to a reproduction ratio of 1:2 (half life-size) or 1:1 (life-size).

maximum burst   The number of frames that can be exposed at the current settings until the buffer fills.

midtones   Parts of an image with tones of an intermediate value, usually in the 25 to 75 percent brightness range. Many image-editing features allow you to manipulate midtones independently from the highlights and shadows.

mirror lock-up   The ability of the T1i to flip up its mirror to reduce vibration prior to taking the photo and to allow access to the sensor for cleaning.

neutral color   A color in which red, green, and blue are present in equal amounts, producing a gray.

neutral density filter   A gray camera filter that reduces the amount of light entering the camera without affecting the colors.

noise   In an image, pixels with randomly distributed color values. Noise in digital photographs tends to be the product of low-light conditions and long exposures, particularly when you've set your camera to an ISO rating higher than about ISO 800.

noise reduction   A technology used to cut down on the amount of random information in a digital picture, usually caused by long exposures at increased sensitivity ratings. In the Canon EOS Rebel T1i, noise reduction is automatically applied for long exposures, and it involves the camera automatically taking a second blank/dark exposure at the same settings that contain only noise, and then using the blank photo's information to cancel out the noise in the original picture. Although the process is very quick, it does double the amount of time required to take the photo. Noise reduction can be switched off if you'd rather not use it.

normal lens A lens that makes the image in a photograph appear in a perspective that is like that of the original scene, typically with a field of view of roughly 45 degrees.

overexposure A condition in which too much light reaches the film or sensor, producing a dense negative or a very bright/light print, slide, or digital image.

pincushion distortion A type of lens distortion in which lines at the top and side edges of an image are bent inward, producing an effect that looks like a pincushion. *See also* barrel distortion.

polarizing filter A filter that forces light, which normally vibrates in all directions, to vibrate only in a single plane, reducing or removing the specular reflections from the surface of objects. Such filters tend to increase the contrast between colors and make blue skies more dramatic, most strongly when the sun is located at a 90-degree angle from the direction the camera is pointed.

RAW An image file format, such as the CR2 format in the Canon EOS Rebel T1i, which includes all the unprocessed information captured by the camera after conversion to digital form. RAW files are very large compared to JPEG files and must be processed by a special program such as Canon Digital Photo Pro or Adobe's Camera Raw filter after being downloaded from the camera.

rear-curtain sync (second-curtain sync) An optional kind of electronic flash synchronization technique, originally associated with focal plane shutters, which consists of a traveling set of curtains, including a *front (first) curtain* (which opens to reveal the film or sensor) and a *rear (second) curtain* (which follows at a distance determined by shutter speed to conceal the film or sensor at the conclusion of the exposure). For a flash picture to be taken, the entire sensor must be exposed at one time to the brief flash exposure, so the image is exposed after the front curtain has reached the other side of the focal plane, but before the rear curtain begins to move. Rear-curtain sync causes the flash to fire at the end of the exposure, a fraction of an instant before the second or rear curtain of the focal plane shutter begins to move. With slow shutter speeds, this feature can create a blur effect from the ambient light, showing as patterns that follow a moving subject with the subject shown sharply frozen at the end of the blur trail. If you were shooting a photo of The Flash, the superhero would appear sharp, with a ghostly trail behind him. *See also* front-curtain sync (first-curtain sync).

red-eye An effect from flash photography that appears to make a person's eyes glow red, or an animal's yellow or green. It's caused by light bouncing from the retina of the eye and is most pronounced in dim illumination (when the irises are wide open) and when the electronic flash is close to the lens and, therefore, prone to reflect directly back. An external flash unit, at a greater distance from the lens, can minimize or eliminate the effect. Image editors can fix red-eye through cloning other pixels over the offending red or orange ones.

RGB color A color model that represents the three colors—red, green, and blue—used by devices such as scanners or monitors to reproduce color. Photoshop works in RGB mode by default, and even displays CMYK images by converting them to RGB.

saturation The purity of color; the amount by which a pure color is diluted with white or gray.

selective focus Choosing a lens opening that produces a shallow depth-of-field. Usually this is used to isolate a subject in portraits, close-ups, and other types of images, by causing most other elements in the scene to be blurred.

self-timer A mechanism that delays the opening of the shutter for some seconds after the release has been operated.

sensitivity A measure of the degree of response of a film or sensor to light, measured using the ISO setting.

shadow The darkest part of an image, represented on a digital image by pixels with low numeric values.

sharpening Increasing the apparent sharpness of an image by boosting the contrast between adjacent pixels that form an edge, either using in-camera processing or after the picture is taken and manipulated in an image editor.

shutter In a conventional film camera, the shutter is a mechanism consisting of blades, a curtain, a plate, or some other movable cover that controls the time during which light reaches the film. Digital cameras may use actual mechanical shutters for the slower shutter speeds (less than 1/200th second) and an electronic shutter for higher speeds.

Shutter Preferred An exposure mode, represented by the letters Tv (Time Value) on the T1i's Mode dial, in which you set the shutter speed and the camera determines the appropriate f/stop. *See also* Aperture Preferred.

side lighting Applying illumination from the left or right sides of the camera. *See also* backlighting and front lighting.

slave unit An accessory flash unit that supplements the main flash, usually triggered electronically when the slave senses the light output by the main unit, through radio waves, or through a pre-burst emitted by the camera's main flash unit.

slow sync An electronic flash synchronizing method that uses a slow shutter speed so that ambient light is recorded by the camera in addition to the electronic flash illumination. This allows the background to receive more exposure for a more realistic effect.

specular highlight Bright spots in an image caused by reflection of light sources, often from shiny surfaces.

spot meter An exposure system that concentrates on a small area in the image, represented by the circle in the center of the EOS T1i's viewfinder. *See also* center-weighted meter.

sRGB One of two color space choices available with the Canon EOS Rebel T1i. The sRGB setting is recommended for images that will be output locally on the user's own printer, as this color space matches that of the typical inkjet printer and a properly calibrated monitor fairly closely. *See also* Adobe RGB.

subtractive primary colors Cyan, magenta, and yellow, which are the printing inks that theoretically absorb all color and produce black. In practice, however, they generate a muddy brown, so black is added to preserve detail (especially in shadows). The combination of the three colors and black is referred to as CMYK. (K represents black, to differentiate it from blue in the RGB model.)

time exposure A picture taken by leaving the shutter open for a long period, usually more than one second. The camera is generally locked down with a tripod to prevent blur during the long exposure.

Through-the-Lens (TTL) A system of providing viewing and exposure calculation through the actual lens taking the picture.

tungsten light Light from ordinary room lamps and ceiling fixtures, as opposed to fluorescent illumination.

underexposure A condition in which too little light reaches the film or sensor, producing a thin negative, a dark slide, a muddy-looking print, or a dark digital image.

unsharp masking The process for increasing the contrast between adjacent pixels in an image, increasing sharpness, especially around edges.

vignetting Dark corners of an image, often produced by using a lens hood that is too small for the field of view, a lens that does not completely fill the image frame, or generated artificially using image-editing techniques.

white balance The adjustment of a digital camera to the color temperature of the light source. Interior illumination is relatively red; outdoor light is relatively blue. Digital cameras like the EOS T1i set correct white balance automatically or let you do it through menus. Image editors can often do some color correction of images that were exposed using the wrong white balance setting, especially when working with RAW files that contain the information originally captured by the camera before white balance was applied.

Index

A

A-DEP (automatic depth-of-field), 20
built-in flash with, 28, 264
color space menu for, 82
focus point in, 28, 147
and hyperfocal distance, 148
with Live View, 185
Picture Styles and, 85
working with, 146–148
A-TTL (Advanced Through-the-Lens), 73
Flash Control menu setting, 267–268
AC adapter kit, 6, 8–9
Live View, working in, 185
for time-lapse photography, 212
for updating firmware, 306
AC power
for studio flash, 275
for time-lapse photography, 212
acrylic/glass shields for LCD, 307–308
action stopping. *See* **stopping action**
Add Original Decision Data function, 128
additional images, viewing, 30
Adobe Camera Raw, 62, 293
with Adobe Photoshop/Photoshop Elements, 295, 298–301
and HDR (High Dynamic Range), 164

Adobe Photoshop/Photoshop Elements, 96, 293–294
ACR dialog box, 299–300
Bibble Pro with, 297
card readers with, 292–293
Dust & Scratches filter, 319
exposure adjustments in, 134–135
High Dynamic Range (HDR) photography, 135
Lens Correction filter, 239
Merge to HDR feature, 160–164
noise reduction, 165
opening RAW image in, 298–300
Photo Downloader, transferring images with, 292–293
RAW images, editing, 295, 298–301
tools in, 299
white balance (WB), specifying, 257
Adobe RGB, 82–84
Bibble Pro supporting, 297
Adorama flash units, 276
Advanced Picture Style Settings dialog box, 96
AE Lock button, 43–44
behaviors of button, setting, 126
in Live View, 188–189
and spot metering, 145

AEB (auto exposure bracketing)
activating, 75, 77
Live View, indicators in, 189
Shooting menu options, 75–77
Shooting Settings display for, 53
working with, 158–160
zero point, adjusting, 158
AF assist lamp, activating, 124
AF (autofocus), 10. *See also* **AI Focus AF; AI Servo AF; focus points; One Shot AF**
AF Mode button, 22–23, 43, 45
choosing modes for, 179–180
circles of confusion, 176–178
contrast detection, 172–174
cross-type focus point, 171–172
evaluative metering and, 143
lenses and, 216, 223
light and, 174
in Live View, 115, 187, 190
for movies, 196, 197
phase detection, 170–172
sensors, 179
Shooting Settings display for, 53
viewfinder, autofocus zones in, 54
AF Live, 190
AF Mode button, 22–23, 43, 45
AF Point Selection button, 23–24, 43, 45, 182
AFD (arc-form drive) lenses, 223, 225
AI Focus AF, 22
working with, 181

AI Servo AF, 22
AE Lock button in, 126
working with, 181
air cleaning sensor, 320–321
Alien Bees flash units, 276
amp noise, 205
**Angle Finder C right angle
viewer, 6**
angles
with telephoto lenses, 239
with wide-angle lenses, 233
**anti-static coatings, 218,
313–314**
aperture, 137. *See also* **f/stops;
maximum aperture**
constant aperture lenses, 219,
223
lens considerations, 216
Shooting Settings display for, 53
viewfinder information, 55
Aperture Priority mode. *See* **Av
(Aperture Priority) mode**
Aperture value (AV) button, 43
Apple computers. *See* **Mac
computers**
APS-C format, 222
**architectural photos, long
exposures for, 205–206**
aspherical lens elements, 235
Auto Cleaning, 114
**auto exposure bracketing
(AEB).** *See* **AEB (auto
exposure bracketing)**
auto exposure lock. *See also* **AE
Lock button**
viewfinder information, 55
Auto ISO setting, 157
**auto lighting optimizer, 124,
133**
flash EV and, 73
Auto mode, 17, 19
ISO settings in, 157
Auto Power Off, 108
auto rotate display, 53

Auto white balance (WB), 78
in Live View, 190
autofocus. *See* **AF (autofocus)**
**Autofocus/Manual switch on
lens, 50–51**
**automatic reset file numbering,
109**
Autumn Hues Picture Style, 98
Av (Aperture Priority) mode, 20
auto lighting optimizer in, 124
built-in flash with, 27, 264
color space menu for, 82
evaluative metering in, 143
exposure equivalent exposure,
changing, 139
flash synchronization with,
119–120
Picture Styles and, 85
working with, 148–149
AV cable, 3–4
axial chromatic aberration, 235

B

back view of camera, 41–47
backgrounds, 278–279
in Creative Auto mode, 156
with telephoto lenses, 237–238
backlighting, 133
barn doors, 279
Basic Zone modes, 17–18. *See
also* **specific modes**
auto lighting optimizer in, 124
built-in flash with, 27, 264
Drive mode, changing, 20
focus point in, 28
image quality for, 20
ISO settings in, 157
list of, 19
Picture Styles in, 85
sRGB color space, 82
batteries
charging, 6–7, 9
dependence on, 304
extra batteries, 5

for movies, 195
saving power, methods for, 108
for studio flash, 275
on updating firmware, 306
battery chargers, 3
car battery charger, 9
LC-E5/LC-E5E battery charger,
7–8
battery grip, 6, 9
tripod socket for locking, 49
battery pack, 3
**Beep option, Shooting menu,
64–65**
**beeper, Camera Functions
display, 53**
Bibble Professional, 293, 297
black and white. *See also*
Monochrome Picture Style
in Adobe Camera Raw plug-in,
300
viewfinder, B/W indicator in,
55
**blacks in Adobe Camera Raw
plug-in, 300**
blower bulbs, 318, 321
Blue/Amber scale, 79–81
blue histogram, 102–104
blue toning effect, 92–94
blur
bokeh and telephoto lenses,
240–241
circles of confusion, 176–178
in Creative Auto mode, 156
long exposures creating, 206,
208
body cap, 3
mounting, 10
bokeh, 240–241
bootstrap loaders, 306
Bosworth, Kris, 148–149, 252
bottom of camera, 49
bouncing light, 272–273
**bowing outward lines with
wide-angle lenses, 235–236**
box, contents of, 2–6

bracketing, 158–164. *See also* AEB (auto exposure bracketing); white balance bracketing
HDR (High Dynamic Range), merge to, 160–164
BreezeBrowser, 297–298
brightness. *See also* HDR (High Dynamic Range)
in Adobe Camera Raw plug-in, 300
in Creative Auto mode, 17, 156
histograms, 102–104, 165–168
LCD brightness, adjusting, 108, 111–112
brush cleaning sensor, 321–322
buffer for Continuous Shooting mode, 198
bugs, firmware upgrades for, 305
built-in flash, 200, 248–249. *See also* Flash Control menu
AF assist lamp, activating, 124
with Basic Zone modes, 264
with Creative Zone modes, 264–265
enabling/disabling flash, 72
range for, 265
Shooting menu settings for, 72–73
working with, 26–28, 263–269
bulb exposures, 204
Bulb settings and light, 137

C

cables. *See also* HDMI cable; USB cable
AV cable, 3–4
calibration for color management, 84–85
Camera & Imaging Products Association (CIPA), 6
Camera Functions settings, 52–53

camera shake. *See also* image-stabilized lenses
in Live View, 185
and short exposures, 203
with telephoto lenses, 239
and wide-angle lenses, 233
Canon EOS Rebel T1i, 3
back view of, 41–47
bottom of, 49
front view of, 36–41
image-stabilization in, 246
multiple flash units, connecting, 276–277
top of, 47–48
viewfinder, information in, 54–55
Canon Extender EF 1.4x II, 243
Canon Extender EF 2x II, 243
Canon File View Utility, 295
Canon 5D Mark II cameras, 214
Canon 5D Mark III cameras, 214–215
Canon lenses. *See* lenses; specific types
Canon Original Data Security Kit, 128
Canon Speedlites, 5–6
basic setups for, 274–275
Custom Functions for, 75
dark flash photos, avoiding, 240
220EX, working with, 272
270EX, working with, 271–272
480EX II, working with, 271
580EX II, working with, 269–271
firmware upgrades for, 305
Flash Control menu settings for, 268
with Live View, 187
sync speed problems with, 262
versatility with, 200
and vignetting, 235
Canon TC-80N3 self-timer, 211
capacitors, 248, 258

"Captivated by Light" (Pierce), 247
Capture One Pro (C1 Pro), 293, 295–296
car battery charger, 9
card readers
with Data Verification Kit, 128
transferring images to computer with, 32–34, 292–293
card safes, 311
Carson MiniBrite PO-25 illuminated magnifiers, 326
cascades, long exposures for, 206, 208
catadioptric lenses, 241
CCD sensors
cleaning, 313
noise and, 164
center-weighted metering, 22, 145–146
AE/FE Lock button with, 44
with Live View, 187
C.Fn *See* Custom Functions
chromatic aberration. *See* color fringes
circles of confusion, 176–178
with telephoto lenses, 241
cleaning. *See also* sensor cleaning
lenses, 318
vestibule, 318
Clear All Camera Settings, 25
Clear All Custom Func., 25
Clear Picture Style, 98
Clear Settings, 25
with Live View, 191
cloning out dust, 319
Close-up mode, 19, 154
ISO settings in, 157
close-ups
lenses for, 227
mirror lockup function with, 124
with telephoto lenses, 237

Cloudy white balance (WB), 78
in Live View, 190
CMOS sensors, 174
cleaning, 313
noise and, 164
Collins, Dean, 247
color balance. *See* white balance
(WB)
color-coded menu tabs, 58
color fringes
with telephoto lenses, 239
with wide-angle lenses, 235
color management, 84–85
color rendering index (CRI),
257
color spaces, 82–85
expanded color space, 83
color temperature. *See also*
white balance (WB)
of continuous light, 253–254
of daylight, 254–255
firmware upgrades for, 305
of incandescent light, 255
color tone, 85, 88
adjusting, 91–92
Picture Style Editor, working
with, 95–97, 281
Colormunki, 85
colors
Adobe Camera Raw plug-in
color sampler, 299
and fluorescent light, 256–257
gamuts, 82–85
Screen Color feature, 111
Compact Power Adapter, 7
for time-lapse photography, 212
compression. *See also* JPEG
format
Shooting menu options, 60
with telephoto lenses, 237

computers. *See also* Mac
computers; PC computers;
transferring images to
computer
Auto Rotate feature with, 109
card readers, transferring images
with, 32–34
formatting memory cards in, 14
Live View, shooting in, 185
constant aperture lenses, 219,
223
contact lenses, diopter
correction for, 10
Continuous Autofocus. *See* AI
Servo AF
continuous file numbering,
108–109
continuous light
basics of, 253–257
costs of, 253
evenness of illumination with,
250
exposure calculation with, 250
flash compared, 248–253
flexibility of, 253
previewing with, 248
stopping action with, 251
Continuous Shooting mode, 20,
26, 198–199
in Live View, 185, 190
white balance bracketing in, 80
contrast, 85, 87
adjusting, 91–92
in Adobe Camera Raw plug-in,
300
auto lighting optimizer, 124
Picture Style Editor, working
with, 95–97, 281
RAW format for adjusting, 168
telephoto lenses, low contrast
with, 240

contrast detection, 172–174
in Live View, 189
converging lines with wide-
angle lenses, 235
copyright information,
128–129
Corel Paint Shop Pro, 294
Corel Painter, 294
Corel Photo Paint, 293–294
Corel PhotoImpact, 295
cost. *See also* lenses
of continuous lighting, 253
of flash, 253
of lenses, 216
of monolights, 275–276
Creative Auto mode, 17–18,
155–156
adjusting settings in, 20
Creative Zone modes, 17–18.
See also specific modes
adjusting settings in, 20
auto lighting optimizer in, 124
built-in flash with, 27, 264–265
color spaces in, 82–85
exposure, calculating, 140–141
flash, enabling/disabling, 72
focus point in, 28
list of, 20
Live View with, 185
metering in, 140–141
crop factor, 213–215
telephoto extenders and,
242–243
with wide-angle lenses, 234
cropping images with Adobe
Camera Raw plug-in, 299
Cross keys, 42–43
cross-type focus point, 171–172
CR2 files, converting, 285
current settings for menu, 59
curvilinear lenses, 235

curving inward lines with telephoto lenses, 240

Custom Functions
AF assist lamp, activating, 124
Auto lighting optimizer, 124
with Canon Speedlite 580EX II, 271
data verification feature, activating, 128
flash sync. in Av mode, 119–120
High ISO speed noise reduction, 123
Highlight Tone priority, 123
ISO expansion settings, 118–119
LCD display when power on, 127–128
Live View, disabled settings in, 187
long exposure noise reduction, 120–123, 164–165
mirror lockup function, 124–125, 210
parts of screen, description of, 115–117
Set button, assigning, 126–127
Shutter button/AE Lock button settings, 126
size of exposure adjustments, 117

D

Dali, Salvador, 201
dark corners. *See* **vignetting**
dark flash with telephoto lenses, 240
dark frame subtraction, 165
noise and, 122–123
darkness, long exposures for, 209
data verification feature, activating, 128

Datacolor, Spyder products from, 85
dates and times, 42
Camera Functions display, 53
entering, 15–16
jumping through images by, 47, 106
Setup menu option for setting, 111
daylight
color rendering index (CRI) for, 257
color temperature of, 253–254
working with, 254–255
Daylight white balance (WB), 78
in Live View, 190
DC Coupler, 77
DC power port, 36–37
defaults, restoring, 25
degrees Kelvin, 254
and fluorescent light, 256
delayed exposures, 209–212
Delete Copyright Information option, 128
deleting
copyright information, 128
images, erasing, 102
My Menu items, 131
Delkin flip-up hoods, 307
DEP mode, 148
depth-of-field (DOF). *See also* **A-DEP (automatic depth-of-field); DOF button**
circles of confusion, 176–178
dust and, 316
Dust Delete Data feature and, 98
with telephoto lenses, 237
with wide-angle lenses, 232, 234
diffraction optics (DO) technology, 230

diffusers, bouncing light with, 273–274
diffusing light, 272–273
Digi4 chip, 62
Digital Image Recovery, 313
Digital Photo Professional, 62, 96
Dust Delete Data feature and, 98–99
EOS Utility, working with, 282–283
Picture Style Editor and, 95, 281–282
as RAW utility, 295–296
vignetting, minimizing, 67–68
working with, 287
Digital SLR Pro Secrets, 314, 322
diopter correction, adjusting, 10–12
Dioptric Adjustment Lens Series E correction lenses, 12
DISP button, 16, 41–42
Camera Functions settings, switching to, 52
in Live View, 188–189
on reviewing images, 30
Shooting Settings display with, 20, 52
display-off sensor, 41–42
displaying images, 30
distance
for built-in flash, 265
scale, 50–51
distortion
bokeh, 240–241
pincushion distortion with telephoto lenses, 240
with wide-angle lenses, 233–234
DOF button, 38–39, 147
with Live View, 187
doughnut effect, 241

DPOF (Digital Print Order Format), 102

dragging and dropping images, 293

Drive mode, 20, 26. *See also* Continuous Shooting mode; Self-Timer/Remote control; Single Shot mode
in Creative Auto mode, 156
in Live View, 190
selecting, 46
Shooting Settings display for, 53

duration of light, 137

dust. *See also* sensor cleaning
avoiding, 317–319
body cap protecting from, 10
cloning out, 319
depth-of-field (DOF) and, 316
FAQs about, 315–316
identifying dust, 316–317

Dust Delete Data, 98–99, 314
EOS Utility with, 282, 285
with Live View, 190–191
with Picture Style Editor, 282

dynamic range of sensor, 134

E

E-TTL (Evaluative Through-the-Lens), 73–74
basic light setups with, 275
Flash Control menu setting, 267–268

E-TTL II
Flash Control menu setting for, 267–268
Shooting menu option, 73

Eclipse solution, 323–324

Edgerton, Harold, 199–200, 202

Edison, Thomas, 255

editing images, 293–294. *See also* Adobe Photoshop/Photoshop Elements; Digital Photo Professional
RAW images, 293, 295–298

EF lenses. *See also* specific types
compared to EF-S lenses, 221–223
distinguishing, 223
mounting, 10–11

EF 15mm f/2.8 Autofocus Fisheye lens, 227

EF 24-70mm f/2.8L USM Autofocus lens, 219

EF 24-85mm f/3.5-4.5 USM Autofocus Wide-Angle Telephoto Zoom lens, 219

EF 28-105mm f/3.5-4.5 II USM Zoom lens, 219, 228

EF 24-105mm f/4L IS USM Zoom lens, 228

EF 28-200mm f/3.5-5.6 USM Autofocus Wide-Angle Telephoto Zoom lens, 219

EF 28-235mm f/3.5-5.6 IS USM lens, 219

EF 28-300mm f/3.5-5.6L IS USM lens, 225, 229

EF 35mm f/1.4L USM Autofocus lens, 226

EF 55-200mm f/4.5-5.6 II USM Autofocus Lightweight Compact Telephoto Zoom lens, 219

EF 70-300mm f/4-5.6 IS USM Autofocus Telephoto Zoom lens, 227

EF 85mm f/1.8 USM Telephoto lens, 230–231

EF100mm f/2 Medium Telephoto lens, 228

EF 100mm f/2.8 USM Macro Autofocus lens, 227

EF 100-300mm f/4.5-5.6 USM Autofocus lens, 227, 228

EF 135mm f/2L lens, 228

EF 135mm f/2.8 lens, 229

EF-S lenses. *See also* specific types
compared to EF lenses, 221–223
distinguishing, 223
mounting, 10–11
suitable cameras for, 223

EF-S 10-22mm f/3.5-4.5 USM Zoom lens, 222, 227

EF-S 17-85mm f/4-5. IS USM Autofocus lens, 217–218

EF-S 18-55mm f/3.5-5.6 IS Autofocus lens, 3, 215, 217

EF-S 18-200mm f/3.5-5.6 IS Autofocus lens, 218

EF-S 55-250mm f/4-5.6 IS Telephoto Zoom lens, 219

EF-S 60mm f/2.8 Macro USM lens, 225, 227

18-percent gray cards, 139–140, 142

electrical contacts on lens, 50–51

electronic flash. *See* flash

electronic focus ring USM lenses, 225

elongation effect, 200–201

Emerald Picture Style, 98

emitted light, 137

EOS Digital Solution Disc CD, 4

EOS Utility, 282–285. *See also* transferring images to computer
card readers with, 292–293
copyright information, 128–129
long exposures, allotment for, 204
for Peripheral Illumination Correction, 69–70
Picture Styles, uploading, 96–97
for time-lapse photography, 211

equivalent exposures, 139

Erase button, 43–44

erasing images, 102

EV (exposure value). *See also* flash EV (exposure value)

adding or subtracting, 75–76

AE/FE Lock button and, 44

bracketing and, 160

changes, making, 151

fast EV changes, 151–152

Shooting Settings display for, 53

slower EV changes, 152

evaluative metering, 21, 143. *See also* A-TTL (Advanced Through-the-Lens); E-TTL (Evaluative Through-the-Lens); TTL (Through-the-Lens)

with Live View, 187

zones for, 143–144

evenness of illumination, 250–251

expanded color space, 83

exposure, 133–139. *See also* bracketing; EV (exposure value); flash EV (exposure value); ISO sensitivity; long exposures; overexposure; underexposure

in Adobe Camera Raw plug-in, 300

backlighting, 133

calculation of, 139–143

continuous light, calculating with, 250

delayed exposures, 209–212

equivalent exposures, 139

flash, determining for, 250, 262–263

histograms, fixing with, 165–168

level increments, setting, 117

Live View, simulation in, 189

Merge to HDR feature, 160–164

methods, 141, 143

overriding, 151

Shooting Settings display for, 53

short exposures, 201–203

viewfinder information, 55

exposure compensation. *See* EV (exposure value)

Exposure Compensation button, 36, 43

extension tubes, 244

external flash, 200. *See also* Canon Speedlites; Flash Control menu; red-eye reduction; studio flash

clearing custom settings, 75

custom settings for, 75

enabling/disabling flash, 72

flash mode setting, 73–74

in M (Manual) mode, 152–153

Shooting menu settings, 73–75

and vignetting, 235

working with, 269–272

zooming with, 75

Eye-Fi Secure Digital cards, 310

eyecup, 3

eyepiece for viewfinder, 41–42

F

f/stops, 137. *See also* exposure

in A-DEP (automatic depth-of-field) mode, 146

in Av (Aperture Priority) mode, 148–149

equivalent exposures, 139

explanation of, 138

guide numbers (GN) and, 263

lens considerations, 216

in M (Manual) mode, 152–153

face detection. *See* Live Face Detection

factory defaults, restoring, 25

Faithful Picture Style, 88

in Live View, 190

FD mount lenses, 220

FE Lock button, 43–44

with Live View, 187

working with, 269

FEB (flash exposure bracketing)

Flash Control menu setting for, 268

Live View, indicators in, 189

Shooting menu settings, 74

fields of view, 232

file management, 64

file numbering options, 108–109

fill light

in Adobe Camera Raw plug-in, 300

working with, 272–273

filter threads on lenses, 49–50, 225

filters

and light passing through lens, 137

Monochrome Picture Style, filter effects in, 88, 92–94

Photoshop Dust & Scratches filter, 319

polarizing filters and wide-angle lenses, 237

UV filters with telephoto lenses, 240

Fine compression, 60

Finelight Studios, 247

firmware

bootstrap loaders for updating, 306

information on, 129

with Live View, 191

reliance on, 304

updating, 304–307

1st Curtain sync, 72–73, 258–259
Flash Control menu setting, 266
ghost images and, 259–260
problems, avoiding, 261–262
fisheye lenses, 235
FL mount lenses, 220
flare with telephoto lenses, 240
flash, 199–201. *See also* **built-in flash; Canon Speedlites; FEB (flash exposure bracketing); Flash Control menu; red-eye reduction; studio flash**
AF assist lamp, activating, 124
Auto ISO with, 157
Av (Aperture Priority) mode, synchronization in, 119–120
basic setups for, 274–275
basics of, 257–263
continuous light compared, 248–253
costs of, 253
in Creative Auto mode, 156
description of, 258–259
evenness of illumination with, 250–252
exposure, determining, 250, 262–263
firing controls, 72
flexibility of, 253
ghost images, 252, 259–260
guide numbers (GN), 263
high shutter speeds, combining, 201
with Live View, 187
in M (Manual) mode, 152–153
previewing with, 250
Shooting menu controls, 72–75
shutter speed and, 201, 258–259
stopping action with, 251–252

sync problems, avoiding, 261–262
viewfinder information, 55
Flash button, 38–39
Flash Control menu, 265–268
Built-in Flash Function Setting, 266–267
external flash settings, 267–268
Flash Firing option, 266
flash mode, setting, 267–268
flash EV (exposure value)
Flash Control menu setting for, 267–268
Set button for, 127
Shooting menu settings, 53, 73–74
viewfinder information, 55
working with, 269
flash hot shoe, 47–48
Flash Off mode, 19, 154
AI Focus mode with, 22
with Basic Zone modes, 264
ISO settings in, 157
Flash white balance (WB), 78
in Live View, 190
flat faces in portraits, 239
flip-up hoods for LCD, 307–308
fluorescent light, working with, 256–257
Fluorescent white balance (WB), 78
adjusting, 257
in Live View, 190
focal lengths
for built-in flash, 265
fields of view and, 232
of lenses, 223
focal planes, 258–259
focus, 169–174. *See also* **AF (autofocus); contrast detection; phase detection**
circles of confusion, 176–178
lens considerations, 216

for movies, 197
selecting focus mode, 22–23
with telephoto lenses, 237–238
viewfinder information, 55
focus points, 174–175, 179
in A-DEP (automatic depth-of-field), 28, 147
cross-type focus point, 171–172
in Live View, 189
manually selecting, 28
selecting, 23–24
setting AF point, 181–182
focus priority, 180
focus ring, 50–51
fog with telephoto lenses, 240
folders for file management, 64
foregrounds
with telephoto lenses, 237
with wide-angle lenses, 233
foreign language options, 113
Format feature, 14, 110–111
formatting memory cards, 13–14, 110–111, 311
low level format, 13–14
reformatting, 312
Freespace, 42
freezing action. *See* **stopping action**
front view of camera, 36–41
Full Auto mode, 154
full-frame cameras, 214–215
Full High Definition, movies in, 195
function key, using Set button as, 126–127

G

GE color rendering index (CRI), 257
Gepe card safes, 311
ghost images, 252, 259–260
glasses, diopter correction for, 10

gravity and dust, 318
gray cards, 139–140, 142
green filter, 92–93
Green histogram, 102–104
green toning effect, 92–94
guide numbers (GN), 26, 263

H

half mirror reflector, 222
halogen light, 255
Halsman, Philippe, 201
hand grip, 36–37
Hand tool, Adobe Camera Raw
    plug-in, 299
haze with telephoto lenses, 240
HDMI cable, 5, 41, 113
    Live View, previewing in, 184
HDR (High Dynamic Range),
    135
    bracketing and, 160–164
HDTV
    HDMI cable for, 5
    Live View, previewing in, 184
    viewing images on, 113
HDMI port, 40–41
High Definition, movies in, 195
High Dynamic Range (HDR).
    See HDR (High Dynamic
    Range)
High-Speed Continuous drive
    in Sports mode, 154
high-speed sync, 262
Highlight Tone priority, 123,
    133
    ISO expansion with, 119
    for low ISO settings, 157
highlights. See exposure; HDR
    (High Dynamic Range)
Histogram Display, 51–52

histograms, 51–52
    brightness histograms, 165–168
    displaying, 103–104, 165
    fixing exposures with, 165–168
    in Live View, 189
    Playback menu options,
        102–104
Hoodman
    flip-up hoods, 307
    magnifiers, 308
    plastic overlays, 307
horizontal focus sensor,
    171–172
hot pixels, 315–316
hot shoe adapter, 258
Huey monitor color correction
    system, 84
hyperfocal distance, 148

I

image editors, 294–295. See
    also Adobe
    Photoshop/Photoshop
    Elements
    Corel image editors, 293–295
    dust, cloning out, 319
    filtration for dust, 319
image quality
    for Basic Zone modes, 20
    in Creative Auto mode, 156
    lens considerations, 216
    in Live View, 190
    of prime lenses, 229–230
    Set button activating, 127
    Shooting menu options, 60–64
    Shooting Settings display for, 53
    of zoom lenses, 229–230
Image Recall, 313
Image stabilization switch,
    50–51

image-stabilized lenses,
    245–246
    benefits of, 244–245
    Close-up mode with, 154
    tripods or monopods with, 203
ImageBrowser
    with Picture Style Editor, 282
    working with, 285
incandescent light
    color temperature of, 253–254
    working with, 255–256
Index mode
    additional Index pages, viewing,
        32
    thumbnails, displaying, 31–32
initial setup, 6–9
instruction manual, 4–5
intensity of light, 135
interleaving shots, 310
International Commission on
    Illumination (CIE), 82
interval photography, 211–212
inverse square law, 250–251
IPTC-compatible captions with
    Bibble Pro, 297
IrfanView, 296
IS lenses. See image-stabilized
    lenses
ISO button, 47–48
ISO sensitivity
    adjusting, 25, 156–157
    for built-in flash, 265
    expansion function, 118–119
    guide numbers (GN) and, 263
    high ISO speed noise reduction,
        123
    light and, 137
    noise and, 121–123, 164–165
    Shooting Settings display for, 53
    viewfinder information, 55

J

JPEG format. *See also* image
    quality; RAW+JPEG format
    color spaces for, 82
    compared to RAW, 62–64
    with Continuous Shooting
        mode, 198
    in Live View, 190
    Monochrome Picture Style
        with, 88–89
    PhotoStitch with, 285–286
    Picture Styles and, 85
    Shooting menu option, 60–62
Jump method button, 43, 45
jump methods, 46–47
    with Main dial, 106
    for reviewing images, 29–31

K

Kelvin scale, 254
Kinkade, Thomas, 247

L

L-series lenses, 224
    EF 24-70mm f/2.8L USM
        Autofocus lens, 219
    EF 28-300mm f/3.5-5.6L IS
        USM lens, 225, 229
    EF 35mm f/1.4L USM
        Autofocus lens, 226
    EF 135mm f/2L lens, 228
    400mm f/2.8 f/4 L-series lens,
        228
    sharpness and, 228
    600mm f/4 L-series lens, 228
Landscape mode, 19, 154
    built-in flash with, 264
    ISO settings in, 157
    Picture Styles in, 85

landscape photos
    built-in flash with, 264
    invisible people, long exposures
        for, 205–206
Landscape Picture Style, 88
    in Creative Auto mode, 156
    in Live View, 190
language options, 113
lateral/transverse chromatic
    aberration, 235
LC-E5 battery charger, 7–8
LC-E5E battery charger, 8
LCD, 41–42. *See also* Live View
    acrylic/glass shields for,
        307–308
    Auto Off feature, 110
    brightness, adjusting, 108,
        111–112
    Camera Functions display, 53
    flip-up hoods for, 307–308
    image playback displays, 51–52
    magnifiers for, 308
    movies, information display for,
        197
    No memory card message, 312
    plastic overlays for, 307
    powering up camera, display on,
        127–128
    protecting, 307–308
    readouts, 51–53
    rule of thirds grid, overriding,
        115, 185
    Set button turning LCD on/off,
        127
Leica
    M film cameras, 170
    R lenses, 220
lens hood, 10–11, 242
lens hood bayonet, 10–11,
    50–51
lens multiplier factor, 213–215

Lens Release button, 38–39
lens switches, 38–39
lenses, 3. *See also* dust; EF
    lenses; EF-S lenses; image-
    stabilized lenses; L-series
    lenses; macro lenses;
    maximum aperture; speed
    capabilities of, 227–229
    categories of, 230
    cleaning, 318
    for close-ups, 227
    compatibility of, 220
    components of, 49–51
    decoding lens designations,
        223–225
    different mounting systems, 221
    diffraction optics (DO)
        technology, 230
    expanding collection of,
        216–219
    FD mount lenses, 220
    first lens, 215–219
    foreign lenses, working with,
        220
    light passed by, 137
    macro focusing with, 244
    motor drives for, 225
    mounting, 10
    Peripheral Illumination
        Correction, registering for,
        69–70
    pro quality lenses, 224
    series information, 224
    sharpness and, 228
    special features in, 229
    special-purpose lenses, 225
    tilt/shift capabilities in, 229
    TS-E lenses, 229
    ultrasonic motor autofocus
        system (USM), 223

light. *See also* **auto lighting optimizer; continuous light; exposure**
AF (autofocus) and, 174
diffusing light, 272–273
duration of light, 137
emitted light, 137
ISO sensitivity and, 157
lenses, light passed by, 137
multiple sources, working with, 274–277
reflected light, 137
sensors, light captured by, 137
shutter, light passing through, 137
softboxes, 273–274, 277–278
softening light, 272–273
source, light at, 135–137
and stopping action shots, 200
transmitted light, 137
light meter, 140
light stands, 278–279
light trails, creating, 206, 208
liquid cleaning sensor, 321, 322–324
lithium-ion power packs, 7
Live Face Detection, 190
contrast detection with, 172
in Live View, 187, 192–193
for movies, 196
Live mode
in Live View, 192
for movies, 196
Live View, 182–184
activating, 186–187
AF (autofocus) in, 115, 187, 190
Camera Functions display, 53
changing settings in, 186
contrast detection with, 172
conventional menu system, working with, 190–191
DISP button in, 42, 188–189

do's and don'ts of, 184–185
Drive mode, choosing, 190
enabling, 185–186
EOS Utility with, 282, 285
grid display in, 115, 185
image quality, choosing, 190
information display in, 187–189
Live Face Detection in, 192–193
Live mode in, 192
M (Manual) mode in, 194
phase detection in, 171
Picture Style, choosing, 190
with Picture Style Editor, 282
previewing in, 184, 188–191
Quick mode in, 191–192
reviewing images in, 186
Setup menu options, 115
white balance (WB) setting, choosing, 190
working with, 187–194
Live View button, 43
long exposures, 204–209
amp noise, 205
bulb exposures, 204
mirror lockup feature with, 125
noise reduction feature, 120–123, 164–165
time exposures, 205
timed exposures, 204
working with, 205–209
longitudinal/axial chromatic aberration, 235

M

M (Manual) mode, 20, 175
built-in flash with, 28, 265
color space menu for, 82
evaluative metering in, 143
ISO settings in, 157
in Live View, 194

Picture Styles and, 85
working with, 152–153
Mac computers
dragging and dropping images with, 293
EOS Utility with, 282
ImageBrowser with, 285
with Picture Style Editor, 282
transferring images to, 32–33
macro lenses, 227–228, 242
special features, 229
Magenta/Green scale, 79–81
magnifiers for LCD, 308
Magnify button for reviewing images, 29
Main dial, 36–37, 48
focus points, selecting, 182
jump method with, 106
manual reset file numbering, 109
manual sensor cleaning, 114
manuals
printed instruction manuals, 4–5
software instruction manual CD, 4
maximum aperture, 223
for prime lenses, 230
for zoom lenses, 230
maximum burst, viewfinder information on, 55
MediaRecover, 313
memory card access lamp, 43, 46
memory card door, 36–37
memory cards. *See also* **formatting memory cards; Secure Digital cards**
Camera Functions display, 53
card readers, transferring images with, 32–34
damaging, 311
dragging and dropping images, 293

eggs in one basket debate, 309–310

erasing images, 102

file numbering options, 108–109

firmware upgrades for, 305

inserting, 12–13

interleaving shots, 310

Mean Time Between Failures rating, 310–311

for movies, 195

print order feature, 102

smaller cards, using, 309–310

for time-lapse photography, 212

troubleshooting, 309–313

Menu button, 41–42, 58

Menu tabs, 58–59

menus, 58–59

Set button displaying, 127

tabs for, 58–59

Merge to HDR feature, 160–164

metering modes, 141, 143. *See also* center-weighted metering; evaluative metering; partial metering; spot metering

choosing, 143–146

with Live View, 187

selecting, 21–22

Shooting menu options, 77

Shooting Settings display for, 53

metering timer

in Live View, 186

for movies, 196

M42 lenses, 220

micro-motor (MM) drive lenses, 223, 225

microphone, 37–38

mirror

dust specks on, 315

half mirror reflector, 222

lockup function, 124–125, 210

mirror lenses, 241

Mode dial, 18, 47–48

for Movie Settings, 131

shooting method, choosing, 17

modeling light, 258

with studio flash, 275

monitors, color management, calibration for, 84–85

Monochrome Picture Style, 88–89

adjusting parameters in, 92–93

in Creative Auto mode, 156

filter effects in, 88, 92–94

in Live View, 190

toning effects in, 88, 92–94

viewfinder information, 55

monolights, 248, 275–276

monoplug connectors, 277

monopods, 203

moonlight, 254–255

mounting the lens, 10

Movie mode, 19

Movie Settings, 131

Movie Share button, 43–44

movies

jump method with, 47, 106

in Live View, 184

settings for, 196–197

shooting movies, 195–197

steps for shooting, 197

with time-lapse photography, 212

MP-E 65mm f/2.8 1-5x macro photo lens, 229

multiple light sources, using, 274–277

My Menu, 58, 129–131

deleting items in, 131

displaying My Menu first, 131

reordering items in, 131

settings, 42

N

naming Custom Functions, 115–117

navigating index images, 32

Neat Image, 293

neck straps, 3

UPStrap, 4

Neutral Picture Style, 88

in Live View, 190

Newton, Sir Isaac, 250

night photos

invisible people, long exposures for, 205–206

total darkness, long exposures for, 209

Night Portrait mode, 19, 154

ISO settings in, 157

Nikon

Capture, 295

F-series lenses, 220

G-series lenses, 220

Nixon, Richard, 201

noise

amp noise, 205

dealing with, 164–165

editing tools, 293

ISO settings and, 121–122

long exposure noise reduction, 120–123

Noise Ninja, 165, 293

Bibble Pro with, 297

Normal compression, 60–61

normal lenses, 230

Nostalgia Picture Style, 98

NTSC standard, 113

numbering images, options for, 108–109

O

Olympus OM lenses, 220
On/Off switch, 48
One Shot AF, 22, 175
    working with, 180–181
100 images, jumping, 106
OnTrack data recovery software,
    312–313
Opteka self-timer, 211
overexposure. *See also* HDR
    (High Dynamic Range);
    histograms
    backlighting and, 133
    bracketing, 158
    with EV (exposure value), 151
    example of, 134–135
overheating in Live View, 187

P

P (Program) mode, 17, 20
    auto lighting optimizer in, 124
    built-in flash with, 27
    color space menu for, 82
    evaluative metering in, 143
    exposure and, 139
    Picture Styles and, 85
    working with, 151
PAL standard, 113
Pantone's Huey monitor, 84
partial metering, 21, 143–144
    AE/FE Lock button with, 44
    with Live View, 187
PC computers
    dragging and dropping images
        with, 293
    EOS Utility with, 282
    with Picture Style Editor, 282
    transferring images to, 32–33
    ZoomBrowser with, 285
PC/X adapters, 276–277

Pec-Pads, 322–323
Pelican card safes, 311
Pentax screw mount lenses, 220
Peripheral Illumination
    Correction, Shooting
    menu, 66–70
perspective
    lenses and, 225, 227
    with short exposures, 202–203
    with wide-angle lenses, 233–234
PF2 files, 282
    downloading, 97
    saving images as, 95
phase detection, 170–172
    cross-type focus point, 171–172
    in Live View, 189
    rangefinder approach to,
        170–171
PhaseOne's Capture One Pro
    (C1 Pro), 293, 295–296
Photo Rescue 2, 313
Photographic Solutions
    equipment, 322–323
Photomatix, 135
Photoshop/Photoshop
    Elements. *See* Adobe
    Photoshop/Photoshop
    Elements
PhotoStitch, 285–286
picture control, Shooting
    Settings display for, 53
Picture Style Editor, 281–282
    creating custom style with,
        95–97
    Tool palette, 95–96
    working with, 95–97
Picture Styles, 85–98. *See also*
    color tone; contrast;
    saturation; sharpness;
    specific styles
    additional styles, locating,
        97–98
    adjusting parameters, 91–92
    creating custom style, 95–97

in Creative Auto mode, 156
    defining, 91–94
    DISP button in, 42
    in Live View, 190
    predefined styles, list of, 88
    selecting, 89–90
    User Definition files, uploading
        custom styles to, 96–97
Picture Styles
    button, 43, 46, 85, 90
    Editor, 85
Pierce, Ed, 247
pincushion distortion with
    telephoto lenses, 240
pixel mapping, 316
pixels. *See also* histograms
    hot pixels, 315–316
    ISO settings and, 137
    long exposures and, 164
    noise and, 164–165
plastic overlays for LCDs, 307
Playback button, 43–44
    for movies, 197
    thumbnails, displaying, 31
Playback menu, 57, 99–106.
    See also reviewing images
    Erase Images option, 102
    Histogram Display, 103–104
    Histogram options, 102–104
    Image Jump with Main dial,
        106
    jump method, selecting, 47
    Print Order option, 102
    Protect feature, 99–100
    Rotate feature, 101
    Shooting Information Display,
        103–104
    Single Image Display, 103–104
    Single Image Display + Image-
        Recording Quality, 51–52,
        103–104
    Slide Show feature, 104–105
    Transfer Order option, 102

playing back images. *See* reviewing images

PNG format with Bibble Pro, 297

pocket guides, 5

Portrait mode, 19, 154
Picture Styles in, 85

Portrait Picture Style, 88
in Creative Auto mode, 156
in Live View, 190

portraits
backgrounds for, 279
telephoto lenses, flat faces with, 239

power. *See also* AC power; batteries
built-in flash, rating for, 26
Camera Functions display, 53
DC power port, 36–37
Live View using, 185
options, 7–9
saving power, methods for, 108

powering up camera, 14–15

preflash, 263

previewing
with continuous light, 248
with flash, 250
in Live View, 184, 188–191

prime lenses, 148, 229–230

Print button, 43–44

print order feature, 102

Print/Share/Live View button, 186, 188
movies, shooting, 197

printers, DISP button and, 42

pro quality lenses, 224

product photography, backgrounds for, 279

Protect feature, 99–100

Protect Images function, 13

Pure Eclipse solution, 323–324

purple toning effect, 92–94

Q

quality of images. *See* image quality

Quick Control screen, 52
Set button activating, 127

Quick mode, 190
in Live View, 187, 191–192
for movies, 196

R

R mount lenses, 220

RAW format. *See also* Adobe Camera Raw; image quality; Picture Style Editor
Adobe Photoshop/Photoshop Elements for editing, 298–301
Bibble Pro with, 297
BreezeBrowser for, 297–298
color spaces for, 82
compared to JPEG, 62–64
contrast, adjusting, 168
Digital Photo Professional and, 295–296
editing RAW images, 293, 295–298
IrfanView and, 296
in Live View, 190
Monochrome Picture Style with, 88–89
noise reduction and, 165
PhaseOne Capture One Pro (C1 Pro) with, 296
Picture Styles in, 85
Shooting menu option, 61–62
white balance (WB), specifying, 257

RAW Image Task, 285

RAW+JPEG format, 62. *See also* image quality
color spaces for, 84
file management for files, 64
in Live View, 190

rear lens cap, 10

reciprocity failure, 200

Recover My Photos, 313

recovery
in Adobe Camera Raw plug-in, 300
memory card images, 312–313

rectilinear lines, 235

red-eye reduction, 70–71
in Adobe Camera Raw plug-in, 299
built-in flash with, 265
Camera Functions display, 53
lamp, 37–38

red filters, 92–93

Red histogram, 102–104

Reduce Image button, 31
for reviewing images, 29

reflected light, 137

reflectors, bouncing light with, 273

reformatting memory cards, 312

registration card, 5

Release Shutter without Card option, 12, 65–66

remaining shots, Shooting Settings display for, 53

remote control. *See also* Self-Timer/Remote control
for movies, 197
sensor, 37–38
terminal, 38, 40

resolution
with Continuous Shooting mode, 198
for movies, 195
Shooting menu option, 60

restoring factory defaults, 25

retouching in Adobe Camera Raw plug-in, 299

revealing images with short exposures, 201–202

Review Time option, 65–67
power-saving with, 108
reviewing images, 28–31. *See also* **Playback menu**
DISP button for, 42
jumping through images, 29–31
on LCD, 51–52
in Live View, 186
and movies, 197
options for, 30–31
single image, viewing, 29
time for reviewing images, adjusting, 65–67
RGB. *See also* **Adobe RGB**
histograms, 102–104
sRGB, 82–84
right angle viewer, 6
ring ultrasonic motor (USM) drives, 225
rotating. *See also* **jump methods**
in Adobe Camera Raw plug-in, 299
Auto Rotate feature, 109–110
Playback menu option, 101
rule of thirds grid, 115, 185
for movies, 196

S

saturation, 85, 87–88
adjusting, 91–92
in Adobe Camera Raw plug-in, 300
Picture Style Editor, working with, 95–97, 281
saving
PF2 files, saving images as, 95
Picture Styles, 96
Scotch Brand Magic Tape, 324–325
scrolling around images, 30

2nd Curtain sync, 72–73, 258–259
Flash Control menu setting, 266
ghost images and, 260
problems, avoiding, 261–262
Secure Digital cards, 5
card readers, transferring images with, 32–34
Eye-Fi Secure Digital cards, 310
formatting, 13–14
inserting, 12–13
Mean Time Between Failures rating, 311
for movies, 195
selected menu items, 59
self-timer lamp, 37–38
Self-Timer/Remote control, 20
for bulb exposure, 204
delayed exposures with, 210
in Live View, 190
mirror lockup feature, self-timer with, 125, 210
for time-lapse photography, 211
working with, 25–26
Sensor Brush, 322
sensor cleaning, 313–326
air cleaning, 320–321
brush cleaning, 331–322
Camera Functions display, 53
checking on, 325–326
liquid cleaning, 321–324
with Live View, 191
mirror lockup feature and, 125
options for, 319–326
on powering up camera, 14
Setup menu options, 114
shutter, locking, 321
tape cleaning, 321, 324–325
sensor focal plane, 47–48
sensor microscopes, 325–326

sensors. *See also* **CCD sensors; CMOS sensors; Live View; sensor cleaning**
AF (autofocus) sensors, 179
amp noise and, 205
cross-type focus sensors, 171–172
light captured by, 137
noise and, 164
phase detection and, 170–171
sepia toning effect, 92–94
Set button, 43, 46
disabling, 127
setting up
final steps, 10–17
initial setup, 6–9
Setup menus, 57, 107–129. *See also* **Custom Functions**
Auto Rotate feature, 109–110
Clear Settings feature, 128–129
Date/Time feature, 111
File Numbering option, 108–109
Firmware Version information, 129
Format feature, 14, 110–111
Language options, 113
LCD Auto Off feature, 110
LCD Brightness feature, 111–112
Live View function settings, 115
Screen Color feature, 111
Sensor Cleaning feature, 114
Video System options, 113
Shade white balance (WB), 78
in Live View, 190
shadows. *See also* **exposure; vignetting**
Highlight Tone priority and, 123
Share button, 43–44

sharpness, 85, 86–87. *See also* **focus**
A-DEP (automatic depth-of-field) and, 146
adjusting, 91–92
in Creative Auto mode, 156
lenses and, 228
Picture Style Editor and, 95–97, 281
Shooting Information display, 16, 51–52, 103–104
Shooting menus, 57. *See also* **Dust Delete Data; Picture Styles**
Beep option, 64–65
color space options, 82–85
EV (exposure value) options, 75–77
flash controls, 72–75
metering mode options, 77
Peripheral Illumination Correction option, 66–70
quality setting options, 60–64
Red-Eye Reduction option, 70–71
Release Shutter without Card option, 65–66
Review Time option, 65–67
white balance (WB) options, 78–81
shooting modes
AE/FE Lock button in, 44
selecting, 17–20
Shooting Settings, 16–17, 19
LCD Auto Off feature with, 110
LCD display, 51–53
Screen Color feature, 111
short exposures, 201–203
shots remaining, Shooting Settings display for, 53
shutter
light passing through, 137
sensor cleaning, locking for, 321

Shutter Priority mode. *See* **Tv (Shutter Priority) mode**
shutter release, 28, 36–37, 48
behaviors of button, setting, 126
for time exposures, 205
shutter speed. *See also* **exposure; shutter sync**
in A-DEP (automatic depth-of-field) mode, 146
in Av (Aperture Priority) mode, 148–149
camera shake and, 203
equivalent exposures, 139
explanation of, 138
flash and, 201, 258–259
ghost images and, 259–260
in M (Manual) mode, 152–153
Shooting Settings display for, 53
stopping action with, 200–201
in Tv (Shutter Priority) mode, 150–151
viewfinder information, 55
shutter sync. *See also* **1st Curtain sync; 2nd Curtain sync**
in Av (Aperture Priority) mode, 119–120
for built-in flash, 72–73
for external flash, 74
Flash Control menu setting
for built-in flash, 266
for external flash, 268
problems, avoiding, 261–262
Sigma
8mm f/3.5 EX DG Circular Fisheye lens, 227
macro lenses, 227, 242
Super Wide-Angle 10-20mm f/4-5.6 EX DC HSM Autofocus lens, 227
zoom lenses, 227
silhouette effects, 133, 151

Single Autofocus. *See* **One Shot AF**
single image, jumping, 106
Single Image display, 51–52, 103–104
Single Image Display + Image-Recording Quality, 51–52, 103–104
Single Shot mode, 20, 26
in Live View, 190
Slide Show feature, 104–105
Snapshot Portrait Picture Style, 98
snoots, 279
softboxes, 273–274, 277–278
softening light, 272–273
software. *See also* **image editors**
instruction manual CD, 4
sound for movies, 197
source, light at, 135–137
special-purpose lenses, 225
speed, 228. *See also* **shutter speed**
image-stabilized lenses and, 245
of prime lenses, 230
of zoom lenses, 230
speedlights, 5–6. *See also* **Canon Speedlites**
spherical aberration and telephoto lenses, 241
Sports mode, 19, 154
with Basic Zone modes, 264
ISO settings in, 157
sports photography
Continuous Shooting mode for, 198–199
JPEG format and, 63
memory cards for, 309–310
in Tv (Shutter Priority) mode, 150
spot metering, 22, 145
AE/FE Lock button with, 44
with Live View, 187
reference circle in viewfinder, 54

Spyder color correction system, 85

sRGB, 82–84

Standard Definition, movies in, 195

Standard Picture Style, 88
in Creative Auto mode, 156
in Live View, 190

stepping back with wide-angle lenses, 232

stills
jump method for displaying, 47, 106
in Live View, 184
movies, shooting stills while shooting, 195

Sto-Fen Omnibounce, 273–274

stopping action
with continuous lighting, 251
with flash, 251–252
image-stabilized lenses and, 245
revealing images and, 201–202
short exposures and, 201–203
shutter speeds for, 200–201
Sports mode for, 154
with Tv (Shutter Priority) mode, 150

straightening in Adobe Camera Raw plug-in, 299

streaks, creating, 206–207

stroboscope, 199–200

studio flash, 248
sync problems and, 262
working with, 275–276

Studio Portrait Picture Style, 98

Sunset white balance (WB), 78

Super Spectra Coating for lenses, 218

super-telephoto lenses, 230

swabs for sensor cleaning, 322–323

Sylvania color rendering index (CRI), 257

sync. See shutter sync

T

taking pictures, 28

Tamron macro lenses, 242

tape cleaning sensor, 321, 324–325

tele-zoom lenses. See telephoto lenses

teleconverters, 242–243

telephoto extenders, 242–243

telephoto lenses, 230
bokeh and, 240–241
flat faces in portraits, avoiding, 239
lens hoods for, 242
macro focusing with, 244
mirror lockup function with, 124
problems, avoiding, 239–241
working with, 237–241

television. See also HDTV
Live View, previewing in, 184
viewing images on, 113

10 images, jumping, 106

Thumbnail Index button, 43–44
playback display with, 45

thumbnails
displaying, 31
viewing thumbnail images, 30

TIFF format with Bibble Pro, 297

tilt/shift capabilities in lenses, 229

time exposures, 205

time-lapse photography, 211–212

time value, 20

timed exposures, 204

times. See dates and times

Tokina macro lenses, 242

toning effects in Monochrome Picture Style, 88, 92–94

Tool palette, Picture Style Editor, 95–96

top of camera, 47–48

transferring images to computer, 13–14, 32–34, 287–293
with card readers, 32–34, 292–293
direct-direct transfer, 288–289
dragging and dropping images, 293
indirect-direct transfer, 289–292
Playback menu option for, 102

transmitted light, 137

transmitter/receiver, connecting extra cameras with, 276–277

transverse chromatic aberration, 235

Trash button, 102

tripods
Close-up mode with, 154
Live View, shooting in, 185
shutter speeds and, 203
socket for, 49

troubleshooting
in Live Face Detection mode, 193
memory cards, 309–313

TS-E lenses, 229

TTL (Through-the-Lens), 73
Flash Control menu setting, 267–268

Tungsten white balance (WB), 78. See also incandescent light
in Live View, 190

Turner, Pete, 85

TV. See television

Tv (Shutter Priority) mode, 20
auto lighting optimizer in, 124
built-in flash with, 27, 265
color space menu for, 82

evaluative metering in, 143
exposure equivalent exposure, changing, 139
Picture Styles and, 85
working with, 150–151
Twilight Picture Style, 98
Twilight white balance (WB), 78

U

ultrasonic motor autofocus system (USM), 223
ultrawide-angle lenses, 230
underexposure, 133. *See also* **HDR (High Dynamic Range); histograms**
bracketing, 158
with EV (exposure value), 151
example of, 134–135
unpacking camera, 2–6
unreal images with short exposures, 202
updating firmware, 304–307
UPStraps, 4
USB cable, 3–4, 288. *See also* **transferring images to computer**
computer, transferring images to, 32–34
USB/Video out port, 38, 40
User Definition files, 85
contrast, adjusting, 168
in Live View, 190
uploading Picture Styles to, 96–97
UV filters with telephoto lenses, 240

V

Velvia film, emulating, 85
version of firmware. *See* firmware
vertical focus sensor, 172
vestibule, cleaning, 318
vibrance in Adobe Camera Raw plug-in, 300
viewfinder
A-DEP (automatic depth-of-field) information, 147
diopter correction, adjusting, 10–12
dust specks on, 315
eyepiece, 41–42
information in, 54–55
with Self-Timer/Remote control, 25
vignetting
Peripheral Illumination Correction for, 66–70
with wide-angle lenses, 235
visible light, 135

W

warranty card, 5
waterfalls, long exposures for, 206, 208
wedding photography, JPEG format for, 63
Wein Safe Sync, 276–277
WFT-E1 wireless file transmitter, 304
white balance (WB). *See also* **white balance bracketing**
adjusting, 25, 257
with Adobe Camera Raw plug-in, 299–300
biasing, 81
Camera Functions display, 53
and continuous light, 254

custom settings, 78–81, 190
flash and, 257–258
library for, 78
in Live View, 190
shift, 79–80
Shooting menu options, 78–81
Shooting Settings display for, 53
viewfinder information, 55
white balance bracketing, 158
biasing white balance, 81
in Continuous Shooting mode, 80
Shooting menu options, 79–81
Shooting Settings display for, 53
steps for, 80
White Balance button, 43, 45
wide-angle lenses, 230
crop factor with, 234
depth-of-field (DOF) with, 234
polarizing filters with, 237
problems, avoiding, 235–237
working with, 232–237
wide-zoom lenses. *See* **wide-angle lenses**
window light, working with, 272–273
Windsor, Duke and Duchess of, 201

X

X-Rite's Colormunki, 85

Y

yellow filter, 92–93

Z

Zoom In button, 43, 45
  in Live View, 194
  for reviewing images, 29
zoom lenses, 148, 227, 229–230
  lens hoods for, 242
  as only lens, 226
  wide-zoom lenses, working
    with, 232–237
Zoom Out button, 43–44
  playback display with, 45
zoom ring, 50–51
zoom scale, 50–51

ZoomBrowser EX
  EOS Utility, working with,
    282–283
  PhotoStitch with, 285–286
  with Picture Style Editor, 282
  working with, 285
zooming in/out
  in Adobe Camera Raw plug-in,
    299
  external flash and, 75
  Flash Control menu setting for,
    268
  lens considerations, 216
  on reviewing images, 30

We've got your shot covered.

Course Technology PTR has the resources dedicated photographers need. Written by experienced professional photographers, our books are filled with the expert tips, techniques, and information you need to master your passion for digital photography.

Selections from Bestselling Camera Guide Author David Busch

The 50 Greatest Photo Opportunities

David Busch's Pentax K200D Guide to Digital SLR Photography
1-59863-802-5 • $29.99

David Busch's Nikon D300 Guide to Digital SLR Photography
1-59863-534-4 • $29.99

David Busch's Nikon D60 Guide to Digital SLR Photography
1-59863-577-8 • $29.99

David Busch's Canon EOS 50D Guide to Digital SLR Photography
1-59863-904-8 • $29.99

The 50 Greatest Photo Opportunities in New York City
1-59863-799-1 • $29.99

The 50 Greatest Photo Opportunities in San Francisco
1-59863-800-9 • $29.99

David Busch's Canon EOS Rebel XS/1000D Guide to Digital SLR Photography
1-59863-903-X • $29.99

Canon EOS 40D Guide to Digital SLR Photography
1-59863-510-7 • $29.99

David Busch's Canon EOS Rebel XSi/450D Guide to Digital SLR Photography
1-59863-578-6 • $29.99

David Busch's Sony α DSLR-A350/A300/A200 Guide to Digital SLR Photography
1-59863-801-7 • $29.99

David Busch's Quick Snap Guide to Lighting
1-59863-548-4 • $29.99

David Busch's Quick Snap Guide to Using Digital SLR Lenses
1-59863-455-0 • $29.99

Other Great Titles

Picture Yourself Getting the Most Out of Your Digital SLR Camera
1-59863-529-8 • $24.99

The Official Photodex Guide to ProShow
1-59863-408-9 • $34.99

301 Inkjet Tips and Techniques
1-59863-204-3 • $49.99

More Than One Way to Skin a Cat
1-59863-472-0 • $34.99

Mastering Digital Black and White
1-59863-375-9 • $39.99

The Digital Photographer's Software Guide
1-59863-543-3 • $29.99